good leaders learn

How do leaders learn to lead? How do leaders set themselves up for success? This book explores the real-life experiences of a wide variety of leaders from different industries, sectors, and countries to bring to light new lessons on the importance of life-long learning.

Consisting primarily of a series of probing interviews with 31 senior and high-profile leaders, *Good Leaders Learn* pulls important and useful perspectives into a robust theoretical framework that includes the importance of innate curiosity, challenging oneself, risk-taking, and other key elements of good leadership. With practical insights complemented by the latest leadership research and theory, this book will help current and potential leaders to build a solid foundation of the leadership qualities vital to their continuing success.

Gerard Seijts received his PhD in Organizational Behavior and Human Resource Management from the University of Toronto in 1998. He joined the Ivey Business School at Western University in 2000, where he is the Executive Director of the Ian O. Ihnatowycz Institute for Leadership (www.iveyleadershipinstitute.ca) and holds the Ian O. Ihnatowycz Chair in Leadership.

good leaders learn

learn

lessons from lifetimes of leadership

gerard seijts

Routledge
Taylor & Francis Group

NEW YORK AND LONDON

First published 2014
by Routledge
711 Third Avenue, New York, NY 10017

and by Routledge
2 Park Square, Milton Park, Abingdon, Oxon OX14 4RN

Routledge is an imprint of the Taylor & Francis Group, an informa business

Library of Congress Cataloging in Publication Data
  Seijts, Gerard H.
  Good leaders learn : lessons from lifetimes of leadership / Gerard Seijts,
  PhD. — 1 Edition.
    pages cm
  Includes bibliographical references and index.
  1. Leadership.   2. Success in business.   I. Title.
  HD57.7.S445 2013
  658.4'092—dc23

                                                            2013017026

ISBN: 978–0–415–65976–5 (hardback)
ISBN: 978–0–415–65977–2 (paperback)
ISBN: 978–0–203–07466–4 (ebook)

Typeset in Minion
by RefineCatch Limited, Bungay, Suffolk

To my Dad

who taught me invaluable lessons about the importance of values and who led by example in doing the hard work of fatherhood and leadership

I miss you Dad

Contents

About the Author   xi
Leader Biographies   xii
Preface   xxxii
Acknowledgments   xxxiii

1. Introduction   1

2. Leadership Character   6

3. Learning to Lead   17

4. The Interviews   23

5. You Have to Be Able to Communicate and Then Be an Example   26
   John Furlong

6. No Task Is Insignificant for Making a Family, a Community, or a Corporation Better   35
   N. R. Narayana Murthy

7. I Am a Better Leader When I Can Represent That in Which I Believe, and for Which My Passion Is Sincere, My Understanding Is Complete, and My Commitment Is Personal   44
   Elyse Allan

8. It Is Critical That Leaders Understand the Concepts of Duty and Obligation   55
   Daniel Akerson

9. I'm a Big Believer That If You Don't Want to Be Criticized, Then Say Nothing, Do Nothing, and Be Nothing   63
   Cassie Campbell-Pascall

10. Roll up Your Sleeves and Work Shoulder to Shoulder with Others   72
    Barbara Stymiest

11. There Are Very Few Things in Life That You Can Control, but the One Thing That You Have Absolute Control Over Is the Quality of Your Own Effort   85
    Rahul Bhardwaj

12. Knowing When to Leave and Do Something Different Is
     One of the Hardest Things for a Leader to Do   96
     Carol Stephenson

13. I Learned It's Not Good Enough to Be Right—People Have
     to Buy Into Your Vision   107
     Michael Deane Harris

14. Life Is a Blackboard That You Cannot Erase   118
     Arkadi Kuhlmann

15. I Didn't Have Time to Think About Courage or Where to Find
     Courage—You Just Have It   129
     Linda Hasenfratz

16. Don't Underestimate the Value of Your Early Career
     Moves—You Can't Make up Lost Time   137
     Stephen Snyder

17. Care With Your Heart, Concentrate Your Heart,
     Relax Your Heart, and Open Your Heart   149
     John Cheh

18. Learn to Accept Accountability and the Consequences
     of Failure: Leadership and Accountability Are Inseparable 157
     Michael McCain

19. People That Mind Don't Matter and People That Matter
     Don't Mind   168
     Kiran Mazumdar-Shaw

20. I Always Felt That My Strongest Role Was as the Voice
     Whispering in Somebody's Ear   176
     Michael Shindler

21. If You Have the Illusion That You Can Do Everything
     Well, God Help You—It Is Going to Be a Disaster   185
     Chaviva Hošek

22. There's Credit in Mission Accomplishment—Don't Bring
     Back Excuses   197
     Lt.G. Russel L. Honoré, USA, Ret.

23. I Constantly Learn Lessons About Letting Go   205
     Robert Bell

24. I Like to Think People Think I Stand for Something   212
     Eileen Mercier

25. Leaders Tend to Be People of Broad Interests and Knowledge   219
      Purdy Crawford

26. Trust Is Built on Behavior, Not on What We Say the Values Are   227
      Charles Brindamour

27. You Have to Create Not Only a Network, but Also a System
      Through Which Information Can Flow   237
      Amit Chakma

28. Coming From a Long Line of Leaders, I Was Raised to Be
      a Leader   247
      Jody Wilson-Raybould (Puglaas)

29. Reach for the Stars—But Keep Your Feet Firmly Planted on
      the Ground   257
      Gautam Thapar

30. There Are Two Things in Life You Should Not Let Go—Your
      Values and Your Family   265
      Umran Beba

31. If You Are Not Creative in Getting Solutions and You Limit
      Your Expectations and Outcomes, You Are Not Going to
      Change the World   277
      Antoni Cimolino

32. If You Are Not Working for People Who Inspire You,
      Who Are You Working for?   286
      Sukhinder Singh Cassidy

33. The More I Learn, the More Exciting My Life Is and the More
      Opportunities That I See   297
      Dennis ("Chip") Wilson

34. There Is No Individual Who Is Ever Bigger Than the Team   306
      George Cope

35. I Went Into Public Life Because I Felt That Was the Place
      That I Could Make the Biggest Contribution   315
      The Right Honourable Paul Martin

36. Reflections on the Interviews   326

37. Conclusions on Learning to Lead   336

38. Leadership Insights for the Next Generation of Leaders   355

Index   368

About the Author

Gerard Seijts received his PhD in Organizational Behavior and Human Resource Management from the University of Toronto in 1998. He joined the Ivey Business School at Western University, Canada, in 2000.

His research activities span conference papers, journal articles, and book chapters, as well as the present publication, and cover a wide range of topics including leadership, organizational change, goal setting, training and development, teams, organizational justice, and performance management. He also enjoys writing for the practitioner audience. He is co-author of *Leadership on Trial: A Manifesto for Leadership Development* (with Jeffrey Gandz, Mary Crossan, and Carol Stephenson) and *Cross-enterprise Leadership: Business Leadership for the Twenty-first Century* (with Mary Crossan and Jeffrey Gandz).

Gerard has taught Executive MBA, MBA, and undergraduate courses in leadership, leading change, organizational behavior, performance management, and staffing. He teaches on executive education programs in North America, Asia, and Europe. He has also worked with local government on issues such as leadership and change.

Gerard is the Executive Director of the Ian O. Ihnatowycz Institute for Leadership (www.iveyleadershipinstitute.ca) at the Ivey Business School. He holds the Ian O. Ihnatowycz Chair in Leadership.

Gerard is the husband of Jana Seijts and the proud father of Aiden and Arianna.

Leader Biographies

Daniel Akerson is chairman and chief executive officer (CEO) of General Motors (GM). He joined the company in 2009 as a member of the board of directors. He and his team moved quickly to re-establish GM as one of the world's largest automakers and a lynchpin of manufacturing after the company emerged from bankruptcy in 2009, during a period of deep global recession. Under Akerson's leadership, decisive steps were taken to transform GM by launching an initial public offering (IPO) of $23 billion—at the time, the largest global IPO in history—and establishing consistent profitability, gaining market share, improving product quality, investing in manufacturing and job creation, and generating significant global growth.

Prior to joining GM, Akerson was a managing director and head of global buyout for the Carlyle Group in Washington, D.C. In this role, Akerson managed in excess of $50 billion in assets and more than 200 portfolio companies with several hundred thousand employees around the world. He was instrumental in helping Carlyle achieve 30 percent gross internal rates of return in the firm's corporate private equity business.

Akerson has also served as CEO or president of several telecommunications and technology companies—including MCI, Nextel Communications, XO Communications, and General Instrument—through periods of explosive growth and dynamic change. Under Akerson's leadership as chief financial officer (CFO) and president, MCI doubled its market share.

A graduate of the United States Naval Academy with a Bachelor of Science in engineering, Akerson earned a Master of Science degree in economics from the London School of Economics. He serves on the board of the U.S. Naval Academy Foundation, the advisory board of Tsinghua University's School of Economics and Management, the International Business Leaders' Advisory Council of Shanghai, and is a member of the Business Council. He received the T. C. and Elizabeth Cooke Business Medallion from the College of William & Mary in 2004. In addition, he has been honored by the U.S. Naval Academy with the 2012 Distinguished Graduate Award for his "lifetime commitment to service, personal character, and distinguished contributions to our nation."

Akerson co-chaired the Leaders to Serve the Nation capital campaign, which raised a record $254 million for the U.S. Naval Academy. He also chairs his family's Blue Earth Foundation Inc, which is dedicated to providing financial assistance to programs serving young people. In 2011, he was named "Humanitarian of the

Year" by SOME (So Others Might Eat), a non-profit organization that serves the homeless and poor in Washington, D.C. In 2012, he and his wife Karin co-chaired the annual Capuchin Soup Kitchen dinner, raising a record sum, and launched the Habitat for Humanity "Leaders to ReBuild Detroit" initiative with a cornerstone contribution. In 2013, he and Karin were named the Habitat for Humanity (Michigan) Sponsor of the Year.

Elyse Allan is the president and CEO of General Electric (GE) Canada and vice president of GE. She is responsible for growing GE's business in Canada and furthering the company's leadership in advanced technology, services, and finance.

Allan's career with GE began in 1984 and has spanned the USA and Canada, as well as several industrial and consumer GE businesses, including aviation, energy, and lighting. She is a passionate champion for Canada's competitiveness, advancing the country's science and technology base and competitive fiscal policy. She actively engages in industry groups, public policy, and the community, and serves on the boards of directors for several organizations, including the Canadian Council of Chief Executives, the C. D. Howe Institute, MaRS Discovery District, the Conference Board of Canada, and the Royal Ontario Museum board of governors. She recently completed her tenure as chair of the board of the Canadian Chamber of Commerce and as director of the Royal Ontario Museum. She has also served on a number of federal and provincial government advisory boards.

Allan has been recognized as a YWCA Toronto Woman of Distinction—Business (2012), as one of Canada's "top 100 most powerful women" (Scotiabank Corporate Executives award) by the Women's Executive Network (2011), and as one of *Canadian Business* magazine's 25 "most influential people in business" (2009). She holds a Bachelor of Arts degree in biology and environmental studies from Dartmouth College, New Hampshire, as well as an MBA from the Tuck School of Business at Dartmouth. An active alumnus, she currently serves on Tuck's board of overseers. Allan also holds an honorary doctorate from Ryerson University, Toronto. She lives in Toronto with her husband and son.

Umran Beba is president, Asia Pacific region, of PepsiCo, which spans 23 markets—ranging from developed markets, such as Australia and Japan, to developing and emerging markets, including Pakistan, Afghanistan, and much of southeast Asia—across more than 23 countries, and includes approximately 6,300 direct and 70,000 indirect employees. She has held a wide range of roles since joining the company in 1994. Prior to assuming her current role in 2010, she was president of PepsiCo's southeast Europe region, covering 14 markets including Turkey, Greece, Cyprus, Israel, and the Balkans. She has also served as the business unit general manager for the east Mediterranean region, comprising Turkey, Lebanon, Jordan, Syria, and Iraq, and she started her PepsiCo career at Frito-Lay in Turkey, where she held several senior positions including that of marketing director, human resources director, and, ultimately, general manager.

Beba is a strong supporter of PepsiCo's "Performance with Purpose" under-
taking to deliver "sustainable growth by investing in a healthier future for people
and our planet." PepsiCo's Asia Pacific division co-founded WaterHope, a collaborative social enterprise that aims to bring clean drinking water to one million
Filipinos by 2015. PepsiCo Asia Pacific has also launched sustainable product initiatives in Australia, Thailand, and the Philippines. Beba is a dedicated advocate of
diversity and inclusion, too. She is an advisory council member for the Switzerland-
based Women's International Network, as well as for "Mentorship for Women for
Board Seats," organized by Praesta and Forbes in Turkey. In 2012, she received the
PepsiCo Steve Reinemund Diversity & Inclusion Leadership Legacy Award.

In 2013, Beba was elected as president of Food Industry Asia, a pan-Asian food
and beverage industry association. She is also a member of the board of Calbee
Group, Japan, and an advisory council member for the Hong Kong University of
Science and Technology Business School. She is based in Hong Kong.

Robert Bell is president and CEO of University Health Network, which comprises
Princess Margaret Hospital, Toronto General Hospital, Toronto Western Hospital,
and Toronto Rehabilitation Institute. An internationally recognized orthopedic
surgeon, health-care executive, clinician scientist, and educator, he brings more
than 30 years of experience in academic health care to the leadership of Canada's
largest research hospital.

In 2000, Bell was appointed as vice president and the chief operating officer
(COO) of Princess Margaret Hospital. Later that same year, the Canadian Institutes
of Health Research awarded him and his colleagues more than C$6 million for
a five-year, interdisciplinary health research team project in musculoskeletal
neoplasia.

From 2003 to 2005, Bell was chair of the Clinical Council for Cancer Care
Ontario (CCO) as well as a regional vice president (Toronto) for CCO. Also in
2005, Bell completed the Advanced Management Program at Harvard Business
School. In 1975, he earned a Doctor of Medicine degree from McGill University,
Montreal, and, in 1981, a Master of Science degree from the University of Toronto.
He completed a fellowship in orthopedic oncology at Massachusetts General
Hospital and Harvard University in 1985.

During his career as a clinician scientist at the University of Toronto, he received
more than C$5 million in peer-reviewed funding and published more than 170
peer-reviewed papers. Bell is a fellow of the Royal College of Surgeons of Canada,
the American College of Surgeons, and the Royal College of Surgeons of Edinburgh.

Rahul Bhardwaj is the president and CEO of the Toronto Community Foundation,
where he works to engage philanthropy to improve the quality of life in Toronto.
Formerly a corporate lawyer with a leading Canadian law firm, he was also vice
president of the Toronto 2008 Olympic Bid Committee.

As part of the mayor's blue-ribbon Fiscal Review Panel in 2008, Bhardwaj was
involved in identifying efficiencies for the city of Toronto. A year later, the Province

of Ontario appointed him to the board of Metrolinx (formerly the Greater Toronto Transportation Authority).

More recently, Bhardwaj was chair of the 2012 Ontario Summer Games, the first multi-sport games to be held in Toronto, and he has also chaired the Toronto Downtown Jazz Festival. His board commitments, past and present, include Upper Canada College and George Brown College (both in Toronto), Community Foundations of Canada, the Stratford Festival (Canada), and United Way (Toronto), among others.

In 2012, Bhardwaj's commitment to city building was recognized as he received a Queen Elizabeth II Diamond Jubilee Medal and was also named one of the "50 Most Influential" people in the city by *Toronto Life* magazine. His vision for Toronto has made him a popular presenter and speaker, particularly on issues relating to the city, community, and leadership as well as the Toronto Community Foundation's annual Toronto's Vital Signs report. Rahul is a frequent contributor on local TV, radio, and in print, and has also been featured on the national CBC News Network, CNN International, and in *China Daily*.

Charles Brindamour is the CEO of Intact Financial Corporation, Canada's largest provider of home, auto, and business insurance. Under his leadership, Intact became an independent and widely held Canadian company in 2009, and engineered, two years later, the largest acquisition in the history of the property and casualty insurance industry in the country. With a market capitalization of more than C$8 billion, Intact ranks among the largest companies listed on the Toronto Stock Exchange.

Brindamour began his career with Intact in 1992 as an actuary and held a number of progressive management positions in the company's Saint-Hyacinthe and Toronto offices. He also served in management and executive roles in Europe with ING Group (*ING Groep*), Intact's former majority shareholder. Upon his return to Canada in 1999, he led the company's acquisition, strategic planning, and capital management functions. Two years later, he became senior vice president (personal lines), and, in 2004, he was appointed executive vice president, responsible for underwriting, claims, planning, corporate development, and investor relations. In 2007, he became COO, a position he held until his appointment as president and CEO in 2008.

A graduate of Laval University, Quebec, in actuarial sciences, Brindamour is also an associate of the Casualty Actuarial Society. He is a board member of Intact Financial Corporation and of the C.D. Howe Institute, chair of the board of the Insurance Bureau of Canada, and a member of the advisory committee of the Climate Change Adaptation Project (Canada), an initiative of the University of Waterloo, Ontario. He is a member of the Campaign Cabinet of the Centre Hospitalier Universitaire Sainte-Justine (CHU Sainte-Justine). He was also a member of the Campaign Cabinet of the United Way of Greater Toronto, and chaired a number of its campaigns among the insurance industry.

Cassie Campbell-Pascall laced up her first pair of skates when she was five years old. Today, she is a heroine of Canadian sport. A passionate and dynamic speaker, Campbell draws on her accomplishments as captain of the gold medal-winning Canadian women's Olympic ice hockey team to explore the themes of leadership, teamwork, motivation, and determination.

As the former captain of Canada's women's ice hockey team, Campbell has taken part in three winter Olympic Games, seven International Ice Hockey Federation World Women's Championships, nine Four Nations Cups, and the Torino Ice Tournament. She is the only captain, male or female, to lead Canada to two Olympic gold medals, and is the longest-serving captain in Canadian hockey history. Her teams have won 21 medals in total, comprising 17 gold medals and 4 silver medals.

After retiring from professional hockey, Campbell joined *Hockey Night in Canada* as a rinkside reporter, and became the first woman to do color commentary (punditry) on their broadcast. Her first book—*H.E.A.R.T.* (Fenn Publishing, 2007), with the title's acronym representing "hard work, experience, attitude, responsibility, and teamwork"—examines her career and offers insight and advice on how to be a better athlete and a better person.

A philanthropist, Campbell runs an annual street hockey tournament that raises more than $200,000 a year for the Ronald McDonald House (Southern Alberta) charity. In 2008, the Cassie Campbell Community Center opened in her hometown of Brampton, Ontario, and in 2002, as a tribute to her captaincy of the gold medal-winning Canadian women's Olympic ice hockey team as well as in recognition of her family connections to the location, Prince Edward Island officially named March 14th as "Cassie Campbell Day." In 2012, Campbell received the Order of Hockey in Canada award, and also received the Queen Elizabeth II Diamond Jubilee medal from Prime Minister Stephen Harper. Campbell has been inducted into the Alberta Sports Hall of Fame (2007) as well as the Ontario Sports Hall of Fame (2012), and was the first female hockey player to be inducted into Canada's Sports Hall of Fame (2007).

Amit Chakma is the tenth president and vice chancellor of Western University. He arrived at Western in 2009, after serving the University of Waterloo, Ontario, since 2001 as vice president, academic, and provost, and as a professor in the department of chemical engineering. Prior to that, he served as dean of engineering and then vice president (research) and international liaison officer at the University of Regina, Saskatchewan. He began his academic career as a professor of chemical and petroleum engineering at the University of Calgary, Alberta. In 2012, Western's board of governors re-appointed Chakma to a second term as president, extending to 2019.

Chakma is a graduate of the Algerian Petroleum Institute (Dip. Ing., 1982) and the University of British Columbia (Master of Applied Science, 1984; PhD in chemical engineering, 1987). The author of more than 100 articles, he is a leading expert in areas related to petroleum research and energy management. His research interests include mass transfer, gas separation, gas processing, membrane separation, petroleum waste management, greenhouse gas control technology, and energy and environmental systems modeling.

In addition to his roles at Western, Chakma currently serves as chair of the World University Service of Canada, as a member of the board of directors for the Ontario Centres of Excellence, and as a member of the Science, Technology and Innovation Council (Canada). He also served as chair of the federal government's Advisory Panel on Canada's International Education Strategy.

In 1998, Chakma was recognized with Canada's "Top 40 Under 40" award, the "pre-eminent business award for young achievers under the age of 40." He is also a fellow of the Canadian Academy of Engineering, and he received the Queen's Diamond Jubilee Medal in 2012 in recognition of his contributions to Canadian post-secondary education.

John Cheh received his Bachelor's degree in economics and political science from McGill University, Canada, and his PhD in economics from the Massachusetts Institute of Technology. He joined the Canadian Government in 1974 and worked for the Treasury Board and Privy Council Office. From 1981 to 1993, he was with Canada's Department of External Affairs and International Trade (now the Department of Foreign Affairs and International Trade), and served in Beijing, Seoul, and Tokyo in senior diplomatic positions. He also worked for two years as the executive director of the Canada China Business Council in Toronto. In 1994, Cheh moved to Hong Kong as the president of Bell Canada International (Asia), in charge of its strategic telecommunications investments and mergers and acquisitions activities. In 2001, he became the president of Bombardier (China), and then joined the Esquel Group in October 2003.

Cheh was elected vice chairman of the China Cotton Textile Association in 2005 and vice chairman of the China Chamber of Commerce for Import and Export of Textiles in 2009. In 2011, he was appointed as an advisory board member of the International Textile Manufacturers Federation.

In 2012, Western University, Canada, conferred an honorary Doctor of Laws (LL.D) degree on Cheh in recognition of his expertise in trade, economics, and labor issues. The Esquel Group manufactures about 100 million cotton shirts annually through its 54,000 workers in China, Malaysia, Mauritius, Sri Lanka, and Vietnam. Its vertically integrated operation includes cotton farming, spinning, weaving, knitting, dyeing, finishing and garment manufacturing.

Antoni Cimolino is the artistic director of Canada's Stratford Festival. He previously served as general director of the festival, managing all of its administrative functions. Before that, he was executive director, during which time he oversaw the successful launch of a stability fund and an endowment foundation, and also improved the festival's infrastructure significantly by leading the design, consultation, and funding process for four major construction projects between 2002 and

2008, including the renovation of the festival's Avon Theatre and the creation of its Studio Theatre.

Beginning his career as an actor at the Stratford Festival in the 1980s, Cimolino began to direct productions for it in the mid 1990s. Since then, he has made the transition to business leader while remaining an integral part of the festival's creative team, continuing to direct some of its most acclaimed productions.

Cimolino serves as the national chair of Culture Days, a nationwide celebration of arts and culture in Canada. He has initiated collaborations with several prestigious theatre companies, including Montreal's Théâtre du Nouveau Monde, Ottawa's National Arts Centre, New York's Lincoln Center and City Center, and the Chicago Shakespeare Theater. He also spearheaded the Stratford Festival's involvement in a joint project with CUSO, Canada's international volunteering agency, to establish a performing arts and educational center in the city of Suchitoto, El Salvador.

George Cope has been the president and CEO of BCE Inc. and Bell Canada, Canada's largest communications company, since 2008. With industry-leading capital investments of approximately C$6 billion in 2009 and 2010, Bell has launched a world-leading mobile HSPA+ network and enhanced broadband fiber infrastructure to deliver advanced television and Internet services.

Prior to joining Bell in 2005, Cope was president and CEO of Telus Mobility, where he was responsible for transforming the company's regional wireless operation into a national competitor. He also previously served as president and CEO of the national wireless carrier Clearnet Communications. He has earned a reputation as an innovative telecoms strategist and builder of high-performance teams, successfully launching three next-generation Canadian digital networks during his career to date.

Cope holds an Honors Business Administration (HBA) degree from Western University and serves on the advisory board of the university's Ivey Business School. He is also a director of Bank of Montreal, BCE, and Bell Canada, and chair of the board of Bell Aliant Inc.

Purdy Crawford is a native of Five Islands, Nova Scotia, and a graduate of Mount Allison University, New Brunswick; Schulich School of Law at Dalhousie University, Nova Scotia (formerly Dalhousie Law School); and Harvard Law School. He pursued his legal career with the Canadian business law firm Osler, Hoskin & Harcourt LLP, practicing primarily in the corporate/commercial area.

Crawford left Osler to join Imasco Ltd. as CEO in 1985. In 1995, he retired as CEO, but continued to serve as non-executive chairman of Imasco Ltd., Imasco's CT Financial Services Inc. business, and its trust company subsidiary Canada Trustco Mortgage Company until February 2000, when Imasco Ltd. was acquired by Imperial Tobacco Canada. He rejoined Osler as counsel in March 2000.

Crawford sits on the boards of several Canadian companies and has been involved with many not-for-profit organizations over the years. He is chancellor emeritus of Mount Allison University, and has received honorary Doctor of Laws degrees from Cape Breton University, Nova Scotia; Mount Allison University; Dalhousie University; and the University of Windsor, Ontario. He was made honorary Chief Rising Tide of the Membertou First Nation. He is a member of Canada's Multiple Sclerosis Scientific Research Foundation's board and is active in its current capital fund raising campaign. In 2013, the Canadian Government provided C$5 million towards expanding the Purdy Crawford Chair in Aboriginal Business Studies at Cape Breton University.

In 1996, Crawford was appointed an Officer of the Order of Canada (OC), and, in 2007, he was appointed a Companion of the Order of Canada (CC). He received the Canadian Council for the Advancement of Education's Friend of Education Award in 1996 for his "significant contribution in a leadership role to the cause of institutional advancement or education in Canada," and, in 1995, was awarded the United Way Canada Volunteerism Award in recognition of his considerable contribution to Canadian communities through volunteerism.

Crawford was inducted into the Business Hall of Fame of Nova Scotia in 1997, and became a fellow of the Institute of Corporate Directors in 1999. In 2000, he was inducted into the Canadian Business Hall of Fame and named "Ivey Business Leader of the Year." In April 2003, he became one of the five Public Policy Forum honorees (2002), and, in October, he was named as the Conference Board of Canada's Honorary Associate 2003. In 2007, he received the Yee Hong Golden Achievement Award and was also honored as a "Champion of Public Education" by the Learning Partnership. In 2008, he received the Canadian Investment "Person of Influence of the Year" award. In 2010, he accepted the Kroeger College Award in Public Affairs—Management.

Crawford was a member of the Joint Securities Industry Committee on Conflicts of Interest and the Toronto Stock Exchange Committee on Corporate Governance in Canada. He was chairman of the Securities Industry Committee on Analyst Standards and of the advisory Five-Year Review Committee, which was appointed under the Securities Act of Ontario. He chaired an expert panel with respect to a single securities regulator in Canada, and was also chair of the Pan-Canadian Investors Committee for Third-Party Structured Asset-Backed Commercial Paper (ABCP) that oversaw the restructuring of C$32 billion of Canadian non-bank, or third party, structured ABCP.

John Furlong has been involved with athletics throughout his life. A former Canadian squash champion, he has competed at the international level in squash, basketball, and European handball.

A long-time member of the Canadian Olympic Committee, Furlong has led many high-profile sport organizations in Canada. He joined Vancouver Whitecaps FC in April 2012 as executive chair—the most senior position of the club's executive team. This comes after his term as CEO of the Vancouver Organizing Committee for the 2010 Olympic and Paralympic Winter Games (VANOC). From the very beginning, Furlong envisioned that the Games could be a true nation builder that would help improve the fabric of Canadian society.

Prior to his appointment as the CEO of VANOC, Furlong was the president and COO for the Vancouver 2010 Bid Corporation. He became the bid's international face and key spokesperson, tirelessly clocking up more than 1.2 million miles in his travels to promote the bid.

Over the years, Furlong—an Officer of the Order of Canada (OC) and Member of the Order of British Columbia (OBC)—has received many honors for his service to sport. To name a few, he was recognized by *The Globe and Mail* as Canada's Nation Builder (2010) and as one of the newspaper's top 25 "Transformational Canadians," as well as being named Canadian of the Year by The Canadian Club of Toronto. Moreover, in 2010, he was dubbed Canada's Marketer of the Year and also Sports Media Canada's Sports Executive of the Year.

In 2009, both *The Globe and Mail* and the Canadian Broadcasting Corporation named Furlong Canada's Most Influential Sport Figure. *Around the Rings* magazine listed him as one of the world's top five most influential Olympic officials in both 2009 and 2010, and he's also Sport BC's Sportsman of the Decade.

For his service to sport in Canada over a lifetime, Furlong was acclaimed as the 2004 Canadian Sport Awards' Leadership in Sport winner. He has also won Vancouver's most prestigious tourism award for the promotion of Vancouver around the world.

Outside of sports, Furlong has been awarded honorary doctorate degrees in law and technology from the University of British Columbia, the Justice Institute of British Columbia, and the British Columbia Institute of Technology, as well as an honorary doctorate in tourism and hospitality from Niagara University in New York, USA.

Born in Tipperary, Ireland, Furlong has 5 children and 11 grandchildren. His book *Patriot Hearts: Inside the Olympics That Changed a Country* (Vancouver: Douglas & McIntyre) became an instant national bestseller when it was released on February 12, 2011—the one-year anniversary of the Games.

Michael Deane ("Mike") Harris was born in Toronto, Ontario, in 1945. Prior to his election to the Legislative Assembly of Ontario in 1981, he was a schoolteacher, a school board trustee and chair, and an entrepreneur in the Nipissing area of the province.

On June 8, 1995, Harris became the 22nd Premier of Ontario. His government's program—dubbed a "Common Sense Revolution"—included reducing the size of government and cutting welfare and health spending. Four years later, Harris was re-elected—making him the first Ontario premier in more than 30 years to form a second consecutive majority government. He and his team at Queen's Park turned an $11 billion deficit into a $3 billion surplus and passed balanced budget legislation. His leadership is considered to have led to 600,000 fewer people on welfare and more than 845,000 new jobs in Ontario.

After leaving office in 2002, Harris founded his own consulting firm. As president of Steane Consulting Ltd., he serves as an advisor to numerous Canadian companies, including Cassels Brock & Blackwell LLP, where he currently serves as senior business advisor.

Harris is also a director on several public and private boards. He served as chairman of Magna International Inc. until 2012. His current public board directorships include Chartwell Seniors Housing (chair of the corporation), Canaccord Financial Inc. (chair of the Corporate Governance and Compensation Committee), Element Financial Corporation, FirstService Corporation (member of the Executive Compensation Committee), and Route1 Inc. (chairman of the board). He also serves on the advisory boards of several private equity funds, including EnerTech Capital and Beringer Capital.

In addition, Harris is a director for the Tim Horton Children's Foundation and is a senior fellow with the Fraser Institute, a public policy think tank.

Linda Hasenfratz was named CEO of Linamar Corporation in 2002. From 1999 to 2002, she was president of the company, and, from 1997 to 1999, she was its COO. She joined Linamar Corporation in 1990, and embarked on an extensive training program to gain familiarity with all aspects of the business. Positions held in the corporation range from machine operator to general manager of the company's Vehcom Manufacturing and Comtech Manufacturing divisions.

Hasenfratz completed an Executive MBA from the Ivey Business School at Western University in 1997. In addition, she holds an Honors Bachelor of Science degree from the same institution. The analytical and strategic planning skills gained during the MBA program, in combination with practical skills gained at Linamar, are key factors in her executive development. Since she assumed corporate-level responsibilities, Linamar sales have grown from $800 million to more than $2.8 billion. The corporation has undergone significant change in terms of formalization, development, communication and execution of a vision, and strategy for future growth, as well as development of communication, performance management, and operating systems utilized throughout the company.

Hasenfratz's board and council memberships include the Canadian Council of Chief Executives' board of directors (vice chair), the Royal Ontario Museum's board of governors (vice chair), the Canadian Imperial Bank of Commerce (CIBC) board of directors, the Original Equipment Suppliers Association's board of directors, Faurecia's board of directors, the Catalyst Canada advisory board, and the Women On Boards advisory council.

She was named one of Canada's "Top 40 Under 40" by *The Globe and Mail's Report on Business Magazine* in 2003, received the Laurier Outstanding Business Leader Award (2007) in recognition of "her demonstrated leadership in an entrepreneurial organization, global experience, and high level of community involvement," and was named as one of the "100 Leading Women in the North American Auto Industry" in 2000, 2005, and 2010.

Lieutenant General Russel L. Honoré retired from the United States Army in 2008. His distinguished military career spanned 37 years of active service, culminating with his appointment as the Commanding General, First Army. He served in a variety of command and staff positions that focused on defense support to civil authorities and homeland defense. Prior to his command of Joint Task Force Katrina, where he led the United States Department of Defense response to Hurricanes Katrina and Rita in Alabama, Mississippi, and Louisiana, Honoré supported the planning and response for Hurricanes Floyd in 1999; Lilli and Isidore in 2002; Isabel in 2003; and Charley, Frances, Ivan, and Jeanne in 2004. He also planned and supported the United States military response to the devastating flooding that swept Venezuela in 1999 and Mozambique in 2000. As vice director for operations, he led the Defense Department's planning and preparation for the anticipated Y2K anomaly. As Commander of Standing Joint Force Headquarters—Homeland Security, under United States Northern Command direction, he planned and oversaw the military response to the Space Shuttle *Columbia* tragedy and the Washington, D.C. sniper shootings.

Honoré is the recipient of many of the highest military service awards. He also holds a Master of Arts in human resources from Troy State University, Alabama, and several honorary doctoral degrees from leading national universities. In addition to serving as a contributor to CNN, Honoré has become well known nationally and internationally for his work on developing the culture of preparedness, a topic on which he both lectures and consults.

Chaviva Hošek is currently a professor at the School of Public Policy and Governance at the University of Toronto. Between 2001 and 2012, she was the president and CEO of the Canadian Institute for Advanced Research; she is now president emeritus of the institute. From 1993 to 2000, she served as the director of policy and research in the Prime Minister's Office of The Right Honourable Jean Chrétien. Previously, she served in the legislature of Ontario and as Minister of Municipal Affairs and Housing of Ontario. She was on the board of the National Action Committee on the Status of Women for eight years and served as its president from 1984 to 1986.

Hošek was educated at McGill University, Canada, and received her PhD in English and American Literature from Harvard University. She was a member of the faculty of Victoria College at the University of Toronto for 15 years. She currently serves on several non-profit boards, including that of the Central European University in Budapest. She has been a member of the board at Inco (Vale Canada Limited) and Maple Leaf Foods, and now sits on the board of Great-West Lifeco. A holder of four honorary degrees, she was appointed as an Officer of the Order of Canada (OC) in 2006.

Arkadi Kuhlmann is the founder and CEO of ZenBanx, Inc., a financial services and technology firm offering a multi-currency, mobile banking account. He introduced the world to direct banking with a simplified customer focus when he founded ING DIRECT Canada in 1996, creating the brand strategy, recruiting the senior leadership team, and, from 1996 to 2000, growing the bank to a successful market position while serving as its president and CEO. He then repeated the process in 2000 by founding ING DIRECT USA and leading its growth to become the nation's largest savings bank and leading direct bank, with more than $84 billion in deposits and 7.8 million customers. Over 12 years, as the bank's chairman, president, and CEO, Kuhlmann established his vision to create a retail-focused bank that offered simple financial products direct to consumers and made it easier for Americans to return to saving.

Prior to ING DIRECT, Kuhlmann served as the president of North American Trust and the president and CEO of Deak & Co. and Deak International. He also served as vice president, general manager, and manager of the Royal Bank of Canada in its corporate cash management and commercial banking marketing divisions. Today, he is serving as general partner of Deak Companies LLC.

In addition to his corporate successes, Kuhlmann taught at the American Graduate School of International Management (now the Thunderbird School of Global Management) in Arizona, USA, where he was a professor of international finance and investment banking. He is the author of *Rock Then Roll: The Secrets of Culture-Driven Leadership* (Toronto: Deak & Co., 2011), *Prime Cash: First Steps in the Art of Corporate Cash Management* (Montreal: Institute of Canadian Bankers, 1983), *The AvCan File: First Steps in Understanding Financial Statements* (Ibid., 1975), and *The Seeker's Way: First Steps in the Learning Process for Students* (Ibid.) and co-author of *The Orange Code: How ING DIRECT Succeeded by Being a Rebel With a Cause* (Hoboken, N.J.: John Wiley & Sons, 2009). His thoughts on banking, leadership, and innovation have also been published in the editorials of major newspapers, including the *Wall Street Journal*, the *Washington Post*, and the *New York Times*.

Kuhlmann has received an HBA and an MBA from the Ivey Business School, Western University. In 2010, he was awarded an honorary Doctor of Laws (LL.D.) degree from Western for his contributions to the world of business strategy.

He has also been honored as American Banker's Innovator of the Year (2006), and as a recipient of the ING Business Award—Revenue Growth Category (2005), the Delaware Business Leader Award (2006, 2008), Habitat for Humanity's Leadership Award (2007), and the Netherlands–America Foundation's Ambassador C. Howard Wilkins Jr. Award (2009). In 2010, Kuhlmann was honored with the Council for Economic Education's Visionary Award, which recognizes champions of economic empowerment, for his "lifelong advocacy in teaching adults and children about responsible money behavior."

The Right Honourable Paul Martin was the 21st Prime Minister of Canada (2003–2006), the 34th Canadian Minister of Finance (1993–2002), and served as the Member of Parliament for LaSalle–Émard in Montréal, Québec, from 1988 to 2008. During his tenure as Minister of Finance, he erased Canada's deficit, and subsequently recorded five consecutive budget surpluses while paying down the national debt and setting Canada's debt-to-GDP ratio on a steady downward track. In 1999, he was named inaugural chair of the G20, an international group of finance ministers and central bank governors.

During his tenure as Prime Minister, Martin's achievements included setting in place a 10-year, C$41 billion plan to improve health care, signing agreements with the provinces and territories to establish a national early learning and child care program, and creating a new financial deal for Canada's municipalities. In 2005, under his leadership, the Canadian Government reached an historic consensus with Canada's provinces, territories, and First Nations, Métis, and Inuit leaders to eliminate the gaps between aboriginal and non-aboriginal Canadians in the areas of health, education, housing, and economic opportunity. This agreement became known as the Kelowna Accord. Further, he introduced the Civil Marriage Act, which redefined the traditional definition of marriage to include same-sex couples.

Since leaving office, Martin has co-chaired a panel responsible for submitting a report on a new strategic vision for the African Development Bank, following up on an earlier United Nations panel report on private sector investment in the Third World, which he co-chaired. He currently co-chairs the Congo Basin Forest Fund. He also sits on the advisory council of the Coalition for Dialogue on Africa, an initiative sponsored by the African Union, the UN Economic Commission for Africa, and the African Development Bank.

Domestically, he leads the Martin Aboriginal Education Initiative, which aims to reduce the aboriginal youth dropout rate and to increase the number of aboriginal students attending post-secondary institutions. He has also founded, along with one of his sons, David, the Capital for Aboriginal Prosperity and Entrepreneurship Fund, and serves on its investment committee.

Prior to entering politics, Martin was a business executive at Power Corporation of Canada, and then chairman and CEO of one of its subsidiaries, Canada Steamship Lines. His acquisition of the latter, in 1981, represented the most important leveraged buyout in Canada at that time.

Martin studied philosophy and history at St. Michael's College at the University of Toronto and is a graduate of the University of Toronto Law School. He was called to the bar of Ontario in 1966.

In 2011, he was appointed as a Companion to the Order of Canada (CC), an honor recognizing a lifetime of outstanding achievement and merit of the highest degree in service to the country.

Kiran Mazumdar-Shaw is the chairman and managing director of Biocon Limited. A first-generation entrepreneur, pioneer of the biotechnology industry in India, and head of that country's leading biotechnology enterprise, Mazumdar-Shaw is a highly respected businesswoman. As the first female brewmaster of India, and with a pioneering spirit to "make a difference," she leveraged her learnings from fermentation science to build a company that manufactures biotechnological products through fermentation-based technology. In 2004, Biocon went public—the first

Indian biotech company to do so. Today, the company operates in two business segments—pharmaceutical and contract research services—and, under Mazumdar-Shaw's leadership, has become a well-recognized global brand.

Named among *TIME* magazine's "100 Most Influential People in the World" (2010; "Heroes" category), Mazumdar-Shaw has made affordable innovation the foundation of her business model. Recently, *The Economic Times* (India) placed her second in India Inc.'s list of the "Top 10 Most Powerful Women CEOs" (2012) while she topped *Nature Biotechnology*'s list of "thought leaders and technology pioneers" in its "Biobusiness in the Rest of the World" category (2006). Her vision and work for biotechnology have drawn global recognition, both for Indian industry and for Biocon in particular.

Mazumdar-Shaw holds a Bachelor of Science degree in zoology from Bangalore University, India, and a graduate diploma in malting and brewing from the Ballarat College of Advanced Education (University of Ballarat), Australia. She also holds several honorary degrees from renowned international universities, such as Trinity College, Dublin (Ireland); the University of Abertay, Dundee (Scotland); the University of Glasgow (Scotland); and Heriot-Watt University, Edinburgh (Scotland). She received an honorary doctorate from the University of Ballarat in 2004.

Mazumdar-Shaw is also the recipient of a number of prestigious awards, including the Nikkei Asia Prize for Regional Growth (2009); the Pharmaceutical Leadership Summit's Award for Dynamic Entrepreneur of the Year (2009); the Veuve Clicquot Initiative for Economic Development for Asia (2007); the Indian Chamber of Commerce's Lifetime Achievement Award (2005); *The Economic Times* Awards for Corporate Excellence, Businesswoman of the Year category (2004); and Ernst & Young's Entrepreneur of the Year Award for Healthcare & Life Sciences (2002), as well as recognition by the World Economic Forum as a "Technology Pioneer" (2002). Her most cherished awards are the two national civilian awards—the Padma Shri (Trade & Industry; 1989) and the Padma Bhushan (Science & Engineering; 2005)—conferred on her by the President of India.

Michael McCain is the president and CEO of Maple Leaf Foods Inc. He and his team have led the transformation of Maple Leaf Foods into Canada's leading food processor and exporter, with approximately 19,500 employees, sales of $4.9 billion in 2011, and flagship brands, including Maple Leaf, Schneiders, and Dempster's. McCain joined Maple Leaf Foods as its president and COO in 1995 and was appointed president and CEO in 1999.

Prior to joining Maple Leaf Foods, he spent 16 years with McCain Foods Limited in Canada and the United States, and was, at the time of leaving in 1995, president and CEO of McCain Foods USA Inc. He began his career with McCain Foods after graduating from university, and held progressive positions in sales, sales management, marketing management, and information systems management. In 1986, he assumed the role of president of McCain Citrus Inc., and was appointed president and CEO of McCain Foods USA Inc. in 1990.

McCain is the chairman and a director of Canada Bread Company, Limited, a director of McCain Capital Inc., the American Meat Institute, the Centre for Addiction and Mental Health Foundation (CAMH), MaRS Discovery District, the Royal Bank of Canada, and the Canadian Council of Chief Executives. He is a member of the Ontario Economic Advisory Panel of the Government of Ontario and of the Ivey Advisory Board. He also co-chairs the current CAMH Capital Campaign and is a past member of the board of trustees of the Hospital for Sick Children, as well as a past director of the American Frozen Food Institute and of Bombardier Inc.

Born in Florenceville, New Brunswick, McCain was educated at Mount Allison University and received an HBA degree from Western University. He has five children and is a resident of Toronto, Ontario.

Eileen Mercier is a management consultant and the former senior vice president and CFO of Abitibi-Price Inc. Her career encompasses 40 years of general management experience in the forest products, financial services, integrated oil, and communication industries. She has held senior positions at Gulf Canada Ltd., CanWest Capital Corporation, and the TD Bank Group. From 1995 to 2003, she ran her own management consulting firm, Finvoy Management Inc., which specialized in financial strategy, restructuring, and corporate governance issues.

Mercier was one of Canada's first female professional directors. She sits on the boards of Intact Financial Corporation, the Ontario Teachers' Pension Plan (chair), Teekay Corporation (chair of the audit committee), and University Health Network (elected vice chair, independent trustee), and is a past director of CGI Group Inc.

Mercier was named one of the "Top 25 Women of Influence" (professional services category) by *Women of Influence* magazine in 2011 and one of "Canada's Most Powerful Women: Top 100" (corporate directors category) by the Women's Executive Network in 2012. She holds an MBA from York University (Ontario, Canada) and an MA from the University of Alberta. She is a fellow of the Institute of Canadian Bankers and of the Institute of Corporate Directors, and was awarded an honorary Doctor of Laws degree from York University.

N. R. Narayana Murthy is the founder and executive chairman of Infosys Limited, a global software consulting company headquartered in Bangalore, India. He founded Infosys in 1981, served as the company's CEO from 1981 to 2002, as its chairman and chief mentor from 1981 to 2011, and as chairman emeritus from 2011 to 2013. Under his leadership, Infosys was listed on NASDAQ in 1999.

Murthy articulated, designed, and implemented the "global delivery model" that has become the foundation for the huge success in IT services outsourcing from India. He has also led key corporate governance initiatives in India, and is an IT advisor to several Asian countries.

Murthy serves on the boards of the Ford Foundation, the Rhodes Trust, the Indian School of Business, and the United Nations Foundation. He served as a member of the HSBC board between 2008 and 2012 and of the Unilever board between 2007 and 2010. He was chairman of the International Institute of Information Technology, Bangalore, between 2002 and 2012 and chairman of the Indian Institute of Management, Ahmedabad, between 2002 and 2007. He has also served on the boards of Cornell University, the Singapore Management University, INSEAD (Paris), the Wharton School of Business at the University of Pennsylvania, and the Graduate School of Business at Stanford University.

Murthy was listed as one of the "12 greatest entrepreneurs of our time" by *Fortune* magazine in 2012. A 2005 study conducted by the Economist Intelligence Unit (with Burson-Marsteller) ranked him among the "world's ten most admired chief executives." He has been awarded the Padma Vibhushan by the Government of India, the National Order of the Legion of Honour by the Government of France, and the Commander of the Most Excellent Order of the British Empire (CBE) by the UK Government. He is the first Indian winner of Ernst & Young's World Entrepreneur of the Year Award (2003) and the Max Schmidheiny Freedom Prize (2001), and he has appeared in the rankings of business people and innovators published by *BusinessWeek*, *TIME*, CNNMoney.com, *Fortune*, *India Today*, *Business Standard*, *Forbes*, and the *Financial Times*.

Murthy is a fellow of the Indian National Academy of Engineering and a foreign member of the U.S. National Academy of Engineering. He was awarded the Hoover Medal in 2012 and, in the same year, the James C. Morgan Global Humanitarian Award by the Tech Museum, California. In 2007, he received the Ernst Weber Engineering Leadership Recognition award from the Institute of Electrical and Electronics Engineers (USA). He has also been awarded about 25 honorary doctorates from universities in India and abroad.

Michael Shindler is the executive vice president, hotels and casinos, of Hard Rock International. At Hard Rock, he is responsible for all aspects of the hotels and casinos portfolio, including both development and operations. Before joining Hard Rock in 2010, he was the president of Four Corners Advisors, Inc., a hospitality transactions consultancy and advisory firm he established in 2007. From 2006 until 2007, Shindler was the vice president, development and asset management, for Las Vegas Sands Corporation. He served two stints with Hyatt Hotels Corporation (2003–2006; 1986–1996) in senior transactional roles, addressing both domestic and international markets. Other hotel development experience includes roles with Mandarin Oriental Hotel Group (vice president, development—the Americas), RockResorts International, LLC/Vail Resorts Lodging (vice president, development), and the Plasencia Group (executive vice president), while his gaming experience includes serving as chairman of the board of directors at Hyatt Gaming Management, Inc. (and its successor) for 18 months. Shindler began his career practicing law in Chicago.

He is married to Andrea Gellin Shindler, founder and executive director of the Foundation for Human Potential (FHP), a 501(c)(3) organization committed to organizing interdisciplinary symposia designed to explore new means of using brain–behavior relationships to enhance and expand educational perspectives. Shindler is the president and a member of the board of directors of FHP; he is also a member of the National Advisory Board of Carolina Performing Arts at the University of North Carolina at Chapel Hill. He received a Doctor of Jurisprudence (J.D.) degree from Washington University (St. Louis) School of Law and a Bachelor of Arts from the University of North Carolina.

Sukhinder Singh Cassidy is founder and chairman of Project J Corporation, which owns and operates an online platform, JOYUS, that enables manufacturers to showcase their apparel, beauty, and lifestyle products through videos. Prior to founding the company in 2011, she spent 18 years as a leading consumer Internet and media executive at global and early-stage companies, including Google, Amazon, Polyvore, Yodlee, and News Corporation.

Most recently, Singh Cassidy served as CEO and chairman of the board at Polyvore, Inc. and as CEO-in-residence with Accel Partners. From 2003 to 2009, she was a senior executive at Google, Inc.; as president of Asia Pacific and Latin America, she was responsible for all of Google's commercial operations in both regions and built the company's physical presence from inception to a multibillion-dollar business across 40 domains and 103 different countries throughout Asia Pacific and Latin America.

Singh Cassidy currently serves on the boards of TripAdvisor and Formspring, Inc., as an advisor to Twitter, and on the advisory council for Princeton University's Department of Computer Science. She has also been a board member of J. Crew Group, Inc. She is a graduate of the Ivey Business School at Western University.

Stephen Snyder was president and CEO of TransAlta Corporation from 1996 to 2012. Previously, he was president and CEO of Noma Industries Ltd., GE Canada Inc., and Camco Inc.

In 2011, Snyder was elected chair of the Calgary Homeless Foundation, and also serves as co-chair of the Calgary Stampede Foundation campaign. He is a member of the board of directors of both Intact Financial Corporation and the Canadian Stem Cell Foundation. He was a member of the board of TransAlta Corporation (until 2012), and also served as a director of the CIBC.

Snyder has served as chair for several charitable and non-profit organizations, including the Alberta Secretariat for Action on Homelessness, the Calgary Committee to End Homelessness, the Canada–Alberta ecoENERGY Carbon Capture & Storage Task Force, the Conference Board of Canada, the Calgary Zoological Society and the Zoo's "Destination Africa" campaign, the Canadian Electrical Association, and the United Way Campaign of Calgary and Area.

He has been awarded the Alberta Centennial Medal (2005), the Conference Board of Canada's Honorary Associate Award (2008), the Chamber of Commerce's Sherrold Moore Award of Excellence (2009), the Energy Council of Canada's Canadian Energy Person of the Year Award (2010), and was named as Alberta Oil's CEO of the Year (2011).

Snyder holds a Bachelor of Science degree in chemical engineering from Queen's University at Kingston (Ontario) as well as an MBA from the Western University. In addition, he has honorary degrees from the University of Calgary (LL.D.) and SAIT Polytechnic (formerly, the Southern Alberta Institute of Technology) (Bachelor of Applied Technology).

Carol Stephenson is the dean of the Ivey Business School at Western University, Canada. Prior to joining Ivey in 2003, she spent many years in the Canadian telecom industry.

A widely respected CEO, Stephenson currently serves on several boards for top Canadian companies, as well as on important government committees. She is a director of Intact Financial Corporation, MTS Allstream, Ballard Power Systems Inc., and General Motors. She is also chair of the federal government's Advisory Committee on Senior Level Retention and Compensation, and was chair of the Ontario Research Fund Advisory Board. Furthermore, she was a member of the Prime Minister's Advisory Council on Science and Technology and of the board of directors of the Vancouver Organizing Committee for the 2010 Olympic and Paralympic Winter Games (VANOC).

In 2009, Stephenson was appointed as an Officer of the Order of Canada (OC). She has also been honored in the Women's Executive Network's list of "Canada's Most Powerful Women: Top 100" three times (2005, 2010, 2011), and inducted into the Canadian Information Productivity Awards Hall of Fame (2005), Canada's Telecommunications Hall of Fame (2008), and the London & District Business Hall of Fame (2012).

Stephenson is a graduate of the University of Toronto, and completed an Executive MBA Program at the Haas School of Business, University of California, Berkeley. She is also a graduate of the Advanced Management Program at Harvard Business School.

Barbara Stymiest, a corporate director, has served as a director of BlackBerry (formerly Research In Motion) since 2007, and has been the chair of the board of the company since 2012. She received an HBA degree from the Ivey Business School in 1978 and became a Chartered Accountant in 1980. In 1997, she received a fellowship from the Institute of Chartered Accountants of Ontario in recognition of her contribution to the profession. In 2011, she received an honorary Doctor of Laws degree from Western University.

From 2004 to 2011, Stymiest served as a member of the Group Executive of Royal Bank of Canada, the senior leadership team responsible for the overall strategic direction of the company. Prior to that, she held positions as CEO at TSX Group Inc., executive vice president and CFO at BMO Capital Markets, and was a partner at Ernst & Young LLP. In addition to her role at BlackBerry, Stymiest also serves as a director of George Weston Limited, Sun Life Financial Inc., University Health Network, and the Canadian Institute for Advanced Research.

She has also served on the boards of a number of professional and charitable organizations, including the Advisory Board of the Capital Markets Institute, the

United Way (Toronto) Campaign Cabinet, the Toronto Rehab Foundation's "Everything Humanly Possible" campaign, and the Hincks-Dellcrest Centre, a non-profit children's mental health center.

Gautam Thapar is the founder and chairman of India's foremost diversified corporation, the Avantha Group. The group has business interests in a number of areas, including pulp and paper, power transmission and distribution equipment and services, food processing, farm forestry, chemicals, infrastructure, and information technology.

Thapar began his education at the Doon School in Uttarakhand, India, and, after studying chemical engineering in the United States, he returned to India, and started his career as a factory assistant in one of the then Thapar Group's manufacturing companies. He rose steadily, and steered the organization through a strategic and visionary turnaround, ensuring that the group attained dominant status in key operating sectors. He became group chairman of the Avantha Group in 2006, and sits on the boards of a number of companies in India and overseas. In 2008, he received the Ernst & Young Entrepreneur of the Year Award for Manufacturing.

Thapar has served as a member of the National Security Advisory Board of the National Security Council of India. He is president of Thapar University, among the top ranked engineering colleges in India, and chairman of the board of governors of the National Institute of Industrial Engineering. He is on the board of trustees of the Aspen Institute, and chairman of the board of the Aspen Institute India; chairman of the Confederation of Indian Industry's (CII) Avantha Centre for Competitiveness for SMEs; and past president of the All India Management Association.

Thapar also takes a keen interest in promoting professional golf in India. He is president of the Professional Golf Tour of India and a member of the board of the Asian Tour.

Dennis ("Chip") Wilson founded Lululemon Athletica in 1998, since which time he has served as chairman of its board of directors. From 2010 to 2012, he served as the chief innovation and branding officer, and, from 2005 to 2010, as the chief product designer. He was CEO from 1998 to 2005.

Wilson received his Bachelor of Arts degree in economics from the University of Calgary in 1980. In the same year, he founded Westbeach Snowboard Ltd., a surf, skate, and snowboard vertical retailer. He served as its CEO until 1995, and as its head of design and production from 1995 to 1997. In 2004, he was named Canadian Entrepreneur of the Year for Innovation and Marketing by Ernst & Young. In 2009, he received the Henry Singer Award, which recognizes "an exceptional leader in the retailing and services sectors," from the Alberta School of Business.

In 2007, Wilson and his wife Shannon launched imagine1day, a charity "committed to the next generation of leaders who will carry Africa into a new era of prosperity." He serves on the charity's board of directors.

Jody Wilson-Raybould (Puglaas) is a descendant of the Musgamagw Tsawataineuk and Laich-kwil-tach peoples, which are part of the Kwakwaka'wakw (also known as the Kwak'wala-speaking peoples). She is a member of the We Wai Kai nation and lives with her husband Tim Raybould at Cape Mudge village on Quadra Island, British Columbia.

Coming from a long line of strong political leadership, Wilson-Raybould was raised to be a leader. After completing a Bachelor of Arts degree in political science and history at the University of Victoria, British Columbia, she went on to earn a law degree from the University of British Columbia. She was called to the bar association in British Columbia in 2000, and then worked as a provincial crown prosecutor in Vancouver's Main Street criminal courthouse in the Downtown Eastside.

In 2003, Wilson-Raybould took a position as a process advisor at the British Columbia Treaty Commission, a body established to oversee the negotiations of modern treaties between First Nations and the Canadian Crown, but was soon elected a commissioner by the chiefs of the First Nations Summit in 2004. As a commissioner, she helped to advance a number of treaty tables and supported the establishment of a "Common Table" of 60 or more First Nations and the Crown.

Wilson-Raybould was first elected regional chief of the British Columbia Assembly of First Nations (BCAFN) in 2009, and was re-elected in 2012 by the 203 First Nations in British Columbia. As regional chief, she has championed the advancement of First Nations' strong and appropriate governance, fair access to lands and resources, improved education, and individual health. In 2011 and 2012, she co-authored the *BCAFN Governance Toolkit: A Guide to Nation Building*. She believes passionately in the need for nation building and empowering indigenous peoples to take the practical steps necessary to implement the hard-fought for rights as set out in the United Nations Declaration on the Rights of Indigenous Peoples (2007), and the promise of the recognition of aboriginal and treaty rights in Section 35 of the Constitution of Canada.

In addition to her responsibilities as regional chief, Wilson-Raybould is an elected member of the council in her home community of We Wai Kai, a role that she credits for strengthening her understanding and commitment to work at the provincial and national level advocating for strong and appropriate First Nations' governance. As a former board member for Minerva Foundation for BC Women, she was instrumental in the development of its "Combining Our Strength" initiative—a partnership of aboriginal and non-aboriginal women. She is currently a director of the national First Nations Lands Advisory Board, and deputy chair of the First Nations Finance Authority.

In 2011, Wilson-Raybould was awarded a Minerva Foundation for BC Women alumni award, and, in 2012, a distinguished alumni award from the University of Victoria. She has travelled extensively to work on indigenous peoples' rights and leadership issues, including to the Philippines, Taiwan, and Israel.

Preface

Are leaders born or made? This question has been debated for centuries and the controversy lingers today. But I believe the answer is clear. Good leaders are made through a life dedicated to constant learning about their careers, their relationships, and the kind of leader they want to become. The only question that remains and the only one that really matters is how do leaders learn to lead? The answers to this question reveal a wealth of important lessons and insights into how we can help people to become good leaders or even better leaders. That's why I chose the title "Good Leaders Learn" for this book.

As I discovered when I studied the impact of the recent financial and economic crisis on leadership, a great deal of learning comes from the uncomfortable and difficult experiences that challenge leaders. Indeed, it is often significant decisions and life-altering situations that both test and develop leaders. But this book is about more than learning from calamities. It is about the learning that happens to good leaders throughout their lives—the experiences and influences that enable leaders to know what to do, how to act and how to lead during tumultuous and trying times. This is a subject that has not been widely examined in the leadership literature—both scientific and practical—until now.

This book also explores why some leaders excel and why others fail to live up to their potential. It shows how good leaders are innately curious and why their thirst to know and understand cannot be quenched. It illustrates how good leaders capitalize on the learning opportunities available to them almost every day . . . the opportunities to learn about new ideas and better ways to do things, the opportunities to build character, and the opportunities to reflect on their commitment to the leadership role.

Good Leaders Learn brings these new insights and lessons into focus by capturing the experiences of a wide variety of leaders from different industries, sectors, backgrounds, and locations. And it wraps this richness of practical and real-life perspectives around the leadership framework of competencies, character, and commitment developed by me and my colleagues Jeffrey Gandz, Mary Crossan, and Carol Stephenson at the Ivey Business School. The fundamental purpose of this book is to help current and potential leaders to build the solid foundation of the leadership qualities vital to their continuing success. It will help them learn how to become effective leaders, in good times and bad.

Acknowledgments

I would like to acknowledge the leaders who participated in this book project, and my colleagues at the Ivey Business School who have been supportive of me writing the book. Special thanks also go to Cam Buchan, Ivan Langrish, Dawn Milne, Kylie Monteith, Kate Palmer-Gryp, Maura Pare, and Debbie Zoccano for their support. I would like to thank Manjula Raman and John Szilagyi from Routledge who guided me in writing the book. A warm thank you also goes to Rosemary Walsh and Tom Watson for all their editorial support with the book and the materials emanating from the book.

1

Introduction

Good Leaders Learn consists of a series of probing interviews with 31 leaders, representing a wide cross section of society—from business, government, health care, sports, and the arts to science and the military. The leaders vary in their ages and levels of experience. And they come from different places in the world, including Canada, the United States, India, Turkey, Bangladesh, Ireland, Germany, Hungary, and Hong Kong.

To give them time to reflect on their answers, each leader received the set of questions in advance of the interviews. Although each of these 45–120-minute interviews was somewhat structured, I told each leader that I hoped we would have a frank and candid conversation about their life and leadership career, the events that affected them, and the people who influenced them. And they did not disappoint me. These leaders shared their challenges, heartaches, and triumphs, providing deep insights into how they learned to lead over the course of their careers.

I became interested in writing a book on how leaders learn to lead for two, interrelated reasons: the discussions and controversies about leadership that arose with the recent financial crisis, and the thoughts and stories about leadership that different leaders have shared with students in my classes at the Ivey Business School.

The Financial Crisis

The global financial and economic crisis that began in late 2007 and continues to influence markets today vividly underscored that the world needs better leadership. In 2008, my colleagues Jeffrey Gandz, Mary Crossan, Carol Stephenson, and I undertook a close examination of this crisis and the impact of leadership—or the lack of good leadership—on this crisis. We engaged more than 300 senior business, public sector, and not-for-profit leaders from across Canada, as well as from New York, London, and Hong Kong, in open discussions on the role that organizational leadership played before, during, and after the crisis.

In a very real sense, we put leadership on trial, not to identify or assign blame, but to learn what happened to leadership during this critical period in recent history. We wanted to use what we learned to improve the practice of leadership today and to inform the development of the next generation of leaders for tomorrow. And as we analyzed the role of leadership in this crisis, we were faced with one major question: "Would better leadership have made a difference?" Our answer was an unequivocal, "Yes!"

We presented our conclusions in the form of a public statement of principle—a manifesto that addresses what good leaders do and the kind of people they need to be (Gandz, Crossan, Seijts, & Stephenson, 2010). A preview of our report is available online: http://www.ivey.uwo.ca/research/leadership/research/LOTreportpreview.htm. Our research illustrates that good leadership is based on the competencies, character, and commitment of leaders. Figure 1.1 shows how these three pillars are reflected in the decisions that good leaders consistently make and in the plans and actions they routinely put into play.

Competencies include the knowledge, understanding, skills, and judgment leaders are expected to have, if not early in their careers, at least in their mature phases. There are at least four competencies: strategic, business, organizational, and people. These are typically acquired through formal education, training, and development programs, as well as coaching and mentoring in the workplace (Crossan, Gandz, & Seijts, 2008). Competencies determine what leaders are able to do.

Underpinning these competencies is general intellect. Being smart matters! It matters because general intellect gives leaders the tools to understand the complex cause-and-effect relationships among the drivers of organizational performance. These drivers include commodity prices, currency fluctuations, competitive actions, tax policies, changing consumer demands, and the other cultural, demographic, and environmental trends that shape the way we live and work.

Character, which can be expressed as a set of virtues, values, and traits, is also fundamental to good leadership. It shapes how we engage with the world around us, what we notice, what we reinforce, who we consult, what we value, what we choose to act on, how we react, and how we make decisions about the challenges we face. Character is developed both early in childhood and in the later stages of life through our experiences and our reflection on these experiences. Character influences what leaders will do in different situations.

Figure 1.1 Leadership competencies, character, and commitment.

Commitment is equally critical to good leadership and it's about more than simply assuming a leadership role. True leadership commitment is about being willing to do the challenging, often grueling work of leadership and to continue to develop as a leader. When that caliber of commitment fades, leaders become mere figureheads. Commitment is forged from an individual's aspirations, from their desire to be fully engaged in their work and their willingness to make personal sacrifices in return for the opportunities and rewards that come with the role of leadership.

All leaders, at some point, will change in terms of their leadership aspirations, how much they want to be involved in their organization's work, and how much they want to sacrifice to remain a leader. When leaders no longer want to lead, they must step aside for the sake of both their performance and the development of new leaders in their organization.

The concept of the "born leader" may be attractive and suggests that good leadership is just a function of natural selection. But, for most people, leadership is learned. It is truly a lifelong process.

Leaders Visiting the Classroom

In addition to my research with others on leadership development, I teach courses in organizational behavior and leadership, wherein I often welcome outstanding leaders into my classroom to talk about leadership. They all told me that they learned to become a leader—and that their development to become an even better leader is an ongoing process. This made me think. How do leaders go through the learning process? What are the formative experiences that influence leaders? How do they reflect on events and truly learn from their mistakes and successes? How do they come to trust others and their own intuition? How do they unlearn dysfunctional habits? How do they become more self-aware?

For example, how did the president and chief executive officer (CEO) of Maple Leaf Foods, Michael McCain, learn to place his leadership on the line during the listeriosis crisis (see Chapter 18)? How did he learn the importance of accountability and taking ownership? He had to make multimillion dollar decisions within minutes; how did he develop the wisdom to act under high-pressure and openly public situations?

Why did the then president and chairman of ING DIRECT USA, Arkadi Kuhlmann, ask all of his employees each year to vote on whether they thought that he should remain in his post (see Chapter 14)? How did he develop the humility—and gain the trust of employees—to confidently ask that question again and again, knowing that some years are better than others?

How do leaders such as Sukhinder Singh Cassidy learn the politics of organizational life early on in their careers, enabling them to quickly assume more and greater leadership responsibilities (see Chapter 32)?

Craig Kielburger was inspired by reading a headline in the *Toronto Star* about child labor when he was 12 years old. How did he act on that inspiration to become a charismatic activist for the rights of children? How did he learn to deal with the cynicism that persists about his youth and perceived naivety?

How do leaders such as Lieutenant General (Ret.) Roméo Dallaire and General (Ret.) Rick Hillier learn to be decisive in life-and-death situations? How do they cope with the fact that all eyes are on them in these critical times? How do they learn to carry the burden of leadership?

How do leaders such as the Canadian Football League's Michael "Pinball" Clemons develop the patience to wait for the right time to make a change in the team or voice an opinion? How did he learn to pick his moments?

Good leaders learn from their own experience and from the experiences of other leaders they have seen in action, good or bad. They learn from their peers, the people who report to them, their competitors, partners, and suppliers. They learn from their critics and their allies. But, to learn in the first place, they must be motivated and have the capacity to learn.

Not every leader is good at learning or is prepared to constantly learn. Some leaders are not open to new ideas. I have seen that in the classroom, too. Others lack the courage to move outside of their comfort zones. There are also overconfident and arrogant leaders who lack the humility essential for learning. Still others are narcissistic, surrounding themselves with "yes" people, who would never suggest that the leader learn something new. Some leaders may simply lack the intellect to learn. Others become lazy about learning, believing that they have reached the peak of their careers and have no more to learn. The fact that these leaders can't learn or don't want to learn undermines their leadership performance. Inevitably, they fail. We have seen too many examples of these types of bad leadership in the recent past.

By contrast, good leaders never stop learning. Even at the higher levels of an organization, they find themselves learning how to lead in new and often ambiguous situations.

Developing Better Leaders

The world craves better leadership. That's apparent from today's headlines alluding to leadership failures in business, government, science and education, sports, the military, and other sectors. For example, the 2012 Edelman Trust Barometer shows an unprecedented gap in the public's trust in both government and business institutions (StrategyOne, 2012). A recent Nanos Research poll reveals that about a third of Canadians distrust scientific findings in the areas of energy technologies, medicine, climate change, and genetically modified crops (Nanos Research & IRPP, 2012).

In 2012, several national and international scandals in sports, science, and the military further fueled this public skepticism about people in positions of power.

There's the story of Lance Armstrong and the U.S. Anti-Doping Agency report that stripped him of his seven Tour de France titles and banned him from the sport for the rest of his life. Consider the Pakistani cricketers Mohammad Amir, Salman Butt, and Mohammad Asif and their conviction for spot-fixing matches. Think about Dutch researcher Diederik Stapel who admitted to fabricating data for his studies. And what about the Pentagon's 2012 survey results reporting that the number of sexual assaults at three military academies in the USA had increased by 23 percent compared to the previous year? One of these academies was the United States Military Academy at West Point, New York, an internationally recognized institution for academic, military, and physical excellence, with an emphasis on leadership character.

Whether the quality of leadership in organizations improves or not depends on the efforts of many stakeholders—families, religious institutions, schools, boards, professional associations, educators, and senior leaders in all segments of societies.

The Ivey Business School is a school of leadership. We aspire to be in the forefront of developing leadership courses and materials for both university-based and corporate leadership development programs. We conduct leading-edge research focused on real-world leadership challenges through the Ian O. Ihnatowycz Institute for Leadership. And our aim is to make this research relevant, accessible, and useful to leaders.

This book delivers on our commitment to leadership and leadership development. Through the interviews with leaders and our most recent leadership research, readers will benefit not only from a new and robust theoretical framework for leadership, but from finding out firsthand and up close how good leaders become better leaders through learning.

References

Crossan, M. M., Gandz, J., & Seijts, G. (2008). The cross-enterprise leader. *Ivey Business Journal* [online], July–August 2008. Retrieved from http://www.iveybusinessjournal.com/topics/leadership/the-cross-enterprise-leader

Gandz, J., Crossan, M., Seijts, G., & Stephenson, C. (2010). *Leadership on trial: A manifesto for leadership development*. London, Ontario, Canada: Ivey Business School.

Nanos Research & Institute for Research on Public Policy (IRPP) (2012). *Green light for science. Caution on scientists* [survey], December 28, 2012. Toronto, Ontario, Canada: Nanos Research Canada Research Inc.

StrategyOne (2012). *Edelman Trust Barometer 2012: Annual global study*. New York, NY: Edelman.

2

Leadership Character[1]

In our conversations with business leaders during the *Leadership on Trial* project (Gandz, Crossan, Seijts, & Stephenson, 2010), they brought up the importance of character and values time and time again. Here is a selection of their observations about what happened during the financial crisis and why:

- "Some people were in denial. Others recognized there were big flaws—but some were unwilling to act or did not have the courage to act, and others thought they were too small to act."
- "It appears to me that, you know, without sort of condemning society as a whole, we seem to lack a moral compass to sort of make the right decision when the reward system is suggesting that we should trade the future for the present. I think as a leadership group we lack the moral vigor to make the intelligent trade-offs . . . I just think as a society we're becoming increasingly agnostic about what we believe in and what we stand for."
- "I did have some incredible mentors at our bank. And the one thing I do remember specifically is that integrity and ethics only mean something when you keep them when it's inconvenient to do so."
- "If you have a sense of what your values are, it becomes a little bit easier for you to figure out what is right or wrong. It becomes a little bit easier for you to be courageous and say, 'I don't like it,' or 'I can live with it,' or 'Here is how I am going to deal with it.' But it all comes from a sense of knowing what's important to you first."
- "I think it comes down to your hiring practices or, in the case of the business school, perhaps entrance standards. And I don't know how you test for honesty and integrity and these sorts of things, but, when we're hiring, I would say character more than ever is a principal determinant."
- "I mean, doctors, lawyers, accountants, everyone has that standard of acceptable behavior, that when they leave the school they know that these are the standards that they need to live up to. I'm not sure that business schools create that same standard among their graduates. And I think that leads to a lot of problems with integrity and character."

Many of the leaders we interviewed underscored the importance of character. However, there wasn't a consistent or shared understanding about what "character" meant and how it could be assessed in people. This underscores the confusion that exists about what we really mean by leadership character. Furthermore, it's odd because we use the term "character" quite often in our language to describe people. Yet, when pressed to specifically assess someone's character, most people find this difficult and are uncomfortable. It seems easier to evaluate another person's competencies and commitment.

A second issue that cropped up frequently in our discussions with leaders was whether character can be learned, developed, shaped, and molded, especially in business schools and organizations. Is character something you are born with or perhaps develop as a child? What can leaders do to help develop good character among their followers? How can they nurture a culture of good character within their organizations? Again, there was no consensus among the leaders we spoke to as part of the *Leadership on Trial* research.

What did strike my colleagues and me during these conversions was that the leaders often looked to us—professors at a prestigious business school—to provide them with the answers to these questions!

In this chapter, I want to focus on leadership character, not because it is necessarily more important than competencies and commitment, but because it is the most difficult leadership quality to define, measure, assess, and hence develop.

Why Character Matters

For some reason, we have lost sight of character. Perhaps this is because our educational system and organizations focus primarily on developing competencies. Perhaps we just don't know what to think about character anymore. Has it become an old-fashioned word? Are we are simply reluctant to discuss examples of character, good or bad, with our colleagues in the workplace? Do we believe that character can't be assessed objectively?

Nevertheless, the fact remains that character is integral to effective leadership. It shouldn't and can't be ignored. Fundamentally, character shapes how we engage with the world around us, what we notice, who we talk to, what we value, how we decide, and so much more.

Our research on why leaders fail points to character as a central theme. Nowhere was this more obvious than in the financial crisis of 2008 to 2009. For example, boldness or instant gratification triumphed over temperance. People knew that bad risks were being taken, but they didn't have the courage or confidence to speak up. People with no integrity sold mortgages to those who could not pay them. Then they bundled these mortgages into fraudulent securities and sold them to others. Some leaders knew about these types of practices and did nothing to stop them. Still others were unable to create the honest, transparent corporate culture that would have enabled them to be in touch with what was happening deep down in the organization. All these were, essentially, failings of character.

Defining Character

I am indebted to my colleagues Jeffrey Gandz, Mary Crossan, and Mark Reno for helping me to define what I consider the most important dimensions of leadership character in today's rapidly changing and turbulent business environment. Together, through our discussions, our examination of the existing research literature, and our research with leaders, managers, and students, we formulated 11 dimensions of leadership character. Although our thinking is still a work in progress, I will offer some thoughts on character and how it can be developed.

There is no consensus in the existing literature on a definition of character. So, allow me to touch on three related, yet different, constructs: personality traits, values, and virtues.

Traits

Personality traits are defined as habitual patterns of thought, behavior, and emotion, considered to be relatively stable in individuals across situations and over time. Traits, however, are not fixed. Introverts may be able to learn how to behave in a less introverted way, while extroverts may learn how to control or moderate their extroverted behaviors when situations require it. For example, the Myers–Briggs Type Indicator assessment suggests that I am an introvert—a personality type that is not always conducive to effective case teaching. But I learned how to act in a more extroverted way in the classroom and, as a result, I developed and matured as a case teacher.

Traits also evolve through your life experiences—such as your childhood, your education, your observations of role models, and other social interactions. You can also deliberately develop traits through coaching, training, and other experiences. The birth of my two children and the death of my father, for example, strengthened some of my traits, and I became more appreciative, mature, and proud. There are, literally, hundreds of personality traits, from "A" (ambition) to "Z" (zealousness), that have been described in the literature.

Values

Values are beliefs that people have about what is important or worthwhile to them. Values influence behavior because people seek more of what they value. A person's values could include autonomy, transparency, the opportunity to do creative work, acting in an environmentally friendly way, work–life balance, and so on. Largely, an individual's values stem from their social environments. For instance, if we are brought up with strong religious traditions, some of us develop values based on these religious teachings. Similarly, our values may be influenced by our home life and friends, the clubs or professional associations we join, our educational choices, the companies we work for, and many other social influences. Values may change at different stages in life or to the extent that a particular value has already been realized. For example, as a person ages (or, as in my case, after a health scare), the value we place on health and a healthy lifestyle may increase.

An important subset of values are those with ethical or social dimensions, such as honesty, integrity, fairness, charity, and social responsibility. These values may be strong or weak and influence behavior accordingly.

Values may also be espoused, but not necessarily manifested. Someone may say that they value courage, but not act with courage.

It's also not unusual for people to experience value conflicts in certain situations. For example, loyalty may sometimes conflict with honesty and sometimes social responsibility may conflict with obligation to shareholders.

Virtues

From the time of the ancient Greeks, philosophers have defined certain clusters of traits, values, and behaviors as "good," and referred to them as virtues. Virtues are like behavioral habits—something that is exhibited consistently. Debates about the nature of "good character" date back millennia.

For example, Aristotle identified and defined 12 virtues: courage, temperance, generosity, magnificence, magnanimity, appropriate ambition, good temper, friendliness, truthfulness, wit, and justice. The twelfth virtue is practical wisdom, which is necessary to live the "good life" and for the achievement of happiness or well-being.

Traits, values, behaviors, and virtues are interrelated. Consider the virtue of courage. Traits such as openness to experience, self-confidence, and persistence contribute to individuals acting in courageous ways, such as putting themselves "on the line". Values such as integrity, treating individuals with respect, and achievement can also predispose individuals to behave courageously. Then there is a set of actual behaviors that individuals engage in and that friends, colleagues, and observers describe as courageous. In effect, these behaviors are societal expectations.

The 11 Virtues of a Business Leader

There exists a gap between the academic and scholarly account of character and the application of character in practice, in particular in business organizations. In my experience, existing classifications of virtues do not always resonate with business

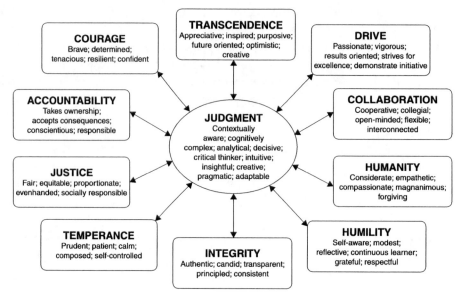

Figure 2.1 Dimensions of character (research underway at the Ivey Business School).

executives. They do not view the materials as particularly relevant or useful. A key question therefore is how character can be brought into mainstream leadership theory and practice.

Based on the existing literature in fields such as philosophy, psychology, sociology, anthropology, and management, as well as our research at the Ivey Business School, I believe that business leaders who focus on the long-term performance of their organizations demonstrate ten virtues plus an eleventh and overriding virtue (see Figure 2.1), as follows:

1. *Humility* is essential to learning and becoming a better leader.
2. *Integrity* builds trust and encourages others to collaborate. People with integrity tend to be consistent, authentic, transparent, and candid.
3. *Collaboration* enables collegiality and teamwork.
4. *Justice* yields decisions that are accepted as legitimate and reasonable by others.
5. *Courage* helps leaders to make difficult decisions and to challenge the decisions or actions of others.
6. *Temperance* ensures that leaders take reasonable risks and that they are calm when others around them panic.
7. *Accountability* ensures that leaders own the decisions they make and can encourage others to share their commitment.
8. *Humanity* builds empathy, compassion, and understanding of others.
9. *Transcendence* allows leaders to take the longer-term view and to do what is right for the future of their organizations, rather than pursue a route that

is momentarily expedient and that may have negative consequences in the longer term.

10. *Drive* implies that leaders act passionately and vigorously in their pursuit of excellence. They set stretch goals and formulate plans to achieve them.

11. *Judgment*, the overriding virtue, allows leaders to balance and integrate the first ten virtues in ways that serve the needs of multiple stakeholders both within and outside their organizations.

Consider what happens when business leaders lack these virtues. The effects on people and organizations can be devastating:

- Without *humility*, leaders are not open minded. They don't solicit and consider the views of others. They can't learn from others. They can't reflect critically on their failures, and, as such, they don't become better leaders.

- Without *integrity*, leaders can't build good relationships with their followers, with their organizational superiors, or with their allies or partners. Every promise they make must come with a guarantee. The resulting mistrust slows down decisions and actions.

- Without *collaboration*, leaders fail to achieve the worthwhile goals that require more than individual effort and skills. They don't use the diversity of knowledge, experience, perceptions, judgments, and skills available through collaboration to make better decisions and to better execute decisions. When leaders don't respect the views of others, it often creates friction in their relationships with others.

- Without a sense of *justice*, leaders are unable to understand the issues of social inequality and the challenges associated with being fair or even-handed. When leaders act unfairly, they demoralize employees. Customers, governments, and regulators react negatively. Inevitably, people rebel. They find ways to undermine the leader.

- Without *courage*, leaders do not stand up to the poor decisions made by others. A lack of courage also means the lack of the perseverance and tenacity required to work through difficult issues. Without courage, leaders will back down in the face of adversity and choose the easy route.

- Without *temperance*, leaders take uncalculated risks, rush to judgment, fail to gather relevant facts, and have no sense of proportion. They frequently change their minds and alter their decisions—with damaging consequences. Sometimes, they even reverse important decisions. Their credibility suffers along with the long-term interests of the organizations they lead.

- Without *accountability*, leaders don't commit to, or own, the decisions they make and cannot secure the commitment of others. They don't demonstrate initiative. They blame others for poor outcomes and inevitably create cultures of fear and disengagement. People stop caring—with potentially disastrous results.

- Without *humanity*, leaders are unable to relate to people, to see situations from the perspectives of other people, or to take into account the impact of their decisions on others. Without humanity, leaders do not act in socially responsible ways. They alienate people.
- Without *transcendence*, the goals of a leader become narrow. These leaders don't see the bigger picture. Consequently, their decisions are opportunistic. They often get bogged down in petty rivalries, personal feelings, and past failures.
- Without *drive*, and the passion, dynamism, and vigor associated with drive, a leader never exerts the mental and physical effort it takes to become successful, to motivate others to excel, and, ultimately, to create value for the enterprise.
- Without *judgment*, leaders make flawed decisions, especially when they must act quickly in ambiguous situations and when they are faced with the many paradoxes that confront all leaders from time to time.

Aristotle states that virtues become vices in their excess or deficiency. For example, in excess, courage becomes recklessness, and, when courage is deficient, it becomes cowardice. Too much humility may lead followers to question the leader's toughness and, consequently, they may lose confidence in the leader. But without humility, leaders make ill-advised decisions, are unable to learn, and people think they are arrogant. Transcendence in excess can turn leaders into vacuous visionaries who can't focus on the here and now and the more mundane decisions that must be made right away. But without transcendence, leaders focus on narrow, short-term goals. Too much drive and the leader becomes hypercompetitive and ruthless. But without drive, a leader becomes too complacent and can't achieve stretch goals. And while collaboration is required to make good decisions and to execute them well, too much collaboration leads to endless meetings and delays decision making.

However, no leader can have too much judgment. Without judgment, all the other virtues aren't enough to guide good actions. Every leader must learn to make decisions and take actions in complex, multi-stakeholder, and often paradoxical situations that depend on sound judgment. The overriding virtue of judgment enables good leaders to balance and integrate their other traits, values, and virtues in ways that suit different situations. For example, while a good leader should be transparent by nature, they are also able to keep a confidence or secret when it is appropriate to do so. And while a good leader is courageous, they also understand which battles to fight and which to avoid.

How Character Develops

People can develop their own character strengths. Their leaders can also help them develop character. And organizations can and should enable character development to take place.

Philosophers such as Plato and Aristotle viewed character as something that is formed, subconsciously, through repetitive behavior that is either rewarded or rewarding. The habit of character is formed along with a myriad other habits that enable and constrain us and which are productive and counterproductive—all at the same time. The interesting thing about habits is that we are often unaware of them. This makes candid feedback on our actions and behaviors critical to the development of leaders. People should always reflect on the feedback they receive from others.

Consider the Apollo 11 space mission.[2] As the story goes, the Apollo 11 space-flight was on its projected path to the moon for only three percent of the mission's time, while for the remaining 97 percent of the mission the spacecraft was off course. Nevertheless, Neil Armstrong and Buzz Aldrin set foot on the moon, as planned, on July 20, 1969. That's because, throughout the mission, NASA managers and the astronauts continuously checked and corrected the trajectory of the Apollo 11 spacecraft. There is a profound lesson in this for all leaders: When leaders continuously collect feedback, reflect, and learn, they do reach their goals. They do achieve success for themselves and their organizations.

Let me bring this down to earth. As part of an executive education program at the Ivey Business School, I teamed up with firefighters in London, Ontario, to take senior executives through a series of mock emergency drills, including the rescuing of dummy victims from a smoke-filled building. We stretched the executives! Powerful lessons about leadership, communication, and teamwork were embedded in this high-impact simulation. It also underscored the importance of character.

After the exercises, the firefighters and executives talked openly about how the drills raised their appreciation and understanding of the role of character and of character strengths such as humility, perseverance, courage, gratitude, prudence, and humor. They readily linked these character strengths to those required to achieve success in their own organizations.

Character, of course, shapes our thoughts, words, actions, and, eventually, our habits. But habits can prevent the development of character. For example, a strong ego built over time to defend one's identity can make it difficult to develop humility and the openness required to learn from different experiences. So when people believe that character is developed at an early age, in some ways, they are right. There comes a time when habits are difficult to break.

For example, I have an acquaintance who I consider to be a humble and quiet person. She found herself in a situation where people were gunning for her and her job. She felt hurt and upset because the same people who did not believe in the initiative she championed six months ago now wanted to take credit for its success. One of her mentors, a former Navy Seal, took her aside, grabbed her arm, pulled her so close that their noses almost touched, and said: "Welcome to the NFL." As her mentor explained: "You want to lead? Now's the time to grow up and realize that leadership means competition. It's part of the game." This became a defining moment to her. She soon changed her behavior, but it was challenging to do so.

It often takes profound life events to liberate us from the cages we construct for ourselves. In these crucible events, people are forced to confront the impact of behaviors and their self-concepts on individual and organizational outcomes. When you are fired or your work is criticized; when you are passed over for a promotion or promoted when you didn't think you were ready for it; when you are accused of harassment, plagiarism, or other forms of unethical behavior, these types of events can shape character.

Less dramatic, but no less important, are those events that reinforce good character. The acknowledgment, praise, recognition, or reward that come to people for doing the right thing or acting in the right way are critical to character development, especially when these events occur during an individual's formative years. Being selected for a treasured assignment or a promotion reinforces these behaviors and, therefore, develops character.

Even routine, everyday occurrences offer the opportunity for character development because these events are simply a part of one's job or life. By reflecting about why you might be impatient, stubborn, or careless you acquire the raw material for examining and developing character.

Senior Leadership and Organizational Commitment to Character Development

Senior leaders can do much to develop leadership character in others. By simply talking about character, leaders make it a legitimate topic of conversation. They stimulate discussion about character and encourage others to reflect on its importance. Organizations can also promote the importance of character by developing leadership profiles that include character as an essential part of being a good leader. Organizations should encourage employees to discuss the importance of leadership character, especially in the context of developmental coaching. When leadership profiles and coaching speak solely to leadership competencies and commitment, they implicitly suggest, if unintentionally, that character is not important.

Equally important, leaders should make sure that their organization's statement of values is more than just a poster or a plaque on the wall. These values must be integrated into the context of the work that people do every day in a meaningful way. Otherwise, employees tend to ignore these values. By the same token, senior managers should speak to the importance of these values, how these values are integral to making decisions, and how they act on these values in their work as leaders. Otherwise, employees tend to ignore these values. Just ask SNC-Lavalin, the global engineering company whose reputation was tarnished by a series of financial scandals.

For the most part, people do not learn values and virtues by osmosis. Values must be addressed explicitly in the organization's coaching and mentoring, reinforced through training and development, and actively used in recruitment, selection, performance evaluation, and succession management. The integration of values into all of these management and development activities is a proven and effective way to foster the development of character.

Personal Commitment to Character Building

The American scholar Warren Bennis often talks about the role of individual responsibility in becoming a better leader. As he says: "The leader never lies to himself, especially about himself, knows his flaws as well as his assets, and deals with them directly. You are your own raw material. When you know what you consist of and what you want to make of it, then you can invent yourself" (Seijts, Gandz, Crossan, & Reno, 2013: 20). This is as relevant to the development of leadership character as it is to the acquisition of competencies and becoming committed. The development of character requires self-awareness, a willingness to examine habitual behaviors, and an attitude that is open to better ways to lead than the ones that have worked for you, more or less, in the past. We limit our development as leaders when we don't have the discipline and courage to assess ourselves honestly.

Character is Critical!

Character is fundamental to making effective decisions. To be sure, leaders can make mistakes because they don't have the right competencies. More often, however, the root cause of these mistakes is a failing of character. For example, not recognizing or not being willing to admit that you don't have the competencies needed to succeed in a leadership role is a flaw rooted in character. Challenging the decisions of others that you believe are wrong also requires character. And, by the same token, creating a culture of constructive dissent that encourages others to challenge your decisions without fear of consequences requires character.

Character is not something that you have or don't have. Rather, it's the depth of one's character that counts. And every situation can present the opportunity to learn and deepen character. That's because character development is a lifelong journey. We may rise to the occasion in some situations, and, in others, disappoint ourselves and those around us. No one is perfect when it comes to character. But as long as you appreciate what it takes to develop habits of character, as long as you reflect on your experiences, and as long as you share your observations with others, you will continue to learn about character and how you can strengthen your character moving forward.

The real question is not really whether or not character matters. The question is why doesn't character get the attention it deserves. That responsibility lies with leaders.

Notes

1. This chapter is based on two previously published articles, "Developing leadership character" and "Character: The essence of leadership," which I co-authored (Crossan, Gandz, & Seijts, 2012; Seijts et al., 2013).
2. I am indebted to my colleague Denis Shackel who shared this anecdote with me.

References

Crossan, M. M., Gandz, J., & Seijts, G. (2012). Developing leadership character. *Ivey Business Journal* [online], January–February 2008. Retrieved from http://www.iveybusinessjournal.com/topics/leadership/developing-leadership-character

Gandz, J., Crossan, M., Seijts, G., & Stephenson, C. (2010). *Leadership on trial: A manifesto for leadership development*. London, Ontario, Canada: Ivey Business School.

Seijts, G., Gandz, J., Crossan, M., & Reno, M. (2013). Character: The essence of leadership. *Developing Leaders, 10* (Winter), 11–20.

3

Learning to Lead

People have debated for centuries—and continue to debate—whether nature or nurture is more important in the development of leaders. I believe this dichotomy is utterly false. Both play a role in leadership development. On the one hand, nature can predispose individuals to develop a set of competencies and leadership behaviors. Studies of twins, for instance, show that the development of certain aptitudes, including leadership, can be partly attributed to genetics (e.g., Arvey, Rotundo, Johnson, Zhang, & McGue, 2006; Avolio, 2007). Nurture, on the other hand, is just as important. Situational factors or external events, such as taking on the role of captain of a sports team, serving on a student council, volunteering in a church group, workplace learning and development programs, coaching or mentoring, and getting involved in local clubs or industry associations, can also foster the development of competencies and leadership character in an individual.

Talent or aptitude, therefore, is a necessary but not sufficient ingredient for leadership success. To become a leader, individuals must want to develop the competencies and to learn the behaviors expected of successful leaders. They need to learn how to excel as a leader.

For example, there is no question that many people would welcome a chance to live the life of Narayana Murthy, co-founder and executive chairman of Infosys (see Chapter 6). However, if it was somehow possible to change places with him, few would likely emulate his dedication to helping out on the home front, where he famously cleans the bathrooms on a regular basis. And that's a shame. After all, Murthy's willingness to get his hands dirty doing a job that he doesn't have to do is one of traits that helped make him a billionaire, not to mention a leader worth respecting.

When Murthy picks up a toilet brush, he isn't just looking to make his wife happy. Learning from Gandhi's teachings and example, he routinely takes on tasks widely considered beneath his station as a reminder that all contributions to society should be valued. "In the corporate context," he says, "it shows that you have respect for everybody's contribution." As he points out, sustainable success requires CEOs to recognize that there are smarter people who do things better. "Once you have that humility, once you have that openness of mind, even when you are doing well, it is possible to learn from people who are doing better than you both within the organization and outside the organization."

Murthy developed into a good leader because he was willing to put in the hard work of learning to lead. There are many individuals who aspire to be a leader, but far fewer who are really prepared to do the continuous and unrelenting work of learning to lead.

My own thinking about learning to lead has been influenced by two books published in 2008: *Talent is Overrated: What Really Separates World-Class Performers from Everybody Else* by Geoffrey Colvin and *Outliers: The Story of Success* by Malcolm Gladwell. Colvin's thesis is that "deliberate practice" explains how individuals like Jack Welch, Chris Rock, Wolfgang Amadeus Mozart, and Tiger Woods became exceptionally good at their trade. To achieve greatness, he argues, people must be extraordinarily motivated or dedicated to practicing their skills. This often requires sacrifice. People need to work furiously hard and, to paraphrase Colvin, the costs are immediate. The benefits only come later, typically after ten years of practice.

Likewise, Gladwell emphasizes that the key to high levels of success in any field is practicing a specific task for a total of about 10,000 hours. He uses the Beatles, Bill Gates, and himself—an award-winning journalist, bestselling author, and venerated public speaker—as case examples for this "10,000 hours" rule.

Good leaders can potentially learn from their every experience and from any leader they've seen in action—good or bad. They can learn from their peers, the people who report to them, competitors, partners, and suppliers. And they can learn from their critics.

But, in order to learn, leaders must want to learn and have the capability to learn. And not every leader is prepared to learn or is good at learning. For example, some leaders have traits that prevent them from being open to new ideas. They may lack the courage to move outside of their comfort zones. Overconfident or arrogant, they may lack the humility essential for learning. They may be narcissistic and surround themselves with people who tell them what they want to hear, not what they need to know to learn.

Some leaders get lazy about learning. They believe they're at the peak of their learning curves and have little more to learn. This may be a psychologically comfortable space. After all, we all like the comfort that comes from the sense that we have "arrived." But the downside is that this comfort prevents leaders from stretching their limits and improving their performance. Eventually, this leads to underperformance and obsolescence.

Leaders must also recognize new opportunities for learning and seize them. People to whom good things happen often say they were in the right place at the right time. But Gautam Thapar, founder and chairman of the Avantha Group, argues that this is not enough (see Chapter 29). Being in the right place at the right time is a good start. But the most difficult part is understanding that opportunity for what it is. To learn how to lead, you must first recognize an opportunity and then actively take advantage of it.

Good leaders see and seize opportunities for learning and development. They possess both self- and situational awareness. Others let the same opportunities pass them by. I am reminded of a sign that the former CEO of IBM, Louis V. Gerstner, Jr., had in his office:

> There are four kinds of people:
>
> 1. those who make things happen
> 2. those to whom things happen
> 3. those who watch things happen
> 4. those who don't even know that things are happening.

Some people may also lack the intellect to learn to become effective leaders. You have to be intelligent to be a leader, especially in today's complex world. Intelligent leaders can isolate the cause-and-effect relationships that will help their organizations to succeed. These leaders grasp the dynamic relationships that exist between a set of inputs and an organizationally relevant outcome. They understand risk and ways to mitigate risk. They are able to process large amounts of information within a short period of time. Some people, in other words, may be willing to learn, but they simply don't have the cognitive abilities to learn. As a result, their leadership career plateaus.

Learning to Lead

For most people, leadership is learned along pathways, which include different jobs, roles, assignments, or mentors, and these pathways will differ from one leader to another. But although these experiences tend to be diverse and wide ranging, there are some common elements to these pathways to leadership, as shown in Figure 3.1.

The common elements illustrated in Figure 3.1—performing, risking, stretching, learning, self-awareness, and trusting—are based on my work in executive development as well as the *Leadership on Trial* project (Gandz, Crossan, Seijts, & Stephenson, 2010). They served as the starting point in determining the set of open-ended questions posed to the leaders interviewed for this book.

Figure 3.1 Becoming a better leader.

Performing

To become a leader, you must be able to demonstrate that you can perform at a high level as an individual contributor. This ability to perform is required at all stages of the leadership development process. For example, Arkadi Kuhlmann, founder and former CEO of ING DIRECT USA, argues that leaders must produce tangible and compelling results (see Chapter 14). Leaders need to win—they need to make a difference in the lives of those they lead.

You can certainly call yourself a leader. You can even don the mask of a leader or fashion yourself to fit a popular caricature of a leader. You may be elected or appointed leader by the people. But at the end of the day, if you don't achieve the goals you set out to achieve, then, simply put, you are not a leader. There is no credit for trying. As articulated by Lieutenant General (Ret.) Russel L. Honoré, credit only comes when the mission is accomplished (see Chapter 22).

Risking

Leaders take risks with their personal careers. Not stupid, foolhardy, or extreme risks, but leaders push for new challenges and volunteer for the tough and sometimes unpleasant assignments that lead to learning. And they make their ambitions clear by voicing their desire for more challenging leadership roles.

For example, Stephen Snyder, former president and CEO of TransAlta, learned a leadership lesson early in his career at General Electric Canada (see Chapter 16). He thought of himself as a humble person. But there came a point when he realized that you have to take control of your career and become more declarative of your ambition. So he signaled to the senior leadership team that his ambition was to become a CEO. As a result, he was given opportunities to develop into a mature leader.

Sometimes learning comes as a result of failure and understanding how to manage that failure. For example, Rahul Bhardwaj, president and CEO of the Toronto Community Foundation, realized that, as a leader, you're fallible and that it's okay to make mistakes (see Chapter 11). In fact, if you're not making mistakes, you're probably not pushing yourself hard enough. If you're not making mistakes, you're not really creating learning opportunities. A preparedness to move outside one's comfort zone is vital to learning.

Stretching

Leaders are constantly stretching, reaching out for new performance levels and innovative and creative ways of contributing more to their organizations. They don't rest on their laurels, hunker down in their comfort zones, or become complacent. Stretching is a planned, concerted effort to master those dimensions of leadership—competencies, character, and commitment—in a way that makes a person a better leader. For example, Umran Beba, president of PepsiCo (Asia Pacific region), made several lateral moves—marketing, human resources, and sales—during her early years at the company (see Chapter 30). She viewed these transitions into different functional areas as preparation for the job of general manager. She was trained to do three things: to manage brands; to manage people and people-related agendas; and to manage and motivate sales teams to deliver results. These three distinct roles offered different perspectives and experiences, which helped her to better understand the big picture—an aptitude essential for any general manager.

Learning

One leadership myth is that the learning curve is steepest in the early years, flattens as one learns to be a good leader, and levels out toward the end of one's leadership career. Good leaders report that there is a learning curve, but it's often shaped the other way. In the early stages of their careers, they learn what others already know. But at the more advanced stages, they learn about what is currently unknown and that is far more challenging.

For example, Elyse Allan, president and CEO of General Electric Canada, was quite blunt in her assessment of learning (see Chapter 7). In the world we operate in today, she believes you're naïve if you expect that your job description will delineate everything that is expected of you. She argues that organizations need to ensure that the leaders they hire or promote are comfortable with ambiguity, complexity, uncertainty, and volatility. Any one of these can be a headwind that you will want to confront or a tailwind that you will want to ride. But the situation will never be neatly described. As a leader, you have to be able to assess the situation and lead in that situation.

Self-awareness

Through learning, leaders become more self-aware. They understand their strengths and their weaknesses, the impact they have on others and the impact that others have on them. They have a better understanding of the competencies, character and the commitment they bring to their roles. This self-awareness strengthens their capacity to lead. That's true for leaders even when it comes to appreciating their own weaknesses.

For example, Charles Brindamour, president and CEO of Intact Financial Corporation, explained that he takes time to step back and reflect on the impact his behavior has on others—in meetings, in debates about projects, and other encounters (see Chapter 26). He analyzes his behavior, assesses if it was calibrated properly, and considers whether it had the desired impact. Were my actions constructive? Was the other party open to my feedback? This introspection and retrospection leads to adjustments, if required, in his leadership behavior. It helps him to become more effective and influential as a leader.

Trusting

Finally, leaders learn to trust and to act in ways that foster trust in others. They recognize that, in order to run successful organizations, they must be prepared to cede control to others, even as they retain responsibility and accountability for outcomes over which they have little or no control. They learn to trust their teams and to trust the knowledge and intuition of others.

For example, Michael McCain, the president and CEO of Maple Leaf Foods, learned to be more trusting and confident in the people around him as he developed as a leader (see Chapter 18). In effect, he realized that necessity is the mother of invention. As your responsibilities in the role of leadership increase, you have to delegate more. As a result, you become more confident in and comfortable with the abilities of the people around you. And the more comfortable you become, the more skilled you become at getting out of the way so the people around you can perform at high levels. Basically, he views the CEO's role as one where you provide your people with the tools they need to be successful. Of course, when trust is betrayed, as is inevitable, leaders need to learn to rebuild trust, for there is no practical alternative.

Figure 3.1 presents my initial thoughts concerning the learning to lead process. I kept an open mind during the interviews and in my interpretations of what the leaders said about their learning to lead experiences. I fully expected to make changes to the figure at the end of the 31st and final interview. These changes, and why they were made, are covered in Chapters 36 to 38 of this book.

References

Arvey, R. D., Rotundo, M., Johnson, W., Zhang, Z., & McGue, M. (2006). The determinants of leadership role occupancy: Genetic and personality factors. *Leadership Quarterly, 17*(1), 1–20.

Avolio, B. J. (2007). Promoting more integrative strategies for leadership theory-building. *American Psychologist, 62*(1), 25–33.

Colvin, G. (2008). *Talent is overrated: What really separates world-class performers from everybody else.* New York, NY: Penguin Group (USA) Inc.

Gandz, J., Crossan, M., Seijts, G., & Stephenson, C. (2010). *Leadership on trial: A manifesto for leadership development.* London, Ontario, Canada: Ivey Business School.

Gladwell, M. (2008). *Outliers: The story of success.* New York, NY: Penguin Group (USA) Inc.

4

The Interviews

Thirty-one high-profile and senior leaders participated in the interviews and I believe that each one of them is a good leader. I know that the notion of "good leadership" is open to debate. There is also no doubt in my mind that the leaders I interviewed offer the best in leadership, although I am aware that at least some people will disagree with my views.

The leaders were from the public and private sector. They led small and large business organizations. They were from non-profit and for-profit organizations. They were leading organizations in North America and in Asia. They were involved in federal and provincial politics. They were from educational institutions and sports, the military and the health sector, the arts and the legal profession. Some were male and others were female; some younger and others more senior; some are still leading their organizations and others have retired. In sum, the sample of leaders is diverse.

I approached these leaders through e-mail, phone calls, and personal connections. I am indebted to Dean Carol Stephenson from the Ivey Business School for her enthusiasm for the project and her willingness to approach leaders about taking part in the interview process. I am thankful to Jeffrey Gandz and his determination to line up leaders for the interviews. My thanks also go to Ramasastry Chandrasekhar, Kelly Cole, Dianne Cunningham, Janet Ecker, Richard W. Ivey, Eric Morse, Solveig Nicklos, Maura Pare, Sami Jo Small, Cathy Vitkauskas, and Dag von Lubitz.

All but two of the interviews took place in person and the other two were conducted over the telephone. All of the interviews were audio-taped, transcribed, edited, and then sent to the leader for approval to be included in the book. The words spoken in the interviews are the leaders'. And I offer my interpretation of the leaders' statements in the three concluding chapters.

I believe the question-and-answer format of the interview write-ups underscores the richness of my dialogues with these leaders. I especially enjoyed the stories that many leaders shared with me. Stories are a great way to illustrate a point and communicate valuable insights and lessons. Peter Guber in *Tell to Win: Connect, Persuade, and Triumph with the Hidden Power of Story* explains that human beings are hard-wired to learn and to be persuaded by the oral narrative. Purposeful stories can serve as powerful calls to action. I discovered a while ago that my students remember the stories I share with them in class long after they have forgotten basic facts, theories, or frameworks.

The interviews contain insights into how these leaders learned to lead as well as their valuable leadership advice. Each interview is followed up with a short "lessons learned," encapsulating the specific leadership themes touched on in each interview.

Good Leadership

I use the term "good leaders" rather than "great leaders" on purpose. I am aware that there is an ongoing discussion in the management and leadership literature on the difference between the good and the great leader. Is "good" a lesser term? I do not believe so. The word "leader" is sprinkled liberally everywhere today, and so are words like "great" and "excellence." This is a problem because I believe it devalues the true meaning of these words. I agree with Cassie Campbell-Pascall, former captain of the Canadian women's ice hockey team (see Chapter 9), who shares this advice with young leaders: "You are not going to be the perfect leader to everybody, but that doesn't mean you're not a good leader." There is a wonderful quote by Jill Churchill, an American author. She said: "There is no way to be a perfect mother, and a million ways to be a good one." I would like to generalize this observation to leaders.

So what does "good" mean in the context of leadership? My colleague Jeffrey Gandz (2007) identified four distinct meanings:

1. Good leadership refers to *effective leadership*. The leader is effective in getting his or her followers to commit to and attain goals that were set or agreed upon. A leader like Michael Harris, the 22nd Premier of Ontario, was an effective leader (see Chapter 13). His Common Sense Revolution struck a chord with Ontarians and he was able to make significant change.
2. Good leadership also means *purposive leadership*. Leaders at all levels of an organization have to be able to communicate a vision or a purpose that inspires and excites others on a very personal level. For example, John Furlong, former CEO of the Vancouver Organizing Committee for the 2010 Olympic and Paralympic Winter Games, explained that the purpose of Canada's hosting the Olympics was not to put on a fancy show that would impress the world (see Chapter 5). Instead, he focused on the bolder purpose of bringing the nation together. And he succeeded. Who was not inspired by the event? Who was not proud of Canada? All of a sudden, Canada had swagger!

   Daniel Akerson, the chairman and CEO of General Motors, observed that people at General Motors were quite shaken after the company came out of bankruptcy (see Chapter 8). Many employees feared for their jobs and the long-term viability of the company. He and his team had to restore a sense of normalcy and convince people that General Motors had a future. An important part of his plan was to reclaim the good name and reputation of General Motors. Akerson had to show that General Motors can design, build, and sell the world's best vehicles.

3. Good leadership refers to *ethical leadership* as well. Good leaders do the right things in the right way. For example, Eileen Mercier, board chair of the Ontario Teachers' Pension Plan, is not shy about discussing ethical transgressions (see Chapter 24). She was a board member of an organization with operations in South America when the internal audit committee discovered a serious violation of the organization's rules and government regulations. She found out that the perpetrator was still with the organization a week later. She demanded action. This person had to be let go and everybody needed to be informed what happened to him and why.

   Being a good leader isn't easy. Nobody cares about excuses. "There's no credit for trying; there's credit in mission accomplishment," says Lieutenant General (Ret.) Russel Honoré, who led the U.S. military's response to the devastation of New Orleans by Hurricane Katrina in 2005 (see Chapter 22). But, despite this focus on results, Honoré points out that successful ends will not justify any means.

4. Finally, good leadership is about *making people feel good* or *feeling good about the leadership provided*. Good leaders never lose sight of the wants and desires of their followers. For example, Steve Snyder, former president and CEO of TransAlta (see Chapter 16), chaired the Calgary Committee to End Homelessness and led the development of Calgary's "10-Year Plan to End Homelessness." His employees wholeheartedly supported his commitment to this cause. They were proud of TransAlta's involvement in an initiative aimed at making a real difference in their community. Chip Wilson, founder of Lululemon Athletica, believes it is critical to engage everyone in his company's success through mentoring, profit sharing, and phenomenal training and development (see Chapter 33). He decided that any employee in the company who wants training can have it, without having to prove that they deserve it. He believes that it's up to him to make his employees feel good and to become better employees.

The leaders included in this book are good leaders. Some may even be great leaders. They all offer clear and compelling lessons to those who aspire to become a leader or a better leader.

References

Gandz, G. (2007). Great leadership is good leadership. *Ivey Business Journal* [online], May–June 2007. Retrieved from http://www.iveybusinessjournal.com/topics/leadership/great-leadership-is-good-leadership

Guber, P. (2011). *Tell to win: Connect, persuade, and triumph with the hidden power of story*. New York, NY: Crown Publishing Group.

5

You Have to Be Able to Communicate and Then Be an Example

John Furlong

John, when did you first realize you were a leader, and what happened to make you realize it?

The first time I experienced leadership, I didn't really know what it was, to be truthful. I grew up around sport. I was a competitor. I was a reasonably good athlete, and sport was a way for me to feel good about myself. In the middle of a competitive season when my team seemed to have the potential to be a great team, I received a phone call from our coach telling me I had been selected to be the team captain. I was very proud to be asked and believed that they had picked me perhaps because I was a nice guy. It felt good to be the captain. Shortly after, we played in a major championship game, in a very large stadium in front of a large crowd, and I led the team out on to the field. We played the game and we won, but it wasn't a great performance by the team and my own performance was no better than average. The coach came into the changing room to analyze the game and directed his scornful commentary at every single person on the team. When he came to me, he told me he was embarrassed by my performance; to use his words, "you were awful." It was a humiliating experience. We had a team bus, but I didn't want to be on it with the others so I walked home. Shamed. I thought about how terrible I felt, and, for the entire week, I practiced harder. Day and night. I thought of nothing else but the team. I ate better and went to bed earlier—all of the things a person should do to play better. The following week, I was ready for the next game in the tournament. It was a bigger crowd. It was exciting. And we won—we won big. It was not a spectacular performance by the team, but I played the game of my life! I felt I had really shown something and been a standout on the field. I was covered in mud and exhausted by the end of the game, but we all felt good about our victory. The coach came in, walked around to the far side of the room, and ripped into the whole team, giving every member a significant telling off. I was sitting in the last booth thinking, "this is going to be fun." He looked at me and said, "Furlong, is there any chance that you're going to make a contribution sometime soon?" At that moment, I knew that he wasn't asking me to play better—he was asking me about leading. He was telling me that he chose me to help him get the best out of these players, to demonstrate by example what was necessary for the team to be successful. He was looking at me and asking me to stand up and lead, and I realized that day that leadership was something entirely different than just having the word "captain" beside your name. I began to understand the responsibility that came with leadership, and the weight of the captaincy. After this, I was always more prepared because I knew more was expected of me. I was always looking for ways that I could do what the coach had expected, to look for opportunities to give the people I was responsible for any advantage I could think of. That was day one. To this day, very rarely does a week go by when I don't get asked this question. I'd like to say that I learned this lesson in some other more sophisticated, formal setting, but that's not how it happened. I learned it in the raw—it happened to me, it was an event, and it was seminal. Out of that, I grew a little, realizing that although you never quite live up to this concept, you constantly try to improve as you go on. That was the one and only lesson.

How did you learn to lead? What were some of the major experiences that helped you develop your leadership?

I realized that it was not reasonable to expect anybody to do anything unless you yourself were prepared to be the first one in and the last one out. *I developed an understanding of what leadership means and its implications—be a good example, show up first, don't say bad things about other people, play fair, play by the rules, win with class, lose with dignity. As I went through my life, situations came about that required these leadership lessons to come together and for me to call on them instinctively. It worked out fine every single time.*

I can honestly say that I've never successfully directed anything that did not, in and of itself, have some powerful core or vision. There was always a higher calling, something that was a privilege to do, where I was driven by something that mattered, like the Olympic Games. This wasn't a job, it wasn't a career—it was a cause. And people would do anything for you if they saw a good example to follow.

Part of learning to lead is to stretch ourselves and step out of our comfort zone. Taking on the role of CEO of the Vancouver Organizing Committee for the 2010 Olympic and Paralympic Winter Games (VANOC) was a major stretch. What made you confident that you were the right person for the job?

A couple of things had an enormous impact on my confidence and willingness to accept a tough challenge. I'm an introvert and not comfortable in big crowds, but, as a leader, I've had to give speeches. I was never comfortable going to the front of the room—I didn't raise my hand to go up. The microphone to me was as terrifying as a weapon—I didn't want to be anywhere near one. Speaking was exhausting, but also an honor. I learned as a young person—when I had the opportunity to sit down with Pierre Trudeau, who had accepted the responsibility to open the

Northern Games—that you had to be able to communicate and then be an example. I was the President of the Northern Games at the time and it was a gritty job. When Trudeau came to open the event, it was my job to brief him. I anticipated that being part of a large group for this that would ease the pressure on me, but, when the door opened, the only person who came in was Pierre Trudeau. He sat down and was very gracious—I could almost see a halo around him and there was a glow to him that made me feel comfortable. My job was to teach him about this event so that he could go downstairs and communicate a message to a large audience. As we talked, I watched him take all of it in without any notes—it was like we were friends talking. After about an hour, we went down to a big room full of people and I introduced him. I was terrified, but tried to do it in an honest way. Trudeau gave the most extraordinary speech with no notes, as if he had been a student of this project. I understood that he had something I had never noticed before in a speaker—he was not telling people what he thought they wanted to hear, but, rather, what was inside of him. I watched and I knew this was one secret to being a credible leader and being able to get people to take you seriously. That day, I made a decision: "from now on, every time I go to that microphone, people are going to hear what I feel as opposed to what I think they'd like to hear." To me, it was the most extraordinary thing, and it has allowed me to be able to stand at the microphone and in front of a room and not be so afraid. Even though I'm still a little terrified, it doesn't show because I'm prepared to be disagreed with. That, to me, was an important realization that made me comfortable with the idea of being the person at the front of the room in the spotlight—the one with the responsibility to offer people a reason to do something important.

As you transitioned to more and more senior roles, what were some of the challenges that you faced, and how did you overcome them?
The biggest challenge has always been the same—the feeling of being underestimated or seen as not as good as you think you are—because there is no proof, no reason for someone to take a chance on you. One of my favorite memories comes from the time Canada was putting together its bid for the 2010 Olympic Games. All I wanted was to volunteer to help—I never anticipated being the leader. But after people heard me talk about things that I felt we should do or not do, my name was put forward as a potential leader for the bid and I was invited for an interview. I was surprised, since I thought the person they were looking for would be somebody from big construction or big government, or somebody with a finely tuned legal mind—a person who had done something remarkable that the community knew about and whose appointment would be celebrated by the community. I'm a sports person and, although I'd had leadership experience, all my instincts come from athletics. I thought the committee was just ticking the sports box, but, as I prepared to talk with them, I realized this was a chance for me to have something to say that counts. I thought long and hard about the interview and imagined that one of the questions they would ask me was, "So, if you were given the chance to lead this

event, what do you think it should be about? What's the vision for this? Tell us what it should be?" I had watched some movie footage from the Nagano Olympic Games and was thinking about what that country had tried to do, and what other countries had tried to do. With that as a backdrop, I considered what Canada should try to do. I realized Canada was the biggest country in the world—in vastness, if not population—to ever take on this challenge. I thought it would be great to have a project in Canada that would effectively unite the country and that would be powerful enough to touch the life of every Canadian. This would be the vision that I would try to communicate. Sure enough, as I sat down next to the chairman, he said to me, "So, John, if you were chosen, what would your vision for the Olympic Games be?" and I replied, "Funny you should ask!" We were looking out the window at the North Shore Mountains and I commented that if the people who live in those homes over there don't care about what we're doing, if they don't talk about the Olympic Games every day, if it doesn't matter to them, if it doesn't touch them, if they can't see the higher calling in this project, then the project really doesn't matter at all and it will not succeed. Countries that we compete against will leave us far behind because they will have something powerful to say that will overshadow this. In my mind, I saw the Olympic flame traveling the highways and byways of the country, entering communities, leaving behind something, and, on the way, letting Canadians come face to face with what they have in common with each other. It would be one of those occasions where Canadians had the opportunity to do something together—something that happens in many smaller countries, but not in a country like this where the distance from one side to the other is almost halfway around the world. After talking about this for half an hour, I was exhausted, and when they responded, "Well, thank you for that. Could you raise the money?" I thought, "Well, that's the easy part." All of the questions in my mind seemed insignificant against this question of "why do it anyway?" As the meeting came to an end, I was feeling very proud of having simply survived. I was waiting for the elevator when the chairman and the headhunter came out with one of the committee members from tourism, who looked at me and said, "You know, John, that was an unbelievable interview. What a vision. Nobody in that room thinks you can pull it off." I realized that day that people are sometimes quick to forget that any human being alive that has achieved anything at all has been in this place where they haven't yet done anything—all of us. My nothing was probably smaller than everyone else's nothing, but I replied, "You know, if I'm given half a chance to do this, there will never be a day from now until the Olympics are over that I won't be on guard for this project." I believed that, and I believed in my head that I knew how to do it. That was my experience of being completely underestimated.

Leaders learn to deal with obstacles, setbacks, and disappointments. There will be days when it looks as if everybody is against you. You had to deal with several nasty headlines in the *Vancouver Sun*. Dick Pound, in particular, said devastating things about your leadership. How did you learn

to deal with people who thought you were a lightweight and questioned your leadership?

I woke up that morning and I wanted to buy every paper in the city. Not only was the headline terrible, but the picture was terrible too. Dick Pound had every right to feel what he felt, but how he chose to express it, to me, was terrible. Implicit in what he said was—I wasn't tough enough, I wasn't strong enough. He actually used the words, "He's a nice guy, but this is way beyond nice." I flew to Montreal, took a cab to his office, walked in through the door and closed it, pulled a chair up to his desk, and looked him in the eye. We had a conversation and I think he probably regretted a bit of what he had said. But, at the time, I wanted him to see that I was not afraid of him, and that I was not afraid of taking the leadership role either. I told him that the one thing he could be sure of was that at no time along the way was I not going to give this my best effort. In the end, I realized something important about leadership: it's unreasonable to think that one person can do it on his or her own. *It is not enough to ask the person at the top, "What will you do?" The more important question is: "What will we do?"*

Has your learning to lead been influenced by other individuals? For example, have you had the benefit of a mentor?

My father influenced me in a couple of ways. I remember him saying to me: "We've taught you the difference between right and wrong. You've been given the best lessons in life that we can give you. We've tried to equip you with the necessities to go out there and navigate your way through the world, and the things you're supposed to know at this stage—you know them. These things are not going to be enough, however, unless you're prepared to step out of the crowd, be a little bit more vulnerable, risk a little bit more humiliation, and do more than the people around you. Will you be that person? Will you be the one? If you're prepared to be the one, you have a fighting chance to be an inspired human being."

However, the greatest lesson I learned came when my father died. We were all gathered around the solicitor's desk to read his will. The first item in his will was a bequest of £500 to the Irish Government for anything he might have taken home from the office—pens, papers, erasers—anything. He was giving money to the Government! I was sitting at the desk thinking, "My dad is the most honorable guy I've ever known. Why on earth would he give the Government money?" My mother, of course, understood and wrote the check and sent it off. The reaction we got from the Government was one of astonishment. They'd never seen anything like it—it was unprecedented. My siblings and I were taken aback because we knew he wouldn't have taken anything. He'd be more likely to give it than take it. What was he doing? We concluded that what he was really saying to us was: "Listen, live a good life. Don't take it if it's not yours. If you break it, fix it. Don't say bad things about other people. Lead with dignity. Learn how to win with class and lose with grace, and make me proud—I'm watching you." I chose to use that lesson quite often in leading the Olympics. I said, "If we can live up to this, Canadians will be there for us when we need them the most. We're going to have problems, but we need to earn their respect. This is how we earn it. Someday, we're going to need the public to say, 'We're with them,' and how will we have achieved that? We need to honor them through our behavior."

My friend Jack Poole also taught me valuable leadership lessons. Jack had this wonderful capacity to take the burden from your shoulders and move it to his. He would share it with you, but it never bothered him that he took it, because he never saw it as such a burden as long as it would reduce yours. He had a way of taking the most extraordinarily complex things and making them insignificant, of demystifying and simplifying things so a mortal could look at them and think that they could go in there. I found myself, over the life of the project, mimicking this wonderful skill that he had. He would phone me to say that he'd been watching me in a complicated situation and wanted to tell me a thing or two. After five minutes or so of telling me about something he was thinking or a piece of advice he wanted to impart, he would say at the end of it, "So then, that is either the best piece of advice you are ever going to get on the subject, or not." He'd leave it to you to decide, but he just seemed to have anticipated everything. I remember on the night of the Opening Ceremonies, when the fourth arm of the cauldron didn't come up, I felt it was a metaphor for the day we'd had and I visualized him sitting beside me and what would have been in his mind. I turned to his wife and said, "This is your husband playing havoc with the Opening Ceremonies." It was one of those moments when he would have said, "What is the big deal? I mean, come on, really!" That was Jack. That was a huge thing for me to be able to acquire some of that attitude.

What were some of the hardest things to learn in becoming a good or an even better leader?

When I started to lead the project, I realized that I had made a commitment to everybody on the team. I said to them, "If you give me your best, I'll get you over the finish line." In fact, it was an unfair gesture because there were some people who were never going to get over the finish line. In a way, it may have been a bit arrogant of me to say otherwise. I had asked people to abandon their careers—to walk away from good work and more money—to come and apply themselves to this project, this noble thing we were doing. I said, "In return for your best, I will protect you and look after you, and I'll get you over the finish line," when, in fact, it was not possible for those who didn't have the right tools. They found out that it was an exam they couldn't pass. It wasn't because they weren't great, it was because it just didn't work—and they've gone on to do other things. It sounded great and I wish I could have fulfilled my promise. I think, as a leader, you have to be a bit cautious, and there are times when you have to do things that you really don't want to do. For me, that was something I remember as being a bit shallow, having said that. But, I said it.

There is always a cost to leadership. What has been the price of leadership for you?

This project lasted for about 14 years, from beginning to end. On one level, I realized at the very beginning that it would take everything I had to give, and my family knew that, and we talked about it, but it was far more than that. It's an easy thing to say, but to experience something that never goes away, that lives on your pillow, wakes up on your pillow, causes unseemly behavior by other people and leads to things happening to you and your family that are so terrible and unforgivable—that was very tough. I would say, as a Dad, I was "missing in action" for a long time. Although my family forgave that in advance, it wasn't something that I should have allowed to be forgiven, but I did. It was very difficult, and certainly had enormous impact on them. It's a high price when you're in public and everyone knows who you are, whether sitting in a restaurant or a movie theatre, and wants to talk to you about something. In the end, I think my children—they are my best friends today—came to appreciate some of the pieces. I hoped that some day, long after the Olympics were over, my kids would look back on this and be proud of what their Dad had been involved in.

Have you ever felt that you stared into the abyss? What made you turn around? And what concrete lessons did you learn from the experience?

There was a time in the early part of the project when I thought I knew things better than anyone else did. I wouldn't say I said that, but I'd say you would have been hard pressed not to see it in the way that I behaved. For example, I made a decision to not make public certain bid documents that we had, as I thought we would effectively be giving the upper hand to our international competition. I was determined that we wouldn't do it, because I thought we had a better bid and didn't want any of the details copied. Why on earth would we show off our best assets to the other countries? Jack thought we should do it, and he thought it wouldn't make one bit of difference to the other countries. I said, "No, we're not going to," and he defaulted to me saying, "Okay, if that's your position, I'll support it." As soon as our position to not go public was made public and we were harshly criticized by everyone and viewed as arrogant by the media, I realized immediately that I had made a perfect fool of myself, putting the project into a tailspin. I felt terrible about it. After that, I was far more thoughtful about how I took positions. One of the things I've always believed is that success at someone else's expense is not success. On that occasion, I didn't follow that rule. It was the first time in the project that I believed my leadership looked suspect. I didn't sleep for ages about it. My team got over it in five seconds, but I didn't.

The Olympic Games were a huge success. What are you learning these days to become an even better leader? Are there any recent "aha" moments?

One of the things I have come to appreciate more than anything else is that leadership is not just being the captain of a team. Also, the capacity for leadership is not in, or for, everyone because there is a high price to pay. I've been in places where there isn't any and I've seen situations where the non-existence of a culture of leadership is so poignant, I don't understand why no one else can see what I see. It's very different to managing. It's almost like our high school coaches used to say, "You know, if you'd just jump off the cliff, you'd learn how to fly." I think part of leadership is trying to convince people to do things they otherwise wouldn't do. Somebody once asked me, "How do you define a Canadian?" I replied, "I'm not sure I can describe the characteristics of a Canadian, but I can tell you when one walks in the room." I think leadership is the same—when you see it, you know it, but it's nevertheless hard to describe. There's something about being able to command a room and get people to say, "Count me in—I want to be part of this."

Situational awareness is critical to good leadership. How have you, over time, developed this aspect of leadership so that the signals you pick up are the right signals and hence you can make an intelligent decision?

As a leader, you have to learn to disarm the environment. I remember trying to navigate in the International Olympic Committee (IOC), and it was brutally hard. I realized that the only way to get in was to simply earn the right to stand inside the wall. We couldn't be threatening or we would be pushed outside the wall again. We had to find a way to gain acceptance. Before going to Prague to bid for the Games, somebody said, "You know, it's really important when we talk to these people that we really talk to them like human beings." I remember the morning we made our pitch. We had a team of about ten people and I had three pieces to deliver—to open, to explain the concept, and then to give the spiritual, "It's us or no one" finish. Standing in front of that crowd, I knew the whole of Canada was watching the presentation on TV and nobody was going to forgive us if we didn't come home champions! I was nervous and a little scared. I said, "You know, I have to say I'm incredibly nervous." And the whole room changed. They let us in. We won in part because we were good, but in large part because they liked us and trusted us. You have to hone that skill over time and hope you have it right. One of the things I came to appreciate more over my time in the front of the room is the more human and vulnerable you are prepared to be, the more powerful and effective you become. I now say to people, "The more willing you are to be vulnerable—because every human being in every walk of life has had that feeling of being in way over their head—the more willing people will be to move a bit and accept you."

I think that one of the best stories in your book, *Patriot Hearts*, concerns the flight attendant who spilled water over your handwritten thank-you letters to members of the IOC. What did you learn from that incident?

I had committed myself to write thank-you letters to all members of the IOC because I thought that it would mean something. But, when the time came, I was exhausted. It was bothering me that I hadn't started the task yet, so I decided I had to start. With all the information I had compiled about people I had met, I started writing the letters on airplanes because this was the most practical place for me to do it. I carried the letters in batches in my briefcase. As I was working, the flight attendants knew what I was doing and they left me alone to write. I was getting fed up with my own words, my hand hurt, and I was tired when the attendant arrived with a tray of water, accidentally spilling the whole thing over me. I wanted to throw her off the plane! She got towels but the damage had been done. She was heartbroken. I threw away a number of letters and started over. It was painful. But, after I had mailed them, and then started receiving phone calls from people who were so touched by the letters that they were going to support us, it meant a lot. Writing these letters was an important detail and every single detail matters. I had finished the task and it was a burden off my shoulders, but I didn't know for sure how it would play out. Then, of course, we won by three votes in Prague.

Here is the real lesson: We can choose to make the effort or not. Much of the time, I think we ignore what needs to be done and accept less than the very best. I tried with the Games not to allow anyone to do that. My advice to my team was, "Look, you want to look back on this and have no regrets, because you'll be the only one who knows what you didn't do. You'll be the only one. Don't put yourself in that place. Everyone else will be happy and celebrating, and you'll know that you took a corner—a shortcut. Don't take that corner. Not now, not ever!"

Leadership Themes

- Be a good example, show up first, don't say bad things about other people, play fair, play by the rules, win with class, and lose with dignity.
- You can choose to make the effort or not. Don't accept less than the very best.
- The more human and vulnerable you are prepared to be, the more powerful and effective you become.

6

No Task Is Insignificant for Making a Family, a Community, or a Corporation Better

N. R. Narayana Murthy

Narayana, when did you first realize you were a leader, and what happened to make you realize it?
That is a very tough question. *I have always believed that leaders are made by circumstances.* Leaders evolve due to a set of challenges. I also believe that it is possible for every individual to become a leader. Every one of us shows leadership qualities in different areas at different points in time. For example, my assistant may have been the captain of his soccer team or cricket team when he was attending college. My driver, who does not get too many opportunities to be a leader in the workplace, is a leader to his family and his children. He raises the enthusiasm, energy, and confidence of his children and makes them achieve what they thought was impossible. So I did not realize at any specific point in time that I could lead people. But, as opportunities came my way, I seized those opportunities and, to the best of my abilities, demonstrated my competence in leading people.

Some people seize opportunities to lead; others don't. People might be reluctant leaders. Have you always wanted to be a leader?
Yes. Whether it was during my school days, when I used to debate, or whether it was in the early part of my career, I sought those opportunities. I offered to take on more and more responsibilities, which demonstrated my desire to lead and to add value. After all, leadership is about being a transformation agent. Most of us have the desire to bring about "big ticket" changes.

How did you learn to lead? What have been the formative influences on you as a leader? From which experiences did you learn the most?
I have had several impactful influences. For example, the principal of my high school was a wonderful leader. I remember an incident when he was conducting a chemistry experiment in our class in the ninth grade. He was very careful about the amount of common salt he put into the test tube. A friend of mine who was sitting next to me in the front bench burst out laughing. The principal stopped the experiment, went to my friend, and asked him why he laughed. My friend was

very honest and said, "Look, I was quite amused that you were so stingy with the salt, which is so inexpensive." The principal said something that I thought was remarkable. He said: "Realize that this salt belongs to the school. It is community property. Therefore, I will treat it with the utmost care. When you come to my house, I will give you a huge sack of salt." That was a very important lesson for all of us. We realized that leadership was all about treating community interest as more important than personal interest.

I will give you another example that had even more impact on me. I was working as a software designer in a French company in the early 1970s. Four of us had been transferred to an important project for the French government. Our charter was to be part of an 18-member team that designed an operating system to handle air cargo for Charles de Gaulle Airport. I had a manager from the Computer Sciences Corporation. One Friday evening, around 5 p.m., when five or six of us were testing our programs, the system crashed. The mistake was mine. I had completely wiped out the disk. My colleagues wanted to leave for home, as it was a Friday evening and their girlfriends and boyfriends would be waiting. My manager came, asked me several questions, and understood what had happened. Unfortunately, the backup tapes were not working and it became clear that the task of recovery would take about 20 hours in order to get the system right by Monday morning. My manager assessed the problem, smiled, and called his wife. They were supposed to go out to dinner. He cancelled the dinner. He told me that he would stay with me and support me in recovering the system. It took me about 20 hours to complete the task. My manager brought me coffee, dinner, and supported me throughout those 20 hours by saying encouraging words. He gave me confidence and hope. When the task was completed, when he was certain that everything had gone well, he said, "Kid, next time you do this, I will spank you." He dropped me off at my apartment near Montparnasse. What a leader, what a fantastic person! He raised my confidence when I had taken up this huge impossible task. When he cancelled his appointment, he did not show one iota of dissatisfaction and anger. He made me achieve what I thought I would not be able to do. And, to me, that demonstrated the finest example of leadership.

What were some of the hardest things to learn in becoming a good or an even better leader?

The biggest bottleneck in being a leader is lack of feedback. In most countries, in the corporate world, leaders are larger than life figures. They are treated like gods. Most corporate employees are a little scared of their leaders. People don't always come forward and say, "You're wrong in this." The biggest challenge a leader has is to create channels for feedback and keep them open at all points of time so that he or she can get the much-needed feedback on where they went wrong. Fortunately, these days, we have tools like the 360-degree review. They have made the job of getting feedback easier. *But we must remember that the day a leader closes those feedback channels is the day when hubris sets in and a leader's downfall starts. I have seen prime ministers and presidents of countries lose their office when they closed the feedback channel.* Therefore, an important lesson I have learned is to keep all my channels of feedback open and to create an environment where nobody is afraid of coming and expressing their disagreement with my policies. It is important that the disagreements are based on data and facts and that they are voiced in an agreeable manner. That is why we, at Infosys, use the adage: "You can disagree with me as long as you are not disagreeable."

Based on such feedback, what have you learned about your leadership you weren't always aware of? What was a profound lesson you took away from the feedback you received?

There are many lessons that I have learned. For example, many colleagues have come to me and said I am too sales oriented and that I value the contribution of sales people much more than the contribution of other people. That was a big revelation to me. So, I asked them to substantiate their view with data. They gave some examples. I then explained to them how all the wonderful things that the company did would have no value if customers did not buy them, and how it was the sales people who convinced the customers to buy what we produced. They seemed convinced. For my part, from that day onward, I listened to everybody with the same level of attention. Here is another example: Oftentimes, people have told me that I was always in a hurry and that I wanted to get everything done in a jiffy. My response was that, in an entrepreneurial organization that has huge aspirations, we had to move as if there was no tomorrow and that, by constantly accelerating what we were doing, we could achieve things we thought were impossible. They accepted my explanation, but they also wanted me not to be in a hurry all the time. So we agreed on a compromise. There have been many, many feedback suggestions and I have learned a lot.

Leaders often talk about their learning during a crisis-like situation, but it appears to me that leaders need to learn throughout the entire business cycle. Can you discuss how you learn during the full business cycle? Infosys has grown at a rapid pace.

An important requirement for success is for us to learn to be humble, to suppress one's ego, and to recognize that there are people who are much smarter than ourselves. Yes, Infosys has been successful, but there are organizations that have performed even better. So, therefore, if you have humility and you have openness of mind, it is possible to learn from people who are doing better than you, both within the organization and outside the organization, even when you are doing well. This is where I believe global benchmarking becomes important. For example, Infosys benchmarked with Motorola in quality when Motorola was a leader in quality. We benchmarked ourselves with Hewlett Packard, an organization that was known for its human resources practices. We learned from General Electric, and Jack Welch's relentless focus on growing the business quarter after quarter. We have learned from the entrepreneurial spirit of Microsoft. So, I believe that we must identify leaders and organizations that have performed better than us and benchmark ourselves against them. But, to do that, you have to suppress your ego. You have to have a sense of humility, and you have to respect people who have performed better than you.

I read a number of interviews in which there are several values and virtues that you keep bringing up—sacrifice, respect, humility, fairness, honesty, integrity, harmony, accountability, transparency, and so forth. These values and virtues guide you in your decision making. Where did these come from?

We are the products of our circumstances. My father was a teacher. We were a family of eight children. I came from a lower middle class family. Our heroes were always teachers. My father would speak about Nehru, Gandhi, and other leaders at dinnertime. He would tell stories from their lives. He would talk about the importance of respect. So, therefore, these conversations created a framework for success in my mind. I came to believe that to be successful is to be respected. That is why, when Infosys was formed, I suggested to my younger colleagues to accept respect as our primary objective. My logic was that seeking respect from customers would help us to exceed their expectations. Seeking respect from fellow employees will help us to be fair with them. Seeking respect from investors will force us to follow the finest principles of corporate governance. Seeking respect from the society will make it easy for us to live in harmony with the society. Seeking respect from the government of the land will remind us to not violate any law of the land. If we did all of this, revenues would come, profits would come, and market capitalization would come. So, that is why our initial mission statement was to be the most respected company in India. Of course, later on, we changed it to communicate our desire to be a globally respected corporation.

How difficult is it to live those values, and to do so on a consistent basis? We talk about values a lot. But leaders tell me that pressures from both within and outside the organization make them, at times, compromise on their values. How difficult has it been for you to live those values? Transparency, for example, can be really inconvenient at times.

There is no doubt that it is very difficult to live out these values day after day. But if we keep our ego, greed, and hubris under control, it becomes easier. If we are willing to lead a simple lifestyle, and if we are not slaves to our money, then it is easier. Therefore, it is very important to have habits that are inexpensive. My father exhorted us to develop such habits. Once, I asked him what those inexpensive habits were. He asked me to read books. When I was small, perhaps even today, every small town in India had a public library where you could borrow books for free and read. Second, he asked me to spend time listening to music. Those days, every small town in India used to have a public park where music was played for an hour every evening. Today, you can do the same with an inexpensive radio. Third, he suggested that I spend time holding conversations with good people. He believed that such conversations would help me to acquire knowledge and wisdom. I practiced my father's advice and found that having inexpensive habits would help me become a master of my habits and that I could keep my greed under control. Similarly, when I remind myself that there are so many people smarter than me in this world, it helps me to mitigate the impact of ego, greed, and hubris.

Business schools have been criticized as producing amoral technocrats. What, in your opinion, do business schools need to do to create better leaders? For example, to help develop leaders with more compassion? You describe yourself as a compassionate capitalist.

Before I can criticize business schools and the MBA programs, I must criticize the leaders of the society. We are the people who have set a wrong example for our younger people. We have chosen the wrong attributes for measuring success in the corporate world. A few years ago, I gave a talk at Columbia Business School entitled "Making respect more respectable." I spoke about how, today, the respect for a business leader comes primarily from market capitalization, the salary that he or she gets, and from the power that he or she wields. I suggested that a global platform such as *Fortune* or the World Economic Forum choose the 100 most-respected global business leaders based on how honestly they conduct their business, how fairly they do business with business partners, how respectfully they treat their employees, how transparent and accountable they are with their shareholders, how enthusiastically they participate in corporate social responsibility, and how they live in harmony with the government. If we did that for five years, the MBA graduates would aspire to be like them. But if, every day, our corporate leaders are vying with each other to get higher salaries, or just to seek market capitalization higher than their competitors by hook or by crook, then it is very difficult to teach MBA students that respect is important. Therefore, I will hold us, the corporate leaders, squarely responsible for not living up to the expectations of the society.

I found it quite remarkable that you founded Infosys with six other colleagues. You operated as a team. I have no doubt that at times there was disagreement and conflict. What have you learned about working effectively in teams?

We followed a set of rules that ensured harmony and oneness as we moved forward. First was to make sure every proposal that anybody brought to the table did not have any self-interest. These proposals had to make the organization stronger, and not any individual or set of individuals. Second, in every discussion, we accepted meritocracy as the basis for judging. Third, every idea was judged purely based on data and facts. Finally, one had to be courteous in how one treated one's colleagues, and argue only in an agreeable manner. This scheme made everybody confident that he or she would win the next argument if they had better data or better facts, even if they lost the current argument. It did not mean that there was 100 % success, but, by and large, it was successful.

I've read that there is something you do every night when you return home, which is to clean the lavatory. Is that true?
Yes, I still do that.

I think there is a profound business lesson involved here. What is the deeper meaning behind this activity?
We have to realize that no task is insignificant in making a family or a community or a corporation better. Second, if there is a task that you don't want to do, but you want somebody else to do, then that person will feel less than what he or she is. There is the concept of "untouchables" here in India—the people labeled by the caste system as "impure," less than human. These are the people who clean the toilets. Mahatma Gandhi said he would clean his toilet because this was an activity that was as important as any other activity. So, I do believe that it is very important, certainly for Indians, to do some of these things because we have to work on our prejudices and reduce our biases. In the corporate context, it shows that you have respect for everybody's contribution. For example, the fact that we have a clean glass to drink from is important to me because we want our visitors to be very comfortable in drinking from that glass. This task is handled by one of the janitors who ensures the glasses are clean.

How did you develop resilience? How have you learned to cope with stress and adverse events, such as setbacks and obstacles in your business? Nothing in life comes easy, in particular in India.
In the early years of Infosys, my two children were young. Spending time with children is very relaxing because of their innocent questions, their ability to enjoy small things in life, their ability to laugh, and their desire for pranks. Such interactions with children release your stress.

I am a fan of Western classical music. It gives me a lot of joy. I spend some of my free time listening to Western classical music. I also believe the most precious things in life do not require much money—affection, love, care, music, books, and conversation. These are good ways of releasing one's stress.

You've talked about books a number of times. I see a lot of books here on your shelves. Is there any particular book that you really appreciate because it helped you think and reflect more on leadership and lessons that you tried to internalize?
Three books have helped me develop my philosophy. They are Max Weber's *The Protestant Work Ethic and the Spirit of Capitalism*, Mahatma Gandhi's autobiography *The Story of My Experiments With Truth*, and *Peau Noir, Masque Blanc* (which means *Black Skin, White Mask*) by an Algerian author named Frantz

Fanon. Fanon was a doctor who took part in the Algerian struggle for independence. In this book, he describes how the attitudes of the rich, the powerful, and the elite in post-colonial societies have retarded the progress of the poor in such societies. Max Weber's ideas help make a society more prosperous. Mahatma Gandhi's idea of leadership by example is a good way for leaders to gain the trust of their followers. I believe that the ideas from these books help a society make fast and inclusive progress.

Coming to ideas of leadership, the book that I like most is *Winners Never Cheat* by Jon M. Huntsman. Jon Huntsman has demonstrated, through his own example, that it is possible to run a business legally and ethically, and that it is possible to win without cheating people. The book is a fantastic read. I have it on my Kindle as well as in print form. I read it often.

Good leaders learn. They mature. How has your leadership evolved over time? Are you a very different person today than when you started Infosys?

As a leader, you have to leverage the strength of people. So, you have to quickly assess their capabilities. You will have to leverage their strengths and mask their weaknesses. *Second, as you start taking on bigger and bigger tasks, you realize that teamwork becomes extremely important. It requires you to suppress your ego, and to give opportunities for other people to shine.* Third, experience has also taught me that not all people have the same level of competence, or the same level of energy and enthusiasm. It is like in a marathon. Different people drop out at different points of time. Expecting everybody to complete the marathon at the same speed is not realistic. A smart leader chooses the right people based on their strengths and weaknesses, protects the respect and dignity of each individual, raises their confidence, hopes, aspirations, and enthusiasm, values their contributions, and instills a sense of meritocracy in the environment. I have learned that there are a few key attributes that are time invariant and context invariant for the success of an organization. They are: openness to new ideas, an environment of justice, meritocracy, speed, imagination or innovation, and excellence in execution.

You are a self-taught entrepreneur. What leadership advice would you give to young entrepreneurs to become better leaders?

Entrepreneurship is about deferred gratification. It is about sacrifice today, with the hope that tomorrow will bring better days, a better future. That means an entrepreneur has to bring together a team of people, create a grand vision, instill hope, enhance their energy and enthusiasm, and make them accept sacrifice today in the hope that tomorrow they will be able to catch a part of the rainbow. *The best instrument that an entrepreneur has, in making people accept sacrifice today in the hope of a better tomorrow, is leadership by example. The leader has to accept bigger sacrifices than those he or she has asked others to accept.* For example, when Infosys was founded, I took 10 percent of the salary and

I made sure that others had a 20 percent higher salary. Similarly, when I asked my other colleagues to be in the office at 7:45 a.m. to handle the time zone differences with our customers in the USA, I used to come at 6:30 a.m. Therefore, the most important advice that I could give any leader is to lead by example, and to walk the talk.

We talked a little bit about virtues. But, as we all know, a virtue can easily turn into a vice. Courage, for example, can turn into recklessness or hubris. Can you talk a little bit about the role that mistakes played in your learning to lead? Has there been a situation where you stared into the abyss? What made you turn around? And what was the major leadership lesson that you took away from that situation?

It's very interesting that you ask that question. From day one, we have operated this company as an enlightened democracy. That is, whenever we had to make a major decision, I would assemble all the relevant people. I would decide the amount of time that we would spend on that topic. We would discuss, listen to every good idea on the subject, and then come to the best possible decision. The good thing about a democracy is that you will never have a disaster because, in a democracy, there is always an opposition. We have been very lucky that we have not had a disaster, because every major decision was discussed and a decision arrived at after getting input from all the major players. That is not to say that we have not had any issues. For example, in 2001, when the Internet boom came to an end and there were serious problems in the marketplace, there was a discussion about recruiting 1,500 engineers for Infosys. Every one of my colleagues argued that we should not recruit, except the head of sales. I finally decided that we would recruit. That was not a great decision. That is when I realized it was always better to listen to the sane voices and not be carried away by one's own confidence.

You have a great quote: "A clear conscience is the softest pillow on which you can lay your head down at night."

It is important that all of us try and maintain a clear conscience through fairness, decency, and honesty. The most important requirement for all of us is a good night's sleep. I have found that I sleep well when I have a clear conscience. Several friends of mine are very rich. Many of them do not sleep well at night because either they have cheated a business colleague, or cheated the government, or done something wrong. So, a clear conscience is very important.

Leadership Themes

- Leaders understand that no task is insignificant in making a family, a community, or a corporation better.
- Leaders create channels for feedback and keep them open at all points in time so that they can get much-needed feedback on where they went wrong.
- Leaders must learn to be humble, to suppress their ego, and to recognize that there are people who are much smarter than themselves.
- Smart leaders choose the right people based on their strengths and weaknesses, protect the respect and dignity of each individual, raise their confidence, hopes, aspirations, and enthusiasm, value their contributions, and instill a sense of meritocracy in the environment.
- Leaders lead by example. The leader has to accept bigger sacrifices than those he or she has asked others to accept.
- It is important that all of us try and maintain a clear conscience through fairness, decency, and honesty. The most important requirement for all of us is a good night's sleep.

7

I Am a Better Leader When I Can Represent That in Which I Believe, and for Which My Passion Is Sincere, My Understanding Is Complete, and My Commitment Is Personal

Elyse Allan

Elyse, when did you first realize you were a leader, and what happened to make you realize it?

At an early age, I knew I was an organizer. As an organizer, I'm not sure I thought of myself as a leader. That realization came at a much later point in my life, when I was at General Electric (GE) and people were talking about leadership. Now, in retrospect, I realize I started leading people very early on. Leadership begins when you start to drive people toward a vision you have created or own, organize people to deliver on that objective, and accept responsibility for the success or failure of the effort. For me, this probably started some time in high school when I rallied folks around ideas to support causes and then organized everyone to take real action to help that cause or make the desired change happen.

Have you always wanted to be a leader?

I never thought about it that way. I have been developing ideas or championing a changed situation, motivating and engaging folks to share that view and work with me to achieve it throughout my life. And I was also always comfortable assuming the responsibility, whether or not we succeeded.

You are the CEO of GE Canada. What have been the formative influences on you as a leader?

I have a few observations. First, I think a critical formative influence is the environment in which I grew up. My parents raised me with a shared belief that initiative and hard work pay off. We were not entitled to lead and accomplishment didn't happen without input. Success, achievement, and respect were earned by our deeds, not our words. That shared value was very important in our family.

A second factor that I also attribute to my upbringing is that I am "comfortable in my skin" and feel well grounded in terms of my values and moral compass. This has proven to be very important for me as a leader because so many decisions we face are not black and white, but gray. *I believe our ability to test our values and to build good judgment through personal experiences and observations helps us establish an internal compass and reduce the "gray" zone. This is very important for a leader.*

The third influence is learning from the actions and experiences of other leaders. I learn so much by watching the way other people interact and handle situations— even those that I think I might not experience and then some day they happen. And, because you paid attention at another point in time and thought about that situation, you have it in your background.

Right now, I am so fortunate to work with an outstanding company where leadership development is core to who we are. I learn every day by watching how my colleagues handle different situations. When I am at a meeting with our chairman and CEO, Jeff Immelt, I pay attention to how he leads, challenges, and influences our team. It's always a learning experience and one I make the effort to reflect upon.

And, finally, there is formal training. Of course, what that means evolves over time and one's career. But, that said, the structured effort focused on particular takeaways and experiences is critical. GE's classroom and experiential learning programs have given me great insights and perspectives that I know have made me a better leader.

There are many different inputs and influences that have developed and shaped my leadership style and capabilities over the years—and I continue to learn and further strengthen those capabilities.

Was there perhaps any particular experience that served as a crucible—an experience that supercharged your learning to lead?

I don't know that there was an ultimate crucible where I walked away and suddenly knew I was a different leader. I find that learning is much more evolutionary for me than having the big "aha." While there was no one event, there were certainly different types of experiences that impacted my leadership development.

For example, you learn a lot from bad decisions or failures. I've been fortunate. I haven't had any major blowouts—but I've certainly had my share of failures or missed opportunities along the way. I think receiving honest feedback— constructive criticism—is incredibly valuable to leadership development. I remember some feedback I received just after I first arrived at GE and was promoted to lead a team of my peers. I was new to the role, pretty serious and over-achieving . . . and my manager said to me, "You've got to go out for a beer with folks and get to know them better outside of work and warm up to them." I think he really wanted me to relax a bit . . . and let them get to know me so we could work better together. I found this advice very useful. Make sure you know the people on your team—who they are and where they are coming from. And let them know the same about you.

Another experience involves job transitions. I almost always accepted roles in an organization where I admired and respected the person for whom I would be working. Of course, I learned the risk in this approach is that you may not like the situation you are left with if that person leaves or moves on.

As I stated at the start of my answer, I do believe in continuous learning and ongoing development in leadership skills, style, and competency. Our roles evolve, companies and situations change, and our leadership capabilities need to change and evolve as well.

You talked about transitions. You started your career at GE in 1984. You left for a few years, but then came back, in 1988, into Canada and returned again as the CEO in 2004. And so, if you just look at your time at GE as you transitioned to more and more senior roles, what were some of the challenges you faced in terms of the requisite competencies, the character that was required, or the commitment to the leadership role? How did you deal with them?

This is a great question. This is my third time back at GE. First, there are always things that you're not going to know in the new role. You have to determine what you need to know and who you need to go to for that information. Recognizing the competencies you require in the next stage of your leadership career is really important. As well as determining your domain expertise versus reaching out and leveraging the expertise of others in the team. In my transition to this role, I weighed the competing needs of internal versus external connections, technology versus market dynamics . . . and the list goes on. How can my leadership best bring value to the company and to my team? What is needed in this role—where do I have to stretch myself to ensure I'm delivering what my team needs to excel?

The passion and commitment to both the strategic vision and the need to combine the strategic vision with execution is something that is fundamental in almost all leadership roles. We have a phrase here: "Imagination without discipline is chaos." Many people have the imagination, the ideas, and the vision. But I think it's also the ability to drive the execution that is so critical in leadership. I believe effective leadership is the marriage of articulating a strategic vision, driving the execution to realize that vision, and being accountable for the results.

The third area I'd like to highlight is needs of the team. The team you have in each situation may well have different needs and expectations of you. Your approach as a leader in terms of motivating, engaging, and developing the team might be different in a large and complex company compared to a smaller, more intimate organization or a non-profit setting. As I moved into different companies and different roles, I learned how important it is to coach your team to excel.

You were the president and CEO of the Toronto Board of Trade and an executive at Ontario Hydro responsible for marketing and technology. What did you learn about leadership in those positions that set you up for your current role as CEO of GE Canada?

I learned a great deal in my different jobs outside GE, especially at the Toronto Board of Trade. I was there for nine years. There, I gained important insights into the intersection of business, government, and the community. At the Toronto Board of Trade, *I learned how much you can get done when you have a compelling vision and the ability to articulate that vision in different ways that motivate different constituencies all around the same vision.* People had spoken to me about the power of grassroots organizations and how impactful they can be. However, this was the first time I saw how that really worked. I appreciated the influence people can have on the media and the power of the media. I learned a great deal about advocating ideas and proposals to politicians as well as how the relationship between media and politicians motivated action. I observed the large number of stakeholders and how some have a lot to say but don't do a lot and will never change their positions.

Overall, my experience at the Toronto Board of Trade helped me better understand how you move something forward in a complex environment when you control very little. I realize now how critical it is to understand what motivates each of the stakeholders and the points of intersection between them. As well, I realized that ultimately you can partner with those least expected, if you can figure out where you both have common ground and points of alignment. This is challenging, of course, but at the same time it's incredibly powerful in terms of getting something done that may be complex and messy. And not a lot of people can do it.

The world today has become more complex and smaller, so we have more global influences that we don't control but need to understand. The stakeholder group has grown. The influence of the government has grown. Social media has emerged as a powerful force that can get a story out before it has officially broken. My role at the Toronto Board of Trade proved to be an incredible classroom in terms of preparing me for my CEO role.

I'll speak briefly about my time at Ontario Hydro. The company was a crown corporation at the time. Government was the primary shareholder, we were regulated, and we had a monopoly. How people think and make decisions both personally and organizationally was quite different than what happens in a traditional private sector company. Appreciating that difference and how it affects your leadership is really important.

Why did you leave GE and, maybe more importantly, why did you decide to return to GE twice?

In both instances, I made the decision to leave for personal and career reasons. The first time I left GE, I was recruited by a group of people who had left GE Capital to do a leveraged buyout of a company. We had worked together before, and I was intrigued by their offer, excited by the opportunity to learn about the capital deal-making world. I was young, risk averse, and respected the folks who were pitching. There was a lot going on in the world of deals on Wall Street at the time . . . so the market seemed hot. I thought, "If this turns out to be a mistake, I have lots of options ahead of me. On the other hand, if it works, it could be quite interesting and I will get exposure to an area that I haven't had

exposure to previously and potentially learn a great deal." So I took the risk. It
didn't exactly work out for the group of us. Fortuitously, as I was planning to leave,
GE found me and called with an intriguing offer. They had heard that I was
engaged to a Canadian. They told me the company could use my skill set and
previous GE experience to launch similar work in Canada. They said, "Some
things that you did for us when you were here we'd like to have you do in Canada.
Will you come back? And are you going to Canada?" This was a great
opportunity for my husband and me to get married and live together! And for
me to come back to GE. You often hear that the company looks for talent and
that it follows people. Here was a great example—I had left on great terms and
kept in touch with everybody. And then, there they were when I was looking for
the next stage in my career and I was there to deliver on something the
company needed. Before I had even called them, they had called me—it worked
out perfectly.

The second time I left, there were a couple of factors at play. The company
wanted me to go back to the United States, where there were several roles
they wanted to move me into. But my husband and I were nesting. We had
bought a house, just had a baby, and we had a perfect care arrangement in place.
My husband was with a firm that was also based in New York, so we
could have moved. But we really made a very important quality-of-life decision.
We both felt we might be better off financially by moving, but it would not be the
balance of life we wanted. We thought we'd lose more control over the balance
that was important to us. Hence, I made the decision to mentally unpack. Canada
would now be home. And once I made that decision, in the early 1990s, I
thought, "I need to learn more about my new home and get based with a company
where I can build a career here." While GE had lots of opportunities for me, I felt
the need to go exploring again. And so when a headhunter called with an
opportunity at a large Canadian company, Ontario Hydro, I accepted the
interview and the role. It was local, so I didn't have as much travel with our young
child at home. So it balanced off a couple of things that were important to us at
the time.

And what made you decide to come back as CEO?
Once again, GE found me and called. I was at the Toronto Board of Trade
and approaching my 10-year mark. I had made it a practice to always reassess
personal and organizational progress around five years in any role. So, after five
years at the Board of Trade, I reinvented my role and redefined the challenge ahead
to make the next five years engaging to me and valuable to the board. As I was
approaching 10 years, I was considering leaving the board to make way for new
blood. Just at that time, GE called and let me know the current CEO was retiring
and, if I was interested, they would like to include me in the competition for that
position. So the timing was perfect. I love GE, and now I had the opportunity to
pursue a role that, earlier in my life, I had aspired to hold. So it was a great fit—and
it worked out.

What were some of the hardest things for you to learn in becoming a good or an even better leader—and why?
The first lesson is the realization that you might be a very good leader in one situation, but, as the dynamics—situation, team, or challenge—change, there are aspects of your leadership approach that you have to change, or you might not be the best leader. You need to learn how to be the most effective leader in different environments. I believe there are certain core attributes that you bring wherever you are—your personal values, your moral compass, and your judgment. That said, your leadership skills definitely change as you progress in your career and have new experiences. *I think it is a real learning process to develop flexibility. You have to be sensitive to this because you may come in with an approach based on your previous experiences and feel you are prepared ... but your effectiveness can derail easily when you are not assessing the situation, your impact, and interaction with the team.*

The second example is the value of the formal versus informal structures. Leaders operate in a complex world. They need to understand the real value of the informal networks. Research shows leaders aren't very good at knowing and understanding the informal networks that exist in their organizations. GE is a global company. Our matrix structure is quite complex. People are spread over great distances. Leaders should be sensitive to the fact that they may not fully understand how the informal network works. *You have to focus time and attention on understanding who in your organization might be really important influencers and critical "knowledge" people to the rest of the team. They may not be the people you thought were the stars.*

As well, it is important to understand the links you need to make to be an effective influencer and leader for your own team. Also, understand your team's importance back into the network.

How did you develop confidence and comfort in dealing with risk in ambiguous situations? How did you learn to live with the knot in your stomach?
I actually like the knot in my stomach. I enjoy the complexity of the problem and the challenge that has to be solved ... the messier, the better. I think you learn to take risks, quite honestly, by taking them. In doing so, I believe it helps us realize that often what you've assessed to be risk isn't really risk. My observation is that people often worry about the wrong things and overemphasize things that are simply not that risky.

I find it valuable to debate risk with others; to ask, "Do you think it's as risky as I do? How do you look at it? What do you see as the main contributors to risk? Why are you hesitant?" People around the table hold different perspectives on risk. I think it is very important to hear these different perspectives, especially when the conversation is with different stakeholders, customers, or groups.

You cannot worry about things that are beyond your control?
There are a lot of things that you simply will not control. There is no action you can take that would stop, or potentially stop, that risk or control that risk. The question

then becomes: Is your solution flexible and robust enough that, if you are wrong, you can deal with it?

Is being able to operate with ambiguity critical?

Absolutely. In today's volatile world, decision making in more ambiguous situations is a critical skill. I think there was a sense, in days gone by, that people needed to know exactly who they report to, what their roles are, and what they should be doing. When I was applying for this position, we discussed a new type of role in the company. Much of it still needed to be shaped because the changes under consideration impacted our entire international organization structure and our approach to globalization. I had a lengthy discussion with my potential new manager. In my thank-you letter to him, I wrote that I really appreciated our discussion and that I was very comfortable with the complete ambiguity of the job that he had attempted to describe.

It is unrealistic to expect, in today's world, that you're going to get a job description that delineates everything that will be expected of you. We need to be ensuring that the leaders we're bringing into our organizations have a comfort with ambiguity, complexity, uncertainty, and volatility. Any one of those can be a headwind at the moment or a tailwind that you want to ride. We need leaders who can quickly assess the situation they are in and have the confidence and the ability to lead the team in that situation. This is a really important lesson for our young people coming through our education system.

I've been a very strong supporter of liberal arts education. Many universities have moved from that because of pressure from people who want more job function specificity. But, in fact, when we look at a liberal arts education, it teaches the ability to think across disciplines and to manage complexity. That approach has a great deal of relevance to leadership today. *Successful leaders today will be able to understand interdisciplinary complexities, work with multiple stakeholders, and solicit broadly for ideas to solve problems.*

Leaders must be transparent and candid in their critical conversations. GE is known for having a culture for candor. What have you learned over the years about speaking with candor and having people listen to you and not becoming defensive? What have you learned about becoming influential?

The world is complex. I find transparency helps. Most of the roles I've had in my career have been around influence and not people directly reporting to me. When I have had larger numbers of direct reports, I still realized that implementation requires a great deal of influence. I find the underpinning of influence is trust. People see through hollow passion soon enough, in particular when they are working with you on the team. Influence is about your sincerity, honesty, and level of trustworthiness. I do believe that business is still personal. You are still two people and you represent an organization, so, when you are making a commitment, maybe sometimes you will not be able to get everyone to deliver, but the person with whom you're working knows you will be doing your utmost to deliver on the commitment you've made. People need to know that you have a high "say:do" ratio. They need to know that if you committed something to the team or to a customer, or you're talking to the government about the way you want to operate, that you will deliver. This goes back to the values and the moral compass that you bring to your role as the leader.

I also find it important to have good alignment between the values of the company and those of the leader. I am a better leader when I can represent that in which I believe, for which my passion is sincere, my understanding is complete, and my commitment is personal. People are hearing from me what I believe we will do and what I will do my utmost to have our company do.

Leadership comes with a price or cost. What has been the price of leadership for you?

Leadership comes with incredible benefits. I think the price or cost of leadership depends on what you're seeking in life and what balance is to you. In my own experience, as I moved through the organization and gained more responsibility, I found it simply takes more time. There is a lot of travel required—and the day still only has 24 hours. As a result, you can't do everything. In my case, the price has been that my group of friends is a more intimate group. I don't see my close friends as often as I'd like. The great thing is that I have a group of friends who know my world and love me anyway. I've been fortunate to find that group of people.

The other comment that I'd make—and I learned this at the Toronto Board of Trade—is that, in the world of media and, now, social media, you become more public. Leadership can be media heavy. Leaders are becoming more exposed. And often the person and the company become melded. You are a spokesperson and you are always representing the company. So I never forget that 24/7 I am the CEO of GE Canada. I have to realize that my behaviors reflect as much on my family and me as they do on our company.

I think leaders always live in a fishbowl so your actions and decisions are public. People might second-guess every action and decision. How did you learn to deal with such transparency and the associated pressures?

When dealing publicly with an issue, I have always had great help ensuring we are well prepared. I think it's something that you really don't fall into—you do have to be coached. You have to learn from experience and from mistakes. You will also learn about trust. You learn very quickly, through your own experiences or somebody else's, that "off the record" is never off the record. You learn very quickly that the mics can stay on when you think the mics are off, or the cameras keep rolling when you think the cameras are off. And sometimes you learn because it happened to other people and you think, "Oh, I never want that to happen to me." The final point is that you need the substance—it's very hard to be in front of the camera when the substance is weak and diluted. Understand the various positions. Make sure you are well briefed. Have great content. You will go into the situation with that much more confidence and that confidence shows.

What have you personally experienced as a barrier to learning? How have you tried to overcome this barrier?
Everybody learns differently. I learn by interviewing others, doing, and testing. As well, I have found GE's new small group experiential sessions very effective. Of course, what matters to me now is different than from five years ago. And the way I might learn that skill or lesson has also changed. I think what you're trying to learn and what is the best way for you to learn varies, not only by person, but also through your experience and life. Consequently, from my perspective, it's critical to stay open minded about new approaches.

Leaders typically learn a lot about themselves during crisis-like situations. Can you please talk a little bit about learning during the full business cycle when everything is going well?
I often tell people that if I ever feel too comfortable, I get worried. Maybe that goes back to the idea of the knot in your stomach. The world is always changing. You always want to be anticipating and therefore challenging yourself as to what are the changes—what are the headwinds that might come your way—and making sure that the team and you are ready for that. So I value testing different scenarios, anticipating actions and reactions. I learn from that. We don't wait for the crisis to happen to learn how to manage in a crisis—we learn by constantly drilling the crisis in the good times.

My second point centers on opportunity. *If things are good, an important question involves your tolerance of risk to take things while they are good now and actually push them faster. Push them harder, have a greater sense of urgency to actually deliver more while you're feeling good and strong.*

You have worked with different leaders. You worked with Jack Welch and Jeff Immelt. What did you learn about working with individuals who have different approaches to leadership?
You learn there are very different types of leaders and they can all be very effective, but in their own ways. My second comment is that organizations probably need different leaders at different times—not all leaders are effective in all situations—a particular style and perspective may be better suited for different times. As I mentioned earlier, there is value in stepping back every so often and assessing whether the skill set, competencies, character, and approach you are bringing to the role is right for the organization, the environment that it is in, and at that point in time.

What advice do you have for women as they embark on their journey of learning to lead?

My advice for women is to develop a leadership style that suits you—it should reflect who you are. You have to be true to yourself and have confidence in building your own approach—one that suits you. Women often have great attributes around multi-skilling, listening, facilitation, and collaboration. These attributes don't come naturally to all, but do come more comfortably to many. These are such important competencies as we look at leadership in our current and more complex environment. Women shouldn't lose those skills just because they may not see them well modeled in male leaders they've worked with. Rather, they need the courage and confidence to bring those skills forward and to develop them.

I read an interesting quote about that in *The Globe and Mail* (Toronto, Canada). You mentioned that women make terrific leaders in part because they listen and in part because they don't rush a decision—correct?

Yes. Often, there's a sense that you need to be able to make a quick decision. Not all decisions are made the same way, or need to be made by you, or need to be made quickly. Leaders gain valuable experience learning from times when decisions were made too fast, too slow, or with too much or too little consultation. I think women, and I appreciate that this is a bit of a generalization, will look at more variables and will reach out to more stakeholders in the decision-making process. This can be valuable when there is time and the input leads to more buy-in or a better decision. But it is not appropriate in all situations.

You have been close to both Jack Welch and Jeff Immelt. GE is known as a company that cares about leadership and leadership development. Is there a difference in focus between these two individuals and how they develop leaders?

I've worked far more under Jeff than Jack, so your question is difficult for me to answer. My comment would be more about the company's approach to leadership. We've never wavered in understanding that we can educate, develop, and help make better leaders. We can make people who didn't think they had leadership capabilities actually be great leaders. We can help those who may not have been as successful as they would like learn to be better leaders. Our organization's commitment to leadership development has been unwavering throughout its history.

The second thing is, throughout my years at GE, we have always started with the concept that we have to understand our values. Values matter when it comes to leadership.

A third consistent theme has been that we can help you understand your personal behaviors and those you should start or stop doing to become a better leader. If we can translate values and attributes of leadership into behaviors, then we can help everyone become a better leader.

And most important is that a prerequisite for leadership is integrity—it is foundational to everything else.

Leadership Themes

- Determine what you need to know and where you need to rely on your team to be the expert.
- Imagination without discipline is chaos. Leadership is the marriage of strategic vision and execution.
- Leaders have to focus time and attention on understanding who in the organization might be really important influencers and critical knowledge people.
- Leaders learn to appreciate that there is a lot of risk that they'll never understand or know about. A key question, therefore, is whether they are flexible enough to deal with what they actually don't know.
- Leaders learn very quickly, through their own experiences or somebody else's, that "off the record" is never off the record.
- Every five years or so, leaders need to step back and ask whether their skill set, competencies, character, and approach that they bring to the role is right for the organization and the environment that it is in at this point in time.

8

It Is Critical That Leaders Understand the Concepts of Duty and Obligation

Daniel Akerson

Dan, when did you first realize you were a leader, and what happened to make you realize it?

When you're young, "leadership" is more akin to a popularity contest. People shove you to the front because they like you. I think "leadership" at that age is based more on popularity than substance. You're the captain of the baseball team, you're the student body representative in your grade school or your middle school, and you start to feel an obligation, a responsibility. Leadership is emergent. It's not clear to you what leadership is. It's good to be well received and respected and liked, but leadership is, as you know, much deeper than that.

Then, in high school and higher education, it gets more complicated. In the United States, we have military service academies, such as Annapolis and West Point, from which we've produced presidents, ambassadors, and war leaders. I went to one of those schools—the United States Naval Academy in Annapolis, Maryland. It is a tough academic program. The admission criteria were focused on the "whole man" concept. The school questioned whether students were seen as leaders by their teachers, coaches, scout leaders, church, and so forth. Candidates were considered for their past participation in positions of responsibility and leadership. Were they extroverted in their personalities and did they demonstrate a desire to be at the head of the class or the leader of a team? The military is a crucible that accelerates your recognition that you might be a leader—that you could evolve to become a leader—and it gives you the opportunity to lead at a very young age.

I truly realized I was a leader and the burdens of leadership when I was a young naval officer aboard ship. As a young naval officer, you have significant responsibilities: an engineering officer had responsibility to run a plant that could produce enough power to light a small city; a weapons officer had responsibility for weapons. At the same time, you're leading men that have professional and personal challenges: they have a job, a duty, and they're away from their families, sometimes for extended periods of time. They're young. Maybe they're married and have children. They get lonesome. Leaders must keep them motivated, focused on the job at hand.

It's there I realized how important leadership was to accomplishing a mission, a goal, and a set of tasks important to the overall output of the organization. While I was a midshipman, the Naval Academy's leadership would bring back successful leaders from the Second World War, the Korean War, and the Vietnam War. These veteran leaders would relate the challenges they faced. This training was not only inspirational but also useful because our class was training for a similar future. What role did their leadership play in these times of stress and crisis?

Our academic and leadership skills were tested every day, to the point where one third of our class did not graduate. From the outset, at Induction Day, we were told, "Look to your left, look to your right—one of you won't be here in four years." Our curriculum wasn't all about academics. It was about character development, leadership, and the honor—these were critical aspects to one's success. *It became very obvious to me that I wasn't being trained to be an engineer; I was being developed to be a leader. This training gave me a huge step up at an early stage in my life.*

Have you always wanted to be a leader?
I think by nature I'm confident (extroverted more than introverted) and I am competitive. If on a team, I wanted the ball. In baseball, I wanted to be the pitcher. I love competition and I enjoy the camaraderie that comes with team sports; the shared experience of winning. I volunteered a lot and got involved every chance I could.

What leadership insights helped you to prepare for the leadership role in business?
Leaders carry the burden of accountability and responsibility. *It's critical that leaders understand the concepts of duty and obligation.* That you are obligated to complete the assigned task for the "greater good." There's an element of honor to be able to lead an organization, but there is also a responsibility and a duty to do it well and to the best of your ability. Fundamentally, one requires three attributes to be a good leader:

1. You must be competent. In the military or business world, people must be confident in the leader's knowledge and capability. The leader doesn't have to be the smartest person in the room, but he or she must have a combination of basic intelligence and experience, and be competent enough to lead the organization.
2. Leaders must have integrity, character. People may feel the leader is able, but if you cut corners, if the leader is unethical, he or she is not going to have the credibility to lead. Nobody will follow an unethical leader for long. You have to be competent and have integrity to be an effective leader.

3. Leaders have to be passionate and have the ability to communicate why the task before the organization is worthy of their efforts, hard work, and sacrifice.

When I became CEO of General Motors, the company was committed to an initial public offering (IPO) in order to liquidate a portion of the U.S. Government's stake in the company. I was essentially given about 90 days to prepare. On a variety of matters, ranging from marketing to engineering to product development, I had to achieve a level of competency. I was offered executive summaries, but chose to selectively delve into intimate details. It was necessary that I demonstrate a high degree of competency so that future owners were assured that the new management was up to the task.

Under the best of circumstances, you learn by observing and emulating good leaders. But, in reality, you will see both good and bad, and ofttimes somewhere in between. ***Perversely, you can learn more from a bad leader—what not to do, and how not to behave in certain situations—than you do from a good leader.*** In the end, your individual leadership style will be a compilation of many experiences, some productive and some maybe not so productive.

I always say about leadership that competencies count, character matters, and commitment to the leadership role is critical to success—individual and organizational.

Agreed. One of the most important people in terms of my personal development used to tell me, "A raise will make your spouse happy for a day or two, but it won't drive you for the next 364 days." Ask yourself: what drives you to identify with the leader of your organization? Do you identify with the team and its goals and what the team (company) is trying to accomplish? I think so, and that's what will make you come back every day and work long hours and strive to achieve. ***People strive to achieve to exceed not for a paycheck but for pride, to be part of something bigger than themselves.*** Leaders at all levels of an organization have to be able to communicate a vision, a purpose that inspires and excites at a very personal, individual level.

As a leader, you will wonder, "How can I establish that dynamic in our organization?" Here at General Motors, it's quite easy. When we came out of bankruptcy, people were really quite shaken. I think many feared for their jobs, the long-term viability of the company. We had to restore a sense of normalcy and convince people that our company had a future. There is a reclamation taking place at General Motors. One aspect of our vision is the reclamation of the good name and reputation of General Motors. That we can and will design, build, and sell the world's best vehicles. Look back 25 to 30 years and you get a sense that we lost our way and strove to "meet the market," to be average. That's a flawed "strategy," a poor vision. Employees see that; they are not inspired by "average" and start to disengage. Today's General Motors exhibits greater energy and enthusiasm because they see the efforts, and initial success, to take our game to greater heights. "Average" can't be part of our future dialogue.

You graduated in 1970 from the U.S. Naval Academy; you served in the Navy for five years during the Vietnam War. How did that particular experience, your military service, influence you as a business leader?
When you are in the military, you don't question what the mission is, the purpose you serve. You serve the needs of our nation; you serve the needs of the Navy. You're not serving for the pay. You serve for the good of our nation as determined by our elected civilian leadership. I always felt service to our nation to be a noble calling, although some of my civilian contemporaries weren't very proud of the military and military service at the time.

I learned how important leadership was to the accomplishment of a job. I better understood the impact positive leadership could have on an organization. Whether in military or business, while in leadership positions, an individual has responsibilities, obligations. Success in discharging the duties of any job may be measured differently—for example, profits versus victory—but "survival" is a common, basic criteria. Prosperity is better in both instances.

So, the responsibility of leadership isn't that much different between the military and business; the mission is clearly different. *Good leaders lead by example, they are able to articulate a vision, a purpose, they must inspire.*

Two important things that I learned in the Navy and that have been very useful throughout my career are:

1. *You must learn to follow before you can lead.* In our culture of cynicism and individualism, there's an unspoken belief the individual knows everything . . . after all, I read it on the Internet! Well, seasoned leaders, either by experience or by where they sit in an organization, ofttimes have better information, and a better perspective. One has to learn to trust. Of course, leaders can be wrong, and have been wrong. That's why there are chains of command, leadership structures, and open-door policies. That's why CEOs have a board of directors. Checks and balances.
2. Great organizations have leaders at every level. People are competent in their jobs; they have unique skills that are not universally shared throughout the organization. An assembly line worker has knowledge of how to build a car, an accountant knows how to balance a ledger, but they share the responsibility of leadership; to speak up about what's right and what's wrong in support of making our company, our ship, a better working, more efficient unit—for the greater good. Leaders support the common goals of organization, and they support one another. They hold one another accountable. *Leadership is not simply top down. To the contrary, great organizations support, communicate, and lead vertically, horizontally, and diagonally.*

You talked about the burden of leadership. Why did you take the General Motors job knowing that it would be a tough challenge to turn the company around?

When the prior CEO left, the board asked me if I would consider the possibility of joining management. It was an "inconvenient" time in my life. I was at a private equity firm that was on the verge of going public. I was a large investor of the business, and would have to forgo the IPO and all that it represented. It would be a radical change to my life, late in my career, in an industry that I had experienced only by way of my board service. So why did I take it? Well, as the old adage goes, "If not me, who? If not now, when?"

I took the job, in large measure, for non-financial reasons, out of a sense of duty and service to our nation. It also happens to be, from a personal and professional perspective, one of the most interesting business paradigms of my lifetime. To my mind, the job has to be multidimensional: interesting, challenging, and fun. There's a lot of personal satisfaction and, yes, hard work, but it has been rewarding. General Motors is an important company. It's an iconic company, it's important to America. This industry represents about 3.5 percent of the total U.S. GDP. It represents 8 million people who are employed by the automotive industry in the United States. In the original equipment manufacturers, there are about 3.5 million people, and about 1.5 million in the dealerships. There are 47 states that have at least 10,000 autoworkers or more, and 20 states that have roughly 100,000 automotive-related jobs. It's a huge company by global standards that competes around the world. It would have been a mistake for this country to essentially give up a fundamental dimension of its industrial and manufacturing base because of structural problems and mistakes of the past by both union and management. I'd rather be part of the solution than the problem; I did not want to be an observer to the demise of an entire sector of our economy. There is something special and noble about our efforts to reclaim and restore General Motors. It transcends any one individual. If you are able to make a difference here, it is multiplied many times over. There have been and will be tough days, and there have been and will be great days. You've got to remember the great ones because they sustain you through the tough periods.

What were some of the hardest things to learn in becoming a good or an even better leader?

You have to constantly evaluate and assess individuals in the performance of their jobs and the potential they may or may not have. You have to be honest in your communication, your feedback. Feedback on quantitative measures is relatively easy. Qualitative assessments, where judgment comes into play, are much more difficult to "measure" and communicate. Nevertheless, one has to be honest and forthright in communicating in both areas. If you accept mediocrity, over time that becomes a hallmark of the organization, and the organization "dumbs down." *You have to recognize that you, too, as a leader, are being observed. If the leader accepts mediocrity, that behavior will be replicated.*

What was the best leadership advice you ever received that helped you develop into a better leader?

I worked for a great leader, named Bill McGowan. He started a company called MCI. He built an organization that took on AT&T and won. His comment was, "Never let them see you sweat." To be a good leader, you sometimes have to be bold, you always have to be persistent, and you have to have tenacity. You can't give in. Winston Churchill said, "Never, never, never give up." There were times that AT&T should have been able to put us out of business, and they tried. They tried so hard, they lost multiple anti-trust actions to the U.S. Government and MCI. In the end, even though we were on the cusp of bankruptcy more than once, we succeeded because we simply would not quit. All companies face hard times, challenges; great companies are persistent and never give up. Bill McGowan was MCI's heart and soul; he never quit and wouldn't let the leadership quit. I was always brought up that way. My Dad was that way.

I was in a race in high school, and broke my fibula in my lower leg. I rolled it, and it broke. I wouldn't quit. I had a half mile to go, but I had to finish that race. The attending doctor thought I was crazy; all I knew was that I had to finish that race.

Leaders learn a lot about themselves and the business in times of crises— can you talk a little bit about learning to lead during the full business cycle? I understand that you've worked for companies that have had explosive growth—what did you learn about yourself during those circumstances?

Credibility in leadership is vitally important. Set the performance bar high, demand consistency in both the up and the down cycles. Demonstrate a degree of grace and poise in both good and bad times. I don't like people panicking around me, and I certainly don't want to show fear or anxiety. Again, "Never let them see you sweat." When things are going well, take it in your stride. Establish a steady pace. In times of stress, the organization will understand the need to quicken the pace and will respond to the challenge. *If you're always in an "emergency" mode—on the balls of your feet—you'll burn people out.* The organization has to know that the leadership has a sense of proportion, what's really important and what's not so important. You need to know when to ask for that extra effort and when to ease off a little bit. I have often said to management, "When things are going really well, we're really not earning our money. We earn our salary when things aren't going well, when times are tough, so prepare yourself and prepare the organization."

You have a knack for telling employees what they don't want to hear. I think people have concluded that you bring candor to the role. What about the

reverse? How do you make sure people around you are not just telling you what you want to hear, but are telling you what you need to hear, which I think is especially important during a crisis-like situation, when you need accurate and timely information?

I'm at a stage in my life where I feel I've learned to read situations and people much better than when I was young. I always try to lead by example. I try to be open and honest in my communications, and I encourage those who work with me to respond in kind. That requires a bilateral relationship built on trust. Subordinates will only trust in that relationship if they feel I will listen and respond in a measured and constructive manner. Based on experience gained over many years, I believe I have honed my listening skills and have learned to sort through what is fact or fiction, emotion or analytical assessment.

Complacency is a killer to organizational success. I've read that you are challenging the organization in significant ways. How did you learn to influence people effectively?

Complacency and mediocrity are killers to an organization. Leadership can and will trump these organizational "diseases." It's a complex formulation of vision that inspires goals that serve as guiding lights, a culture that is open and honest, commitment by the leadership that serves as an example, crisp execution, and accountability.

To inspire the organization, I speak of the reclamation of our good name and how important that is to our nation, our communities, and our families. How do we go about achieving this "reclamation?" What are the rallying points that the organization can focus on? We have articulated four basic building blocks that serve as guiding lights throughout the company: producing the best vehicles, strengthening the brands and their value, growing profitably on a global scale, and maintaining a "fortress" balance sheet. These are simple, clear goals that provide an overarching construct for every organizational unit to support when building operational goals and objectives. The organization then has to create and support a culture of "openness," which calls accountability to the fore.

Central to organizational goals and objectives is our external perspective. In order to keep the organization sharp and to avoid complacency, external benchmarking is critical. In the end, competition will be the arbiter of success.

What are you learning these days to become an even better leader? Are there any recent "aha" moments?

I think I'm much more self-aware and self-critical. I did not "grow up" in the automotive industry; I grew up in the technology/telecommunications industry. Leadership and management skills are transferable, but industry-specific knowledge is an area that I am intensely focused on. *I have had to hone my listening skills and allow that, every day I come to work, I learn as well as contribute. I find that exhilarating and humbling.* I hope that enthusiasm is infectious and helps me to become a better, more inspirational leader.

Leadership Themes

- Leaders must inspire people by their example.
- Leaders need to know how to follow.
- Don't accept mediocrity, it reflects badly on you.

9

I'm a Big Believer That If You Don't Want to Be Criticized, Then Say Nothing, Do Nothing, and Be Nothing

Cassie Campbell-Pascall

Cassie, when did you first realize you were a leader, and what happened to make you realize it?

I was named captain or assistant on almost every team I played—soccer, volleyball, or hockey. By university age, I began to realize exactly what it means to be a captain. I played for the University of Guelph—I was chosen to lead a great group of people. I thought, "Hey I'm the leader. I have certain things I need to do."

Have you always wanted to be a leader?

I don't know if I always wanted to be the captain. I don't think I ever set a goal that I wanted to be captain of the national women's hockey team. But I always wanted to be a leader. I always wanted to be someone who had an impact on the ice and on people's lives—to try to make people around me better. That was always a part of my character. But I think I would have been the same person regardless of being given a letter [the "C" for captain or "A" for assistant captain] or not.

What have been the formative influences on you as a captain or leader? What did people do to help you learn? What experiences did you learn the most from? Was there any particular experience that supercharged your learning to lead?

First and foremost, my parents influenced me. My parents were divorced, but they were very supportive of me through all my sports. They taught me about the importance of working hard. They both had their own businesses. My parents were hard-working people; they built their businesses from the ground up. I also learned from them that you treat people the way you would like to be treated. I remember an incident in minor hockey. A girl got a penalty on me. I was very upset about it and I hit her as she was on her way to the penalty box. My mom took away my skates when I met her in the arena lobby. It was a quick message—treat people properly off and on the ice. These two elements—hard work and respect—are the foundation of my leadership.

My older brother also played hockey. He made it up to the Junior C level and was a great player. But he never had an opportunity to make it to the big leagues.

He was captain and assistant on his teams. He played every role—defense and forward. He was a versatile player and I think that is why he was chosen for his leadership. I learned from him the importance of versatility, or a willingness to do everything for your team.

I learned a lot from the captains of the national women's hockey team. Sue Scherer was the very first captain in the 1990s. She was also my coach at the University of Guelph. I learned from her the importance of professionalism. She spoke well. She conducted herself well. She had a real presence. She also told me to just be myself. Those words have stuck with me forever—just be myself. ***People who struggle with leadership are often trying to be something they're not. And people see right through them.*** I haven't met one leader who is perfect. I can say that about me and I'm sure all the great leaders of our time would say that about themselves. But I think the best ones know they're not perfect so they decide to just be themselves. The moment you try to be perfect, people are going to see right through you and see you as fake. That stuck with me throughout my career: "Cass, just be yourself." She probably doesn't even remember saying those words, but they were pretty powerful.

The second captain of the national team, Stacy Wilson, was a grinder of a forward. She led by example and would do anything for the team. I learned from her that you don't necessarily have to be the best player on the team, but you can still be a great leader. In my opinion, it is very rare if the team's best player is the best leader.

Is there any particular experience that supercharged your learning to lead as a captain?

The 1998 Olympics in Nagano. We lost the final and won a silver medal. I was a young assistant captain and pretty immature. Maybe I thought I was a little better than I actually was. A lot of new things were coming at women's hockey during that Olympics—things we'd never experienced before. I allowed my head to swell a little bit. My leadership got away from my foundation. I didn't reach out to people and ask for help or lean on people as I had done before in my career. I realized that you can quickly become a different person if you allow it to happen.

I didn't perform very well during that Olympics and I will always live with that regret. We had a lot of veteran players who'd been around a long time and this was their only kick at the can for the Olympics. I still live with that regret today—I did not play as well as I should have. I learned a lot about myself that year and I changed to become a better player, person, and leader after that experience.

You said you changed. Did people around you correct you on your behavior?

People tried, I think, but I didn't want to hear certain things. Furthermore, I think people felt they couldn't say certain things to me, as the assistant captain, because I was supposed to be a leader. I wish more people who really knew me had taken me aside and said, "Shape up," or "What are you doing?" They should have been more blunt with me, particularly all those great veterans on the team. I would have really respected what they had to say to me. But it was a new experience for everyone, and all of us were going through the Olympic experience for the first time.

I also remember that a coach was trying to reach out to me that year through a sports psychologist. I brushed that off. I didn't think it was important. Of course, it was very important to get the opinions of experts and people around me. I was just too cocky to think they had anything of value to give me. My immaturity showed for sure that year.

How did you prepare for the role of captain of the national women's team? What did people do to instill in you the confidence to take on the captain role?

I relied on my assistants, particularly Vicky Sunohara. She easily could have been the team captain. Danielle Goyette was another player on the team. She was a very good friend and I leaned on her a lot. We also had a sports psychologist, Peter Jensen. I leaned on him if I needed to vent about my personal issues with the game. I always found that difficult as I never wanted to go to my teammates a lot because my job was to get them to play their best, and I never wanted to take away from that. So I often looked to outside people to chat. My husband was a big supporter of me. I remember one particular story in the 2002 Olympic year. We had lost eight times in a row to the United States. He luckily was on the trip with the team. He worked for Hockey Canada. So I went to him after the game—our eighth consecutive loss—and I just asked, "I'm the captain of this team, what am I doing wrong? Why are we like this and why can't we win?" He looked at me and said, "Cass, what a story this is going to be. You guys are losing all these games, but you're going to win the one that really matters." If I hadn't heard those words from him at that particular time, I would have put so much pressure on myself and so much blame on the lack of our team performance. That conversation changed my whole way of thinking. I kept telling the girls, "What a story this is going to be. We're going to beat the American dream team on its own soil. What a story it's going to be after losing so many times." I often looked outside the team just because I wanted to make sure they knew I was positive and focused on the goal at hand. My job was to make them the best they could be. I felt that if I was venting or frustrated, I wouldn't be the great leader that I should have been.

The team beat the United States during the 2002 Olympic Final in Salt Lake City. Was this an incredible boost in your confidence as captain?

I look back at that 2002 Olympic year and people are always shocked to hear me say that it was the worst hockey year of my entire career. We had so many things thrown at us. We had a veteran cut at the last minute and replaced by a rookie. We had injuries. There were so many things that went on behind the scenes that took a lot of my energy. I internalized a lot of these events and felt that it was reflective of my leadership.

I kept questioning myself and I had to make some pretty tough decisions. For example, I had to call out a veteran on our team. At the time, she was one of the best players in the world, in my opinion, but she never had her best performances when we played against the United States, year after year. We really needed her to perform. As a last-ditch effort, I called her out in front of the team, which is something I had never done before and never really believed in. I knew it was going to be tough. I knew some people were going to agree with me and some would not. But I knew it was the right thing to do because she needed to know that this was the way I felt. We had tried other things in previous years, but nothing really worked. She was mad at me for a good month. But she came out of her little slump and played some of the best hockey of her career. We are good friends today. That was one of the hardest things I ever had to do, and I was taking a chance of losing her good play altogether, but I knew she was a great leader too and I knew that she would realize that if I was able to say those things, then they must be true. Only she knows the previous conversations she had with other leaders, including myself, on the team, and she eventually figured out that what I had said was true, and, once she realized that, she played some of the best hockey I had ever seen from her.

I really struggled with that decision. ***Being a leader sometimes involves communicating tough things and making hard decisions. I believe that, by saying nothing, you can actually make things worse. At least you show you care when communicating a tough message. I think everyone realized that I cared.*** I was willing to talk about a friend in front of the group and let her know we needed her to be better. It all worked out and, yes, it boosted my confidence.

Sometimes we have to put our leadership on the line.
I would rather make a mistake than do or say nothing. I'm a big believer that if you don't want to be criticized, then say nothing, do nothing, and be nothing.

Leaders often model themselves after other leaders they admire. Other than Sue Scherer and Stacy Wilson, I don't think there were a lot of high-profile female captains in hockey at the time you played. Did you model yourself after a captain from the NHL?
I was a huge fan of Steve Yzerman. He was a fantastic player and captain. One of my former teammates, Jayna Hefford, told a story to *Sportsnet* magazine. She commented on my leadership, and basically said that I always knew what to say in a difficult situation. I think Steve Yzerman was a lot like that. I admired his humbleness. For example, if an article was written about him, he always tried to bring in his teammates and make it about the team. I think that was my big focus. Even though I was getting a lot of the attention, I always tried to deflect things to the team to really pump up the other girls and make them understand how important they were. So, yes, Steve Yzerman was definitely someone I looked up to. He's probably only about five or six years older than me, but I idolized him and watched him a bit more closely than others. He didn't talk all the time as he picked his

moments, and he also was willing to do whatever it took on the ice to make his team better. He was an elite player who also changed his style of play to benefit the team to win.

Did you ever have conversations with the other NHL team captains or did you just communicate from a distance?

Most of the communication was from a distance. But I will tell you a funny story about Steve Yzerman. He couldn't go to the 2006 Olympics in Turin because of a bad knee. I'm at the opening ceremonies and my cell phone rings. I answer it and someone says, "Hey Cassie, this is Steve Yzerman." I thought someone was playing a joke on me. Sure enough, it was Steve. He wished my teammates and me the best of luck for the tournament. I remember sharing with my teammates what Steve had said and they were so excited that he had called. That's the kind of stuff that I try and do now. I talk to some of the girls now and I text them before tournaments and wish them luck. I try to pump up their tires. Little messages and a bit of communication can really make a big difference. Some of the best things I have done people don't even know about and I like it that way. I think Steve is like that as well.

What were some of the hardest things to learn in becoming a good or an even better captain?

I'm a pretty vocal person, but I think I became a better listener over the years and that was important for me in order to become a more mature leader. I wanted to go listen to speakers, including other leaders, and get their books. I began to reach out. I think my listening skills evolved over the years. I picked my moments to speak better as my career went on. I also, later in my career, did a lot more to help develop the future leaders of the national team. I really encouraged them to step up a bit more, even when they didn't have a letter on their jersey.

How did becoming a better listener help you to become a better leader?

I always took the time to get to know people. I now wanted to better understand what made people tick. I wanted to know what I had to say to certain individuals prior to a big game to help them to elevate their game. I wanted to know how people played their best game, so I would simply ask them questions and listen to their answers. I asked them questions such as, "When do you play your best game?" or, "When do you feel at your best?" I became a bit more of a "people knowledge" person. I just took more and more time, as my career went on, to really get to know people around me and what was going on in their lives.

What have you learned about building relationships and trust in high-performance teams?

Despite our successes together, we're not all best friends. Some of the team members are now retired and we did not stay in contact. We may see each other at functions and different things. But we trusted each other on the ice and we went to war on the ice, so to speak. We were all responsible for our actions on the ice and off the ice. I truly believe we built that trust by spending a lot of time together. We really knew each other and understood what made us tick. We also understood that it was okay if we had differences with each other. I think when teammates get to a point where they know they don't have to like each other, but they understand each other and know what makes each other tick, then they trust each other. Building a relationship is so much about trust.

One of the biggest mistakes in the corporate world right now is the emphasis on work, deadlines, and meetings. Organizations don't spend enough time having fun. I'm a big believer that the more fun you have as a group, the more you will get to know each other and trust each other, regardless of your roles and differences. We just had a lot of fun together. We all enjoyed what we were doing and that was important. We all cared.

But we also worked very, very hard. For example, we had boot camps that mimicked the Olympics and preparation. We would have these three-week-long boot camps where we trained numerous times a day. You saw the worst in everyone because we were exhausted. I remember a particular camp, in Prince Edward Island, for the 2006 Olympics. It was May or June of 2005. We did a triathlon in which one girl swam, one girl biked, and one girl ran. We had different teams competing against each other. We ended up having two or three people go to the hospital because we were so competitive—people were crashing on their bikes. It was just complete exhaustion, but everything we did throughout those three weeks was team oriented. At the end of camp, I remember sitting in the restaurant and we had a team meeting to discuss where we were as a group. Everyone was completely exhausted. The big thing that came out of that meeting was that we finally had players who were truly there for each other, despite the fact that we were competing against each other to make the team. Based on all the activities we had done that week, we realized there were times when players could have left other players—just keep riding their bikes or do their own things and leave players who were struggling—but they didn't. That boot camp was really big for us. It was about building relationships. I think our coaches did a great job of putting us through the worst-case scenarios so that if we came out of the experience as a team and trusting each other, we could overcome any circumstance.

We have an expression at the Ivey Business School—competencies count, character matters, and commitment to the role of leadership is critical to success. Can you talk a little about how you see competencies, character, and commitment applying to the role of captain?
Being humble is one of the most important aspects of leadership. *A leader should be a good communicator. You can be a quiet leader, but you still need to communicate your thoughts. I believe that if you can't communicate, your leadership will be diminished.* We all have our insecurities. But I think good leaders are people who are secure with their lives and positions on things. They are not afraid to make mistakes. I think someone who has an open-door policy and is willing to take ideas from other people is a good candidate for captain. A good leader is someone who

is happy with other people's successes. He or she equally celebrates their own and others' successes. To me, those traits represent good leadership.

Sometimes leadership is not a lot of fun. There might be disappointments. You talked about the 1998 Olympics. How did you as a captain develop resilience?

Surround yourself with people and touch base with them. Make sure you balance your emotions by putting yourself more with the "givers" in your life and monitor your time with the "takers" in your life. Leaders have to deal with both types of people, but you can't let the takers bring you down. For example, I really used our sports psychologist, Peter Jensen, a lot, particularly during my last Olympics. I knew I was close to the end of my career and had just come off a major injury. Deep down inside, I knew some of my passion was gone. But I did not want to show this to any of the players. I relied on Peter a lot to help give me strength. He was one of my givers, and I used my givers a lot more toward the end of my career than I did early on. I learned to filter everything a little bit better. I understood my takers a bit more, too. I didn't let them bring me down as much.

I think my teammates always knew I fought for them behind the scenes, and they knew I would never ever go behind the scenes and throw them under the bus. In 2002, Nancy Drolet was cut from the team after our eighth loss to the United States. She was a veteran of 10 years and I played with her for a long time. Nancy was replaced by Cherie Piper, a young player. Nancy decided to file an appeal, and so the case went through a court. I was asked to testify at the proceedings about logistical things the team was told and about Nancy's character. I said, "Guys, you can ask me any logistical question you want. You can also ask me about her performance. But I will never say anything negative about her character, and you'll never get me to say anything negative about anyone's character. I'm never going to throw a teammate under the bus." I stuck to my guns on that. In my discussions with coaches, I was honest about players' performances when asked, but I would never throw a teammate under the bus, no matter the situation and no matter the person. I could never justify that as a teammate, whether former or current.

What has been your most rewarding experience as a captain and why?

It is rewarding to have the current players calling and texting me and asking for my advice. That's been the most rewarding thing throughout my career—having friends and colleagues still wanting to talk to me about life and stuff they are going through, and still valuing my opinion and what I have to say. I get texts from the girls when they're at tournaments and things. I just give them my two cents, but mostly I try to encourage them to figure things out on their own; that's important for their own personal leadership. That means more to me than any gold medal. I had one of my former teammates go through something difficult in her life. I was the first person she touched base with to say, "Hey . . . I need your help." She ended up staying at my house. That is the most rewarding thing to me—my friends and colleagues still come to me for advice and help and they trust me.

All things considered and knowing the roles and responsibilities of being the captain of the national women's team, would you take on the role again?
Would I? Yes, without a question. Would I need to? No.

That is an interesting answer. Explain that to me, please.
I don't think I ever aspired to be captain of the national women's hockey team. You always want to be the best player and the best person you can be. But I don't think, when I was 10 years old, my wish list included being captain of the women's national team. First, I didn't know we had one. Second, my goal was just to win games. I wanted to help my team win. So, would I do it again? Yes. But would I need to? No. I would have made the same decisions. I would have stepped up and done the same things whether I had a "C," an "A," or nothing on the front of my shirt.

What advice do you have for people as they embark on their journey of learning to lead?
Two things: listen and learn. I was captain of the team, but I still had so much to learn and so many great people to learn from by listening to them. *You can learn so much from people around you. You do need to listen, though. You should never think you're the best you can be. You can always be better, so you should continue to learn about being a better leader.*

People are often afraid to be leaders. They may fear criticism or doing something wrong. I think fear stops people from stepping up in the dressing room and just saying whatever they feel needs to be said. People are afraid of the repercussions. I'm a big believer that, if you don't want to be criticized, then say nothing, do nothing, and be nothing. And that's how I've lived my life.

Even now, as a broadcaster in the National Hockey League, I'm criticized all the time. Sometimes legitimately, and sometimes just for being a woman in a man's sport. I can stay at home and sit on my couch and watch television or I can do something with my life. *Don't be afraid to fail. Don't fear failure. It's a part of life and leadership and it is the only way you can really learn.*

But such criticism must hurt. How do you deal with that?
I'm actually the first captain in female hockey to lose a World Championship for Canada. We lost in 2005 to the United States. It was also the year of the lockout in the National Hockey League, so there was a lot of attention on us. I remember we landed in Toronto and I was given a newspaper. There was a picture of me on the front page of the *Toronto Star*. I was standing on the blue line crying because we had lost the game. I was wiping the tears from my cheeks. It was just an awful and ugly picture. My dad was at the airport and he, too, was disgusted. The picture was published across Canada. My approach after settling down was to embrace the fact that women's hockey had made the front page of the newspaper. It may have been the ugliest picture ever taken of me, but it was there and people cared! People actually cared! I remember cutting that picture out and folding it up as I was training

for my last Olympics. When things got tough and I couldn't find the passion and all those things, I pulled that picture out to remember what losing a final felt like. We failed.

Some of the biggest moments in my life are actually the failures. The failures are the events I talk about the most when I'm speaking to groups. The failures are the events in my life that I remember the most details about. People see players win the gold medal at the Olympics and the Stanley Cup. They think we were perfect. We were far from perfect. *I think that's one thing that I would tell a young leader—you are not going to be the perfect leader to everybody, but that doesn't mean you're not a good leader. Listen and learn. And don't try to be perfect.*

Leadership Themes

- Be yourself. People who struggle with leadership are often trying to be something they're not. And others see right through them.
- Being a leader sometimes involves delivering tough feedback and making hard decisions. By saying nothing, you can actually make things worse. You show you care when you communicate a tough message.
- If you don't want to be criticized, then say nothing, do nothing—and be nothing.
- Organizations don't spend enough time having fun. The more fun you have as a group, the more you will get to know each other and trust each other, regardless of your roles and differences.
- Being humble is one of the most important aspects of leadership.
- You can be a quiet leader, but you still need to communicate your thoughts. If you can't communicate, your leadership will be diminished.
- Don't be afraid to fail. Don't fear failure. It's a part of life and leadership and it is the only way you can really learn.
- You are not going to be the perfect leader to everybody, but that doesn't mean you're not a good leader. Listen and learn. And don't try to be perfect.

10

Roll up Your Sleeves and Work Shoulder to Shoulder with Others

Barbara Stymiest

Barbara, when did you first realize you were a leader, and what happened to make you realize it?

I first realized it when I moved into a leadership role in public accounting at Clarkson Gordon (now called Ernst & Young). Accounting firms have a business model where, first, you're a staff person, then a manager, and, ultimately, a partner. The manager role is a leadership role because it's the first time you have direct reports and you have to organize them and run it as a little business. What's implicit and never really said is you're also responsible for the mentoring of the staff, and the morale, and some of the softer issues. Interestingly, though, you were only held accountable for the business results, not for the softer skills—at least, that was the case back then. When I became a manager in the early 1980s, I also joined a not-for-profit board, which was going through significant financial challenges because there was a recession and its funding model was challenged. The chief executive officer (CEO) had retired and the company had become unionized—and I was asked to serve as chair. That was truly a leadership position for me. I was leading the board and leading the organization through a transformation, which involved getting a new CEO and putting in place a new business model. That was challenging and a true test of my leadership skills.

I'm still not sure that the penny dropped and I thought, "aha!" I didn't wake up one day and say, "I'm a leader." I very much enjoyed my role and ended up volunteering with that organization for 10 years, and as chair for 4 or 5 years, during that difficult period. I believed in its mission. I felt that I was learning and growing as a citizen because of the public policy issues the organization addressed. That was very early in my career. I had only been working for five or six years when I embarked on that not-for-profit leadership journey, and I think it helped me as I progressed in my career. As I built my career, I drew upon the skills and experiences that I had as a leader in the not-for-profit sector.

I have heard that before—when you want to learn about leadership, you should work in the not-for-profit sector or volunteer. Is this because you have little or no formal power and you cannot direct people to do things?

I actually wrote a speech about that and it articulated that power comes from ideas, processes, and decision making. As a leader, you have to put all those things together. *There is no innate thing that is power, but, rather, it is your ability to make things happen.*

I was often asked to give speeches about leadership, and I didn't like to just say, "I'm a leader and this is how I did it." Instead, I tried to figure out how to talk about leadership in a way that was constructive and could help people to learn to be leaders.

So, let's talk about that journey. How did you learn to lead? You told me that the journey started at Ernst & Young, and then you went to the Bank of Montreal, followed by the Toronto Stock Exchange (TSX) and the Royal Bank of Canada (RBC), and now you are the Chairman of the Board at BlackBerry. How did you learn to lead?

I think the biggest jump for me was moving from chief financial officer (CFO) to CEO, and I actually have thought and reflected a lot about this. When boards select CEOs, they tend to focus on skills, rather than leadership capabilities. Unless you've been a CEO, I don't think you understand what it really takes and how much you have to draw upon your leadership abilities to actually do a good job. For me, that was the biggest jump.

I learned from observing the leaders to whom I reported. For example, when I was a CFO, I probably had 150 to 200 people working for me. I had people in the USA and the UK working for me. I had to learn a lot. I wondered if I should sit on the executive floor or with my team, because those decisions and activities send messages to people. I decided to be with my team. I saw enough of my colleagues on the executive committee and met with them regularly, but I thought it was important to be with my team and to be seen and to always be available.

Eventually, the moment arrives when you're actually in a defined leadership role that's not volunteer or part time, and then you wonder how to execute on the leadership role. I was very lucky in my role at the TSX to have had an extremely capable head of human resources (HR) who was a great coach and helped me to be a strong internal leader. That was important. She couldn't help me with the other part of it—being an external leader and a change agent—but having her to help me with the internal stuff was huge. Right from my first day on the job, she was very thoughtful and gave me advice about things such as seeing staff, having town hall meetings, what might be expected of me, what I should say, and how to restructure our internal communications. She also helped me to make the tough leadership calls when putting together my leadership team. Those things weren't easy to execute, so having her help with all of that internal stuff was great. I had to figure out the external side of things by trial and error. There was no handbook or manual telling me how to do it.

Some of my seminal moments were around thinking about how to split my time as a leader between internal and external stuff. I became pretty regimented about how my time was allocated. My time was divided about 40 percent internal, 40 percent external, and 20 percent on other stuff. On the external side, I saw customers and listened to their needs and met with many shareholders, especially when the exchange became public. Investor relations and broader stakeholder community relations were very important to the exchange, and we had a couple of important meetings each year with heads of exchanges from around the world. At these meetings, we shared what was going on in a fast-changing industry and discussed our individual leadership challenges.

My early days at the TSX were also interesting. The exchange was being criticized for breaking down regularly because its technology was on its last legs. We faced a 21st-century market with a 19th-century set of rules, organization, and mindset. Canada's capital markets were at risk. We brought in a very good head of public affairs early in my tenure. He felt very strongly that we needed to control and shape the external messaging so that, rather than always being defensive, we'd establish the exchange as a leadership brand. We began to premeditate how we could shift people's perception of the exchange. Instead of them seeing the exchange as failing, we wanted them to see it as a leadership institution that was a symbol of Canadian leadership and capital markets. For our strategy, we picked an issue that was important to a key group of shareholders and many stakeholders in general—the national securities regulator proposal—and became vocal on it. That was a deliberate strategy and we spent a lot of effort executing it. It helped us to think about the issue through the eyes of branding. I didn't learn about branding until I became a CEO. Until that time, I hadn't really understood what a brand stood for and how to execute a brand strategy. You never learned about a brand when you were CFO. You never learned about public affairs or just managing the executive team. As a CEO, there were new challenges, and I think I learned a lot about leadership that continues to serve me well.

Can you talk a little bit about the learning curve—does it ever level off?

I would say it ebbs and flows. I think that you learn things and then you get comfortable in executing them. If I learn something in a day, then it's a good day for me. It doesn't matter if I'm learning something about my industry, my family, or technology—just that I'm learning. I derive great pleasure from learning in any situation.

Well-run companies set objectives and leaders hold themselves accountable, but, in my opinion, you can't actually deliver on the objectives if you don't have the leadership piece in place. It was important to me, especially when I was at RBC, to have a very diverse group of professionals. Our group had auditors and accountants in the finance and internal audit functions, lawyers in the general counsel function, a branding group, and an HR group. Trying to get these highly skilled, dedicated individuals working and thinking as a team, as opposed to just individual professionals in their own separate roles, was a real leadership challenge. I once received some very good advice at a leadership training session and I knew I had to figure out how these groups under my leadership were going to add value to the success of RBC for the next year. We had various frameworks that we tried to use, but I was most proud of one later in my tenure that I learned from a professional outside of the bank. Under this framework, we had to deliver on three things: caramel bars, strings of pearls, and chemical fusions. "Caramel bars" referred to things that are fairly self-contained, but complex. Each one of my professionals had a set of caramel bars—things that would make the bank run better—to deliver. "Strings of pearls" referred to the larger objectives that we had as a group. We called them strings of pearls because, although you could do your piece individually, you couldn't create something beautiful, like a string of pearls, unless you connected with other functions. For example, for a successful merger, you need HR due diligence, the mergers and acquisitions team has to execute well on the negotiations and pricing, and the law group needs to do the legal documentation—and, together, you create a string of pearls. "Chemical fusions" referred to the really big things, where you would have multiple disciplines working together on highly complex and interrelated problems and projects. For these, everyone involved works as part of a collaborative team and all the expertise comes together to create something where you can't actually see the individual pieces. If not, then you don't really accomplish the objective. We had to focus a lot on determining what chemical fusions were needed, and how we would need to structure ourselves and operate and deliver to deal with the bank's really challenging issues. My group was very involved in such things as looking at the impact of regulatory reform post financial crisis and that took a lot of input from the treasury function, the law group, and government relations. All of these pieces had to meld together. This was a great way to work because my team could sit around the table and think differently about how it was going to structure its objectives, and be very clear on the ones that were dependent on successful teamwork rather than individual excellence. It wasn't an "either/or" situation, it was always an "and" situation. It was great fun.

You said earlier that a good day is a day where you learn something new. What have you learned most recently, as chair of BlackBerry, about leadership?

I think that board leadership is different to management leadership, and I've never underestimated the importance of alignment. There are two levels to alignment. First, the board doesn't necessarily need to be unanimous, but must be generally aligned or in agreement broadly on what it's trying to achieve. Second, the board should also be aligned with management. For an organization to be successful, particularly when you're driving a lot of change, getting everybody on side is crucial. I knew this, having chaired a lot of things since my first not-for-profit experience, but I ended up learning more about this while chairing the exchange for a couple of years when it was going through a big change agenda. It was my first experience in a complex, changing organization where I realized how much time is actually spent as the chair—as the leader of the board—in the bilateral conversations to try and build consensus so you can come to a meeting with a lot of the hard work done ahead of time. That doesn't mean the work is done outside of the boardroom, but that you've prepared the way for the deep and rich discussion and an environment in which you can actually debate and make the key decisions. That lesson was reinforced for me when I stepped into the BlackBerry chair.

You indicated that mentors facilitated your learning and people tell you stuff—how difficult was it for you to open up yourself for information that, perhaps, at times you did not expect or want to hear?
I think that I have trouble with the concept of formal mentoring because I find, if it is forced and structured, it's not terribly effective. Informal mentoring, on the other hand, has had a huge impact on me. I wouldn't necessarily even call very many people my "mentors," but you can learn a lot from observing people who are effective and successful. I was always open to learning from people either directly, by observing them, or by asking for their opinions on my challenges. I would also call people. I still have people today who I call my "thought partners" who are very important to me. They have helped me immensely to think through the really tough stuff. On the other hand, you are right—you're going to get a lot of unsolicited advice. I think listening is a key skill because, even if some advice is unsolicited, there may be some great kernels of wisdom in it. As CEO, it was important for me to balance the time I spent internally and externally. I wasn't going to hear very many new or different perspectives from inside of the organization, so it was far more important to learn the diverse views outside of the organization. That said, it was really important for me to build one of my internal teams to focus on strategy. We were always thinking about, and studying, and trying to understand the changing environment that we were in. You need deep analytical resources to think about change, and then your other leaders can execute in a very open and collaborative way on these strategies that have been developed. You get lots of advice, but advice without a good fact base is not necessarily very valuable. Advice that causes you to actually do research and think things through, and that then causes you to change a course of action towards execution, is highly valuable.

You talked a little bit about collaboration. I think you need quite an amount of candor for true collaboration to happen. What have you learned about facilitating candor in conversations to build trust?
I think that's a very important element of the structured hierarchies in the business world. I remember having a conversation with Roger Martin, a fellow BlackBerry board member who has been one of my thought partners for a long

time, about understanding hidden agendas. We were discussing what to do if you're sensitive to them and ways you can counteract them. An example of a hidden agenda is the fact that your staff are always encouraged to make you think that they're doing a good job since you ultimately promote, compensate, and reward them. When you're talking to your staff about an issue, you need to remember that they have that motivation, but to also establish some openness and let them know that they can challenge you. This way, the important conversations can happen. *I learned very early on, from chairing many meetings of both executive leadership teams and the board, that when you're in a defined leadership role, you never state your point of view first or else there will be a natural tendency for people to jump in and support your view.* To create openness and allow constructive debate, it's better to say, "I may have a view, but I don't know the answer and I want to consider all the elements," and to have processes where you can have the dialogue happen in an open, constructive, non-challenging way. It's basic common sense. You don't tell people they are idiots—you listen carefully to what they are trying to say and you try to get the quiet people to open up. You do all of those things to get tough debates going. Many things in business have high degrees of complexity and the only way you're going to figure them out is through engagement and having the intellectual diversity to solve the problems. I don't have all of the answers and I never thought I did. It's not about having all the answers, but having a reasonable sense of your own limitations and the ability to be open and to engage your team to get to the better answers.

That sounds straightforward, but we know enough to understand it doesn't always happen that way. How have you developed confidence in yourself and the leadership role to engage in the activities described? And how would one avoid becoming overconfident?

That's a good question. I think you always have to have a sense of skepticism about your own abilities and realize the world is just a complicated, fast-changing place and you just don't have all the answers. I've never believed I had all the answers. *I think the recipe to success is having two tablespoons of hard work and a good dose of skepticism.* In my experience, you always had to watch the macro stuff. You had to watch the outside-in view of your organization or the issue with which you were dealing. You had to think about long-term, structural trends and overlay those on your business model. Without that outside–in perspective, you could fall into the trap of becoming overconfident. I'll be quite blunt. There was an often-discussed issue at RBC—and maybe this is a trend in large organizations because they are large and pyramidical—that there are people at RBC that do RBC really well. They have PhDs in RBC—they know how to get things done, get promoted, and play the political game. But they would fail miserably if you took them out of RBC and put them in a leadership role in any other organization because their skill set is working in bureaucracy. The leaders that I valued were the great thinkers. It's important in a large and complex organization to know how to get things done, but you need to have much more than that to be a successful leader.

You are high profile. You live in a fishbowl. Is there anything that you fear about the role of leadership?

This is quite practical, but I really feared public speaking. I think innately I'm pretty shy, and I was not the most outgoing person. Even back when I was sitting in the Ivey classroom, we all knew that a huge percentage of marks was for participation. It became clear to me pretty fast that the people who raised their hands, but didn't have a lot to say, were trying to exploit the model, unlike the people who always made important contributions. Anyway, I did eventually learn to speak in public, but I still don't feel really comfortable in a large group of people. When someone gives a presentation and asks, "Any questions?," I'm not going to raise my hand first if I'm in a room with 40 people. In those situations, I worry about what people are going to think of my question, and whether or not they are going to second-guess me. I'm much more comfortable speaking in front of a group from my team. Initially, though, I was scared to death of standing up and speaking in front of anybody, on any subject. I recognized early on that it is a very important skill to have, and I was quite deliberate in doing it enough that I overcame most of my inhibitions about speaking. How did I do that? In my Ernst & Young days, all the internal staff training was done by internal people, so I volunteered to teach the technical courses for the staff. Learning how to be an instructor was a great opportunity to stand in front of a group of 30 or 40 people and discuss a subject with which I was confident. I still remember one of the first speeches I ever gave when I was chair of the board and had to speak at the annual meeting. I was very proud of it, and I had worked hard with the CEO on what I was going to say. I invited my mom and my sister to come and hear me! I've come a long way since then. I still remember what I've learned. I think there is a time when you put your notes aside and then you can actually talk to people about important issues in a straightforward, thoughtful, logical way without talking too long or muddling up your thoughts. Being able to speak on important issues—having done your homework—is an important skill, but it's a learned skill. It comes by doing it a lot.

What have you personally experienced as a barrier to learning and how have you tried to overcome this barrier?

My challenge for the last 25 years has been to continue to inform myself in a rich way about what's going on in the world. From that comes the additional challenge of balance. I have always had a messy desk because I have across my desk the 50 items I want to read. I have time-management challenges. I know how important it is to be well informed and thoughtful and understand issues deeply, but there are only 24 hours in a day. *For me, the biggest challenge is how to learn and absorb information in as efficient a way as possible given there are only 24 hours in a day.* The easy part is the learning you do through talking to people—whether your thought partners, customers, or staff. I enjoy that. I think I am a relatively social person because I like to learn through dialogue, but I think it's also important to read to get the complexity and details. That's why I still have six books on my desk that I want to read. You also need to balance that reading with books you want to read or movies you want to watch just for fun. It's an even bigger challenge in the Internet world today where we have unlimited access to information. I wish someone could tell me the secret sauce for that!

I guess lots of learning takes place when we put ourselves on the line in crisis-like situations. Of course, learning should take place during the full business cycle, including when things are going smoothly for the organization. Can you talk a little bit about learning in a crisis situation, and learning when things are well executed and going smoothly?

They are very different. I think being an effective leader in the broadest sense—you have a good knowledge base, a good team, you're on top of the issues, and have good relationships—means that all the important ingredients necessary in the day-to-day stuff can come to the forefront during crises. For instance, I remember 9/11 quite distinctly because no one knew what was happening or what to do next. The relationships and informal relationships that existed in this country so that you could have dialogue with the key decision makers in Ottawa were important. I had open lines of communication to the New York Stock Exchange, the NASDAQ, and U.S., and Canadian regulators—and we were all trying to figure out what was the right thing to do. I had my colleagues and my team to help me to think through what was going on, and I also had the relationships and the ability to interact with people who were faced with the same things. We were trying to make the right decisions. We had questions such as: Do we open the market or not open the market? What was going on next? How bad could it be? Should we close? Should we send people home? All of those decisions had to be made in a moment of crisis, but it helped that we had the building blocks in place. I didn't make those decisions lightly. We had other crises where we had technology problems at the exchange and we wondered whether or not to close the market, what's going on, are we running a fair and orderly market? We had to have a decision framework, but we also had to have enough people that understood it so that we could get together in the flash of an eye and make the tough calls. When you have a good team that's well informed and that you trust, you can have the quick debate to find an answer and then execute.

What role did mistakes play in your learning process? Can you talk about a mistake you made as a leader and what you learned from that mistake?

I would by no means say that I haven't made lots of mistakes, but it's hard for me to pick one defining mistake. For me, it was much more about making little mistakes along the way and learning the hard way. You learn by making those small mistakes. I remember, back in my public accounting days, being in a tough situation and learning a tough lesson about not overpromising. It was related to an insolvency and my natural human instinct was to help the poor banker whose loan was clearly at risk. I was going to deliver all this information and help him to do his job, but I didn't need to do that. The person that I was working with helped me to understand the implications of me overpromising something that didn't need to be promised. I'm hesitant to make commitments that I haven't clearly thought through and aren't within my scope and purview and necessary to do. I wanted to be helpful and nice and co-operative, but I've learned that sometimes you have to be a bit more ruthless when something is important and in your mandate.

You have done great things in the financial and technology sectors. Has being a woman operating in those industries affected the learning process in any way?

I think the gender aspect is a little bit overplayed and I've always thought of myself as being a little bit gender blind. I found myself in situations where I was the only woman or one of a few women, and I just stopped noticing that after a while. I had chosen to do things where there were a lot more males than females. We had a course at the Bank of Montreal to build awareness of issues when men and women work together. I realized that, while men may have biases against working with women, I had equal biases about working with men. What really opened my eyes to this were conversations with co-workers about home life. I thought a lot of my male colleagues had stay-at-home wives and therefore didn't have to deal with the mundane stuff you have to do just to make your life work. During these conversations, I learned that a lot of my male colleagues in fact had high-powered, professional, working wives, and they shared the tasks of picking up the dry cleaning, dropping off the children at daycare, making meals, washing dishes, planning holidays, and other duties. I had assumed they had much better support networks than I had, which made their lives easier, but I was wrong. In fact, the very next day, I think I saw one of my colleagues at the dry cleaners and thought, *Yep, we're the same.* I think that I've been attracted to the industries I've worked in because they are fun, interesting, challenging, and fast paced. I don't think that it's really anything more than that. I wasn't attracted to them because they were male dominated, but I wasn't un-attracted to them because they were male dominated, either. I spent most of my career in financial services because of the complexity and pace of change. Other people were attracted to it for those same reasons and that's why I liked to spend time with those people.

Did you ever feel that you had to prove yourself more or work harder than your male counterparts? Were there any differences between the men and women you have encountered?

I don't think so. I thought about that a lot. I know I'm pretty driven and I wondered if I was more driven because I'm female, but it turns out I'm just a driven person. I think women can work in multiple dimensions and multitask better. I don't know if our brains are wired differently for that. For example, I can have a conversation with the team about something very technical and, at the same time, watch the dynamics of the team and think about my next meeting as well as the implications of the meeting's outcome. I'm on three levels all the time. I think some men are wired like that, but not all men. My ability to integrate multiple thoughts has been helpful.

What expectations do you put on yourself in the leadership role?

My dad was an entrepreneur and taught me many lessons. I used to work with him in my summer jobs and he was adamant in his belief that leaders should be the hardest-working people at an organization to set the standard and tone there. I never forgot that and I struggled to live up to his expectations sometimes. For most of my career, I was the first person in the office because I heard my dad's voicing telling me I had to work harder than everybody else. Working harder doesn't mean putting in more hours, but being there—being present—and letting people know that you are there. In large organizations, you can't be the first person in to the office and also the person who turns the lights off at the end of the day, or else you'd never sleep. ***The fundamental message my dad taught me is to be committed and show people you care. As a leader, you need to roll up your sleeves and work shoulder to shoulder with others.*** My dad did that and that taught me a lot.

What sustains you as a leader? What continues to motivate you? What do you like about being a leader?

The answer is simple—having the influence to shape the outcomes in the best possible way. I like that I can set an agenda, work with other leaders, and push the right things forward. I truly believe that when you get out of bed in the morning, you want to have a fun day. I think you get to shape the enjoyment in your life when you're in a leadership role, and that includes shaping the balance and morale, as well as the outcomes, at an organization. I remember when I first started at the exchange, I wanted to take my daughter to her first day of school. We were planning our next management meeting and these were generally held on Tuesdays. The next one would fall on the Tuesday after Labor Day, which was the first day of school. Since I was the leader, I could just say, "We're not meeting on Tuesday. We're going to move the meeting to Wednesday because I know a lot of you have children you need to take to their first day of school—that's what I'm going to be doing." I really relished the fact that I could set a tone that could balance home and work, and that was as important to me as driving the outcomes in the organization.

Now the flip side—what drains you?

I think it's clearly the effort. I stepped down from my 24/7 responsibilities almost a year ago, and I know I worked extraordinarily hard for 35 years and sacrificed a fair bit. There were not a lot of holidays and I missed a lot of family time.

Is that the price of leadership?

Yes, and there are always pictures of the Canadian prime ministers and U.S. presidents at the beginning and end of their term. They certainly have more gray hair!

What have you learned over the years to be transparent and candid in critical conversations, and to do so effectively? What major challenges did you have to overcome?

I think it's difficult to communicate effectively in a way that provides constructive feedback. My style has always involved giving compliments and then giving the constructive feedback. It was always difficult to give criticism to the under-performers. It's tough to figure out how to make them better at their tasks. But it's great and so rewarding to coach the coachable and the high performers to a higher level. You want to surround yourself with coachable high performers because a leader is only as good as his or her high-performing team.

Has it been difficult to stay true to yourself despite the success and accolades you have achieved?

It is difficult because there are times when your ego gets in the way and absolute power can corrupt. *I've seen a lot of leaders who are self-centered and they stop listening and are not constructive anymore.* I think your family keeps you grounded. For example, my daughter is now 14, so she, of course, has a computer and has been using Google for a while. It was quite an eye-opener for me to watch her Google my name because, for her, I am just mom who leaves in the morning to go to the office and then comes home late at night. Now, it's fun as she's hit these teenage years to see her reaction to what she learns about me. When I get an award, we actually giggle and joke about the fact that I was chosen as one of the most powerful women. She'll say, "Yeah, Mom, and you can't even make a good omelet!" We talk about it in an amusing way, and that is nice. I don't want her to think of me as anything more than her mother.

Good leaders learn. They mature. How has your leadership evolved over time?

In the last 15 years, I've learned the importance of building strong teams and making teams work together effectively. I think the more senior you are, the more important that skill becomes. I also think I've gotten better at assessing talent. As you get more senior and experienced, your thinking becomes more integrated. You start to see problems in multiple dimensions because you now have experience in all those multiple dimensions. Earlier, I mentioned coming to the exchange and learning about government relations, branding, and media relations. I could think about things more broadly and get different perspectives and integrate my thinking to produce better outcomes. Experience got me to that point. I've been working for 35 years and, boy, if 20 or 30 years ago I knew what I know now—not just in terms of technical stuff—I would have been better at doing my jobs then.

Situational awareness is critical to good leadership. Can you talk a little about the importance of context?

One of my favorite words is "context." You need to have the context to make sound decisions. We haven't talked about communication. We referred to it only in regard to public speaking, but not in terms of being able to communicate effectively. It doesn't matter whether you're giving a speech, preparing a one-page note to your staff, or doing an intervention at a leadership meeting, it's important to communicate effectively. When you're talking about complex things, you always have to link to something more understandable—that bridging is important. Think about the context of the point you're trying to make and figure out a way to link it to something that is understandable. A leader of a public company needs to be able to communicate effectively to its shareholders. Communicating effectively to employees is also critical and needs to be done in a thoughtful way. It's really difficult to communicate both well and consistently.

Can you elaborate on the contextual part of leadership? Is there anything you learned over the years that perhaps enabled you to become more adaptable or flexible in your leadership approach?

You have to be different in different situations. I think I'm different with my colleagues than with my board of directors. I think you need to be adaptable, because different people expect different things from you. You need to understand the context of what is expected, but that doesn't change the content. You know the content, but what changes from situation to situation is what you do with it—how you use it in different situations or with different stakeholders to educate people, lead, and set direction. Your brain is always processing these things and you may not even know it.

I sense you want to add something to the communications piece?

I'm glad we talked about it because it's so critical. *If your leaders can't stand up and tell you where you are going, how will you ever get there? You need everyone in the boat, paddling in the same direction, to get to your destination.*

I remember during my first year at Ivey, our cases were marked twice; once for content, and once for English. I learned a lot from this and decided to take an English course because I thought it was important to learn to write and express myself well. I never regretted it.

Leadership Themes

- Leaders aren't above their team members—they are part of the team, and need to work along with the other members.
- Leaders should encourage constructive debate at their organizations.
- Leaders need to be able to communicate effectively.
- There is no innate thing that is "power," but, rather, it is your ability to make things happen.
- The recipe to success is having two tablespoons of hard work and a good dose of skepticism.

11

There Are Very Few Things in Life That You Can Control, but the One Thing That You Have Absolute Control Over Is the Quality of Your Own Effort

Rahul Bhardwaj

Rahul, when did you first realize you were a leader, and what happened to make your realize it?

I don't think there was a moment when I thought, "You are a leader." Leadership is not a role—it's far more complex than that. *Years ago, the person at the top of the pyramid was the leader. Today, you're at the hub of a series of spokes on a wheel, and your role as a leader is to integrate all of that because collective leadership has real power. Leaders shouldn't dictate, they need to bring everyone along.*

You are, and have been, in influential positions where you can make a real difference—have you always wanted to be a leader?

I didn't decide to pursue leadership positions. My organization is small and, when I started there, I asked, "Will the people on the leadership team please put up their hands?" A lot of people didn't raise their hands because they didn't see themselves in that role. I told them, "The next time I ask that question, everybody should put up their hands." Everybody has leadership capabilities and aspects contributing to overall leadership. I've been lucky that the organizations I've been at have had a culture where everyone contributes to leadership, so I'm not the sole leader. I'm merely part of a leadership group focused on advancing the organization. I never set out to actually aspire to a leadership role.

Do you think leadership just happens?

No, other people provide you with leadership opportunities. People saw that I had the capabilities to contribute to city-building activities, and to advance that through some sort of leadership role. Those people opened the door and I stepped through, delivered, added value, and created something. Then other doors start opening and the pattern continues. *Leadership doesn't just happen on its own and, in many ways, is facilitated by other people—people who give you opportunities.*

How did you learn to lead and prepare for your current leadership role?

You are always learning, so it is a lifelong process. Learning involves both looking forward and backward. I'm sure some of my childhood experiences contributed to my leadership and my outlook on life. Everything I've ever read or written has contributed. Every mistake I've ever made and every success has contributed. The culmination of everything in my life enables me to lead as I do. The variety and breadth of my experiences made me a leader.

Can you reflect on a few experiences that helped you grow and develop as a leader?

My volunteer roles were exceptionally good and gave back to me far more than I gave. When I was a young lawyer and joined a particular board, I observed the brain trust and seniority around the table. I listened and learned, and, as a result, began to understand how people speak, arrive at decisions, and the role of vision and strategy. My comfort level increased as I saw how seasoned leaders behaved. I didn't always aim to imitate them, because sometimes you see things and say to yourself, "Gee, I don't want to do that," but just being in that milieu was very helpful. *Volunteer opportunities provided me with a remarkable testing ground and opportunities to grow.* Also, reading and my liberal arts education exposed me to such topics as history, philosophy, and political theory, so I began to see leadership in different ways. My education allowed me to experience different styles of leadership in various contexts. Those experiences—non-profit and education—made me appreciate leadership. When you get close to leaders, you learn about what they do strategically and tactically, what they achieve, and how connected they are to other people in their organizations. At the end of the day, you become more comfortable with leadership and understand the importance of authentic leadership.

You mentioned that in your network you had access to people from whom you learned a lot?

I enjoy talking about leadership and speaking with people who like talking about leadership. Leadership is an art, not a science. Speaking about leadership with people who really like it is like talking about art. As a result of my conversations with people about leadership, I learned that the key to leadership is knowing what to do with it. I thought a lot about what leadership means, whether I formulated the right vision for the organization, articulated the direction properly, set goals high enough, and am doing everything to enable the organization to move in the right direction. From these conversations, I also learned not to confuse managing with leading. I don't think a week goes by where I don't ask myself, "Did I lead enough this week? Did I manage too much?" People challenged me to make sure I was not just simply managing, because that is easy to do. Instead I had to consciously think about being a leader and what that entails. I also had to understand what to do with the leadership platform given to me.

What does leadership mean to you?

First, let me tell you that it is not managing. Managing is an important part of a leadership role, but so is communication; having clarity around a vision and articulating it; infusing values into an organization; and bringing people along. Managing is just one aspect of those very important things. Leadership is about being authentic. It's about being passionate about what you're involved with, whether it is producing widgets, being involved in politics, or art. Leadership comes from within—it's not a role. It's who you are. There are moments when people are aligned with their organizations and they're a good fit. That's likely not because they are smarter or luckier, but rather because their personal values and mission were authentic and aligned with their organizations.

You've been at a number of organizations and have done many great things. Good leaders learn. They mature. How has your leadership evolved over time?
Let me share a little anecdote from a meeting a number of years ago. I was asked to attend a meeting between some groups that were trying to move ahead on a collaborative venture. There were some stumbling blocks as well, and, going into it, I thought, "I probably can't add a whole lot, but I'll go because I was asked to participate funnily." I listened, and there were some very bright, motivated people, and the discussion was going back and forth, and it evolved, and, funnily enough, I felt I just didn't need to say much and I was there to support. I left, and a First Nations gentleman walked out with me and said, "I know you're Indian." I replied, "How do you know that?" He said, "You learned the same thing I did." I said, "What's that?" and he replied, "God gave us two ears and one mouth for a reason!" I thought, "Isn't that an interesting observation, because what I've seen evolve over time is really the ability to listen better—actively and to synthesize information. We can all hear. But do we really listen?"

The second part of the answer is that I trust myself much more now. I allow myself to make mistakes and I internalize the notion that a mistake is a learning opportunity. In many ways, when I have a success—and, of course, I love to have successes—I'm really hard pressed to tell you what went right. When something goes wrong, I can really look at that and say, "Ah, Okay, now I understand. It wasn't the right time. It wasn't the right way of thinking about this. I was too quick on this or too slow on that." I can look at that situation and file information away. You learn to trust yourself as a result of these situations.

Learning requires reflection. Do you reflect on your leadership?
At the beginning of my career, it was more deliberate, but I was always thinking about it in some way. I think about it when I'm driving. I think about it at the end of the week when I'm unwinding. I ask myself, "Did I manage too much? Did I lead enough? Am I doing enough with the platform for leadership I was given? What am I doing with this?" I also try to look at leadership in different ways. I have discussions with friends and peers about leadership. I listen to them and we brainstorm. We don't dissect leadership, analyze it, or prescribe advice, but simply just boot the issue around and it's wonderful. Also, when I read books, whether biographies or literature, I ask myself, "Are these people demonstrating leadership? How did they create their vision? What is their vision? How do they see the world?" ***Part of***

leadership is recognizing that I am unique only in the sense that my experience has me looking at the world differently than others will, and there are so many different ways of looking at the world.

You read a lot. What books on leadership would you recommend? What books made you think about leadership?

I had the pleasure of studying political theory, and I still go back to some very fundamental books on that topic. Plato's *Republic* and Aristotle's *Politics* are phenomenal, very rich books. I also like *One Hundred Years of Solitude* by Gabriel García Márquez. People likely won't think of this as a leadership book, because it's not a "how-to" book. I wouldn't read how-to books about leaders, but, rather, books about people who demonstrate leadership and authenticity in given situations. That, to me, is the essence of the discussion about leadership. If I read a golf magazine, I'll ruin my golf swing. I am not likely to open a book that specifically says "how to be a better leader." I don't want to imitate somebody else's life and leadership. A key issue for me around leadership is authenticity and how to bring that out.

As you transitioned to more and more senior roles, what were some of the challenges that you faced, and how did you overcome them?

I found it exciting when I leaped to those roles. When you're junior and reporting in to a manager, you need to understand what's in your manager's mind. Reading people's minds is difficult. I found it liberating to be in a senior role because then other people looked to me to help shape and define the organization's vision. There are also certain skills you need to have for these roles. I needed to learn how to integrate my thinking and how the different parts of a business—finance, marketing, operations, strategy—fit together. *The big leap forward, though, is getting in touch with who you are. You need to trust the sum of all your experiences and marry the vision and view that you have of the outside world. Then, you need to bring all of that to your leadership role at the organization. If you don't do that, people won't see you as authentic.* Good leaders empower others to be leaders. They need to leverage their own leadership to create an even greater collaborative leadership within your organization. As you move through these steps, you build the skill base and the confidence to run an organization. Hopefully, this process will also help you to trust in who you are, because that's what makes you a leader.

You live in a fishbowl. You are one of the civic leaders in the city of Toronto. You manage numerous stakeholders. There is potential for conflict.

Yes, it's a multi-stakeholder environment. There are obviously conflicts that arise from time to time, but that's not the key thing. The key is there are multiple activities, strategies that are unfolding in different files and portfolios, any way you want to look at it. You've got to trust yourself to be consistent in who you are across situations and how you deal with those. It's almost like you can't jump into one scenario and be one person, then jump into another and be another. You have to be grounded in who you are in terms of that consistency. I think you raise a very interesting question, which is: "How do you prepare yourself to deal with a multi-stakeholder environment, which is inherently more complex than a less multi-stakeholder environment." *I think part of the learning is to expose yourself to the complexities more often. Expose yourself to diverse files. Introduce yourself to complex situations. These offer opportunities to learn about who you are and to get grounded in who you are in that environment.* I was given opportunities to work in those multi-stakeholder environments and, over time, started to build the required toolkit to be effective. You always hear that, with professional athletes, the better they get, the slower the game gets for them. It is somewhat similar to working in a multi-stakeholder environment, but it takes time to develop those skills and your confidence, and, hence, how comfortable you feel in those situations.

You talked a lot about trust and confidence. How has that developed for you? How did you develop the confidence to put yourself on the line and really try to make a difference?

One of the best things is to make a mistake early on, because then you learn that you can fail and that keeps you humble. Through mistakes, you also learn to embrace that tomorrow is another day. You toughen up and realize that you're fallible and that it's okay to make mistakes. *In fact, if you're not making mistakes, you're probably not pushing yourself hard enough. If you're not making mistakes, you're not really creating many learning opportunities. You gain confidence when you make mistakes and manage to move on and learn from them.* Part of that process is knowing you've had successes so you're confident that you'll have more successes. Humility is also part of that because you know that you've both been successful and made mistakes. You also need to recognize that you don't always have to be confident. You can still function very well and demonstrate leadership when you're perhaps not at your best or feeling the most confident. For example, I have a lot of public speaking opportunities and some go better than others. On some days, I get up and I just don't feel I've got the mojo. On other occasions, the first 30 seconds of speaking are not smooth and that gets me on a roll, fighting that little piece. When you do this enough times, you realize you can right the ship again. That's a good feeling. Sometimes, those situations are even more fulfilling because you had to struggle to right the ship. You need to trust yourself to work your way through it, and not put so much pressure on yourself that it's a win-or-lose situation all the time. You also can't get too cocky. Quite frankly, if you're a successful leader, you've had your own booboos and failures, too, so you realize that failure is always a possibility. It can be lurking around the corner at any time.

You are a visible leader in the community of Toronto. Is there anything that you fear about the role of leadership?

As a leader in an organization, you want to push and grow your organization, and make real impact through change, so you need to take risks. You need to stick your neck out personally, professionally, and organizationally. In many ways, you're the beneficiary of a lot of the success when things go right. You're also the beneficiary of criticism when things go wrong. As a leader, you're always cognizant of the fact that you could make a mission-critical mistake. You live in fear of that, and your own natural risk management process internally tries to keep you from making a mistake. You don't want to always live in fear, so you need to trust yourself and tell yourself, "You've built a good team around you and built a good governance structure around you." You have put all those things in place to mitigate mistakes or failure from happening, so that should help to reduce some of that fear. There is always a risk, in a very public profile, that you might say the wrong thing or it might be taken out of context and damage your organization's reputation. You need to be mindful of this, but also trust yourself and, as you gain confidence, you see that this possibility is remote. There's always a notion in the back of your mind—in particular, when you're in the philanthropic world, because that's a very different space from the traditional commercial environment—that things could go awry very quickly. You don't want to live in fear of that, but you want to look over your shoulder.

Leadership is about ongoing learning. You reflect often on your leadership. What are you learning these days to become an even better leader? Are there any recent "aha" moments?
Trust yourself more. It's remarkable—even people who are very successful hold themselves back. So, I think what I learned recently, and it's an ongoing thing, is to push myself more, and to let that come out more. *We need to give ourselves permission to really think big.* That's what gives us purpose, and that's what really brings us together to do great things. We should trust ourselves to commit to the things we yearn to do.

What have you personally experienced as a barrier to learning and how have you tried to overcome this barrier?
I think, inside of all of us, we gravitate towards things that we like to do—things that we see as success and that we do because we find them fulfilling. There are always aspects that we procrastinate on, and I think a part of being a successful leader is you don't procrastinate on things that are really important because those will come back and bite you. The aggregate of those things, though, that we don't look at because they are not so comfortable and they're just not that fun to do are things that could become problems. Part of my own dialogue with myself, too, is to be able to identify those weaknesses and try as best as I can to face those head on, to say, "Okay, I need to get better at this, it's not going to happen overnight, but let's put in an honest effort and go in over here, and let's make sure that I do get better at doing that over time." It's a difficult discussion to have with oneself because nobody enjoys that piece, but it's important to have that conversation. It's good to have a governance structure around you and a process where you've got people who can talk to you about your challenges. A process or relationship that's built on; where people will say, "You're good at these things, we really like that, and here's an area that you can focus on a little bit more." You need to be able to put your ego aside long enough to say, "Okay, that's important so I'm going to go work on that."

So what is it that you have to do to step out of your comfort zone and stretch yourself?

Sometimes you don't have a choice. You could have a board of directors that suddenly, in a consensus discussion, would say, "Great, we need to do this, this, and this," and, intellectually, you agree very much—that's the place to go. But suddenly you'll go, "Well, geez, I've never been there before—how do I do this?" And that's when you've got to go back inside of yourself and say, "You know, I've trusted myself to learn how to do new things before; this is a new thing, I will learn to do that." It could be an entirely new way of looking at things or a new way of doing things. Your role now is to give that life; to translate it into a way that you can do it. You may not yet know what that looks like. But you've got to step in and learn a new way of doing that. You may be uncomfortable with this, but you have to convince yourself and say, "It's got to get done, I'm going to go there with a positive attitude, and I'm going to learn as much as I can about it."

Transparency and accountability are important concepts in the area of philanthropy. How did you learn to take accountability, and what were the challenges in learning to take accountability?

I think, once you've personally crossed the hurdle of recognizing that you have made mistakes, that you will continue to make mistakes, and that you've learned from those mistakes, it builds within you, hopefully, the capacity to say, "I was wrong, I made a mistake." There are some people for whom, for whatever reason, it's too much of a debilitating thing to admit that they were wrong. They just can't see themselves as being wrong, or it's such an admission of weakness that it's just overwhelming—it paralyzes them. Have we made mistakes? Sure. Are we pleased to stand up and say, "Gee, we made a mistake"? Not particularly. I hope we can move on. Once you're comfortable with this notion, it takes the notion of accountability as an issue off the table. We are accountable to our stakeholders. We are accountable to the city of Toronto because we're all about the vision of making this city as good as possible. We want to live up to that responsibility, so I really want to take the fear element out of it, and say, "Let's liberate ourselves to go do the best job, with the best commitment, the highest levels of integrity and motivation, and with transparency."

That sounds so easy. Don't you think there can be a significant cost associated with taking accountability?

In the political realm, clearly, everybody wants to see you fired, and everybody wants your job—that's the nature of that beast. It's very difficult to stand up and say you've made a mistake. It happens from time to time, but it's rare. In the corporate context as well, depending on the culture of the organization, some leaders are comfortable taking accountability whereas others won't be able to do that. If an organization is truly committed to transparency and accountability, I think it will create a safe environment for people to acknowledge that. For example, if people know that they are going to be fired for making a mistake, you're never going to get accountability. I think we've created a governance structure and an environment with our board of directors, our stakeholders, and our staff that we know is a safe environment to be able to be transparent and accountable.

What have you learned about building trust? What are some of the things that leaders can do to build trust in organizations?

It's about understanding the notion of stewardship. *Leaders are stewards for the organization. I think a deep sense of stewardship is important because it's the recognition that you're holding this position and role in trust for those who came before you and will come after you.* You also have to build trust in relationships. In my view, that requires a great deal of authenticity. There's that word "authenticity" again. You can't pretend to build trust. It has to be who you are. People are very, very bright. They will see if you're not authentic. They'll know if you're not comfortable in your own skin; and they'll know if you're not consistent and, for example, treat one group dramatically different to another group. If you're espousing values over here, and obliterating the same values over there, you will not have trust and consistency. You will get a cynical group of people instead. The "trust" part is very personal. People need to see that. People need to know who you are, and that doesn't develop over a week or two. Trust develops over years—people seeing you in circumstances of crisis and circumstances outside your comfort zone. People will see you in all kinds of circumstances interacting with others and they'll want to know, "Who are you?" If they don't know who you are, they aren't going to trust you. It is important to be open and honest, authentic and transparent, all those things—but also to be someone who can converse with them and who they believe has actually got the best organizational interests at heart and wants to work with them. For me, it is also about delivering on promises, providing support to people, and caring about people as individuals. That's, in my view, how you build trust. The scary reality about trust is it takes a long time to build and a very short time to lose.

What sustains you as a leader? What drains you?

The art of the possible—the possibilities of what your organization can do—it's endless. There are moments when a plan comes together, or you've done something new, or you've taken an idea and created something out of it. There are times when you're building something, and seeing it grow, and it's getting better than you ever would have thought because other people are adding good things to it as well. The chances of doing that again in different ways are extremely exciting, so those moments sustain you. Every time you do something like that, you give a lift to the organization and yourself. Those moments remind you that you can do bigger things collectively, and you build that into the DNA of the organization, so that you start to see other people doing it as well. When this happens, there is a beautiful collaborative leadership that just gets bigger and bigger. You start to really believe in and be the change that you seek. There is a great sense of purpose that comes with that. That's what sustains me.

What drains me is fear that the spigot will turn off, the creativity will dry up, and I'll suddenly become misaligned with what's going on out there and, as a result, lose momentum. When you're in a resource-constricted environment, it's a constant grind to make sure that you are resourced. It's draining when you have this great vision, but you know you're missing something to accomplish it. It's tough when you don't get to see your vision live out its fullest potential. Sometimes leaders worry about things such as will they run out of steam, become disconnected with the organization, or will the organization no longer need them? We're living in a world of great uncertainty, and it can be draining to dwell on uncertainty. Part of being a leader is to live in the gray zone and with intense uncertainty—and still being energized in that space. Leaders need to be believing, hopeful, and optimistic.

What expectations do you put on yourself in the leadership role?

I'll share with you a story from my days with the Toronto Community Foundation. I was being introduced to staff for the first time. There is a saying that you never get a second chance to make a first impression, and I was aware that people knew me by reputation. That first meeting was important because I needed to settle people down and start off on the right foot. I wanted people to feel comfortable. There will be lots of time for discomfort as you move forward, so you want to start off on a good note. I felt it was very important for me to convey to folks my mindset and orientation about life. When I spoke with them, I shared with them a quote that I happen to believe in: "There are very few things in life that you can control, but the one thing that you have absolute control over is the quality of your own effort." That's all I ask of my team—if it puts in the effort, we'll figure out the results. I've also learned along the way that if you only focus on results, that's all you ever get. If you focus on the effort, people may go far beyond the results you imagined. That's my orientation and the piece that keeps me feeling really comfortable in terms of leadership.

What has been your most rewarding experience as a leader and why?

There have been a number of them, but they all have one common characteristic— bringing people together to dream a big vision and be absorbed by it. I enjoy feeling their energy and excitement, and watching them take the first step in that journey. In some cases, that journey ends successfully, and that's the most exciting thing to see. It's fantastic when you watch people grow to new heights because you gave them the opportunity to do so. It's great to look at their faces when they achieve what they never thought possible.

You talked about leaders and the importance of self-awareness. There is also the situational awareness piece, because leaders and their organizations operate in a context. Can you talk about that a little?

Part of developing greater self- and situational awareness is enduring the school of hard knocks and the culmination of growing up. In my case, growing up as a visible minority—as an immigrant in a new country and city—at a time when there weren't many visible minorities made me want to fit in. I had to understand the context and be nimble and aware. My antennae had to be up. If I made a mistake or goofed up, it would be more painful because then I might stick out a little bit more. I learned to be more self-aware. In some cases, I also think I was intrigued by what others said and did, and had to be awake and alert to catch it. I like word games and nuances. You need to be awake to catch those kinds of things and that's part of being aware. Being aware is important. You want to be sensitive to the people that are around you as well, because that helps to build a better team and get things done.

Do you like being a leader?

This is a really interesting question because some people confuse leadership with the most senior manager position in the organization. Some people don't like decision-making and managerial duties. I personally think most people would want a leadership role if they really understood what it allowed them to do. It allows you to dream and work with others to shape that dream and vision. It allows you to inspire and be inspired by others to do really neat things. If you told people that's what leadership is about, I think most would say, "Okay, I'll do that—what I don't want to do is all that grunt work." The grunt work is the managerial part of it. I often hear people say they'd be a great number two in an organization because they are afraid to really stick their necks out. When we talk about sticking yourself out there, boy, you do lead with your chin. You can be quite alone in that space. You can develop alliances and relationships and things like that, which are great to have, but you are fundamentally out on your own. I'll give you an analogy. When you're the artist walking through a gallery and you painted that piece that's up on the wall that people are staring at, knowing that they're either going to love or hate it, you can't run and hide from the fact that you created it—that is part of who you are. Leadership can be a very lonely sphere. *The other challenge is that you can't turn leadership off. You are a leader all of the time, and, at times, that can be a burden. It creates a little bit of an island that can be quite lonely.* You asked me if I like being a leader. The answer is overwhelmingly "yes." Leadership provides opportunities for me to grow in ways I never imagined. I get to work with people who amaze me. Their commitment and desire to do great things make me feel privileged to be at the organization through its own journey in history. I'm inspired when I look at the people on my board who come to our meetings and want to be a part of it. I feel fulfilled when I look at the people who walk in as my staff every day and I know that their lives are full of purpose. I feel fulfilled when I go to community groups and give speeches in Toronto and see people getting excited about creating a better city and a better world. Leadership creates an opportunity for purpose that would be very, very hard to replicate. It comes with a burden, but the opportunities and the possibilities are significant.

Leadership Themes

- The key to leadership is to know what to do with it.
- We can all hear. But do we really listen?
- One of the best things is to make a mistake early on, because then you learn that you can fail and that keeps you humble. You also learn to embrace that tomorrow is another day. You toughen up.
- If you're not making mistakes, you're probably not pushing yourself hard enough.
- If you only focus on results, that's all you ever get. If you focus on the effort, people may go far beyond the results you imagined.

12

Knowing When to Leave and Do Something Different Is One of the Hardest Things for a Leader to Do

Carol Stephenson

Carol, when did you first realize you were a leader, and what happened to make you realize it?

I don't think there was a defining moment where suddenly I woke up one day and decided I was a leader. I think it was the culmination of a lot of experiences that gradually shaped me as a leader. Those experiences started in childhood. I got along well with my friends. I would often lead the games at the playground. There was no defining moment. I think it was just a culmination of life experiences, and then, suddenly, you just find you're leading.

Did you want to be a leader?

No. In fact, when I was young, I was a bit shy. I remember pretending I was sick so I wouldn't have to go to school and make a public speech because it terrified me so much. Of course, we all know that leaders have to be great communicators. *I don't think I was thinking about whether I wanted to be a leader, but, at the age of 8 or 9 years old, I found out I wanted to make things happen. I liked working with people and, as a result, I would find myself in positions where I was leading.* I also had a strong sense of wanting things to be done well. I had high standards even at an early age. This probably developed my leadership.

What have been the formative influences on you as a leader? What did people do to help you? What experiences did you learn the most from? Was there any particular experience that supercharged your learning to lead?

I was at Bell Canada. I was doing well, but I had a vice president who took me on as "a project." I remember having my first performance review with him. I was going to see my boss in his office and I was armed with stacks of performance indicators and results to prove that I was doing well in my job. He looked at me and said, "just put those away" and "let's talk about leadership." And I'm thinking, "Oh . . . I didn't prepare for that." He then told me some of the things that he did and he had learned throughout his career. He took me under his wing, and it did make a difference in my career.

One of the things that he stressed was the importance of communication. In one of our sessions, he would have a professional come in and help me learn to communicate well. I remember thinking, "I communicate just fine. What is this all about?" I watched the video of my performance and then I realized that he was right. My boss had many lessons on how to influence people, how to get things done, and how to accomplish what you think you might not be able to.

The vice president was a formative influence in my business career in terms of my leadership development. He never gave up on me; he was like a dog with a bone. He was instrumental in arranging a transfer that was totally out of my comfort zone. I really had to rise to the challenge. He moved me into a regulatory job, which was populated with lawyers. I had line experience, I was not a policy wonk. This was at the time when competition in long distance was just starting. I was in the spotlight in terms of making sure that Bell's position was put forward. There was absolutely no room for being shy, no room for not doing the job really, really well, because so much depended on it. I would say he was someone who really did propel my career forward.

It is always challenging to step out of your comfort zone and start doing things that perhaps do not come naturally. How did you develop the confidence to step out of the comfort zone?
I think practice is a big determinant in getting comfortable doing things that you might think are out of your comfort zone. Once you do them, you find that they aren't that hard. You realize that you can do more and more of them. Earlier in my career, I was running a downtown Toronto switching center. It was a technical job. I had only men reporting to me. Many of my friends said that this job was a career ender—"What are you doing?" they asked. I also had a boss at the time who did not believe women should be in these jobs. He didn't talk to me for a week. Finally, he said, "I guess we better talk. I guess if I have to take a woman, you're the best of a bad lot." I thought, "There's a crack here!" It actually turned out to be one of the easiest jobs. But what I learned about myself is that, sometimes, these assignments that everybody says are difficult, or not in your comfort zone to do, are not that hard and that, once you keep doing them, you get the confidence that you can take on things that you don't know you can do.

As you transitioned to more and more senior roles, what were some of the challenges that you faced and how did you overcome them?
Let's start with competencies. Often, when you're going into a new environment as a leader, you don't know everything there is to know about the job. I think the really good leaders understand what they don't know. I'm not a big believer in this "first 100 days" plan. I think your first 100 days should be about listening and learning, and getting to understand the people better. What are their issues? That has always been my approach when I go into a

new job: To listen very carefully, to get involved, and to learn the issues. But don't pronounce on what you think needs to be done because, quite honestly, within a year it might be very different than your first initial impressions. I would say I'm sure we all feel a little nervous and have our nagging doubts when we go into a new job, but, if you listen really well and you understand the people, I think you actually gain the required competencies to be successful more quickly.

I've never had a problem with commitment. I don't know that I'm a workaholic but I have such high standards for myself that I do roll up my sleeves and I do work hard. There's always more work to do. I'm not satisfied unless I think that I have achieved what is possible for me to achieve.

And with regards to character, I think we all are challenged from time to time with gray areas where your character is tested. My values are strong. I have strong values from the influence of my parents; not that they are the same values, but they are strong values. *I've always been encouraged to follow my heart so I try and stand back. And I say this to our Ivey students: "Get off the treadmill, and then reflect and consult with people around you that you trust. But, most importantly, listen to your heart and, if it doesn't feel right, it probably isn't right."* So, I use my own internal sense of what's right and what's wrong to make the right decision.

You said you take time to reflect on your leadership. What does that reflection look like?

I take time to reflect on leadership, in part through mentoring other people. When people are asking me about their leadership, it causes me to reflect on my own. The second thing I do is I observe a lot. This may sound strange, but I've probably had only two really bad bosses in my entire career. I learned a lot from those two individuals, in terms of how not to lead. I think observing other people in leadership roles really helps you understand leadership and figure out how you can do it, too. It also helps you see the worst in leadership.

Can you give an example of a bad boss and the profound lesson in leadership that you learned?

In my very first meeting with this person, he said to me, "I want to get one thing straight with you. I tangled with one employee once and he is no longer in the company and I am. I hope you understand that I am the one with power." And I remember thinking that this was the strangest way to develop a relationship with a new employee in their first meeting. It was a threatening remark and it didn't make me want to work any harder or better. Actually, it made me want to move somewhere else, because this is not the aspiring leadership that you're looking for from your boss. The fact that I can still repeat that sentence is remarkable because it was many years ago. The lesson that stuck with me is about motivation: Certainly, threatening people is not the way to do it.

What then do you believe is the essence of good leadership? For you, what is the key to good leadership?

Leadership to me is about influencing people and getting them to do their very best. Leadership is also about raising the bar: Making sure that people reach their potential and that they are excited about what they're doing. I also believe a leader owns the culture of the organization. What is it that we're trying to instill in the culture? The leader is the keeper of that culture. People watch you. A lot of people assume that nobody listens to the CEO. Studies have shown that the two people that employees are most likely to listen to are their immediate boss and the CEO or the leader of the organization. *You are being watched for what tone you set in the organization. And if you deviate from the set of espoused values, or the culture that you believe is important for your organization, then people will say, "I don't need to do it because the leader's not doing it."* These are two of the most important things a leader can do: Understanding people, and helping them achieve their potential, and owning the culture.

Where does your commitment to the leadership role come from?

It comes from my upbringing. I came from a family where everybody worked. My father was a teacher and my mother was a nurse. My grandmother also worked. There was a mantra in the family: "You can do anything you want, if you put your mind to it." And, secondly: "If you choose to do it, do it well." That could be anything from volunteer work to your job. There were no barriers ever suggested to us, but there was an expectation that you would do your very best at something. I don't know that I realized it at the time, but my parents always let me make decisions. There was a faith in us as kids that we would do the right things and we would also do the right things well. So I think the commitment started there. And it came from inside; if I don't do it well, then I've let myself down.

What were some of the hardest things to learn in becoming a good or an even better leader?

I mentioned earlier that I believe communication is really important for a leader, and I had to work hard at becoming a good communicator. I have a natural shyness. I have a natural listening tendency as opposed to a speaking tendency. So, I worked hard at figuring out how to communicate well, when to communicate, and to really enjoy it, because, if you don't enjoy it, you actually don't do it very well.

   The second thing is gaining confidence, to know that you can do the job of a leader. I sometimes get asked by students, "How old did you want to be when you got your first CEO job?" My answer is that I thought they were going to fire me at my first job and that kind of doubt about my abilities carried on in my first five or six years until I realized I was getting promoted. So, I think confidence is another thing that you need as a leader. One of the culminating things that really helped me with confidence was I acquired my formal business education a little bit later in life. I went to Harvard and there were about 150 people from around the world; there were only 10 women in the program. I remember thinking, "If these are the cream of the crop from around the world and they're leading really impressive organizations, then I am just as good as they are." I actually came back from that experience with a lot of confidence. Confidence is something that you have to acquire. Some leaders pretend to have confidence. But there's a difference between having that inner confidence and putting up a show.

We often talk about leadership and the importance of self-awareness. But situational awareness is as important as self-awareness. People will eat you up and spit you out if you read the situation the wrong way. Did you have to learn the importance of situational awareness the hard way?
I'll give you an example of where I was really wrong in terms of reading the situation. I was the CEO at Lucent Technologies Canada. We went through the big downturn in the telecommunications sector. I had been through business cycles before, certainly at Bell. So I knew how this would all work out in the end. At that time, the employees at Lucent were quite young. I thought it would be really helpful if I explained to them what it was that we will go through and how long it will take to recover. I thought that, having been through business cycles before, this will be really helpful information for the employees. It may help relieve their anxiety. That presentation was the worst thing I could have done. *What I forgot was to pay attention to the emotional cycles that people have to go through. I hadn't allowed for the anger and grief to happen. I was into remedies and solutions, and so it was a terrible misjudgment on my part in terms of reading the situation and how people might be feeling.* I realized that the employees were upset with me, but I recovered. I have often reflected on that episode. Your knowledge is useful, but you have to know when to apply that knowledge. I certainly missed the boat on that one critical factor: People need time to release their emotions.

What have you personally experienced as a barrier to learning and how have you tried to overcome this barrier?
I think sometimes if you have been successful doing things a certain way time and time again, you can close your mind to new ways of doing things. The second thing though, and I remember this well, is you can get bored. Boredom closes your mind to new learning. This happened to me when I was in the telecommunications sector for more than 25 years. I knew the sector well. I had seen all the cycles and I knew what to expect every time. I also knew everybody. I almost knew what they were going to say before they said it. *And I suddenly realized that I was bored, and that wasn't good, because, once you think you know everything and everybody in an industry, you quit listening or you jump over a few steps that you should, in fact, take.* It was time for me to make a change and so I did. So if you get stuck in that sort of boredom spot, it can be a barrier to your learning.

This is a remarkable observation. It is hard for leaders to step aside when they start to doubt their commitment to the role of leadership and their engagement.

Knowing when to leave and do something different is one of the hardest things for a leader to do. There are a couple of reasons why this is so hard. No one's going to tell you, unless you're really making a mess of things and then they'll fire you. And, if things are going well, people aren't going to suggest to you that you should leave. Things can also become comfortable. In the end, you must rely on yourself. This doesn't mean that you hate your job or that you don't love what you do. People think that stepping away from a job or organization means something was wrong. Actually, a lot of things can be right—you've just decided it's time to do something different. This has been a hallmark of my leadership. *I never said "no" to an opportunity without thinking about it; and they weren't necessarily opportunities that fit my background. People can stretch. No one should be afraid to take on opportunities.* It is important to know yourself well enough to realize when it's time to go. This is really a hard thing to figure out.

What sustains you as a leader?

People sustain me. I get great satisfaction from things that involve people. I'll give you an example here at the Ivey Business School. There was a young man who we admitted into the MBA program based on a conversation he and I had. He did not have an undergraduate degree. But he had started a business in high school. I knew, from listening to him and having him visit the school, that he had what it took to succeed. I took a risk and I broke a few rules to make sure that he was admitted. He went on to do really, really well. I saw him in San Francisco a month ago, and he gave me this nice little card saying "you were so important in terms of what I've achieved to date." That may sound kind of sentimental, but to think that you can have an impact on somebody's life is a good feeling. Of course, it wasn't just me alone. Obviously, he had a lot of talent. But to think you have opened some doors for people, that you somehow allowed them to achieve their potential, is to me a huge satisfier.

What drains you?

People. Good leaders care about people. They like people to do well and to reach their potential. So, if people aren't getting along and performing well, and if they aren't getting the opportunities you think they should, it requires a lot of energy to help solve those problems. That can create stress.

You worked with different leaders. What did you learn about working with individuals who had different approaches to lead?

You have to respect different leadership styles. I remember taking a course and I've never forgotten some of the learnings. The course was about how to get results through other people when they have very different leadership styles. I remember, at the time, I was working for a boss who was highly analytical and I tend to be more verbal. I couldn't figure out why he wouldn't agree to some of the things I wanted to do. But, after taking that course, I realized I wasn't providing him with the necessary analytics. That's what made him comfortable with decisions. I changed the way I presented information to him, and, before I knew it, things were going a lot better. There was another category called "the persister." The worst thing you can do to the persister is not listen to his or her ideas and just ignore him or shut her down. Once you know somebody's a persister, the best thing you can do is listen to their ideas. You may not necessarily implement the ideas or agree to them, but, if you haven't listened, you don't have a hope of getting the individual on your side. *I learned that you have to understand other people's leadership styles and to be able to adapt to that style over time. I guess you could say it's as simple as putting yourself in the other person's shoes.* If I were in their shoes, what would I be concerned about? What would I be thinking about? How do they think? And then try to solve those problems. And always be respectful. That's when you can have an open and transparent conversation.

You have been a CEO. You are the dean of the Ivey Business School. Leadership is not always a bed of roses—there are obstacles and setbacks; there might be disappointments; and, of course, things are happening that are beyond your control. How did you develop resilience?
I've learned not to take things personally. That is hard to learn, especially if you've invested a lot of energy and time into something and it fails. It's really easy to say, "I personally failed." Over time, I've become better with this. There's a great line: "Don't grin and bear it, groan and get over it." I think sometimes we grin and bear things too long, as opposed to groaning and moving on quickly. It didn't work? Get over it and move on to the next thing!

Second, if things get pretty stressful and you're ready to tear your hair out, I actually take a personal break. I'll take a day at the spa or I'll do something for myself. It re-energizes me, because you can actually drag yourself down too much. I recall a situation in which I was miserable in my job. Somebody pointed out to me that I was not myself. This caused me to reflect and I left the job that I was in. I think I was in the mode of blaming the organization, and it suddenly dawned on me: Big organizations aren't going to change because you're not agreeing with them. I was the problem and what had happened is I probably had grown beyond the culture of that particular organization. We often need to step back and say, "Is there anything I can do that will make things better?" or "If I'm totally unhappy, then maybe I shouldn't be doing this. I should be doing something different." So I left the organization, went on, and did something new.

How important have networks been to your learning and success?
When I started at Bell, there was a group of us—all women—who started together. We were all on a management rotational program. The deal was that, if we

didn't do well in the first year, they would fire you. So we were all in this together. Fast-forward 30 years—we are still having dinner at least twice a year. We've lost a couple members; and none of us is at Bell anymore. But the friendship and the openness to share more than just work issues have sustained us. There is also family. They know us sometimes better than we know ourselves. Therefore, getting their input on things is important. The same applies to your business associates. *Networking just to network is fun and it's interesting, but I think you do need a group of friends, or some group that sustains itself over a longer period of time, that can be your sounding board.* The people who have made the most impact on me are the people I have known for a very long time.

What are you learning these days to become an even better leader? Are there any recent "aha" moments?

The more experienced you get, the more self-aware you become. I say to the younger leaders, just chill out a little bit and learn more about yourself. Learn what you're good at, find out what you're not so good at, and don't be afraid to say that you're not good at something. People will see it and place the right people around you who are good at those things. So, self-awareness is really important, and especially in younger people who are just starting out their careers. They're so busy trying to prove themselves that they sometimes lose sight of their own self-awareness. I sound like I'm somebody's grandmother here, but self-awareness comes with age and experience.

The second thing that I would emphasize is something I've always called peripheral vision in leadership; your ability to look beyond your organization you're leading, and beyond the country in which you're leading. Scan the world, be global, look outside your industry. Here at the school, I like to call it cross-enterprise leadership. I would say, the more experience I gain, and the more things I've been exposed to, the more I understand the importance of cross-enterprise leadership. It's so important to have that peripheral vision that goes beyond your own little piece of the action or your own little piece of the world. I learned it over time, but I think the earlier you can learn it as a leader, the better you're going to be as a leader.

What advice do you have for people as they embark on their journey of learning to lead?

I do believe that you can learn to be a better leader. I think back to some of the courses I took and the early experiences I had. Second, I would encourage leaders to get feedback and to try and establish relationships with people who will give them honest feedback, because you learn through that feedback: What you're doing right, what you're not doing right, and what you can do better. And the third thing is that leadership takes courage. *I would encourage people to continue to be brave enough to lead in turbulent times, not to give up, to be persistent, and embrace the impact that you can have as a leader.*

You talked about feedback. We talked about mentors. But sometimes we get unsolicited feedback that I think can be valuable. We need to open ourselves up to that feedback. What unsolicited feedback have you received that in hindsight was good feedback, but perhaps at that time you didn't want to hear?

I will never forget this episode. I was having my performance review at Bell and, at the time, the head of the organization was in the hospital. They had done my performance review around the hospital bed. My boss came back to share my performance review. They had some interesting feedback. My boss was not the classiest guy in the world. He said, "We think you need pizzazz." I said, "What?" "You need pizzazz." "What do you mean?" He said, "Look at that woman [a colleague]. She has false eyelashes and great clothes. She just looks fabulous all the time." And I think, "This feedback comes from a guy that wears white socks and green pants! What has this got to do with my performance? And look at who's delivering the message!" Anyway, I was pretty annoyed with all of this and I was taking it personally. I doubted they were telling the guys they needed "pizzazz." I don't know what possessed me to do this, but I went out and bought this fashionable dress. I was making a presentation to the executive team in this dress, and I had bright red lipstick and lots of makeup. The person that had been in the hospital said, "If I were younger, I would ask you out on a date." I'm thinking, "Oh goodness." In hindsight, I think what they were probably trying to tell me, in their own way, was that you need confidence, you need to look professional, and you need to have a business approach to things. And they were right. I didn't wear the red lipstick anymore and I didn't wear the extreme dress, but I was a lot more conscious about the importance of presence, if I can call it that, in the business environment.

Have your views on leadership changed over the past five years? You are on the board of General Motors. You are on several government committees. You are the dean of the Ivey Business School. In all these positions, you deal with a very complex and interconnected world. Are there leadership qualities that change with the times and that maybe in today's business world, as complex and interconnected as it is, become even more important?

One of the things that I've learned is the increased pace of change. General Motors is a good example. *Leaders have to make decisions that are impacting people and businesses around the world. You would like to have more time to consider the implications of your decisions. But often time is a luxury. How do you speed up some of the things you have to do as a leader?* You're traveling around the world and sometimes you're exhausted. Time is never on your side in a hypercompetitive world. Getting that balance right between acting quickly on things that you really need to act on versus taking a little more time on those that you can take time on is really challenging for a leader these days. We talked about some of the mistakes that I made. When I look back over my career, some of the things that I wish I had done differently would've been acting more quickly on people issues. I tend to be an optimist. I think I can coach people. But perhaps I let things go on for too long in some instances and I should have acted more quickly. I've learned that, especially in the fast-paced world that we're in now, you can't afford to have leaders who can't lead for too long. There can be huge negative implications. You have to act quickly in today's world. You should not let decisions about people and leaders, in particular, linger longer than needed.

Is there any specific advice that you might have for the next generation of female leaders who are in the process of learning to lead?
First of all, my experience as being a female leader is that, at the entry level, there probably isn't a huge difference vis-à-vis our male counterparts. But as I got into more senior positions, that's where I actually saw some differences emerge. And the difficult part is that it can be quite subtle. I would rather have somebody as a boss who tells me that he believes women should not be working here. That is a lot easier to deal with than the dozens who use the right words, but all of a sudden you're not invited to meetings or you're not involved in decision making. It's subtle and it's because you're in a position of power that sometimes you can be viewed more of a threat. I think you have to be sensitive to that.

The second thing is to stick to your own leadership style. I think that, as a female leader, we do have some characteristics that are more natural to women and, quite frankly, they're really great characteristics of leadership, so don't abandon them. Be who you are and stick to that style because if you're not authentic, people will see through it.

Third, I think women have to support other women. I've been supported by a group of women through my entire career and we continue to support one another. I think it is important to understand that, as you become more senior, you can actually have an impact on women who may be considered for leadership positions. I'll give you a good example. I was on a search committee at a university— they were looking for someone to do the vice president, international, role. The committee was talking about this one particular woman who would be a good candidate. I remember that some people around the table said she would never take the position because there is too much travel involved and she has children. She couldn't possibly do the job effectively. I said, "How do we know that she can't travel? She might have a nanny. She might have a husband who stays at home. Why are we jumping to conclusions?" So this is an example where the committee might have eliminated a potential candidate because of a preconceived idea. I don't think it was mean spirited; it was just assumptions. Of course, we do not want to have women in leadership positions when they are not qualified. But we should be supportive of other women getting an opportunity to lead.

The fourth thing I would say to women is be confident, be persistent, get advice, and don't pigeonhole yourself into an area that you think is the only area in which you can work. I remember somebody one time said to me, "How did you get so lucky in your career?" *I love the line: "Luck equals opportunity plus preparation." I have followed that adage. I took opportunities that were not anything I would have contemplated in my life until they were presented, and I prepared myself, whether it was through education or hard work. Luck does play a role in life, but my advice to women is don't close your mind to opportunities and prepare yourself.*

The fifth thing is outsource a lot of your work. I couldn't do all the things I do today without having someone clean my house and do some gardening. Don't think that you can do absolutely everything yourself. Figure out the things that are really important to do, including your family needs, but then don't feel guilty about outsourcing the things that you don't have time to do.

Leadership Themes

- Practice is a big determinant in getting comfortable doing things that you might think are out of your comfort zone.
- Leaders are being watched for what tone they set in the organization.
- You have to understand other people's leadership styles and to be able to adapt to that style.
- Leadership takes courage. Continue to be brave enough to lead in turbulent times, not to give up, to be persistent, and embrace the impact that you can have as a leader.
- Having fun in whatever you do is essential for your success and for your wellbeing. Feel good about the opportunities you are given, the challenges you encounter, and your achievements—big or small.

13

I Learned It's Not Good Enough to Be Right—People Have to Buy Into Your Vision

Michael Deane Harris

Mike, when did you first realize you were a leader, and what happened to make you realize it?

I didn't realize it at a young age. It was certainly later in life. I had a very dominant father who was also my employer. He was in small businesses, so there were not a lot of opportunities for me to lead—I was a follower and a doer. That said, I learned a lot about leadership from my father, just not at an early age. I didn't learn about leadership at school either. I wasn't a star athlete—I was average. But I was always in the game and my opinions were respected. I had no awareness at that time that there was anything leadership-wise in me.

I left North Bay [in Ontario, Canada] and went off on my own for the "find myself years," as I call them, to a resort in the Laurentian mountains. I was a ski instructor. I got the job before the management staff saw me ski. I wasn't that good and had never taught skiing. But, at the end of the year, I was invited to come back the next year as the ski school's assistant director. I was the worst skier in the group, but I was a pretty good teacher. Here was a group of quite talented individuals who could all ski better and had more experience than me, and they still accepted me for a leadership role—the ski school's assistant director. That was the first time I felt maybe I do have something in me, and, subsequently, there were many events that reinforced that feeling. I was in my early 20s.

Did you want to be a leader?

No, and I had never thought about being a leader. I didn't grow up with leadership or need it to satisfy me. I was quite happy being on sporting teams, but not as the team leader.

I want to go back to my late father—and if my mother ever reads anything about this, forgive me, mom, but he was very dominant. There weren't many opportunities in the home or in his businesses to lead. You were a follower and did everything you could to win satisfaction or look good in his eyes.

What have been the formative influences on you as a leader? What did people do to help you? What experiences did you learn the most from? Was there any particular experience that supercharged your learning to lead?

I was a teacher at a public school in North Bay. Then, I left teaching to pursue business interests. But I continued to have a great interest in education and ran for the school board. I was elected as a trustee. I was surprised to learn we had some trustees who had been there for quite some time and were considered gurus of education. I was so much younger than them. I was surprised how often they would turn to me for my opinion. I was just the new kid. I was in my late 20s.

There was a man named David Doney who was head of the Northern Ontario Trustee Association. He was well regarded in the education community. He was probably my first mentor in something outside of the family business and my own recreational interests. He clearly saw something in me that I didn't know was there. He wanted to step down as chair of the board. Two years after I was elected as a trustee, I was elected as chair of the school board. I ran against another long-standing trustee and won overwhelmingly. At that time, I realized a lot of other people saw something within me that I wasn't sure was within me. So, to be frank, it was a scary time for me. But it was probably the defining moment for me in understanding that I had leadership qualities and abilities. People were prepared to entrust me with leadership—in this case, of the school board—so I went from there.

You said it was scary for you. What was scary?

I think going into the unknown is always scary. Kids are nervous the first time they stand up in front of the class to speak. Putting your name on the ballot is a little risky. How is this all going to be received? But, generally, what you learn from this is that there may be things unknown to you, but, if you have enough confidence in yourself and in your ability to learn, then you ought not to be afraid of it. So, every time I went into something new, there was a certain apprehension. Usually, it's the fear of the unknown. "What is this all about? What are the expectations here? There's a whole group of people here who are smarter than me in various areas; how am I going to come in and lead this group and be accepted?" There is also the fear of doing something stupid that demonstrates your lack of knowledge. You overcome it by educating yourself and realizing that, if you're new, people don't expect you to know everything. You also learn to realize that leadership doesn't necessarily mean you're the smartest person in all areas. Leadership is about being comfortable having smarter people working with you. Your goal is to get the best out of all of them to take you where you want to go.

In a sense, leadership is a journey—you were a ski and golf instructor, teacher, school board trustee, Member of the Provincial Parliament, Cabinet Minister, Progressive Conservative Party of Ontario (PC) house leader, PC party leader, and then Premier of Ontario. As you transitioned to more and

more senior roles, what were some of the challenges that you faced, and how did you overcome them?

You need to demonstrate that you know where you are going and are able to work collectively with everybody on how to get there. Each step was a challenge. Your previous accomplishments help you go forth into new areas. For example, being a Minister of Natural Resources when you don't necessarily know a lot about it, you got all these experts to give you advice. How are you able to grasp it all? You are the Minister by virtue of the appointment. You sit around the table listening to the briefings. People are waiting for you to be the final arbiter to make the decision. These are pretty important decisions and they're waiting for you to make them. That, in itself, is scary and drives you to understand, study, research, and read about the implications of the decision you have to make. I think that's probably the most important lesson in leadership. You are the leader and, at the end of the day, the final arbiter of what you're going to do, where you're going to go, and how you're going to get there. But, each step in the leadership journey gives you more and more confidence that you can do that.

Do your responsibilities get larger and larger?

Yes. It's important to have confidence that you have the right people giving you advice. *You need to have the right people in the positions of responsibility and the right people at the level you used to be at before you moved up through the organization. My own view is that I had to be comfortable enough having people smarter than me in all the knowledge areas.* When I say that, my critics will say that it was pretty easy for you to have people smarter than you in these positions. You need to be comfortable with that, and good leaders do that. But bad leaders, and those who make mistakes, don't always want people smarter than them around. They don't want to be second-guessed; they're afraid those people are after their jobs. I always believed I wanted people to be after my job, because if they move up, I move up. We keep getting the job done and we get it done better.

For you, what is the key to good leadership?

Good leadership requires those who are going to follow you, be part of your team, and accept you as leader, to buy into where you want to go. Great communication is key. People need to understand where we want to go and the changes required to get there. If they don't understand these things, they're not necessarily going to follow. If they don't understand the steps along the way—what you have to change to get there—it's going to be very difficult for them to follow.

I spoke to two of your former colleagues—Dianne Cunningham and Janet Ecker. Both told me that you are good at building teams, particularly the Cabinet. The Cabinet was a strong and united team. What have you learned about building and leading successful teams? And what I find of particular

interest is that you put Dianne Cunningham on your team. She was, at one time, your rival for the PC party leadership.
Bill Davis became the party leader in 1971. I had just started to get interested in politics. Davis was a mentor to me. He was the overwhelming favorite to win the leadership race. But Allen Lawrence almost upset him. Davis looked at the team of people that ran the Lawrence campaign and said, "Those are the people I want." He brought his rivals on board. He recognized that these were good and smart people. That was a great lesson for any leader in any area, but particularly for a political leader. I realized you need good, smart people to work for you. You need people who are in it for the right reasons—not just to win, but to win for a reason—and who cared about the province. When I won the leadership, I looked for those people. For example, the leadership team that led us to success in 1995 had two people—Tom Long and Leslie Noble—who didn't like or trust each other. They didn't really talk to each other. I picked Tom for chair of the campaign and Leslie to manage the day-to-day campaign. They both said "no" because they couldn't work with each other. But each of them had great strengths and I had confidence in them. I told them that, and literally forced them to work together. This not only led to my campaign successes in 1995 and 1999, but, today, they are really good friends with a lot of respect for each other. So it wasn't just Diane Cunningham and some people from her team; there were others I identified as important and the best people.

So, how do you do it? You have to have a common goal. In our case, the province needed a new direction; it needed help. We had a vision of where we wanted to go. People were brought together by their shared vision of a better Ontario. This helped us to overcome dislikes and personal differences. I believe the key to my success from the leadership to the premier's office was that we shared a vision of a better Ontario. We were changing a lot of things in the province. The changes created a lot of turmoil and uncertainty. Most people don't like turmoil or conflict. Most people don't like confrontation, so the end result had better be worth it—and that's the most important part. We all felt we were going to a better place. That gave us a unified team. It also required dismissing people who did not share the vision—including lifelong Conservatives—from the team.

You became Premier of Ontario in 1995. It was clear at that time the province needed change. The change you implemented—the "Common Sense Revolution"—was a tough change for many. Some would say this was radical change—certainly not incremental. You believed in that change, but, as in business, one can never be sure at the outset that the change will be successful. How did you develop confidence and comfort in dealing with the change and, quite frankly, putting your leadership on the line?
You need conviction. You have to believe you're going to be successful. You have to believe the change you are making will produce a better province, economy, education system, or health care system. You have to believe things are going to be better when you finish.

We had spent a fair bit of time developing the Common Sense Revolution. We did something quite radical—we put the platform out a year before the election. I felt I couldn't balance the books unless I got Ontarians back to work. The only way I could get them back to work was to be more tax and regulatory competitive.

We looked at other jurisdictions—states and countries where change had been implemented. For example, we looked at the success of Christine Whitman, the former governor in New Jersey. She had campaigned on a 30 percent tax cut as a way to leave more money in the hands of people earning it and less in the hands of the state. We also looked at the ideas and policies of Margaret Thatcher. We were confident, from looking at other jurisdictions and their successes, that we would get the results we wanted. The truth of the matter is there were many examples where these policies had been successful; they weren't brand new, we pulled them from other jurisdictions.

If you have confidence, the team around you will have confidence or people around you will develop it. If they don't, they'll leave. I didn't have too many people leave. Some did, but many more joined. Was I confident we would win the election? No. But I was confident that, if we won the election, we would have the mandate to make the changes. Was I confident I was going to be able to make the changes? No. But I was confident that, if we could make the changes, we'd have more jobs and better education and health-care systems and more people would stop being dependent on government assistance.

What were some of the hardest things to learn in becoming a good or an even better leader?

I learned it's not good enough to be right. People have to buy into your vision and ideas. It takes time to bring the team along with you. The team that actually has to implement the policy, for example, has to understand where you're going and why you're going there. It takes a lot of time before you can actually pull the trigger on an initiative. An example is the education system changes. We did not have total buy-in from the school boards because we proposed some changes that affected their powers. We studied and consulted for about two years with the various teacher associations on the changes that we felt had to be made. We didn't get buy-in from the associations and we went ahead and made the changes anyway. We just thought they were so important. We then went directly to the parents to explain what we were doing and why. Standardized testing would be a good example. We used a lot of political capital in making some of the required changes. We felt Ontario was falling behind other jurisdictions, particularly in math, science, and literacy. It was a difficult time. If we had had buy-in from the teachers, if they had spent half the time and money getting up to speed in the new math curriculum as they did fighting me, we would have had a better result. That was a pretty important lesson, in that it ought not to have been that difficult for all of those involved with education—the teachers on the front line, the school board and the administration, parents, taxpayers, and business. We all have an interest in having a better-educated workforce. That shouldn't have been a tough fight. But we didn't have buy-in. Should we have gone ahead without that buy-in? I ultimately made the decision that we couldn't afford to keep waiting—it was too important. I think it was the right thing to do. But it would've been so much easier and better had we had buy-in.

Here's another example. I had won the leadership race. I recall a caucus meeting. I talked about the Common Sense Revolution. I said we're going to do this, this, and this. People looked at me and there was nothing there. I was not going to be able to lead the caucus. It didn't take long for me to realize there was a lot of preparation time and inclusiveness required, and they all had to be a part of the development process. They would accept me to lead them through that process, but they were not going to accept me saying this is the way it's going to be. My father would have said, "This is the way it's going to be," and he drove a lot of us to aspire to do the best we could because we wanted to please him. We wanted his acceptance. That works in a family setting, but doesn't work very well outside.

I read that when you became leader of the PC party, you were a relative outsider. You were from North Bay and not part of what some people call "the elite" or "the circle." What lessons did you learn about earning credibility and becoming influential?

I was an outsider. I think it's important, if you are an outsider and not part of the establishment, to figure out who is part of the establishment. These people may be part of the same establishment that's going to be there in the future. So, you better become part of it, get accepted, and be respected by them. It's the same in a business—you have to raise money for the business and have credibility if people are going to give you money. You couldn't get elected leader of the party with just North Bay people financing you. You had to get to know the movers and shakers. And you should find out whether there is a group of people who really haven't been part of the organization for one reason or another—maybe there wasn't room for them—but who would like to be part of the organization. I did both of those things. Attracting and spending time winning over those of the establishment who were good in the past, but also wanted to be there for the future. That's the most important thing you need to understand. Take Jim Balsillie as an example. He wanted an NHL team. In my opinion, he didn't understand the owners. He had the money, passion, and vision, but he didn't spend enough time on the process of understanding that the NHL wasn't owned or run by the sports writers or the Canadian public. It was all about the owners of the teams. In my opinion, had he understood that, and tried to be part of that establishment, we would probably have a third team in Ontario today. So, you must understand the movers and shakers, the money people, and the decision makers. If you're not going to be accepted by them, you better make sure you're replacing them with a group that is powerful enough to succeed in the future.

What role did mistakes play in your learning process? Can you talk about a mistake you made as a leader and what you learned from that mistake?

I have made lots of mistakes and they've affected me along the way. I'm sure all leaders have made mistakes along the way. If you don't learn from mistakes, you are not learning and you're not going forward. Communication is a large part of your success in the political world. There was a great learning moment in the 1995 election. We had laid out a message for every day. I can't remember how long the campaign was—maybe 35 days—so we had 35 messages. I knew months before the campaign what I would be doing on Day 17, the message we wanted to drive on that day; and we wanted to dominate the 6 p.m. and 11 p.m. news. I was in London, Ontario, on Day 1 or Day 2 of the campaign. I don't remember today what the message was—it was probably a tax-cutting message. I get a question from a local reporter about professor tenure: "Is it time to re-examine tenure?" I said, "Maybe it is." Hence, that became the story for the next 24 hours. We lost the whole tax-cutting message. We lost the opportunity to drive the message we had wanted to dominate the news. We got phone calls, including one from Dianne Cunningham, who ran in London, Ontario. We had told the whole team, "Here is the message for today. When you get questions in your riding, here's what you talk about." We all wanted to be on the same page. It is critical to be disciplined in executing on an agreed-upon plan. A leader had better demonstrate leadership if he or she wants the whole team to follow the plan. So, we had a one-day disaster on our hands. We were able to overcome the incident, but we figured we had to be flawless in executing what we wanted to do each day.

I recall another example. This one involves the three Dionne quintuplet survivors. The quints were born in Corbeil, Ontario, in 1934. The babies were born two months premature and quickly became a worldwide phenomenon. The Ontario government withdrew custody of the babies from the parents to "provide better care for them." The perception, however, was that the quints were not well served by the government trusteeship. In 1998, the three surviving adults were living in a small place just outside of Montreal. They had made a request through their nephew to the Ontario government for money. The previous Liberal government had turned them down. The government opined it had no legal responsibility for what happened to the babies in the 1930s and 1940s. The subsequent New Democratic Party administration responded in a similar fashion. And so representatives for the Dionne survivors approached our administration when I was elected. I felt an obligation to them because they were part of my history growing up. Our lawyers said there is no legal reason here. But I offered them $1 million—it was a "take-it-or-leave-it" offer. Two days later, one of them is on television saying the cruel Premier said, "Take it or leave it." I got absolutely slaughtered in the media for about three days. In the end, $3 million was offered and accepted. My intention was right. I wanted to help and be part of the solution. There was no legal requirement for compensation. I'm sure there are many cases in business where there might not be a good business reason why you're doing certain things. You might not be able to explain to the board of directors or shareholders at the annual meeting that you should do something just because it is the right thing to do and then do it in the right way. I knew the right thing to do, but I didn't do it in the right way and paid a price for it. You learn quickly from these things.

Leaders live in a fishbowl. Your actions as Premier of Ontario were public. People will second-guess every action and decision. How did you learn to deal with such transparency and the associated pressures?

This is the toughest thing. There are sleepless nights when you think, "Why doesn't this group like me? Why do they think I hate them?" I don't want to say this is all part of the game of politics—it's not fair to call it a "game." Politics is too important to everybody's lives. People will say a lot of things that they might not necessarily mean. When you are making changes, people are affected. They are affected negatively and they don't like it. It's not always easy as a leader having to make very difficult decisions that affect people's lives—you learn coping mechanisms. Certainly, having somebody to talk to—talking to friends and supporters who get what you're doing and what you're going through—can help. Talking to others who have gone through the same thing may help. I guess you have to get back to the basics—understand that what you are doing is the right thing to do and, yes, there are consequences and, yes, not everybody agrees and some respond in a nasty manner.

I'm not sure your family ever gets it. That's the toughest part. How do I help my son understand that not everybody loves his dad? I had a son in ninth grade at a time when we were making major changes to the education system. He was attacked at school by a few teachers. He remembers being singled out in class by one of the teachers, who clearly felt strong enough to voice his displeasure. All you can do is take a life learning lesson that not everybody will love you or agree with what you are doing. You have to look in the mirror and ask, "Am I doing the best I can do? Am I doing what is the right thing to do?" Humor also helps, and being able to laugh at yourself.

There is always a cost to leadership. What has been the price of leadership for you?

There is a cost at being recognized. I had lots of threats. I treated them as people blowing off steam or anger. But you have to learn to deal with that. *The higher up the ladder you are, the more likely you are to get people who don't understand what you are doing or why you are doing it and get upset.*

These are significant costs to bear. Why does anyone want to lead? What explains your commitment to the role of leadership?

Wanting to make a difference and see the change. There's a certain amount of ego involved to be the leader of a province or company. I think you have to have a little bit of that. But if the ego is, "I'm the Premier," that's not a good thing. If the ego is, "This health-care system is better today," or, "Over a million Ontarians found jobs," or "700,000 people are off of welfare rolls," then that's more productive. But I'll tell you, to this day, once in a while I get stopped on the street by a person saying, "You ruined my life."

Still?

The odd time. But I get the greatest satisfaction from somebody who stops me on the street and says, "You know what, I used to hate you. I was on welfare, and I had a young daughter at home. You forced me to get a job or go back to school. In the end, though, you changed my life for the better." Another one of those people worked at a law firm. She said to me, "I want to thank you for changing my life. Initially, I was mad at you. In fact, I hated you." But, she went back to school and worked hard for her success—a rewarding job and a new life. You get satisfaction from these kinds of individual stories about lives. This is what makes leadership worthwhile, at least for me. Nothing is more scrutinized than politics. So, there has to be a reward there for you personally. There must be some satisfaction in it for you to want to do it. In business, some of the rewards may be financial, but that's certainly not the reward in politics. I am very proud of my time in office and the changes we made. I'm very proud of the lives we impacted. I wish they could have all been positive impacts, and I know they weren't, but, by and large, I feel pretty good.

People have described you as a regular guy and very personable. How difficult has it been for you to stay true to yourself? A lot has changed since you became the Premier of Ontario. Are you still the Mike Harris from North Bay?

I hope so. I try to be. There's no question things change when you walk into a room as leader of the opposition or premier. The reception is different and you feed off that and react to it. You treat people differently when they have those titles. You have to learn to understand that it's the Office of the Premier of Ontario they're acknowledging, not Mike Harris or Dalton McGuinty. I'd like to think I'm the same person. I've certainly grown and probably changed in my understanding of things and people. I think I've learned from every experience, both positive and negative. Most leaders will tell you they learn from mistakes perhaps more than successes, because often you're not exactly sure what you did to be successful. But I'd like to say I'm still Mike Harris from North Bay, son of Deane and Hope Harris and father to my kids. I'd like to say I stayed the same.

You said that you've grown as a leader. How is your leadership different today than it was earlier in your career?

First, it is about confidence. I was in a school play once. I remember being behind the curtain getting ready to come out. Up to that point, it was the most terrifying moment of my life. I'm trying to go over my lines and I can't remember a single one—and I'm on in 30 seconds! You get out there and the lines come to you somehow and you get through it. The next moment when I was that scared was probably the leaders' debate in 1990. I was absolutely petrified, because there's only one debate in the Ontario elections. Of course, everybody tells you not to make a mistake or a gaffe. And, if that is all you are thinking about, then it's hard to communicate the message you want to get out. In 1995 and 1999, while still nervous, I was far more confident. And, even today, I'm far more confident of the unknown. I feel far more capable because of the experiences I've had along the way.

I've also discovered I don't need to lead all the time. As premier of the province, you are under the spotlight all the time—you are leading all the time, in every decision. It is a challenge to go into a meeting and having everybody think, "I wonder what the Premier is thinking and what he wants me to say here?" The constant scrutiny, even on little decisions that really don't matter that much, was a big challenge for me. I had to learn how to deal with that. Today, I can be a little bit of a follower. If people don't hear my opinion before the decision is made, it's not the end of the world. It is important to know when it is critical your view is heard.

What are you learning these days to become an even better leader? Are there any recent "aha" moments?

I'm leading on some boards that I chair. My opinion is sought out, even if it's in an area that I absolutely know nothing about and I shouldn't necessarily be respected in such area. I've learned to be very, very careful about what I say in those areas until I'm quite sure I understand the issue. I think I do add value to the boards on which I serve, but I add the most value when I'm a little more reflective and take a little more time to make sure I understand what the issues are all about. Companies may ask my advice because of who I was in the past, as opposed to who I am now, and look for my opinion on a problem they are facing. The important thing for me as chair is to facilitate a full discussion by all board members and senior management before coming to a conclusion on any issue.

This book is about learning to lead. What question did I forget to ask you about the learning process? What did we not touch on?

I don't think leadership is rocket science. I was elected Premier of Ontario in 1995. The province was heavily in debt and running a large deficit. The province had borrowed money from the Germans, French, British, and so on. Hence, the Minister of Finance and I traveled to the financial capitals of the world. We wanted to let people know who we were, the changes that we were making, and that Ontario was once again more business friendly. I was in Tokyo as part of that trip and the Canadian Embassy had arranged for a meeting with business leaders of the Keidanren—a major economic organization—who had an interest in North America. I remember we sat around a table of about 30 people. I was there as Premier and told my story. There was a good dialogue. Japan was going through a tough time, in part because it had relied on the unrealistic value of the yen. The yen appreciated and Japanese companies had difficulties competing. Then the banking sector collapsed. So these executives—all from leading companies such as Sony and Samsung—started asking me questions: "What did we do wrong?" I grew up thinking the Japanese built better cars and electronics than us, that they were an economic powerhouse. And now they are asking this kid from North Bay, "Where did WE go wrong?" I thought to myself, "How can this be? They're asking ME all these questions?" That's when you realize none of these people are any smarter than you are. These individuals—heads of great organizations—all came from a

North Bay somewhere and they've had experiences and learned along the way. Meeting with the Keidanren that day gave me great confidence in moving forward.

Leadership Themes

- Going into the unknown is always scary. But, if you have enough confidence in yourself and in your ability to learn, then you ought not to be afraid of it.
- Be comfortable in having people smarter than you work with you. You don't have to be in control all the time.
- It's not good enough to be right. You have to bring the team along with you.
- The higher up the ladder you are, the more likely you are to get people who don't understand what you are doing or why you are doing it.

14

Life Is a Blackboard That You Cannot Erase

Arkadi Kuhlmann

Arkadi, when did you first realize you were a leader, and what happened to make you realize it?

Ironically, the first time I realized I was a leader was at the Ivey Business School in my first undergraduate year. We were in study groups. There was a group project and a deadline. The group was dysfunctional and couldn't get itself organized, and I just basically stepped up and got things organized. Somebody had to step forward and start saying, "Do this, do that," or "I'm going to do this." It quickly became apparent that, when there is a challenge in front of me, I just put my hand up and lead. I just tend to get involved in things. So, one of the reasons why I really enjoyed my time at Ivey was that I was able to actually sort of inject myself—whether it was in the classroom, or in a study group, or on a project—and be proactive. That feeling of proactiveness kind of settled in me as leadership. It's something that I feel really good about. I feel a responsibility to it and it feels natural to me. I like to be in charge. I think it's probably in my nature that I just want to be proactive, which I think translated into leadership.

Did you want to be a leader?

Yes, but I don't think I articulated that I was a leader when I was young. I think I did demonstrate those proactive qualities that, later on, turn into leadership. I think what it comes down to is, if you really like what you do, and you want to basically meet that challenge, then you're the one that wants to climb the mountain. You're the one that wants to win. You're the one that wants to get it done, whatever "it" is. If you have the ingredients of hard work and curiosity and you love what you're doing, then it brings out those qualities. And if you have those leadership qualities, which means you like to infect other people with the ideas and you like to have other people win with you, then it's kind of like somebody leads the charge. I don't think anybody really thinks, "You know, I'm just going to wave the flag and I'm going to jump out front." I think people just do it.

This question reminds me of something that happened 15 years ago. I was sitting in Amsterdam with the top 250 executives of ING and a professor was giving a speech at one of our international conferences. He took out a bill of 100 guilders.

He held it up and he asked, "Who wants this?" I walked to the front and took it from him. He then said, "This is what you all need to be able to do." I didn't ask for permission, I just took it at face value. He asked, "Who wants it?" and, usually, everybody thinks that question is rhetorical, right? I took it at face value and just went up and took it. Everyone laughed and said, "Now, you can buy us all beer," and all that kind of stuff. But the point was it was then—those kinds of moments— that you realize you don't have to apologize for it, you just live by it. So, that's how that comes.

How did you prepare for the role of leadership?

For me, it was pretty easy—I needed money. When I went to high school, I had a job after school so I didn't play a sport. I went to the factory and worked. I had a paper route. From a very young age in my household, there was a focus on working—my mother worked, my father worked, we worked part time, we worked weekends. Everybody worked. That gave me some great lessons to live by. I remember once while at Western University I was clear out of money. I went to the unemployment office and tried to get a job as a day laborer. I went to Red Path Sugar and, for a whole weekend, I basically unloaded railway cars of sugar. Those moments stay with you. *My belief is that the tougher your challenge is, the better you rise to the occasion.* So, if you have a handicap, I think you struggle to over- come that handicap. If you have no money, you struggle to overcome that, right? If you have a difficult relationship with your family, you'll struggle. The human spirit is really about stepping up to whatever challenge life gives you. I think that shapes you. Even today, I'm sort of in the golden years of my career, but if you ask me, "How do you manage yourself?" I'd say, "I work." It's engrained in me. I never relaxed when I was young. I never relaxed as I got older. Why would you somehow expect me to relax now? You kind of become a collection or a composite of what your experiences are.

As you transitioned to more and more senior roles, what were some of the challenges that you faced, and how did you overcome them?

The answer to that is really simple. I was an outsider. When you have a name like Arkadi Kuhlmann in the late 1960s and early 1970s in an Anglicized world when being foreign was not a good idea, you are clearly an outsider. My background wasn't very widely accepted here [in Canada] either. I was not going to belong to the clubs. I was not going to be in the right circles. I was in the working class circles. The great thing about Canada, though, is that it gives you opportunities. I think being an outsider caused me to know that I might get ahead only if I could perform or deliver. I would get a break—and I'm forever indebted to those people who gave me a chance. At the end of the day, though, it was clear that you had to earn it. It was engrained in me that it was all about performance. I knew that people were always watching me. As I got into executive roles, the only reason why I ever got a promotion or opportunity was because when I got an opportunity, I delivered. And that takes hard work.

Is there anything that you fear about the role of leadership?

I think I fear letting other people down. For me, it's personal failure, whether for a task or on a job. You can't win it all. You have setbacks. You have to deal with those in terms of character. You have to be realistic about that. I fear letting down the people who have faith in me. They work with you, whether in a study group or at a job or company, and when things don't go well, it gets emotional because you are emotionally committed. To deal with that, you have to have a truly clear conscience and know that you've tried everything possible to the best of your ability. That means that you have to constantly think things through. You don't want to have regrets. ***You can't take any shortcuts. I learned that pretty early in my career. You can't take shortcuts with people or in situations. That's where the danger is.***

Has your learning to lead been influenced by other individuals? For example, have you had the benefit of a mentor?

I've had the privilege of having four mentors in my life. I think there are two things about a mentor that are critical for a leader. One is that the mentor reinforces your own value set because you like to actually have your value set reinforced by the actions of a mentor. So, the way your mentor deals with you, and the way the mentor behaves, is pretty critical in terms of validating your own style. People generally like to be with people who are like them. That's why I think a mentor takes you on and why you stay with a mentor—because you have the same kind of value set and you're learning. You're trying to get more insight, which I call wisdom. The other thing that I think happens is you need to learn quickly from mistakes. ***It's amazing to me how many people won't do the postmortem. They'll do the homework and they'll do the exercise, but they won't take enough time to reflect on whether that could have gone differently and how that could have been done. I learned very quickly from my mentors that the postmortem is where the value is—good or bad or indifferent.*** It's funny—as a society, we do this with sports. We will argue for hours about why a goal was scored, or not scored, and how an individual played, and so on. In business, and even in family situations, we just won't do those kinds of postmortems. We don't do them enough. We get the results and just move on. The reality is that really good leaders take time to reflect. This isn't just quality time for bonding or thinking of new ideas, it's about reflecting on the performance. My advice would be to consider how much time you spend looking back.

Learning requires reflection. Can you give me an example of an "aha" moment?

I got along very well with a chief financial officer (CFO). Then, I accidently found out that he had a side business in the same building that we were in. If I recall correctly, he had a little accounting business on the side. When I first heard that, I said, "Well that's crazy. He's the CFO so he can't be doing that. It's just not right." When I asked him about it, I said, "I heard this, can this be right?" He said, "Well, it's a business that my wife has." So then I forgot about it—and I don't know why

I forgot about it. I should have dug a little deeper. I should have had more conversation, but I just made an assumption. I didn't try to join the dots. It turned out it was his wife's business, but he was involved, and there was a level of disclosure and dishonesty that should have been talked about openly. So, of course, when I found out, he left, and afterwards I asked myself, "Why didn't you think about this? How did you miss this?" I'm pretty focused on detail—detail is a big thing with me. It was totally out of character for me. It's not that I needed to grill him or investigate him, but I ran on the wrong assumption and that bothered me for so long. Why, at this moment, did I pass it by? Did I wish it away? Did I not want to face the challenge or the embarrassment? Did I misread him?

You talked about the importance of mentors. What was the best leadership advice you ever received that helped you develop into a better leader?
Mike Leenders [Professor Emeritus, Ivey Business School] is one of my mentors. I was a case writer and research assistant with him. I remember once, while sitting in his office, I asked him, "How do you get all this done? It's incredible how much you do." He gave me advice about time management that I'll never forget. He asked me, "So, what time do you get up in the morning?" and I replied, "6:30 a.m." He asked, "What do you do then?" and I told him that I got up, got dressed, had breakfast, read the paper, and went to class. "So, how long do you take for breakfast?" he asked, and I replied, "Half an hour." "How long do you read the paper?" he asked, and I replied, "About 20 minutes." Once he heard it all, he said, "Well, that's almost an hour! You could do breakfast in 15 minutes." *I learned that you chew up a lot of time, you waste a lot of time, and you get sloppy about time.* If you organize better and you're more disciplined, you have breakfast in 15 minutes and you don't just dally around. He told me it takes 15 minutes to read the paper, so he just found me another 20 minutes. He made me so conscious about time management that I got really good at it. I can get more done in a day than most people can. That's the only reason why I'm disciplined about time. I don't think I ever would have realized that if it hadn't been for Mike pointing that out to me. I think it was in his nature to be pretty disciplined. You need to think about what is most effective for you. I've always been an organized person, so that piece of advice put it together for me.

Part of learning is to be open to information, whether solicited or unsolicited. How difficult was it for you to open yourself up to information that you perhaps did not expect or want to hear?
It was difficult. I didn't feel that I was favored by my mentors. As a matter of fact, all four of the mentors were pretty critical of me—I've got some pretty tough love. I remember my mentor at the Royal Bank of Canada. He was pretty upset with me fairly regularly and very critical of some of the things I did. People have this idea that mentors are always people who are nurturing and supportive and bringing the best out in you. That wasn't so in my case. In my case, I don't think any of those mentors really saw me as a favorite. I think they saw some potential in me, but they

never said to me, "I'm going to be your mentor." I'm the one that basically looked to them for mentoring, and they called it the way it was.

I think one of the reasons why I listened to them and not the others is because they were kind of bigger personalities than you would think. So, maybe in that sense, if you're a leader, you look to leaders for advice. I looked for someone that was different as well. Dave Maltby at the Royal Bank of Canada—he passed away some time ago—smoked cigarettes and put his feet up on the desk and had some very weird sort of behavioral characteristics that were out of sync from the Royal Bank of Canada standard. He was a bit of an oddball, so of course that made me gravitate to him. He was kind of harsh and tough, and I felt more comfortable that way. I'm very leery about compliments. I got that from my early upbringing. Compliments don't work very well with me. Maybe that's one of the reasons that I worked so well with the Dutch for 16 years. For me, when someone said, "It could have been worse," I figured that was about the best compliment I could ever get. That resonated with me because I don't like pats on the back and being told I'm doing great. My mentors pointed out good things to me, but they also didn't hold anything back. I remember once playing golf with Mike Leenders and he said to me, "Are you going to do the next shot as bad as the last one?" That was a little harsh! I'm not a good golfer, and I just wanted to play with other people, but there were two other people there and that was a pretty harsh comment. It got me determined again. This sort of critical pointedness triggered in my personality something very unique. I realized that, if you push me to the wall, I will fight back. And so, for every obstacle I see, my emotional response is to challenge back. I don't retreat very much. A mentor pushing me probably gets the best out of me, so that was probably the best learning experience that I could get. You have to have that personality link, though. It might not have worked for someone else.

What were some of the hardest things to learn in becoming a good or an even better leader?

The hardest thing to learn is to be a bit humble. You remember humbleness is now the total opposite of being proactive and stepping forward and saying, "This is the way and let's do this," and promoting a view or a vision. It's difficult to do that and, at the same time, be a bit humble and respectful of people.

It takes a lot of time to learn that you have to temper your proactiveness with the people with whom you work, that are following you, or with whom you're partnering. You have to be a bit humble. It is so easy to get the ego involved, and I think it sneaks up on people and they don't even realize it. It's a nicer office. It's that nicer suit. It's that better meal. Your ego gets involved and you think, "I deserve this." And then, all of a sudden, you begin to forget that real ***leadership, in its purest sense, is about service.*** To a cause, to a goal, or to a group.

So how do you stay grounded?

I have one technique that I've developed, and I don't know where it comes from, but I basically believe that every day is the last day of my life. So, I figure if tonight at 8:00 p.m., after our session with the students, if I die on the way to the airport, I'm pretty well happy. I work every day. I've been like that for my whole life. It's an emotional thing. Obviously, some of my affairs are not totally set—I haven't written my epitaph yet—but it's a mindset that is really important. The mindset is really good because what happens is that we always look to the next lead—if I could only get that promotion, if I could only get that next opportunity, if I could only marry this person, if I could only write this book, if I could get tenure, if I could become president of the university. You're constantly looking ahead and thinking that, when you get to that level, you'll be okay. The earlier you recognize that it's just the journey of life, and that's kind of interesting, but you're missing the point about where you are today, which is a student. If you died tomorrow and they said, "Well, this student died," are you okay with that? That's an emotional point of freedom, right? Two things happen then. First, today, being here right now with you, is an absolute blessing. I feel very positive about what I do today. Second, I have absolutely no expectation about tomorrow. I know what I'm doing tomorrow, but tomorrow is another gift. It may sound a bit Zen, and maybe even a bit Buddhist, but I am a Christian so I make no apologies about that and I've come to grips with this emotionally. As a leader, you'd be surprised how much motivations drive you in different directions when everything counts on what's going to happen tomorrow. It's your reputation, your success, your results, and all that other stuff. You're born naked and you're going to die naked. It's an 80-year journey. I'm okay if I'm going to die tonight.

How have you developed confidence in your leadership?
You only get confidence by results. It's quite different to determination; it's quite different to willpower. *Confidence in leadership is when you have to work at something and it has to work out right. You have to win. There's no way around this—you can't be a leader if you're not scoring points. If you're not winning pennants, If you're not making profits . . . you can call yourself a leader, you can act like a leader, you can be the appointed leader, you can be given the opportunity to lead—you can do all those things—but, I'm sorry, at the end of the day, if you don't get the goal, you don't get paid, you don't get promoted . . . you are not a leader.* So, practicing leadership is quite different to being a leader, and being a leader means you've got confidence in yourself as a leader—and you can only get that if you get a track record. There's no other way around it.

There is always a cost to leadership. What has been the price of leadership for you?
I don't agree with that statement at all. Leadership has rewards, and it has personal prices you pay. You make those trade-offs, whether you sacrifice your family, or you sacrifice money, or time, or whatever. But, look, you're going to spend time in one way or another. I think leaders kind of do what they want to do. The payoff is in the vision and the mission and the goal and the accomplishment. If you step back, what are the two things you're going to think about? First, these are the

people that I journeyed with, and I was able to lead in this team, or this group, or this partnership. Second, this is what we accomplished, and we made a difference. Wow. That's what you want to do. Whether you paid some price for that is sort of a bit academic—it's sort of like saying athletes sweat . . . and business people don't have enough time for golf or didn't get enough time to get married.

What have you personally experienced as a barrier to learning and how have you tried to overcome this barrier?

Well, one is it would help to be smarter. Intelligence is a big piece of that. I had to work a little harder because I'm probably not quite as intelligent as I would maybe like to be. I'm smart enough to understand that there are some things that I just intellectually can't do. You have to work through a handicap. My solution is to work harder. Maybe somebody else can get through something in an hour, but it's going to maybe take me two. The sooner you recognize that, the better off you are. The other thing is you've got to be very selective about what you focus on. When you're in a job experience, or you're in a work experience, there's so much stuff going on that it inhibits your ability to pick up the things that are meaningful for you. Being in touch with what you need to know and what you need to learn is really important. The best recent example that I have is I switched to a new cell phone device. That is an interesting problem. You have a set of habits about how you use the first device, and now you go to the second device. There are two ways to solve this problem. One is that you read the manual, and the second is you just learn along the way. If you learn along the way, you know intuitively that you're going to have lots of problems and it's going to be an agonizing process and you're not going to get up to a proficient level for a long time. On the other hand, you dread the idea of reading the manual and doing the tutorial. If you're very smart, you don't need to do that, but, if you're not that smart, you need to find another way around the handicap. The way I did this was I figured out the five things I need to do—those were my higher priorities. Those things I figured out how to do, and the other stuff—the secondary stuff—I decided to just go through the agony of learning. That's how someone with my abilities works through a problem.

What expectations do you put on yourself in the leadership role? Where does your commitment to the leadership role come from?

I am always reflecting on the leadership I provided. Was it worth doing? Did I deliver a successful value-add? Did I improve my leadership reputation? I think I just have this thing about keeping score. Am I winning or am I losing? I respect my responsibility enough that I've always put myself up for a vote with other people. You [Gerard] might remember this story. I was asking my employees to vote on whether they would like me to serve them another year. I wanted the validation to basically say, "Well, if you're willing to follow me, I have a higher obligation to lead, and I want to do it because I respect your commitment to work with me, and, therefore, I have a higher commitment to stay with it until the finish." To me, the whole commitment is see it through until the end. It has been a problem. I've stayed too long with things. Also, in the work situation, there were opportunities where I probably should have left earlier, but I stayed. I didn't stay for any other reason than I felt I owed it to people to see it through to the end of the game. I don't stop 10 minutes before the end of the game and say, "Well, the score is 10–3, so we might as well quit since we've lost." I just have that obligation to play it until the end, and then take my accounting. That's so engrained in me that, you know, I tend to stay to the end, and then someone will say, "Well, you know, you could have made more money," or, "You could have been more opportunistic," and, "Why didn't you leave?" People ask you, "Why didn't you play the smart game and move every three years?" I feel like, when I'm in something, I have to finish it.

Have you ever been in a situation where you started to realize that you crossed the line? What made you turn around?

I ran a trading company. We did a lot of what now would be considered black market transactions. It did feel like we were crossing the line because you knew that you were dealing with bad people and you were doing things that, in principle, were wrong. They weren't, at the time, wrong in the rules, but they were wrong in principle. Bribery payments and things like that. You're thinking to yourself, "Well, I'm just sort of the middleman—I'm not doing it, I'm just passing the money along". I began to justify my actions—I wasn't getting any personal benefit out of it, so I figured I was sort of innocent. The truth was I wasn't innocent. You're touched by it, and I didn't do anything to step away from it or change it. Ultimately, I think the reason why I didn't go that way was because I could have made a lot of money, and I was really tempted, but I don't think I felt sure, at the end of the day, that I could live with that. I think the only thing that held me back was not because I was overly virtuous, but I think I was scared that, if I went there and did that, I couldn't reverse it. *What I've learned as a leader is that life is a blackboard that you cannot erase. Everything counts. There's no such thing as a time-out. There's no such thing as "it doesn't count." There is a blackboard and it'll never be erased.* If you really understand that, then you know this whole idea about—well, you can cross the line, you can make some money, but then you can give it away and ask for forgiveness and somehow it will all be forgiven—is wrong. There is a thing about forgiveness and second chances, and we do accept that in society, but it's not a standard for a leader. For a true leader, that's not a standard. It's okay to fail. It's okay to win. But you can't cross the line. I just do not believe that it's okay to be wrong on the moral front, and then somehow cross the Rubicon and it's okay and you're sorry. I kind of live with this world of no forgiveness on that stuff.

What drains you as a leader?

What happens in a lot of situations of leadership is that you just can't get the mix right all the time. This is what drains you. I would like to have 20 percent laughter today, and I would like to have 20 percent constructive conversation, and I'd like to have 20 percent of arguments, and I'd like to have 20 percent tears, and I'd like to have 20 percent of relaxation. That would be kind of an interesting balance for the day. Unfortunately, most days are weighted or skewed one way or another and that is draining. It's the unpredictability and the volatility when you're up. When you're on all the time, you just don't get the mix right. And so that gets to be very draining, because you have to adjust as your own biorhythm goes in one way. Some days, you feel a bit more energetic and a bit more positive—you maybe had a good run of things. Other days, you feel kind of down—but you know that you have to always be pretty consistent. People will follow you only if you're consistent. People will look and say, "Oh, Arkadi—he's happy today," or "Oh, Arkadi—he's a little down today." People want to basically gauge you. It's natural. What you have to do as a leader is try to avoid that as much as possible. You can't totally avoid it because people can see it on your face and on your body, because you're a real, involved leader, so you have characteristics. You have to be so conscious of the fact that you have to try to modulate it. Modulating that is draining because you try not to be overly happy. You try not to be overly depressed. You've got to basically be transparent and open, but, on the other hand, you have to keep some things to yourself. *The first obligation of a leader—the ONLY obligation of a leader—is to eliminate doubt.* You can't eliminate doubt if a person's looking totally into you and saying, "Wow, he's depressed today; therefore, I don't think he's so sure about what we're going to do, so why should I follow him?" If my responsibility is to eliminate doubt, I need you to see enough of me as a human being to see the ups and downs, but not to the point where it erodes my primary responsibility. To do that, you've got to be a really good actor; you've got to be really good.

You live in a fishbowl. Close confidants might disagree with you. The press might be all over you. How did you develop resilience or the ability to cope with stress and adversity?

I think it's about faith—that's an important piece. I am spiritual. I think some kind of hobby or activity is really important. For me to get this resilience, I have to write or I have to paint. I have to do some other things that I really enjoy doing. It's really a mental time-out. I probably internalize too much. My life probably would have been better if I would have exercised more, ate less, slept more. That's probably true. The heart of resilience is really distraction—doing something totally different. In the financial industry, it's pretty depressing and so you have to have a bit of faith and a spiritual meaning about the broader prospect of life. The only way you can contain this problem, and not get absorbed by it, is to put it in the broader context, and then the way to get resilience is to be able to distract yourself. Whatever hobby it is, I always tell everybody to, please, have a hobby. I don't even want to work with you if you don't have a hobby. I don't care if you're a cook or a painter or you like to play the banjo, but, if you don't have a real hobby that you have some passion about, you've got some real weaknesses. I'm not saying you have to be good at any of those things, but it's for the resilience part that I think it is important.

What has been your most rewarding experience as a leader and why?

Oh, that's pretty simple. It's absolute love and affection from people that I work with. The hugs and the letters and the kisses and the gifts are treasures. What people are saying is, "You know, whatever we had together, I think you gave me a gift, and I'd like to give you something back." It's tremendous. Yesterday, I got a book from one of the people I work with, with a beautiful note. It's a 365-page book on daily sayings from Buddha, with pictures. It's a beautiful gift, and of course it was all heartfelt. People say, "The last five years working with you have been the best years of my life." I get hundreds of those kinds of things. They are around my office and I look at them and I think, "You know, you've touched people. You've made a difference in people's lives. Here are some of the examples." Those are great memories. A great family is a family that has great memories. A great leader is a person that has great memories. The battles we've fought, the people that we've touched—that's a measure that I think about at the end of the day. I know what I want to accomplish when I'm 80 and I have another few more years before I die, hopefully. The last thought I want to have is, "I've served the very best I could. I didn't hold anything back. I didn't reach for more than I deserve, but I did the right thing."

You personally touched me with this answer—a great family is a family with great memories. I recently lost my father because of cancer. I have great memories of him.

So, look at your father. As most of us have, we sort of think of them as a key to the family. If you look at that in a positive sense, you know what a father's responsibility is—to give opportunity and insight and build memories with the family. When we pass, all we can give to the next generation is the memories and the ideas and the stories. And, since people were cave dwellers sitting around the fire, all they did was tell stories. Look, the money will disappear, the body will disappear, but somewhere down the line, somebody will read a case or hear a story from a book and say, "Gee, that's an interesting thought. That's a great idea. We should try that." And so that moves society along, and that moves people along. I think leaders need to be a bit philosophical.

The challenge is making sure that you don't have too many regrets about all this stuff as you move ahead in your years and you validate your leadership capabilities and how you want to measure it to yourself. Maybe society thinks you're a leader and gives you awards and whatnot. The constant thing to keep you balanced is to say, "Well, is there anything else that I'm not doing?" You'll never have time to make it up, so you're almost always thinking about what else you can do. I think back now on my early career, and I had a few years when I probably could have done more; I probably should have done a bit more. Thank God I woke up early enough to keep that going. I think the reason I woke up early was because I just had a simple need for money. It wasn't about wanting to get wealthy—it was just money to get on with life.

Leadership Themes

- Practicing leadership is different than being a leader. Leaders produce results.
- The first obligation of a leader—the only obligation of a leader—is to eliminate doubt.
- Organize and you'll be more disciplined with your time.
- Life is a blackboard that you cannot erase. Everything counts. There's no such thing as a time-out for a leader. There's no such thing as "it doesn't count."

15

I Didn't Have Time to Think About Courage or Where to Find Courage—You Just Have It

Linda Hasenfratz

Linda, when did you first realize you were a leader, and what happened to make you realize it?

I don't think you wake up one day and think, "I'm a leader." You learn from people you've worked with. You read a lot of books about leadership and attend conferences or seminars on leadership. You hear leaders speak on leadership. You learn what works and what doesn't work in your approach to leadership and, most importantly, what feels right for you. Leadership is a process that evolves, and, over time, you begin to feel more confident in your ability to lead.

When was that first moment you had confidence in your leadership and realized you were leading something significant?

This probably occurred when I ran my first plant. I had been in management positions before. I had worked in many different departments, but this was my first shot at running the whole show. As the plant manager, I now was in a position to pull all my knowledge and abilities together. I interviewed people and put the team together. That was really exciting. I realized I was fully responsible for a profit unit.

You said it felt exciting to be in the leadership role. Did you want to be a leader?

I've always been inclined towards leadership, enjoyed positions of leadership, or taking charge of a situation. I see people in our organization, and other groups I have been involved with, who are natural leaders. People turn instinctively, naturally to these individuals for direction or guidance. *I've always been inclined to quickly assimilate information around me, figure out what is happening, make decisions, determine who needs to do what, and then get the people aligned. I think there is definitely a natural inclination to be able to do these things instinctively, which is very helpful to those who aspire to be leaders.*

You had a natural inclination to lead. What have been the formative influences on you as a leader? What did people do to help you? What experiences

did you learn the most from? Was there any particular experience that super-charged your learning to lead?

As you work with different people, you're exposed to different leadership styles. From birth, I had the privilege of being exposed to the leadership style and capability of my father, Frank Hasenfratz, who is a fantastic leader. I have learned, and continue to learn, a lot from him. For example, I learned from him to move quickly; to do things today and not to wait for tomorrow. I learned to put a solid team together; and to hire the best people you can find. He taught me to be enthusiastic and excited about growing our business and to look for opportunities in every corner and in every person I met. He also taught me to ensure we are operating efficiently and effectively and to balance that with the big picture of growing and evolving our company. He taught me simple rules to evaluate performance and visual clues to look for when visiting a plant. He taught me simple rules of thumb to make managing easy.

But I learned just as much from other people. For example, I learned a lot from Jim Jarrell, our president and chief operating officer (COO). His leadership style is different from my father's, but equally successful and impactful. I worked for Jim for quite a few years before I came to corporate. Now, Jim is part of my team. I learned from Jim to balance decision making between our customers, employees, and shareholders. This is a core philosophy we employ today company-wide. I learned from him a lot about effective communication, aligning and motivating a team, and effective sales and marketing techniques. Jim is also a fantastic negotiator. He's fair, but also firm, creative, and determined. We are lucky to have him as a key member of our team, leading and inspiring a whole new generation of leaders at Linamar.

I like the way you can take elements of leadership from different people and bring them together in your own style. I learned from leaders. I read books and attended seminars. I interacted with good and bad leaders. I sorted through all the information and experiences to develop my own leadership approach and identify a leadership profile that I wanted in our leaders at Linamar. We identified six leadership behaviors we thought were important in terms of making a successful leader at Linamar.

What are those six behaviors? And are those the behaviors that you are most comfortable with?

I wouldn't say that I necessarily embody each of these behaviors perfectly, but I do fit the profile overall. I think these are important leadership behaviors. I wouldn't expect a person to necessarily be fantastic at all six. But I would expect that, if a person is a little less fantastic in one of them, he or she would know enough to hire somebody who is fantastic at that so they have that capability on their team.

The first behavior is passion. You need to be excited and motivated about what you're doing or where you're going in order to engage people. Planning is the second important element of leadership. You need to be able to put together a plan that outlines where you're going and how you're going to get there. Third, it's not good enough to have an exciting plan and get everyone revved up about it. You need to be able to get things done: execute. You need to meet milestones and develop a track record of excellence. Fourth, people need both acumen and edge. People need to develop an instinctive sense of the right direction. This comes from knowledge and experience. Do people take the time to read and learn what's happening in the world around them? Do they understand what's happening in the industry? Do they understand the organization itself? That broad knowledge base gives people the ability to make insightful decisions. "Edge" refers to being able to deal with challenging situations and conflicts as well as make tough decisions. Fifth, people need to be able to communicate with a wide variety of people, including customers, investors, bankers, employees, the community, suppliers, and so forth. For example, you need to articulate your plan properly and do a good job of motivating and instilling confidence both internally and externally. The sixth element is care. *You need to show that you truly care about what happens to your people. The best example of care can probably be found in military leadership. Are you going to follow somebody into battle? You are not going to feel confident to follow the leader in battle if you feel the leader doesn't care what happens to you. I think care is just as important in business.* You need to have a clear relationship with your people so they know you care about them, and that, together, you're going to succeed and meet your goals.

You are a graduate of the Ivey Business School. What was the impact of your education on your learning to lead?
I completed my MBA in 1996–1997, when I was launching my first and second plants. I found the education invaluable. I was literally learning something on the weekend and then going to work on Monday and doing it. The formal education in finance, marketing, team building, and strategy was exactly the right complement to the more practical hands-on training I had completed on the floor at Linamar.

Before you became the CEO of Linamar in 2002, you had companywide experiences. You made several vertical and horizontal moves. For example, you were a machine operator, operations manager, general manager of several divisions, chief financial officer, and COO. Can you please talk about how those transitions helped you develop into the leader you are today?
Having had tangible experiences in virtually every area of the company was invaluable to me in being able to take on increasingly larger responsibilities. Starting out on the shop floor and running the machines was really important for my development. I needed to understand the nuts and bolts of our business, or the basics of what we are doing. This experience also helped me to understand and appreciate each and every role or position in the company. It helped me to understand what it's like to be that person on the shop floor who is running a machine and working 8-, 10-, or 12-hour shifts and what that feels like. That was important

because how can you give orders to somebody to do this or do that if you don't have a good understanding of what it means to perform those job duties? These experiences made me conversant in that particular area—quality control, finance, or engineering. It gave me the understanding and language to talk to people in those areas in a way that enabled us to have meaningful conversations about what was happening.

I always encourage young people who go into business to try and get a multidisciplinary experience. They shouldn't worry if there are lateral moves. You can move up once you've got that broader-based experience. Having that broader-based experience will always give you a better perspective of a business that better suits you, versus just stepping into a general manager or executive role in a company.

As you transitioned to more and more senior roles, what were some of the challenges you faced and how did you overcome them?

Regarding competencies, there were big learning curves involved, in particular in the area of finance because it was something brand new for me.

I don't think my values really changed as I went along the leadership journey. I had been taught from a young age to work hard. I had been taught to be respectful of people.

I think what changes is your maturity, your approach to decision making, and how you interact with people. People interact with you in different ways. *You can't paint people with the same brush. As you get more experience, you realize people aren't all the same and they don't all respond the same way. They don't think the same way. They don't listen the same way. They're not motivated the same way. This is something that you truly learn with time.*

I also learned about the time frame that I should use in decision making. Again, when you're young, you tend to move quickly and make decisions quickly; or at least I did. The "do things today, not tomorrow" approach was instilled in me from a very young age. I learned over time that not every decision should be made quickly. You will need to make some decisions quickly. But you should be more thoughtful about other decisions. For example, if the consequence of a decision is something that might have an impact for years, then you should spend some time thinking about that decision. Gather more data. Evaluate a couple of different scenarios. And then go ahead and make that decision.

You are the daughter of the founder of Linamar. How did you work on building your credibility?

This proved to be a big challenge. I made a lot of transitions, both in terms of jobs and plants. Every time I encountered a new group of people, I knew some were thinking, "She isn't smart" or "She won't want to work hard." I knew some were also thinking, "If that isn't bad enough, she is a woman, too!" That was difficult to deal with because I had to prove over and over and over again that I was going to work hard, I was going to be here until the job got done, and I wasn't sailing out the door at four or five o'clock. I was able to do the job and enjoyed doing the job. I enjoyed working with people. I always had a lot of respect for them. I learned from them. So, over time, you build relationships and foster mutual respect, and, as a result, build your credibility. Just having to do it over and over and over again was challenging. I remember at one point saying to my dad, "Why can't they just talk to the people at the last plant?" But, in any case, I think it was time well spent because I now have a network of people throughout the company that I've worked with. It's a lot of different people! I still like to touch base with them from time to time. They can be your supporters in the organization.

Can you tell me about a time when you really had to stretch as a leader and step out of your comfort zone? What did you learn?

I never feel panicked in a crisis-like situation. I go straight in and address the challenges. We faced dark days in 2008–2009. Automotive is a big part of our business. Two of our top five customers were on the brink of bankruptcy. Automotive volumes had gone from 17–18 million units a year to 8 million. Our heavy truck business was down dramatically. Our Skyjack business fell 80 percent. These were just shocking changes.

The crisis really required my team and I to step up and be very perceptive of what was going on in the environment, our industry, and the company. It required us to go above and beyond the communications side. First of all, we put a plan together identifying what we were going to do in the midst of the crisis, and then we went out of our way to over-communicate with our employees, investors, customers, and suppliers. We told them, "Here's what's happening. Here's what it means to you. Here's what we know. There are things we don't know." We were not afraid to say, "We don't yet know what's going to happen." We had a three-pronged approach: cut costs, conserve cash, and find growth opportunities. We wanted to grow our way out of the crisis. For example, we looked at companies that were struggling—we acquired some or just took over their contracts.

I remember going to visit with investors. I've always tried to visit our investors in Toronto and Montreal each quarter. I didn't stop doing this during the crisis. I remember the investors told me, "You are the only CEO we've seen in months." They really appreciated these visits because they were scared, too. And they wanted to know what was going on at Linamar. Even if I didn't have all the answers, at least I could tell them what I knew. I think my communication efforts made them feel more comfortable with us. Of course, our stock price still sank—we were between $2 and $3 during our lowest point. We are now at $26.

We spent a lot of time communicating with our own employees. For example, when General Motors filed for bankruptcy, we were ready with an internal communication. We outlined how this development would affect the employees. We were proactive and transparent. I think we helped to stop the panic by over-communicating. We also had to find the right balance between urgency and panic.

There were things we had to do and we needed to get people motivated enough to do those things so that we had a chance to survive and thrive. You can't create the perception that you're going to lose the business and they are all going to be out of a job. But you need enough urgency so they get things done and therefore meet the plan you laid out. Achieving that balance is tricky!

The situation was certainly drastic. We made some very tough decisions. We had gone from 12,000 to about 7,000 active workers. It was a huge reduction in the workforce. About 1,500 people were temporarily laid off. Today, we are at 17,000 employees. This means we added 10,000 new members to the team in three years. That's no small challenge to hire, train, and motivate!

No business and on-the-job training can realistically prepare you for a crisis of this magnitude. How did you develop the confidence or wisdom to take the actions you took?
I think it comes from inside you. I remember at the time I was extremely determined and very focused on putting together a plan that outlined where we needed to be. I felt confident the situation could be managed and we were going to find a solution. We communicated that from the first moment we felt the effects of the crisis. I had a great team around me. We were quite analytical in our approach. We worked very closely together during that time frame. We sat down and said, "Okay, here's what we need to do." I wasn't scared. I didn't have time to think about courage or where to find courage, I just had it. Only later did the impact sink in.

I remember once being caught in quite a bad lightning storm on a boat with my husband and children. It was a very frightening situation, but, at the time, I recall not being frightened at all. I was so determined we were going to make it to shore and my husband was completely calm and in control as well. I was counting down the meters to safety: "100 meters. 90 to go. Okay, we are there." It was only after we were safely on shore that the seriousness of the situation and what could have happened sunk in. It is interesting how that works in business as well!

How did that experience help you to become a better leader?
I think having lived through the crisis absolutely helped make me a better leader. It taught me a lot about the importance of communication. It got a lot of us a step closer to the action in the company. We learned there were areas in the company where we could do things a little better or a little bit differently. The experience also proved to all of us that we could handle a crisis. This built confidence going forward. A crisis such as the 2008 financial crisis is a humbling experience. You mature as a leader. The experience and the associated learning give you a better perspective going forward and on the challenges we face today.

Is there anything that you fear about the role of leadership?
I don't know that I fear anything about leadership. I will say there is always the weight of knowing 17,000 families are relying on my leadership and my team's

leadership to make the right decisions. That is a lot of responsibility and it is always in your mind. For example, the impact of the crisis on our people and their families was very tough to manage through.

It is important to always be a step ahead in the marketplace. There are a lot of examples of companies that were really successful and made a lot of money. But they did not see the truck coming that all of a sudden took their business away. You need to be absolutely vigilant. You continue to plan towards the future. Set a goal. Meet the goal. Set another goal. You continue to march forward. There are always opportunities. There were opportunities as a direct result of the crisis and the subsequent recession and there will be opportunities in the next couple of years. For example, we are now keeping an eye on what is happening in Europe.

What were some of the hardest things for you to learn in becoming a good or an even better leader?
I think the toughest things for me to learn were, first, how to step away from the action and delegate and, second, to take more time on important strategic decisions. I grew up from the floor. Not only am I familiar with the action there, but I loved it! It is hard to step away and let someone else take that on. We continue to evolve as a company and it's hard to hand over the reins and rely on people to be accountable. It's hard to give people the tools and information they need and then hold them accountable to meet goals. Timing around decisions is tough, too. I always want to decide fast and act quickly. I have to constantly remind myself to take time on certain more strategic decisions and think them through, get input and feedback, evaluate options, and then decide.

You referred to building a team of capable people. What have you learned about building trust and learning to trust others?
Building trust is a two-way street. *You need to be trustworthy for people to feel they can rely on you. They need to know they can follow your lead. People need to know you're leading them in a direction that makes sense. Trustworthiness is rooted in how you treat people.* Do you show people respect? You show people respect until they violate that respect. Then trust will have to be rebuilt. If someone has violated your trust, it is very difficult—sometimes impossible—to rebuild.

Good leaders learn. They mature. How has your leadership evolved over time?
My style has evolved in at least two ways. First, I learned to let go. I came from the shop floor. I ran a plant and was very hands on. Then I ran 2 plants, then 3, then 17, and now 40. You must learn to let a little more go every time, but still be engaged enough that you can come down and help when you need to, or that you can come down to look and see if things such as operations still make sense or whether you have to redirect. I need to be able to operate at 40,000 feet, but be able to go down to 2 feet. This is something that evolves over time. Second, I learned to be more

inclusive, more team oriented, and less autocratic. I learned that I don't always have the best answer. Hence, I've learned over the years to listen more, to table an idea, to get some feedback, and then make the decision. I'm not looking for consensus. I'm looking for input and feedback and buy-in. You don't achieve a lot if you don't have people's buy-in.

What advice do you have for people as they embark on their journey of learning to lead?
My advice is to listen more and recognize that a diversity of opinions is important. It is critical to get input from people from a variety of different areas. *The sooner you learn to listen more, talk less, and get people engaged, the better your decisions tend to be and the quicker you'll be successful. Of course, having a strong team around you is also critical.* My advice is to hire the best people you can find, because the smarter and more capable your team is, the better you look.

But not everybody shares that belief. To some people hiring the best people—those that are smarter than you—can be very threatening. So how did you become comfortable with that?
My father taught me many years ago to never be afraid to hire people smarter than me, because they will only ever make me look good. I think it's absolutely true. You're right—not everybody believes this. It is not a good sign if you're afraid to hire somebody who is smarter than you.

Leadership Themes

- You need to show that you truly care about what happens to your people.
- Don't paint people with the same brush. As you get more experience, you realize people aren't all the same and they don't all respond the same way. They don't think the same way. They don't listen the same way. They're not motivated the same way.
- You need to be trustworthy for people to feel they can rely on you. Trustworthiness is rooted in how you treat people.
- The sooner you learn to listen more, talk less, and get people engaged, the better your decisions tend to be and the quicker you'll be successful.
- Live through a crisis—it will make you a better leader.

16

Don't Underestimate the Value of Your Early Career Moves—You Can't Make up Lost Time

Stephen Snyder

Steve, when did you first realize you were a leader, and what happened to make you realize it?

I always thought that leadership was a by-product. The only goal I had in my career was to do the job I had better than anyone else and then move on to the next job. Performance takes you to the next step in your career. Leadership is based on what you are able to accomplish. I never said, "I want to be a leader." I never said, "I want to be a CEO." There is a big difference between saying, "I want to be successful," and actually doing things and delivering results. You need substance and you have to have a track record of delivering. I was very performance driven and I think what happened was that I became a leader by default.

I didn't consciously think about leadership until an incident at General Electric (GE) Canada. GE used to have these human resources (HR) forms that you were required to complete. It included a question that focused on what you wanted to be "when you grow up." I filled this form out every year. One day, the head of HR for GE Canada came to see me after I had handed in my form. He said, "Steve, I saw your form. You didn't put down that you want to be CEO." I would have been in my mid-thirties when this happened. I always put down I wanted to do the next job up or maybe the job up after that. I thought it was a bit arrogant to put down "CEO." I think of myself as a humble person. The head of HR asked whether, at some point, I would like to take on the role and I replied, "Yes," but that I was not going to put that down on paper. I thought, "We'll see what happens over the coming years." The head of HR responded, "Steve, they are expecting you to put it down and they would be disappointed if you didn't." I went home and thought about what happened. ***I came to the conclusion that, at some point, you have to take control over your career and be a bit more declarative of your ambition.*** So, I put down that I wanted to be CEO. This is what got me thinking more consciously about leadership.

You never set out to be a CEO? How did you make the transition to CEO?

Careers have a lot of timing and luck to them as much as they have skill behind them. My good fortune was to be part of the GE system at the time when Jack

Welch was re-creating how to run the company. At GE, I got a wide variety of experiences early in my career. The company had a number of different businesses, so there were lots of opportunities to get exposure to different challenges. You also had Welch trying to have a different type of leader coming into the organization. He wanted to make GE more global; I wasn't an American, I had an MBA, I was doing well in the company, and I was part of the right age group. The senior leadership at the company started to move me around a lot. This is one of the pieces of advice I always like to give young people: "Don't underestimate the value of your early career moves. You can't make up lost time. If you don't get your experiences by 35, 38, or 40, you're probably not going to get them." Those early years are really critical. I always trusted the company to make the next move. *I think I was very fortunate to get a wide variety of experiences quite young. The GE system was pretty ruthless, so you learned quickly or you sank.* That little fear factor, that paranoid factor, was a little juice to keep you going.

What have been the formative influences on you as a leader? What did people do to help you? What experiences did you learn the most from? Was there any particular experience that supercharged your learning to lead?
There were three leaders who influenced me early in my career. They are all from GE, because that's where I had the bulk of my experience. Number one would have been a gentleman called Bill Blundell. He was the CEO of GE Canada for many years. I think he is one of the most underrated Canadian business leaders of the last 25 to 30 years. Bill shepherded my career through GE. He was the key interface between GE Canada and the United States and he was well respected by Welch. What I saw in Bill was a person who was just absolutely dedicated to success. He taught me the importance of being involved in the community, which Bill felt was a part of developing leadership skills. He had a strong sense of community and believed it was important to give back.

Bill said something that took me many years until I understood what he meant. He said, "Always be prepared." I thought that was a weird thing for him to say . . . of course, you're always prepared. It took me four or five years to realize what he meant. As a leader, you had to go into the week ahead of everyone else. You had to have your work all laid out. Things happen you didn't plan and you can get behind your schedule very quickly, and then you begin to struggle for time. Bill taught me that you work over the weekend to get ready for Monday and the rest of the week. So, when unexpected things come up during the week, you have got time and you can deal with them.

Jack Welch was about numbers. He believed that if you have a good accounting system, then you don't get tied up by emotion. The numbers never lie, so let them guide you. I learned two things from Welch: The importance of communication and HR. I think the importance of communication is now well recognized. Yet, I think that some CEOs still feel that, if they say something, then people will listen, and that somehow things will get done. This is not typically the case. I learned from Welch the importance of repeating messages and to have only a few messages for a large organization at any given time. People can't absorb too many messages. I look back on my time at GE, and he never had more than one or two things that he drove, ruthlessly, at a particular time.

A lot of CEOs continue to view HR as something on the side. In my opinion, Welch was really innovative in HR. He spent a huge amount of time thinking about how to best develop leaders, how to motivate people, how to measure performance, and how to promote people. He did this at a time when most CEOs spent a token amount of time on these and other critical people-related questions.

The third person that had an influence on my leadership is also from GE—Larry Bossidy. In the GE system, you never got to a general manager's role without a meeting with one of the vice chairmen or the chairman. A bad meeting with Bossidy, one of the vice chairmen, or Welch, and your promotion could be derailed. I went to see Bossidy in typical GE fashion. You go to headquarters in Fairfield, Connecticut, and you meet him in his office. He had five minutes for our meeting. He was a very busy guy, and I was this little guy from Canada. Welch had characterized the Canadian business as a "popcorn stand" in GE terms. He only had one question, "Steve, name me two leaders who influenced you and what do you remember about them?" I talked about Blundell and Welch and observed that they had two different styles of leadership. He said, "You never forget that. There's no one style of leadership. A lot of styles work . . . Now, get out of here and make good things happen." That was it, but it stuck with me. *Leadership style has really very little to do with success.* We like to think and talk about style a lot and that it's what makes you a leader. But at the end of the day, people would do things for Blundell and Welch for totally different reasons, but equally committed, equally devoted, and equally believing in that leader despite their very different styles.

I could go into any bookstore or university library and would locate tens if not hundreds of books on leadership. Thousands maybe? This tells me that no one can distill leadership into something straightforward. Leadership is so complex and so varied that you can describe it in multiple ways. *I believe it is critical to be you and get clarity on a number of key issues. "This is what I am about." "This is the way I am going to do things." "I have to stay true to these principles." This doesn't mean that, when the world changes, you shouldn't change. But you have got to bring consistency with your leadership style and your approach in getting things done.*

I like your last observation. People often want to know which style is best. We discuss leadership style, but forget about the substance that individuals bring to the leadership role.

I agree. But more important, I believe, is the consistency with which we lead. People knew what to expect with Welch. He never varied. He was always quite consistent in the way he processed information and implemented decisions. He had his views about what was right and wrong, and, in most instances, he stuck to those views. The same applied to Blundell. They weren't always right, but people knew what they were getting into.

Welch was incredibly dedicated and focused. I recall a specific initiative around employee engagement that he wanted to implement. The head of GE Aircraft Engines didn't buy into the program. He thought it was crap and stupid. Everyone kept asking Welch, "Are we on with this program or not?" So, Welch took him out—he fired him. This person was one of the most senior leaders in the company and well respected in the industry. Welch was sure the program was the right one. The initiative was not optional! His leadership style is not a style that works for everyone. But when it comes to style, I believe the one thing you can't be is wishy-washy, because, if you are, no one really knows what you are up to.

People should find the style that works for them. *I tend to be an instinctive manager, and I observed that, when I stopped being instinctive and bold, I began to make mistakes. I found out that when I overanalyzed a problem and potential solution things didn't work very well.* I didn't really know what went wrong because there were just too many inputs to know which one of those was the one that caused our decision to go awry. What worked for me was to take my shot and correct mistakes quickly. But that only worked when I was instinctive. That is one of the things that I learned from the system at GE—the importance of speed.

How did you develop that instinct and be more right than wrong?

I don't know. I am not sure if I developed this as part of the learning process. I think the instinct may be part of your genes. GE identified it early. They always did a very intensive testing of people going through the officer ladder. They said, "Steve, you're at the high end of being instinctive. This is not perfect. You have to find some offsets." What I learned from that is that I was best served by a chief financial officer (CFO) who was as numbers oriented as possible and whom I respected. The person needed to have the strength to tell me, "Steve, this is a great idea, but the numbers don't line up." I needed to have that resource to offset what I was good at. *I think good leaders recognize that they're not good at all things, so they need to get those gaps filled and be quite comfortable getting these gaps filled with very strong people.* I've had trouble, in the past, as a leader in situations where I haven't been able to work with people whom I could trust and count on.

You need to build a group of trusted people around you who are willing to give you candid feedback. People that will tell you that you have a piece of spinach stuck behind your teeth. What have you learned about building trust?

I was always quite deliberate about trying to find people who brought candor. For example, I took the time to tell people about my expectations. Of course, they all say, "Yes, I'm going to do that." Hence, I carefully observed people to find out about fact and fiction. I think people selection is among the biggest challenges of any leader.

I had one CFO who was very good at bringing that candor to our relationship. The problem was he also applied that style below him. This contributed to distrust and we had to find a way out of that. There was another CFO who was really good at managing down, but I didn't have the confidence that he would really tell me what was going on in the company, and, hence, that was a problem the other way. Both situations had to be acted on for different reasons.

Oftentimes, you get a team together and everything is jelling and fantastic and you wish it could go on forever, but it never does. Someone leaves, or someone gets sick, or someone quits, or someone screws up, and then you have to build the team back up again. You have to be prepared for that cycle. Personally, I believe it takes about two years—you can't change people that quickly and building trust and confidence in a person takes time.

You were building your leadership career. GE provided great opportunities. You were also a single parent with young children. How did you learn to integrate family and work?

Becoming a single parent was obviously a major event for me because it coincided with a couple of things. First, it coincided exactly when I was asked to run the major appliance business for GE in Canada—Camco. Camco was the result of a merger of three companies, so it was a tough situation. What made the situation even more challenging was that there was a 40 percent minority shareholder in the new company who was in the process of suing GE for oppression; in essence, there was a disagreement regarding transfer pricing. That's a challenging situation for an experienced CEO, never mind a first-time CEO.

I started the job of CEO in January and my wife passed away in February. I was six weeks into the job. What do you do? I had to consider a couple of things. First, I knew I had to make a tough decision, because it wasn't like I could take four weeks off. I was the new CEO of a brand new company. You can't just take four weeks off, no matter what the reason is. Second, as I stated earlier, the situation at Camco was quite serious and confrontational. Hence, I had to make a decision quickly. Was I going to stay in the job or would I resign? If I was to stay, then I would have to go back to work quickly. The third consideration was the age of my children, who were three and five years old. I realized something had to give. I decided to stay in the job. That forced me to change a lot of things around me. I basically dropped all of my outside personal events overnight. I stopped golfing. I stopped bowling. I stopped playing cards. I stopped all those activities—I went to zero instantly. I just did two things: worked with the kids and worked at work.

Losing your wife is something that impacts you dramatically for a long time. But there was a profound immediate lesson for my leadership and the business—learning when to be efficient and when to be inefficient. I will elaborate on that. At work, everything is about efficiency. I've got this new job. I'm trying to show GE that I can be successful. I have to deal with a lawsuit. I also knew the kids would be time consuming. I realized efficiency was going to be critical. I had to manage my time minute to minute. I'm pretty good at that. I did that for about a month, and then I realized that this was not working at home. I'd get home from work about 6 p.m. I'd get supper ready, get the kids organized for the next day, do the laundry, and get them in bed. Then, at 8 p.m., I'd start to do my work for the next day. But that's not what the kids wanted. They want the exact opposite! They are inefficient users of time. They want and need quantity. So, I had to get home and shift to being inefficient. If the laundry didn't get done, it didn't get done. If I didn't start my personal work until 9 p.m., then I didn't start until 9 p.m. Those extra hours on the weekend became theirs. It was very hard for me to shift from efficiency at work to inefficiency at home. But I feel I got there. And I think it is a very helpful skill.

But there was an important business lesson I learned. There are times at work when you need to slow things down, and other times when you need to speed things up. I became much more conscious of that. I was just go-go-go, drive-drive-drive. That's fine early in your career, but, as you get more responsibility, and you have to work with a lot more people, then you begin to recognize what I call the "muckiness" of people. *People have issues; they have personal problems that need to be addressed if you want them to be effective. If you don't like taking care of those, then don't be a leader.* You learn to appreciate that there are times when you have to back off and slow things down.

You once said you knew nothing about the power generation industry when you came to TransAlta and that you faced a very steep learning curve.

The reality was that I didn't know the power business. I didn't know about regulated businesses or capital-intensive businesses. In my career, I moved up through mostly consumer durables, which were fast-cycled and less capital-intensive businesses. The benefit of that route was that you learned about speed in decision making, and speed is always helpful in any job. I think it's very difficult to go from a long-term capital-intensive business into a fast-cycled business. Going the other way is a bit easier. This is why GE puts a lot of people in their consumer business, initially—to learn about pace.

I did a couple of things to learn about the power generation industry. I met with lots of different experts who told me about the business. I got heavily engaged in industry associations so I could meet other CEOs and industry leaders. I heard a lot of different perspectives, which was very useful. Quite often, industry meetings are a waste of time, but when you are brand new to a business it's a great way to meet, talk to people, and learn. I'd also spend a lot of time after the meetings to meet people informally for coffee and talk about the industry and what people were doing in their jobs. I also tried to reach out to community people here in Calgary. I went to a lot of social functions because these events were a good way to meet people and hear about things. Dick Haskayne, the chairman of the board at the time, was very helpful. He knew everyone and introduced me to a lot of people who could tell me about the business community and share their views on what was going on. It was a conscious effort to overload. Of course, your involvement with all of these activities and events drops off over time, but, initially, you seize these opportunities as ways of reaching out and learning.

These must have been incredibly long days.

That is right. Typically, I was at work at 6 a.m. and would be home at 9 or 10 p.m. By that time, my children were 12 and 13 years old, and so we were able to manage things a little better. But it was just sheer hard work. I really tried to learn as quickly as I could. What is the business model for success in this industry? What are the four or five things you just have to do right to survive and make a profit? Following that, it is all about the fine tuning that needs to take place so that you can make the business model, and execution, even better. This was a major challenge because our business was in transition. We went from being regulated to becoming non-regulated. And this was one of the reasons why they brought in an outsider as the next CEO, to help the company move through that process.

You had a funny story about Dick Haskayne?

I was there a couple of weeks and Dick said, "Steve, let's go to the golf club and have lunch." I knew Dick by reputation—I didn't know him that well personally. We're having lunch and people start coming over and to say "Hello" to Dick. He would say, "This is Steve. He is the new TransAlta CEO." And then the next person came to the table, and the next one. This went on for about an hour and a half! I couldn't eat my lunch. I told people after the meeting that, if you ever go out for lunch with Dick, then you should order a cold sandwich because your food is going to get cold anyways. He just knows everyone.

What a great resource to have.

Indeed, Dick was incredibly helpful. I faced a messy transition and he was a very proactive chair in helping me to engage with the community. He also had great views on corporate governance, long before they became the norm. He wasn't saying, "This is what I want you to do in the company." His approach was more along the lines of, "I want to help you to do your job in the company." It was helpful that he introduced me to so many people. I always knew that Calgary was a business community where it's important to know the other leaders. It's a small yet powerful community. *It's very helpful that you can call on people, but, to do that, you've got to be in the game. You can't just phone up someone you haven't talked to for two years and ask for their advice.*

You have a very outspoken style of leadership. Did that style always work for you or did you have to hold it in check occasionally? What have you learned about becoming influential in communication?

I would not have thought of myself as being outspoken at the time. I always tried to clearly communicate what I thought the issues were. You're trying to be outspoken in order to get people's attention and show them where you stand. But, like anything in life and business, you can carry things one step too far.

There's a point where you're too outspoken and you become divisive. Consequently, people will say, "Forget it!" and they will go the other way. I probably crossed that line a number of times without realizing it. When that happens, it is good to have people around you whom you trust and who will give you honest feedback. For example, I would go out in the community and someone would say to me, "Steve, that statement the other day was pretty strong." I would reply, "It was? I didn't think it was." And the answer would inevitably be, "Well, that's the way it came across." That made me think about how to communicate better.

I think I had a tendency to keep pushing the next step, and the next. You need to develop an awareness to step back and say, "Hold it. Am I pushing that too far, too soon, and too fast?" *I always felt, as CEO, you had to stir things up a little bit. But the question was how much—and when. I guess my view was you're better off to go a bit too far than not enough.* But you can still go too far, and, when that happens, little goes forward. You have to decide whether you can take small steps or big steps, but you have to take a step.

Learning requires reflection. Do you reflect on your leadership?
I did not set aside planned time to reflect as often as I perhaps should have. There were times I did. I cleared time on my agenda and sat in my office, thinking about the company and how my leadership supported or undermined its success. If I observed that the company wasn't doing well, I reflected, *Is it me?* Again, much of my leadership was instinctive. On those occasions when I thought I was off base, I would step back and talk to people I trusted.

How did you decide to step down as CEO of TransAlta? Did anyone give you advice? Did you know the right time through self-awareness or reflection?
It was 100 percent my own decision. The time was right. It was an instinctive sense I got that the time for something different was approaching. No need for a forced search, but time to start getting organized for an eventual CEO change.

I always use the "feel good" barometer. If you got a call on Sunday night saying you got to come into the office because there is a problem, you can either say, "Yes, let's go," or you think, Aww, crap. Once you think, Aww, crap, then it is time for you to leave as the CEO. It was not that extreme when it came to my decision. But I realized I was becoming more aware that there was something else out there for me to do, and I decided to start planning for my departure because these transitions may take several years to complete.

People sometimes have difficulty understanding that they no longer have the passion or the drive to lead and they stay.
I knew it was time. I've been the hired gun and professional manager all my career. I worked hard at it and loved it, but I felt I wanted to do something different. The

way I described it to people is that it's time for me not to work for a salary or to a forced schedule. If you work for a salary, then you work to a schedule. I loved doing that for 35 years. I now want to do something else, to have more control over my time. And to have more free time. I still want to earn money. I just don't want to do it via a salary.

You once said, "I always came to work paranoid that this could be my last day at the job. I always felt I had to come in and earn my job every single day." Can you elaborate on that statement?

It's absolutely true. I think that I always was a naturally humble person. I never took anything for granted and I felt I always had to earn whatever I did. Furthermore, the employees always win over any CEO. If the employees decide they can't stand you as a CEO, then most boards have to react to that. It's like a hockey team. Typically, the coach goes when things are bad. Why? You can't fire 20 hockey players. The coach goes, even though he may be a great coach. There is no other option. The same happens in a company. If, for some reason, the employees decide that you're a jerk, and the board knows that, then what choice do they have? Try to convince 2,500 employees that you are not a jerk after all or bring a new person in? You need to realize that feeling self-satisfied or arrogance is going to lead to problems.

The quote you mentioned has a lot to do with self-discipline—to always try to do better. The point is that, if you don't deliver, then you should be gone. *You should be coming in with the attitude that you have to earn your job and employees' respect every single day. Once you no longer have that attitude, I'm not sure if you're delivering your best performance.* I think the mindset I brought to work is a positive one, and I encourage all leaders, managers, and employees to bring that mindset when they come to work. You do that and you're going to work hard, you're going to deliver, everyone will be happy, and you'll be happy with what you've accomplished.

The word "humility" has come up several times. Where did your humility come from? Your upbringing? From a particular experience early in your career?

I think your sense of humility comes largely from your upbringing. I got it from my dad. My parents were Saskatchewan farmers and came from humble beginnings, so they didn't tolerate a lot of fancy stuff. My dad was a Depression baby. He didn't get through high school; he was successful in life through incredibly hard work. *What I learned over the years is that hard work is 80 percent of your success and intelligence is the other 20 percent.* What do you get when a really smart person doesn't work hard? Not much. I've seen people who are average in skill set, but work very hard and do extremely well.

I remember my early years at GE. I was in a leadership role at a fairly young age. I always had people much older than me working for me. Sales managers had significantly more experience than I had. They worked for me, but I would always say, "Mr. Smith, what do you think we should do here?" Growing up when someone was older than you, you always said "Mister." You always showed respect. That is the way I was brought up.

Why would people say anything to you if you come across like a jerk? They're just going to shut you out. I decided that I was going to learn to work with these people out of respect for people. I made mistakes of course. I got mad at the wrong times and I didn't see things that I should have seen because people put the smoke over your eyes. But these were all learning opportunities. For example, *I quickly learned to ask a lot of questions to make sure that there was substance behind what people were saying and not just gamesmanship.*

You have a distinguished career in business with lots of success. You are the recipient of several leadership rewards and recognitions. How difficult has it been for you to stay true to yourself?

I like to think I stayed true to myself. I think part of my personality is that I don't necessarily want to get any recognition for things. We were trying to create something great at TransAlta. *Our successes were always team efforts, and, hence, the CEO should not get singled out for success.* There was an early learning moment at TransAlta. I used to go to a lot of external functions so I could meet people, get to know our community better, and see things for myself. However, the press want to take your picture because you are a CEO. I suddenly realized that, about every second Saturday, my picture was in the social column of the newspaper. I thought that sent the wrong message to the people at TransAlta. I had to tell people to stop taking my picture, even though perhaps my ego encouraged it. I think employees want to see a bit of you in the news, but not too much. For example, when I decided to chair the homeless program in Calgary, I was a bit worried about the visibility, as I had a lot on my plate already. But then I got feedback from the employees and they liked my involvement with the program. They understood that homelessness was a real problem—it is not right that 3,000 people are homeless in the winter in Calgary on any given day. They were very supportive that the company and I were supporting the effort to make a difference. To most of our employees, this was a great use of my time.

You've done a lot of community service. What motivated you to do this and did your leadership style change as a result of working in that particular environment?

The motivation goes back to my early leadership days and the mentoring of Blundell. Over time, I began myself to recognize that employees spend a lot of time in their communities. We all have skills to make our communities better and doing so is bound to help employees, and then, hopefully, even make the company a better company. I was asked to contribute and I thought I could help out. Once you are engaged in something, it sort of snowballs.

I also realized there was a lot I could learn from managing a diverse group. I often ended up being chair of committees. These organizations, by their nature, tend to be input based. Output is often less than hoped for. As chair, you can't just sit there and just listen to all the points of view; someone has to galvanize people to do something a bit different.

You get a lot more diverse views in social institutions than you do in business settings. Members can be very passionate and dedicated—and they don't always listen to one another. You have to learn how to bring extreme points of view closer together and achieve balance . . . and outcomes. And that's a helpful learning for any leader.

Being engaged in community work gives you a much better sense of how to handle diversity. I learned that getting people who don't directly work for you to buy into things is a different skill set than to get a commitment from people who work for you. These people are volunteers—this is not a job for them. They are there because they want to help and they typically are very passionate about the cause (and opinionated).

I think one of my skills was that I could get these diverse people around a table to discuss important issues—homelessness and other social issues—in a comfortable and pleasant atmosphere. *People around the table knew way more about issues than I did, but my ability was to get them to work together and then come up with something that was actually constructive and could be supported by a strong majority.* That skill is very important in a work environment as well. I definitely felt I benefited as a leader from my community involvement.

What were some of the hardest things to learn in becoming a good or an even better leader?

To undo what I did—to recognize a decision you made was wrong or not as good as it could have been, or that the world had changed and a different approach is now required. It takes a lot of energy to restart. But often it's the only good choice. I have looked back on some situations and come to the conclusion that it would have been better if I had acted sooner. Instead, I let things go on too long before I acted. My mistakes overall as a leader tended to revolve around not being bold enough and not acting quickly enough.

What are you learning these days to become an even better leader? Are there any recent "aha" moments?

I continue to learn about the importance of what I would call "slight mellowing." Being on edge and driven contributes to becoming a CEO. But mellowing the edges is important—to show a bit more tolerance for things, to provide more freedom to act, to pace your decision making a bit better, to learn to take the extra input, to know when to take the extra input, to step back and think through a few more ramifications of your decisions. But, you have to watch you don't lose that instinctive boldness to move when you want to move, and I would think that degraded a bit with me over time when I shouldn't have let that degrade. Getting that balance right is tricky and requires constant and thoughtful introspection. You can't lose sight of that. But, overall, a leader must always remain energetic, drive to do better, recognize their shortcomings, and find ways around them. And that's the beauty of a large organization. There are always deep resources to draw on to help you. You just have to reach out to them, put ego aside, and let the results speak for themselves.

Leadership Themes

- Take control over your career and be declarative of your ambition.
- Good leaders recognize they're not good at all things and that they need to get those gaps filled and be quite comfortable getting these gaps filled with very strong people.
- People have issues; they have personal problems that need to be addressed if you want them to be effective. If you don't like taking care of those, then don't be a leader.
- Leadership style has very little to do with success.
- Hard work is 80 percent of your success and intelligence is the other 20 percent.
- Bring the attitude that you have to earn your job and employees' respect every single day.
- Success is always a team effort.

17

Care With Your Heart, Concentrate Your Heart, Relax Your Heart, and Open Your Heart

John Cheh

John, when did you first realize you were a leader, and what happened to make you realize it?
If I had to pick a defining moment, that would be nine years ago when I was invited to give a lecture on leadership to a group of international MBA students at Zhongshan University in China. In preparing and giving that talk, and in the active exchange with the students that followed, I realized that I could consider myself a leader. I have since been re-invited by the university to give a talk each year!

I think being a leader comes in stages. A key attribute is one's aspiration to do well, to excel. Even as a student, I was an "overachiever," always trying to do well in class, get into the best schools, participate in extracurricular activities, and be fully engaged with my peers and with the school. When I first began to work, I was very much feeling my way. In each case, starting a new job, taking on a new role, not without some fear or trepidation, I tried to overcome that, to learn and to perform. This went back to my first job at the Treasury Board of Canada, where, as a newly arrived analyst, I had to learn the job context and try to excel, not to impress anyone, but to prove to myself that I had what it took to succeed.

You indicated there was always a little bit of fear or trepidation. But you strike me as a calm and confident person?
Be humble—know that there are always things to learn. We should realize that any new role comes with its own set of challenges; its team of people to work with and the need to gain their confidence, their support, their engagement. *The leader should have some trepidation, rather than behaving like a superstar who thinks: "I can do it all; you listen to me, follow my orders, and you will do well!" That is not the proper way.* But, of course, nor should one show fear. I realize many people are afraid to change roles or positions. People leave their comfort zone when they take on a new assignment or a new position. It is natural to experience those feelings, but you have to learn, adapt, and stay calm.

How have you learned to step out of your comfort zone and stretch yourself? How challenging was that?
There is no easy answer. In a way, it comes with trial and error. It comes with experience. Perhaps I will use the word "maturity"—as one matures, by having gone through different experiences, the learning curve or the adjustment period gets shortened. I was in the Canadian public service for 19 years. Those years were not static at all. Then I made the transition from the public to the private sector. Stepping out of the comfort zone is a function of one's personality. For example, I enjoy change. I look back and feel blessed that I have had the chance to move to a new position, a new role, a new location, a new country, a new sector. I have learned to adapt and then contribute.

What have been the formative influences on you as a leader?
After almost 38 years in the public and private sectors, so many experiences helped shape me. Let me be selective and draw on several experiences across different roles and positions. One thing stood out from my time in Ottawa. I had just joined the Treasury Board. The vice president of finance and treasurer from a large Government-owned corporation came to my office to meet me. After a brief exchange of pleasantries, he abruptly told me that the corporation was facing a cash crunch and needed a massive capital injection to avert bankruptcy. This was a difficult and complex endeavor. And remember—I was the new kid on the block! After a few very demanding weeks of analyzing complex financial restructuring alternatives, we came up with a sound plan that was presented to the Treasury Board and was approved. I remember people told me, "John, that was a really tough assignment, but you did it well." I had to learn a lot within a short time. I had to put the different pieces together, draw on the expertise of many people, and not pretend that I had all the answers. A lot of the work involved coordination, making trade-offs, and negotiation. We ended up with a workable and viable package. That was a critical experience in my early years in government.

Years later, there was the 1993 G8 Summit in Tokyo, with Kim Campbell being the Canadian Prime Minister who attended it. I was asked by the Ambassador, Doug Campbell, to chair the Embassy Taskforce to support the Canadian delegation to the summit. It was a difficult role that required liaison, coordination, and consultation with different Japanese Ministries and with Ottawa. Even arranging the communications and logistics aspects of the summit was a complex task. But the whole event went flawlessly—we executed well. After the conclusion of the summit, the Prime Minister came to the Embassy and personally thanked the team members for their support. That was a special and memorable moment!

The third example comes from my days at Bell Canada International. We were scouting for strategic investment opportunities in Asia's telecommunications services sector, and became the only North American player bold enough to invest in a Korean mobile phone carrier during the Asian financial crisis. We assessed the opportunity and performed our due diligence thoroughly. The deal had multiple challenges, but we managed to proceed with the investment. Then, just as the dot-com bubble was bursting three years later, we decided it was time to exit. There were many hurdles along the way. Even after the sale and purchase agreement had been signed, the buyer insisted on our taking a "haircut" in the selling price during the last two weeks of the deal because the value of our stake in the company was diminishing day by day. We bargained hard, made some tactical trade-offs in those final negotiations, and successfully closed the deal at a significant return to our investment. What a thrill: I could see how one could become a "deal junkie" in doing mergers and acquisitions!

Through experiences like these, I learned a lot about leadership.

What did people do to help you in the process of learning to lead? Have you had the benefit of mentors?

I have been very blessed in terms of people who have supported and encouraged me. I can name several individuals who guided me and gave me opportunities. One example came from my days at the Privy Council Office. The then Canadian Trade Minister—Ed Lumley—included me in his trade mission to China, which gave me exposure in the field of foreign trade and investment promotion. It was a great learning experience to see how effectively Minister Lumley handled the meetings and built up relationships and trust with his counterparts. A year later, I sought and was given the opportunity for a posting as a trade officer at the Canadian Embassy in Beijing. I still jokingly tell people, "I'm the guy who Ed Lumley took to China and left behind!"

When I made the transition to the private sector and was appointed the president of Bell Canada International in Asia, Derek Burney was my mentor. I have tremendous respect for Derek. He is a former senior statesman, having served as Canada's ambassador to Korea and the United States. He was also chief of staff to Prime Minister Brian Mulroney. Derek Burney was chairman and CEO of Bell Canada International Inc. from 1993 to 1999. He guided me, supported me, and encouraged me in making a number of large telecom merger and acquisition deals in Asia. One memorable occasion, in particular, was when I accompanied Derek to call on the late President Kim Dae Jung in relation to our investment intention in Korea. Derek was warmly welcomed by President Kim, who knew Derek from his days as Canada's ambassador to Korea, and the two of them reminisced fondly about their past encounters. Derek went on to explain succinctly the rationale and significance of our planned investment—and received the President's strong indication of support.

Then, of course, my current role as the CEO of Esquel. I have known the chairman, Marjorie Yang, for many years. I left Bombardier China for Esquel in 2003—and this is when I would use the cliché "the rest is history"! I have been having both a wonderful and a fulfilling time. I have been learning on the job; after all, I had no prior experience in the textile and apparel sector! I am managing the company—with 54,000 staff and workers worldwide. Together, with Marjorie, we have almost tripled our revenue since 2003 and have achieved significant improvements to our bottom line. We engage and motivate our staff. We strive to improve the livelihood of our staff and workers in multiple locations. We support local communities and are putting real meaning to the term "corporate social responsibility."

But what, specifically, did they do to help you? What made them good mentors or sources of support?
I will use Derek Burney as an example. He was a very demanding chairman and CEO! You could not slip anything past him if you did not have a solid case to fall back on. He was strategic and had strong business instincts. He supported me in making the case to the board to approve a C$150-million investment in Korea. In the actual execution of the project, it was all about guidance. He would not try to second-guess me, but, whenever I felt I needed some guidance, he would give it and then leave me to do the job. This is what I am doing now in my role—pointing out the direction, but not doing the job that could be better done by my staff and subordinates. There are senior executives who feel that they are the superstars and they can do everything better than their subordinates, and they set out to prove this. Marjorie is not like that at all. She is truly visionary. We discuss long-term direction and strategies together, then she gives me the autonomy to manage and execute. I believe it is far more important to let the staff perform. A vision or strategic direction has to be set, but let the staff do their job. When they succeed, recognize and reward their achievements. Give credit to the staff. Make sure that people understand that we are executing and performing as a team.

What were some of the hardest things to learn in becoming a good or an even better leader?
I think the common challenge is how to relate to people, understand people, and then give them support and general guidance. Not instructions to do this or to do that. Figure out who is best suited to perform what role, rather than force-fitting. Not everyone is adaptable. There are technical people, there are financial people, there are general management people, and so forth. I think it is incumbent on the leader to judge people, utilize them properly, encourage them, and give them positive feedback. The opposite is also true. You asked me what has been a mistake or a painful experience in leading organizations. I think it is making wrong judgments about people. Sometimes, a person comes through as a strong candidate, but then fails miserably on the job. I have had cases like that, and then it is a matter of knowing how to deal with the situation in a professional and fair manner. Make the necessary changes—bite the bullet.

I have heard you talk about the importance of values. Can you tell me about the core values at Esquel?
We have coined what we call the "Esquel 5-E culture." Five core values that begin with the letter E: ethics, environment, exploration, excellence, and education.

Ethical behavior is indispensible. Be ethical, be moral at all times: There is zero tolerance for unethical behavior. Environment—be green. Achieve reductions in energy and water consumption. This is not just good for the environment, but there is also a solid business case when we reduce energy and water consumption: We improve efficiencies and achieve lower costs. Exploration—we invest in research and development, in product development, in innovations, and in deploying new technologies and processes. Excellence—we are in the cotton shirt business. We are a vertically integrated manufacturer, from cotton to yarn to fabric to shirts. We are very focused on the product—high-quality cotton shirts—and we aspire to be the best! The fifth E is education. It is continuous learning. It is career development and training for our staff and workers. We support education in our communities where we are based. We donate funds to help rebuild schools and provide school equipment. And it is not just the company—many of our staff members are involved, by being instructors or sponsors of students with financial needs.

It may surprise you to hear me as a representative of a traditional industry saying all of this. At Esquel, we aspire to be an innovative, non-traditional company in a traditional sector!

How difficult has it been for you to stay true to those core values and not to take any shortcuts? Sometimes, our stated values can be quite inconvenient.

This is a key point—there can be no compromises, because we will not be true to ourselves and our staff. If we say one thing and then behave in an opposite fashion, how can we stand up to ourselves, our people, or our customers? We have to live and breathe our core values because they define our brand equity. This is how our customers look at us. Our values are how people have come to understand and respect Esquel. We are not doing this just as a selling tool. First, we define and live our values for ourselves—to have meaning in what we do. We want to make a difference for our staff, our workers, and our communities. This is the mission! It is not just about making money. Now ... the two—our values and making money—in our view, are not in conflict. We have a strong brand. Our staff and workers are committed to the organization. And our customers sleep better at night when they have us as their supplier–partner.

I read your convocation speech and you talked about leadership. You talk about "caring with your heart, concentrating your heart, relaxing your heart, and opening your heart." Can you talk a little bit about how these principles have guided you in your leadership career?

I am touched you read my convocation speech! The main theme that I built on was "doing things with your heart" in one's career, one's occupation, one's business, and, indeed, one's life. I made four points all based on the word "heart" in Chinese. First, "care with your heart" means caring about the impact of what you do on people, your colleagues, staff, the environment, and society. Have a set of values to care for and pursue. Second, we hear a lot about the need to concentrate. "Concentrate your heart" denotes focus, discipline, not getting distracted. Take up the information, anticipate, act, and apply your skills to achieve the best possible results. Third, "relax your heart." Relax does not suggest that we should just be laid back. It means that we should not be timid in whatever we do. It means not being negative or insecure. Instead of worrying, be bold in order to try new things and to effect change. Last, but not least, always strive to "open your heart," which means be happy and have fun! *I believe having fun in whatever you do is essential for your success and for your wellbeing. We should feel good about the opportunities we are given, the challenges we encounter, and our achievements, big or small.*

For you, what is the key to good leadership?

In China today, it is still common in formal meetings with government or corporate leaders for subordinates to ask: "Leader, what instructions do you have for us today?" This line probably originated from the military during official parades. To me, this is not what leadership means. *If leadership is simply giving instructions, then you will not get the best out of people, nor give them true satisfaction. People just become executing agents—like machines or robots.* The two words that mean "leadership" in Chinese do not translate into "giving instructions." The first word is "*Ling,*" which conveys the setting of a direction, vision, or goal. The second word is "*Dao.*" *Dao* does not mean instruct. It means guidance. It means support. So, the essence of leadership consists of the setting of a vision or direction, followed by guidance and support. This forms a virtuous circle. For the team, if there is no direction, they can easily get lost. If there is no vision, then how does one measure the results? As for guidance or support, leaders should not spell out step by step how the subordinates should carry out their jobs. To give a simple anecdote, I certainly don't instruct my team how to stitch a shirt: They know far better than I do!

What have you personally experienced as a barrier to learning and how have you tried to overcome this barrier?

I am, by nature, an impatient person. I am demanding on myself, always chasing things, wanting to do and accomplish things. Hence, I expect and demand that from my colleagues and staff. Over time, I have learned to size up the situation and evaluate people to get the best out of them. This means that, in some cases, I have to be more patient. People are not all alike. There are some who respond well to the pressures I put on them. There are others whom I have to allow more tolerance in order to perform well. I know I am more patient now than when I was a young executive. One thing I would say, though, is that, no matter what, I don't let up on myself very much. I always demand the most from myself. That is not to say I suffer though. I get the satisfaction when the job is done. I can relax. And I sleep well at night while handling all the pressures from the job during the day.

You talked about the importance of remaining humble. How do you stay true to yourself? How do you remain humble? We learned from the financial crisis that there were leaders who had lost that sense of humility.

It is not hard to stay humble when one looks at the big picture. I consider myself very fortunate to have a job that I enjoy. I am supported by a visionary chairman. I have a good team: The team members are the people who are making things happen—day by day. I am privileged to work with such a team. I am fortunate that, together, we have been able to generate amazing results. The last thing I want to do is gloat. If I were to lavish praise, I would lavish it on the staff. In return, to be honest, I hope that they would say, "Hey, John, you treat us well, you support and encourage us." These are things that I am supposed to do, and I enjoy having the chance to do them. I guess I can say that I am proud, but not arrogant.

Good leaders learn. They mature. How has your leadership evolved over time? What changes or adjustments have you made in your leadership?

I would like to illustrate this by using the example of different vintages of wine. Consider a bottle of young Bordeaux red wine, one that just came out—it is strong with tannin; it is pushy; it wants you to notice it by rushing its fruity smells and tastes through your nose and your palate. Now, take a vintage Bordeaux red, perhaps a 1961 or 1982—that wine has matured . . . it has that sublime quality. The different fruits and flavors have blended together, have become more subtle yet balanced and elegant. The young executive tends to be more aggressive. This might be a reflection of his or her insecurity. Wanting to impress. Needing to impress. Wanting to get ahead on a fast track. I think we all went through that.

People are not all alike. If you apply the same standard of performance and measurement, then there will be many staff members who won't cut it. So, give people some allowance. Coach them and help them achieve their potential. We should not ignore incompetence or misbehavior. But we all have examples of where people do not quite measure up and we coach them. Help them rebuild their confidence. Some people blossom later on. People grow—they are not static.

What was the best leadership advice you ever received that helped you develop into a better leader?

I will go back to the more philosophical line to say we all live and strive for meaning. If we make our own lives and our work meaningful, and provide meaning to others so that they can live and work meaningfully, then I think we have got true leadership.

We also must have a sense of humor. Try to "open your heart" and make the work fun. I know that is a tall order, but, if there is no fun, then the work becomes a chore. We should remind ourselves that we are not perfect and should be able to laugh at our own mistakes. This also means we will be more tolerant of others.

Last night, I had a great dinner with our sales team. We celebrated the fact that we had a strong third quarter. We washed down the food with some nice wine.

I have a second job title at Esquel: Aside from being its CEO, I am also Esquel's "CFBO," which stands for "chief food and beverage officer". Cheers!

Leadership Themes

- The leader should have some trepidation rather than behaving like a super-star who thinks: "I can do it all; you listen to me, follow my orders and you will do well!"
- I think the common challenge for leaders is how to relate to people, understand people and then give them support and general guidance. Not instructions to do this or to do that.

18

Learn to Accept Accountability and the Consequences of Failure: Leadership and Accountability Are Inseparable

Michael McCain

Michael, when did you first realize you were a leader, and what happened to make you realize it?

That's a very difficult question to answer. I don't necessarily view leadership as an event, hierarchy, or position. Leadership is not about the stripes on your shoulder. Leadership is not about the location of your office or the size of your paycheck. To me, leadership is more of an attitude. Leadership is an attitude that engenders followership. People can demonstrate leadership of some form in all walks of life. And I think people are predisposed to do that. I've always had a desire to accomplish things in my life, have an impact, and do interesting things with people. Hence, I have tried to practice leadership.

I certainly had good role models in leadership. I have been involved in the family business from the day I could walk. I had a good relationship with my father, who was an extraordinary leader.

You indicated you always had a desire to have an impact and to do things. Where did that come from?

These things are always a combination of nature and nurture. It's almost impossible to dissect the nature and nurture components of leadership. I don't know that there's any clear answer as to which is the root source of the desire to have an impact in your life.

What have been the formative influences on you as a leader? What did people do to help you? What experiences did you learn the most from? Was there any particular experience that supercharged your learning to lead?

Leadership is a journey. It's not a single experience. It's an evolutionary process that starts with a desire—the passion to have an impact. I look back on my own journey of leadership and there are countless touch points. There are dozens of people who have played an extraordinary role in my life and in terms of my learning—all contributed in different ways.

Educational experiences are also critical. But these experiences don't necessarily take place in the classroom. There are critical experiences in all kinds of settings—both personal and professional. I also think great leaders mature and learn the most from their failures—more so than they do from their successes. For example, at an early age, I probably had more hubris and cockiness than I undoubtedly should have had around leadership, ambition, and goals. I think those things are healthy, but you need to learn to keep them in check.

I believe there is a tremendous cocktail of influences that occurs over a lifetime and coalesces into a leadership model, a belief system around what constitutes leadership for you as an individual. You recognize very clearly that there is no blueprint for leadership. There are tens of thousands of articles and books written on the subject of leadership. People have so many different points of view and none of them are wrong—they are just different. Great leaders have their own views of what is right or wrong—and they live by those beliefs. For each of us, there is a leadership model that emerges out of the thousands of points of light, and, hopefully, it coalesces into something that's successful.

What does your personal leadership model look like?

First, leadership is an attitude, not a level on an organizational chart. This attitude is reflected in everyday behaviors. And these behaviors yield committed followership. Second, leaders demonstrate passion. They care deeply about the things that are important to them, act on what they care about, overcome any obstacles to succeed, and are fundamentally optimistic people. Third, great leaders have an impact on others. Leaders have emotional intelligence; serve their people; are great communicators; have energy and the ability to energize others; respect and gain respect; and are driven by an internal ego, but not demonstrated ego. And fourth, leaders deliver results. They are decisive and incisive; and have the skills of execution, beginning with the end in mind.

You referred to your educational experience. You are a graduate of the Ivey Business School. What was the impact of your education on your learning to lead?

I think all of the business schools will probably do an equally good job of imparting the tools of business. The tools in, say, accounting, finance, operations management, marketing, and so forth are relatively well known. I also believe these tools are relatively easy to impart in a sort of commodity way. I think three things differentiate the Ivey experience and are what I took away from my experience. First, the teaching method at Ivey is clearly focused on the decision-making process. You focus on both the mental and emotional processes of making a decision. You are put into situations where you have to make a decision with either too many facts or not enough facts, and a paradox or situational dilemma attached to that. You learn to develop judgment. All of these elements of the decision-making process—and the urgency of just making a decision—seem very trite, but it's very real in terms of the teaching experience at Ivey. Second, you will acquire tremendous communication skills going through the Ivey experience. Those who immerse themselves in the experience learn the art form of dialogue and debate associated with the case discussion in the classroom setting. Furthermore, when I went through the program, the instructors put a heavy weight on your writing skills, and that was really developmental for me. So, two insights: learning the importance of communicating your ideas, and the fact that, if you have an idea that seems so profound in your own mind, it is really worthless unless you communicate it well. And, third, you develop a strong network. Several people from my graduating class are still friends and colleagues today. The network is an extraordinary source of strength—both personally and professionally—through an entire lifetime. So, these are the three takeaways above and beyond the tools of the business. And learning the tools is a layer you can probably get anywhere in any business school.

You talked about your father and the fact that he was very important in your development as a leader. You must have learned countless leadership lessons from him. What was the most profound lesson that helped you become a better leader?

It would be very hard to pinpoint one specific lesson. Of all the mentors I have had in my life, my father was certainly the leader of the pack. He was an extraordinary man in so many different ways. I loved him dearly and learned a tremendous amount from him. He allowed me to be different—we were certainly not the same in many dimensions of our leadership. I valued that as much as he did actually. We used to talk regularly about those points of difference.

I was exposed to the family business and talked about the business from a very early age—as early as I can remember. Business was discussed around the dinner table. We visited the plants as soon as I was able to walk.

The attributes that I valued the most in him, and tried to emulate as much as I could, were his action orientation and decisiveness. He was on top of every little detail in the business. He was the most persevering of action-oriented leaders. He would smash right through the brick wall in front of him. So, I got an appreciation of his action orientation, decisiveness, and just getting things done. He was a doer—not so much a talker. I also learned he was an incredibly talented relationship builder. He was a people person. He had tremendous skills to connect with people from all walks of life.

My father always maintained a balance in his personal and professional life. I learned as much about being a leader as being a great father from him. I learned about the importance of maintaining an appropriate perspective in life—to understand what is truly important in life and that the business is just part of your journey in life. I could go on and on, but those are some key lessons I learned from my father.

You also talked about failures, and that good leaders learn from their mistakes. Can you talk about a mistake you made as a leader and what you learned from that mistake?

Our family experienced a seismic event in a very public way. As you know, family and business often collide, and, in the early 1990s, it exploded in a public setting.

I think I was a key protagonist in that. I look back on that period in my life and I am not proud of my behavior. The event was, to a large extent, a family failure; but, more importantly, it was a personal failure as well. *One curse of youth is that, sometimes, you don't necessarily value the emotional intelligence of leadership. This dimension of leadership evolves over time. I probably didn't value emotional intelligence as much as I should have, or put as much effort as I should have into understanding the importance of relationships in both family and business.* But, in the end, you consider the failure and then you learn from it. This event offered profound leadership lessons. But I should remind you that this failure was just one of dozens. There were more failures than I can count—and every one of them is a source of learning.

You started your career in the business in the sales department and you then became the president of McCain Citrus, CEO of McCain Foods USA, and then returned to Canada as COO and eventually CEO of Maple Leaf Foods. As you transitioned to more and more senior roles, what were some of the challenges you faced, and how did you overcome them?

I was blessed with some great experiences when I was in my pre-20s. I was exposed to the business. I started on a construction crew, tarring a roof. I started at the lowest level and this helped me to understand the importance of people. And then, post graduation, I had several functional experiences: sales, marketing, and a stint in information technology.

I was sent to the USA to run a business. We had an $80 million book of business and nobody to run it. We had to quickly assemble an organizational team to run this business from scratch. We discovered the business was fraudulently misrepresented. Needless to say, I found myself, very early on, in the middle of a transformative, bottom-up restructuring. These kinds of experiences are certainly interesting and instructive. For one, I learned about industry structure and conduct, as we had to embark on something of a roll-up strategy in order to create some degree of success in that particular business.

I came back to the Maple Leaf Foods organization when we acquired it in 1995. The business was on the precipice of demise. The financial results were in dire straits. We engaged in crisis restructuring to salvage the future of the business. Again, that was interesting and instructive in terms of learning to lead change. And then, throughout the Maple Leaf Foods journey, there have been different chapters of that evolution as we've tried to build a successful business.

The big learning is that building a great company takes a lot of time—you can't build a great company in a short length of time. It's more luck than good management when that occurs. Thus, we've taken our time and dealt with lots of obstacles. We've had extraordinary obstacles to overcome and I'm very proud of my team in dealing with those obstacles and setbacks.

I have been involved in turning around troubled businesses or difficult situations, as opposed to managing the status quo. I have often said, jokingly, that I am not sure if those types of situations attract me or I attract them. The element of leadership through change has probably been one of the more dominant themes of my time.

You said you've often found yourself in turnaround situations. This requires a great amount of resilience. How did you develop resilience over the years?
The stresses of life are not necessarily those associated with leadership in a professional context. There are lots of personal and professional obstacles that life will dish out to any of us at any time. And developing resilience as a skill set is important in life. I believe resilience is an important dimension to personal happiness going through life. I don't know whether there is an instructor's manual on how to accomplish that. But I do know there are different paths for different people at different times in their lives.

I think some people will develop resilience just by having confidence they will do their very best and be comfortable with the outcome. People do what they feel is principled under the given circumstances, and accept that whatever happens, happens. My father was a huge advocate of that. You behave according to your principles or deeply held convictions. You work hard and do the very best you can. You do your best to manage the downside as best you can. When it's all done, whatever happens, happens. If you have your health, you move on—you take care of that first and everything else doesn't really matter. You develop a certain amount of tranquility.

Resilience in life goes well beyond the professional elements, which, at times, are the easiest with which to deal. Take life challenges such as facing a terminal illness or having a death in the family—these are the most stressful events. The need for resilience is so much more important in those types of situations, and things such as faith or your intimate personal relationships can help get you through.

What were some of the hardest things for you to learn in becoming a good or an even better leader?
I think the most important thing people learn, or should learn, in leadership is that you start at a very young age with this extraordinary confidence in your intellectual capacity and business-related skills. I gave a talk at Ivey to the undergraduate students a couple of years ago. I used a David Letterman-style list of the "top ten things" you'll never learn at Ivey, but need to know about leadership. The list contains imperatives people need to develop; and these imperatives are mostly rooted in your emotional intelligence rather than your intellectual intelligence. You learn, over time, that those emotional intelligence components are infinitely more valuable to you than any measure of your intellectual capacity in your leadership journey. There are many layers to that evolution of your emotional intelligence. And I do not believe these layers can be taught. They're like wine that needs to age—they mature with successes and failures, your personal and business interactions, mentoring, and so forth. All of the very intricate components of that emotional intelligence layer in your leadership develop over a period of time

and at various paces according to your experiences. That's the "secret sauce" of leadership.

Can you share some of the items that were on the list?

Certainly, number one is that emotional intelligence is more important than your intellectual capacity. Other items on the list are things such as followership is more important than leadership; your passion is more important than your intellect; people who are humble are usually confident, whereas people who are cocky lack confidence; your success is not about you—it is about the people around you; and your success is about knowing what you stand for and what you don't.

"Followership is more important than leadership"—explain that to me please?

The essence of leadership is to gain followership. It is to impact people in a way so they follow the leader in a willing, constructive, enthusiastic, compassionate, and collaborative way. So, the statement is not about what leaders purportedly do; it really is about the ability to gain the followership of the people you purport to lead, towards the goals of a specific result.

We ask leaders to make decisions in high-stakes situations. We want leaders to be visible and we expect them to be accountable. But leaders often have to make decisions with imperfect and, at times, incomplete information.

At times? Always! If you wait for all the information you think you need, you'll either never make a decision or you'll be too late.

I agree. So, how did you develop the confidence and comfort in making decisions in ambiguous situations and, in essence, put your leadership on the line?

I don't know the answer to that. I think that is one of the things Ivey does best. As I mentioned earlier, through the case method, the instructors put you in a position of internalizing the importance of making a decision. You learn to address the ambiguities and paradoxes embedded in the decision-making process. So, that's the layer that an educational experience brings. But that still doesn't necessarily make you comfortable in the stretch zone. Because I've spent most of my time in difficult, turnaround situations, I've developed a certain amount of tranquility and think, "That's just the way it is." You know you have to make those difficult calls. And, certainly, some are more difficult than others.

We have what we describe as a values-based leadership model at Maple Leaf Foods. That values-based leadership model is quite explicit about the desirable, acceptable behaviors attached to our leadership beliefs. The leadership model spells out the normative behaviors people are expected to demonstrate inside the Maple Leaf Foods organization. I do not profess to know the holy grail of leadership. But the model spells out the behaviors that work for us. And, because we've spent so much time being explicit about our values-based leadership model, it does make the decision-making process pretty clear. We have a clear decision-making architecture, if you will—a values-based architecture. We have been in some stressful crisis situations and it's really astounding how—if you just bring things back to what the core values of the organization are—the necessary decisions become pretty clear pretty quickly. But, beyond that, it is hard to articulate what contributes to my comfort or discomfort with decision making in ambiguous situations.

I would like to push on that a little further. Take the value of "dare to be transparent." We would like to see more of that in our leaders—to be transparent and visible when the situation demands it. You lived that value during the listeriosis crisis. Other leaders have failed to live up to that value.

Again, it's a cocktail of personal experiences that helped shape my values over a period of time and, eventually, into a blueprint that 20,000 people in our organization aligned around. Take transparency as an example—this is very much the DNA of my father. He was one of the most transparent people. You never doubted what was on his mind. Never! He wore every emotion he ever felt on his shirtsleeve. He told you exactly, to a fault maybe, what was on his mind. He was genetically hard-wired to behave that way. He couldn't behave any other way. It was just not possible for him to be anything but transparent. I think I happen to be the same way—perhaps through genetics or through exposure to my father. I feel a lot more comfortable that way, actually. You take the good with the bad. I just find it a much more authentic space to be, whether you're in private or public. And, hence, transparency became a very clear part of our culture. We are very explicit that being transparent is essential to us in this organization.

When we crafted the language of our values, one of my colleagues suggested we put the word "dare" in front of it. This was a very explicit add—as we thought about it, we said that really makes a lot of sense because to be transparent requires a tremendous amount of courage. *Transparency feels authentic in the first instance, but it does, in many circumstances, require a fair amount of courage. Transparency has some risk attached to it. And, hence, we felt we should put the word "dare" in front of "transparency" to acknowledge that fact. The value of "dare to be transparent" has become a defining feature of our organization.* We're not necessarily perfect all the time, but it's a defining feature of our culture. And so, when we hit a crisis, we know we have to be true to our organizational values; and I think we were.

Leaders must be transparent and candid in critical conversations. What have you learned over the years to do this effectively?

Being candid and direct is core to our culture. It is one of the leadership values we've adopted in the organization. There are a number of tools that help to deliver on candor and directness.

The first is the belief you should be factually provocative, but personally respectful. You can debate and talk about facts, and even your own perspective or opinions interpreting those facts, but you should never personalize things. And you should never make somebody feel like things are personalized. I believe this is an incredibly useful architecture.

Second, you should act with candor and directness, but with an element of humility that is attached to your behavior. An example is the willingness to say, "This is my perspective. This is my opinion. This is what I see. But I could be wrong." You could demonstrate a simple acknowledgement of somebody else's perspective while you're being candid and direct about your own. Too often, we demonstrate an attitude that suggests, "You are an idiot for thinking this way. I'm right and you're wrong."

And third, always make sure you give people balanced feedback. Perspectives should be offered in balance. For example, there's always a positive, and, if you look into the positive, the recipient of the message will be much more willing to accept the candid and direct nature of the message if it is stressful or might breed conflict.

The final tool is probably how to deal with the defensiveness itself—inevitably, you're going to get defensiveness. Who amongst us is not defensive? We're all defensive at particular moments in time. So, dealing with the defensiveness that emerges as a result of our candor is an important skill as well. How do you deal with the defensiveness? One approach is to allow people to be defensive in the first instance. They may be defensive today, but accept the message tomorrow, when they have had a chance to think about it. But the main message, again, is that it is really about the tools that you wrap around your unwavering candor and directness.

Leaders learn to manage paradoxes. Leaders need to be optimistic and realistic. Confident and humble. Aggressive and patient. Intuitive and analytical. And so forth. How did you learn to manage those paradoxes in your leadership career?
Roger Martin wrote a book called *The Opposable Mind: How Successful Leaders Win Through Integrative Thinking* (Boston, MA: Harvard Business School Press, 2007). His thesis is you can resolve the tension in two diametrically opposing perspectives by forming an entirely new idea that is superior to either opposing perspective. He emphasizes that we need to learn to appreciate constructive tension. I agree with him. I think you need to show an appreciation for finding a balance in those paradoxes, and finding the "third path." We should learn to value those paradoxes and the necessary balance between the yin and yang of the leadership dimensions to which you referred. Find the right balance and with it an equal appreciation of both perspectives. I know that being uni-dimensional on any of those dimensions of leadership often is a huge liability.

Did you learn some of this the hard way?
Totally. I have been overly intuitive in the past. You learn that you should have known or discovered more about a problem through a more careful analysis. You

learn the value of a divergent perspective. A friend of mine, David Baum, has this wonderful little graphic he uses in some of his work. It shows a person who is abandoned on a remote island with a little palm tree. He is looking out and sees this other person in a rowboat heading towards land. The person on the island says, "Boat!" looking for rescue and the person in the boat says, "Land!" looking for security. And they are both right. It's just an illustration of perspective. I think valuing perspective is one of the emotional intelligence elements that develops over a period of time. As a leader, you have to learn to value perspective. You should be able to put yourself in somebody else's shoes. You should learn to look at a challenge from another angle. You should develop the discipline to look at something intuitively versus factually and vice versa. This, too, is probably difficult to teach in school. You have to go through experiences, and often you learn about the importance of perspective the hard way.

What have you personally experienced as a barrier to learning and how have you tried to overcome this barrier?

I think all of us have a change-resistance gene embedded in our psyche. We are human beings and, by nature, we are creatures of habit and, hence, have an element of change resistance. And while it exists in everyone, I think some people have a better ability to pierce through that or look beyond change than others. I think, sadly, sometimes experience can be a barrier to learning. You think you're so goddamned experienced that you don't need to learn anymore. The older or more experienced you get, the more you rely on pattern recognition. So, people may think, "I've seen that pattern or event before," "I know what is unfolding," "Don't mess with me . . . This is the answer," and, "This is the way to proceed." And that, of course, is totally inappropriate. It takes a conscious effort to break out of that loop and decide not to rely solely on your past experience.

I think intellect can be a barrier to learning. Some of the smartest people I know really have the biggest blocks around learning because they are overconfident in what they already know. They don't have the humility to learn. They are too proud to admit their ignorance.

Experience can be a barrier; intellect can be a barrier; and your change-resistance gene can be a barrier. But, if you have an innate desire to continue to learn, then, number one, you'll become a better leader and, number two, it will keep you younger. I personally think I am totally committed to the mindset that every day I'm going to wake up and learn something new. And, as soon as I don't, then it's probably time to call it quits. So, that will be my definition of age—real age is when you decide that you've stopped learning.

You talked about humility. How difficult has it been for you to stay true to yourself?

Not at all. I refuse to do anything but to stay true to myself. It's an absolute life conviction—I won't do anything but that.

I know you as a constant learner. What are you learning these days to become an even better leader? Are there any recent "aha" moments?

I think that, as you age, you learn to be more trusting and confident in the people around you. So, I think necessity is the mother of invention in that regard. As your responsibilities increase, you largely have to delegate a little bit more and so you become a lot more comfortable in the competence of the people around you. As I've aged, I think I've become much more comfortable and skilled to get out of the way so that people can perform. My role is to provide people with the tools to be successful.

As I mentioned before, learning is a journey. The good leaders have an acute self-awareness around their strengths and their developmental areas, as well as understanding their perennial developmental needs. You work to refine your skills over a long period of time.

What has been your most rewarding experience as a leader and why?

I'll give you two things. First, the most important thing to me is that I have five children, of which I am extraordinarily proud. I collaborated with their mother to support, nurture, develop, and guide my children and do all those important things that parents do. We raised five amazing people, each unique. I have no doubt that, when I look back on my life and career, I'll say that's the real legacy of my life. I've always said running a business such as we have—Maple Leaf Foods has C\$5 billion in revenue and 20,000 people in the organization—is an absolute piece of cake relative to the challenges of parenting.

Second, and probably a distant second, we've accomplished some great things in the Maple Leaf Foods organization. Our financial results were a little disappointing for a period of time as we persevered through some pretty extraordinary challenges in our history, but we got through that and now have a blueprint to deliver great results. We persevered through those obstacles and have that blueprint largely because, over the last 15 years, we've created the DNA of a great organization populated by amazing people who have a passion for the business. They have incredible competencies. And we're doing some really great things to make a difference in the Canadian food industry, society, and the communities in which we live and work. We work to solidify the long-term future of our business. We feel great about these achievements. This is a source of pride for me and all my colleagues. I'm most proud that I had the opportunity to work with some amazing people in my life and here in this organization.

What advice do you have for people as they embark on their journey of learning to lead?

It would be largely to have a clear view of what your own leadership model is. *I can describe in some granularity what our collective leadership model is. Our model, of course, is not the only path to success. But, individuals who aspire to lead must articulate a very clear view as to their own leadership models and why they will be successful for them. And we should always keep in mind that the greater purpose of leadership is to create followership and have a positive impact—that is, deliver a winning result.*

I would like to conclude with five thoughts. First, lead from your heart, not your head or your hands—it's the only way to know what is right for you. Second, show vulnerability; it makes you real—people respond to authenticity. Third, learn to accept accountability and the consequences of failure. Ultimately, leadership and accountability are inseparable. Fourth: do, don't talk. Many leaders talk a good game. It takes courage to act on what you say and believe. And, fifth, as I mentioned earlier, leadership really is about followership; it is not about you. No one can lead except by getting others to follow.

Leadership Themes

- Individuals who aspire to lead must articulate a very clear view as to their leadership model and why it will be successful for them.
- One curse of youth is that sometimes you don't necessarily value the emotional intelligence of leadership. This dimension of leadership evolves over time.
- The good leaders have an acute self-awareness around their strengths and their developmental areas, as well as understanding their perennial developmental needs.
- The essence of leadership is to gain followership; to impact people in a way so they follow the leader in a willing, constructive, enthusiastic, compassionate, and collaborative way.
- Intellect can be a barrier to learning. People may be overconfident in what they already know.

19

People That Mind Don't Matter and People That Matter Don't Mind

Kiran Mazumdar-Shaw

Kiran, when did you first realize you were a leader, and what happened to make you realize it?

As you know, I started Biocon on my own. I was leading the way, but was not really conscious that I was a path breaker. I was just very self-assured as a person, as I knew I was doing something different. I knew it wasn't going to be easy. I knew that it was going to be a long struggle. But I was willing to take on the challenge. I think that's what eventually gave me the ability to lead from the front. Leadership is not about realizing that you are a leader. It's about your ability to make decisions with limited and imperfect information. *I have learned that leadership is about the willingness to fail, and to pick yourself up and move ahead. I was willing to do all of this right from the time that I started my business.* I was leading, but I didn't look at myself as a leader. My main focus was on who is going to share my excitement about what I am doing? I managed to get a few people to share that excitement, and to join me in the journey to build a pioneering Indian biotech enterprise and make a big difference.

It's only when I started forming an organization of about 50 people, and developing a structure, that I started realizing that I had to play a leadership role as well. I think there's a difference between recognizing yourself as a leader and playing a leadership role. I felt, in my early years, I started playing the leadership role because I had to. I realized I had to make tough decisions. I realized that, when things didn't work out, I had to solve problems. That's when I realized I had to play a leadership role; otherwise, my company wouldn't evolve.

When you founded Biocon in 1978, you had your youth—you were 25 years old—and gender work against you. You founded the business on an untested business model. I imagine you had many doubts during those first few years. How did you build your credibility?

I felt that I had to show that I was capable of demonstrating my abilities. Yes, I had several credibility challenges. And my behaviors and actions were about countering those challenges. I had to prove to the people that, just because I was a woman, just because I was 25 years of age, and just because my business model was unique, that should not put me at a disadvantage. That was the first thing I wanted to prove to people. I started by focusing on my technology and the products I was trying to develop. I did not have a technology barrier. I could actually go to industry and have a one-on-one conversation with the customer on a technology plane. That gave me a lot of confidence that I could convince people that what I was developing was quite interesting. The second challenge was to have bankers accept me as a financially credible businessperson. I had a number of failures along the way, but the moment I succeeded by convincing one banker to offer me a loan, I felt I had overcome that challenge. I had been able to convince this person that Biocon was a worthwhile business to back. Others soon followed. The first two years of my business life were spent creating credibility and a belief that what I was trying to do was worthwhile. I think I went through a number of failures in doing that, but I carried on.

What have been the formative influences on you as a leader? What experiences did you learn the most from?

I certainly believe that, when I got into this business, I realized that I was doing something different from what anyone else was doing. Because I was doing something so different, I realized that a differentiated business model actually gives you an advantage. It's one thing I learned along the way. I think it's important to pursue differentiation as a business strategy. Even today, every time I get into a new business, I make sure the business strategy is about differentiation. I don't want to be a "me too." I am a path breaker—that has always been my guiding force, to do things differently. Don't be one of the pack. People should follow you, you should not follow people. That has been my style. Why do I get noticed? Why am I always singled out as an example in innovation? Because Biocon is different. We deliberately committed to differentiation as a business strategy.

The second big lesson I've learned is how to deal with failure. I know everybody talks about failure in leadership. This is a cliché, but, if you don't go through an experience of failure, you don't really develop strong leadership qualities. What is your role as a leader? I believe the role of a leader is to carry people with you, saying: "We may have failed, but I believe we can solve this problem; we can move ahead. Failure doesn't deter us; it shouldn't stop us." *I've always used this phrase: "Failure is temporary, giving up is permanent." Don't give up. Even if you fail, you should pick yourself up and learn from that failure and move on.* That's been my style. I've failed a lot. Failure is an integral part of innovation. You must learn to deal with failure. For example, we are trying to develop the world's first oral insulin. That process is, and continues to be, a challenge. We fail a lot, but we learn along the way. Innovation is an endurance test. It is a learning process that challenges you all the time. It's not predictable. It is a process that will make you learn in a very difficult way, but you must be willing to do that. Mastering leadership is the same.

How do you lead at Biocon?

I am an open person. I am like a sponge: I absorb a lot. I like to hire people who are smarter than me. I think that is very important in this particular business. There are two styles of leadership. There are leaders who want to command and control. The other kind of leader focuses on collaboration and empowering people. I like to do the latter. I don't like to command and control. I like to empower people, I like to delegate. I like people to learn how to make decisions.

You stated that the leader must be able to inspire individuals.

I like to spend a lot of time with my people. I like to get people to feel that I am engaged and that I know exactly what they are doing. If you're on top of things, and you know about the challenges that people face in the innovation process, then people know that you're engaged. That's another way of inspiring people—showing that you are informed.

I don't inspire people by just patting them on the back. I hold meetings with my various teams, which keep me up to date. In these meetings, I make it a point to appreciate and encourage good work.

Our company is structured into verticals. I have quarterly business vertical meetings where I meet with all the key people in that vertical and I understand what's going on. I like people to focus on problems. I don't want to keep focusing on the great things we've done. I used to see a lot of presentations where people would be boasting about all the great things they had done. I said, "I don't want to see all the great things you're doing because I can see that all the time. Have you been smart enough to identify our challenges and ways to address those challenges?" That, to me, makes good leadership. That's how I'm trying to develop people, through setting up challenges and coaching them to address those challenges. I don't want to get accolades for all the good things we're doing. I judge myself as being a good leader if I know about the challenges and problems and what change of course or corrections we need to make.

I think people get really inspired by my approach because they develop leadership skills; and, when they solve problems, it makes them very confident. I inspire confidence in people. That is my strength.

Forbes listed you among the "World's 100 Most Powerful Women." *TIME* magazine included you on their list of "100 Most Influential People in the World." You have received numerous other accolades. How do you stay grounded?

That's a very important question. My husband keeps me grounded. And he always reminds me of a very important saying, and I keep using that saying a lot: "People that mind don't matter and people that matter don't mind." I'll just explain that to you. When you are a celebrity, when you're a person who is very well known, you almost expect to be treated a certain way. And when you're not treated a certain way you get . . . uppity. That's not a good trait. You're demeaning yourself. Whereas, if you're humble, and you are not expecting to be treated in a special way, but just give your best, you end up getting recognized, even though you are not doing things because you want to be recognized. I don't think any of us on the *Forbes* list are doing things because we want to be recognized. We are recognized because of what we are doing. I feel that, if you are being recognized for what you are doing, you should be secure enough not to mind trivial things. People who make the list and who are insecure tend not to be humble. *I just want to do the things I do because I want to make a difference. I think I want to do something in my lifetime that I can be remembered for. I shouldn't bother about trivial things.* I must be humble because, after all, I am what I am, not because of myself. I am what I am because of a set of circumstances; because of the people who have joined me and helped me in realizing all these things. And if I really believe that it's all because of me, then there's something wrong with me.

Your father taught you the importance of meritocracy. I read that he didn't want to give you the money to get into medical school. You had to earn it. That must have been a hard lesson. Can you talk about leadership and how you had to earn it?

I always tell people you earn respect. You don't just demand it. That was a lesson that my father taught me a long time ago. He said, "If you can't get into medical school through meritocracy, then you don't deserve to go to medical school. If you really want to go to medical school, then work hard. You'll get into medical school through merit. If not, do something else." *I will carry this lesson with me for the rest of my life, because he taught me a very important value in life: "Don't pay your way through life. It's only through hard work that you will achieve things."* I see people buying their way through life and I think that's wrong. I will never do that. So that is why I am so concerned about corruption in this country. I am so concerned about greed in this world. People really feel that they can buy their way through life, and, unfortunately, people look up to people with this amassed wealth. Nobody questions how you got that wealth.

What is your purpose in life? To become rich or to create something that is of value? I have created Biocon with my bare hands. I am proud of that. I have created value and wealth came with that. I always tell people that, when you want to create value, wealth will automatically be a part of that value. But, if you want to just create wealth, then you may not create value. There are different ways in which you can amass wealth.

You are a self-taught entrepreneur. What leadership advice would you give to young entrepreneurs to become better leaders?

First and foremost, I always tell young entrepreneurs that there are no shortcuts to success. Everyone is in a hurry to succeed. I keep telling young people, "Don't be in a hurry to succeed, because there is a certain path or course you have to go through. You have to spend five years of your life working hard. And success comes with material sacrifice." I also tell young entrepreneurs that it is okay to make mistakes. But we should learn from our failures. Only then can you become a sustainable entrepreneur. If you are too much in a hurry to succeed, you may succeed—no one says you can't. But you may give up easily at the first failure. Or at the first exit opportunity that will not allow you to develop your company even further. I find that this is happening today. In this haste to make money, young people who are doing something really smart in their start-up companies are willing to just give up on that smart idea by giving it to the first person who comes along and says, "This is a smart idea—I will buy you out." You may feel great and think, "Someone is giving me $10 million for just an idea." But you don't realize that, by just developing that idea to another level, that $10 million would have been worth $100 million. So don't be in such a hurry.

I also believe that I am one of those old-fashioned entrepreneurs. I'm not looking for an exit. I'm looking to build an enduring company. Why would I just blow up everything and exit in one big swoop? I wouldn't. So, that's another side of me where I feel that I may be old fashioned because, after a point in time, money should not matter. I always tell people, "What if I'm offered billions of dollars for my company? What am I going to do with those billions of dollars?" First and foremost, I should do something very important with it in this lifetime, because, after I'm dead, what value has that money? And am I sure that the people who I'm entrusting the money to will know what to do with it? So, that's why I believe a lot in philanthropy. I should make a difference in this lifetime. And I actually have a big problem with people who don't give back to their community. *I always quote Indian scriptures as they have some powerful sayings. For example, the scriptures indicate: "Wealth and knowledge if not shared are useless." If you don't share your knowledge, but just keep it to yourself, it's a waste! The world will not know of the good insights you have.* In the same way, if you just hold onto your wealth and don't share it, again, what good is that? Philanthropy is about investing in your future. Maybe you won't be there to enjoy it, but you are investing in the future of your own community. Why did I build the cancer hospital next door? Because I felt that a city of this size—Bangalore—didn't have a good cancer hospital. Cancer treatment is expensive. So I said, "Can't we do something about that?" Nobody was willing to do anything and, hence, I said, "I will do it." I'm doing it for the future of my community and the hospital is already making a difference. I'm glad people are benefiting from it.

Has your learning to lead been influenced by other individuals?

I've always looked up to a number of people. I'm always inspired by people who are doing things differently. Who are change makers? Who are the path breakers? Who is daring enough to do something inventive? I remember my first mentor—Mr. Vaghul. He used to be with the ICICI Bank. He was the one who invested in my first research project. Nobody would touch it because it was seen as a project with a very high risk. I knew him as a man with a strong set of values and principles.

He is also the one who hired numerous women in leadership positions at ICICI. And, as a result of that, these women have a significant influence in the Indian banking sector today.

I really looked up to my father. He was so different. He was the chief brewmaster at United Breweries Ltd. I remember that, as a young child, I used to think that it was not a good thing to be the daughter of someone who works in the alcohol industry. I had the idea that a brewmaster must be drunk all the time and that he encourages other people to drink alcohol. *My father taught me to never, ever look down upon any profession. Every profession is a very worthy profession. He taught me that it is important how we conduct ourselves in life, and add value.* My father was someone who believed in moderation. He always said beer is a very healthy drink. He used to do a great job of selling his product. And he explained to me that you need a lot of scientific skill to make beer. My dad was the one who made me excited about biotechnology.

Another person who really inspired me was Narayana Murthy, one of the co-founders of Infosys. He was a person of my time. Infosys was founded in the 1980s. We were trying to change India, so it was a very exciting time. I work very closely with Dr. Devi Shetty of Narayana Hrudayalaya Health City, Bangalore. He has brought in a lot of change into the health-care model.

Every time I meet people who are doing things in a very different way, they inspire me. I used to read a lot about Jack Welch of General Electric and Steve Jobs of Apple. Each one of these individuals inspired me in different ways.

How did Jack Welch inspire you?
Jack Welch came up with the concept of the boundary-less organization. I built my company on that principle. Percy Barnevik from ABB believed in the same principle. I was looking for ways to let ideas flow and have people collaborate with one another. This tends to be a problem in most organizations. We put people in boxes and they never speak to each other. So the concept of the boundary-less organization inspired me a lot, and that's what I want to do in my organization.

I see what excites you about leadership. Is there anything that you fear about the role of leadership?
I think the biggest fear I have is that once you have become successful and enter the spotlight, any little wrongdoing is magnified. People can pull you down really fast. One little wrong step and you will be crucified. For example, look at what happened to Fareed Zakaria. I think he is a wonderful writer. He is fearless when he expresses his opinions. He made a mistake by lifting a passage from an article in the *New Yorker*. He did not credit the writer. It was plagiarism. But this could happen to anyone. He has apologized and I think he has realized what a serious error he made. But you shouldn't crucify a person for that. Look at all the good things he's done.

I remember Jack Welch and one of his quotes: "The higher the monkey climbs, the more his ass is exposed."
It's true, and that's what I'm saying. The bigger the leader you are, the less you can afford to have faults. You almost have to be this ideal person . . . this perfect human being . . . which you can't. You cannot be a perfect human being. You have to have flaws. The problem is that people are not willing to see those flaws in you. No matter how small they are. Then, they start sort of crucifying you for whatever you say.

I will give you an example. Last week, there was this mischievous social media fear mongering that led to ethnic violence. People from the northeast fled Bangalore after hate messages were spread through social media. There were threats that they would be killed if they stayed in the city. I made a public statement—I said that it is so sad seeing the northeastern people are getting so threatened. I said, in fact they are such hard workers, adding so much value to our economy in Bangalore. I added that these people are so disciplined and hardworking compared to our locals. Of course, I got a barrage of tweets. "How dare you say that!" "How can you say the locals are so bad?" Of course, I didn't say that the locals are bad. I just said that these people are more disciplined than the locals; and it's a fact. But, of course, this is my opinion and I expressed it. And this is what happens. People look up to you, and, the moment you voice an opinion that people do not agree with, they put you in the hot seat.

You lead Biocon. You sit on boards. You are involved in the business, medical, cultural, and educational sectors. I'm sure that you've seen talented people whose careers derailed. How do people with potential derail a promising leadership career?
I think the biggest enemy of anybody is insecurity. These insecurities are often unfounded fears. People have a fear of the unknown. They lose confidence. It could be because of a personal tragedy; it could be an emotional disappointment; or it could be a failure on some project. And I ask, "Why are you giving up? You are so capable." A lot of people ask me whether there was a time when I was thinking of giving up on something. The answer is "no."

My niece is at Stanford. She is doing her PhD in cancer immunology. She said to me, "I don't know whether I'm doing the right thing. Maybe I should do medicine." I said, "Why, Claire? You're in such a fascinating field and you're doing so well. You're a top-notch student. Why should you feel like that?" Then I realized her experiments were not going well. So, I told her, "No experiment will go like a dream. You must understand that not all your experiments will go well. But you shouldn't give up for that reason. Don't shift your focus so much and say, 'I'll do something else.' You're doing very well. Give yourself time."

And, sure enough, she sent me an email yesterday saying, "I'm so proud of you! You are on the *Forbes* 100 list again. You have climbed 19 spots. Big jump!" I called her and I said, "How is everything going?" She said, "Great. My experiments are going well. I'm enjoying my work. My qualifying exams for the PhD are in two weeks' time. I'm feeling really great." I said, "See? Don't give up so easily. This is what happens." And she said, "Thanks a lot for pushing me into that spot."

Leadership Themes

- Leadership is about the ability to make decisions with limited and imperfect information.
- Failure is temporary, giving up is permanent.
- Never, ever look down upon any profession. Every profession is a worthy profession.
- People must see that you are engaged as a leader. Show that you are informed about the challenges that people face.
- You develop people through setting challenging goals and coaching them to reach those goals.

20

I Always Felt That My Strongest Role Was as the Voice Whispering in Somebody's Ear

Michael Shindler

Michael, when did you first realize you were a leader, and what happened to make you realize it?

My parents referred to me as a "cocky kid." I guess cocky kids present self-assurance and try to take charge. But I don't think I truly realized I was a leader until I was going into the eleventh grade. I must have been 15 or 16 years old. I had just been elected to an office of a regional youth group. We had a camp every summer. A series of activities was organized each day. I remember taking the last jump into the swimming pool, even though we were a little behind schedule that day. As I got out of the swimming pool and reached for a towel, one of the rabbis took me aside and said, "Michael, you are a leader of this group. You need to set an example." That conversation always resonated with me. I realized then that being an officer put me in a position of leadership.

Many years later, when my children were away at camp or school, I closed all of my letters to them by saying, "Treat others the way you want to be treated." Not only did I tell my kids that, I tried to live it, too. Leaders need to set an example. The rabbi told me that when I was 15 years old. You need to show you care. Be straightforward. Be honest.

Did you want to be a leader?

I don't think I ever expressed a desire to be a leader. I started my own consulting company in 2007. I actually wrote a piece on my website saying I didn't start it because I had some overwhelming desire to be the president. Over time, things just evolved.

Perhaps you didn't give the topic of leadership a lot of thought. But you have been in various leadership positions. Where did the motivation to be at the forefront of action come from?

I have a very strong perspective on what I think is doing things the right way. I express that. I want things to be done right. Sometimes, I wear my emotions on my sleeve. To me, there is a very clear black and white; or right and wrong way.

I want my opinion heard. I think it is far more important for me to be heard than to be followed, so I accept that my recommendations are not necessarily followed. I recognize the corporate hierarchy says certain decisions get to be made by the CEO, even though I might not make those decisions. I have no problem with that. I have a problem when I have limited say about something that affects me.

What have been the formative influences on you as a leader? What did people do to help you?

First, and most important, I've been fortunate to have had people whom I consider to be my mentors. I finished my undergraduate degree, then law school, and went to a law firm. I identified with one person in particular. He was a partner. I was just a young associate. I looked up to him and sort of strived to be like him. I wasn't in his department; he was not my supervisor. We had an annual one-on-one lunch at the end of the year. He would give me guidance on where I was in the firm at that particular time. His approach consisted of warmth and guidance, mentorship, and communication. And that prevailed throughout the time I was practicing law at the firm, and even after I left the practice of law. He took an interest in me, not just as a lawyer in the firm, but also as a person. He was interested in how my career would advance. I left the law firm eventually and went to work for one of our clients. When I told him I was considering leaving, he asked me why. Our subsequent interaction made me think about what I was looking for in life. His mentoring was critical to me.

Second, over the past 30 years, I have held several jobs and this gave me an opportunity to observe the leadership at each. I was able to take experiences and compare different bosses and their leadership. I learned from those experiences and observations—small, bite-sized pieces. I try to teach my children that negative lessons sometimes are much more valuable than the positive ones. For example, everybody should get a pat on the back and be told they are appreciated. You quickly realize that every academic and corporate leader says you need to identify and recognize when people do good things. In fact, the opposite probably teaches us better lessons; that is, when the leader scapegoats employees or doesn't express gratitude. You realize you don't want to be that person, and try to distill that into a concrete leadership lesson. *These negative leaders helped me become a better leader because I don't want to be that person.* I've managed to learn from everybody, good and bad.

You talked about the importance of a mentor. Sometimes we get unsolicited advice from people or information that we don't want or expect to hear. Do you have an example of such unsolicited advice that helped develop you into a better leader?

I have been told to develop a better "poker face." As I said, sometimes I wear my emotions on my sleeve, and, all these years later, I haven't completely overcome that. I've gotten better at expressing my opinion when it needs to be expressed. The one lesson I wish I had learned earlier is that you fight the battles you can win. I'm getting better at it. But, even now, it's a challenge for me to figure out which battles to fight and which to not.

Was there any particular experience that supercharged your learning to lead?

I made a mistake taking the job I had before I set up my own consulting practice. I took that position for the wrong reasons. I was at the company for about four months when I realized my mistake. The substance of what I was doing was terrific. However, the milieu in which I was working didn't allow me to do what I did best. But, after four months, and considering my age then, one doesn't easily say, "I'm done." My wife and closest friends all said I really needed to play this one out. And then, six months later, I realized I couldn't play it out too much longer.

In business, you either have to learn to go along or you have to get out. *I realized it was time for me to move on, because, at the end of the day, you are only as good as your environment allows you to be.* That's not to deflect responsibility for my own performance, by any means.

I needed to plan my exit in a way that made sense for me. Upon talking to people, I realized I never had a burning desire to be in charge. I had always felt my strongest role was as the voice whispering in somebody's ear. In baseball terms, it's the bench coach. I don't think of myself as a visionary. However, I am very good at taking the little steps that need to be taken to get to the end goal. I always thought I could advise the person who has the big idea. And, so, I realized I could create a consulting practice where I could help people navigate through the world of the hotel business. I knew that business well, and it is a bit of an odd industry. It took me a few months to formulate my plan and line up a couple of clients so that I was able to pay some basic bills.

This event made me reflect on who I was and where I wanted to take my life. At the time, I realized I had another 10 or 15 years left in my career and I didn't want to feel I was in the wrong place. The event also encouraged me to write down some of my ideas about leadership, even though I had never run a business. I reached out to Aaron Nurick, a professor at Bentley University, Massachusetts. I wanted feedback on whether the things I observed in businesses and wrote about made sense. Aaron and I were friends and fraternity brothers in college. I knew he was exploring, from his academic perspective, many of the same issues, and I wanted to see if I was off base. Apparently, I was not.

You made a number of transitions. For example, you went from being a practicing lawyer, to a consultant, to being in a business role. You had to adjust the way you look at and feel about things. Can you talk about those transitions?

First, you have to learn to move outside the cocoon of being comfortable. For example, I needed to learn the hotel business. It was foreign to me. I did everything

I could to educate myself. I talked to people, I read books, I taught myself, I observed, and so forth. I learned to stretch myself. The industry that I have now chosen for my life's work is not rocket science. I don't have to operate on somebody's brain and make sure it is wired correctly. But, with each step, you have to stretch yourself a little bit to learn.

I learned an important lesson from these transitions: Always learn about your boss's job, your subordinates' jobs, the job of the person sitting next to you, the job of the person across the desk from you, and so forth. This is important because I believe it will make you a well-rounded person and you will understand where your job fits into the bigger organization. To be frank, the challenge at the time was not so much around whether I was the right person for the job. The issue was, really, could I learn fast enough what the job was all about? And this, of course, is an ongoing study.

This brings me to a second lesson. There are components of my job at Hard Rock that I may not have complete expertise for, even after almost three years here. Hence, I've hired people who know that particular area better than I do. I try to be a devil's advocate. I challenge them to articulate and build a foundation for the recommendations they make. The lawyer comes out in me—did we look at the issue from all sides? At the end of the day, if they can rationally and reasonably articulate about why they believe certain things to be true, then I'm going to allow that to go forward because they know it better than I do. I think you have to rely on them to do the right thing.

It is hard to give the team even more responsibility. You have to assess when the team is ready for the next step in its development. You don't always get to hire everyone on your team. Sometimes, you inherit people. I want to make sure that I push and stretch people to provide them with more skill sets because it's good for the company and it's good for their career paths. I cannot promise a complete career path in this company, but I can promise the building blocks of a successful career. I think, as a leader, I owe that to my team and the people that work for us. For example, if somebody gets transferred, or a spouse gets transferred, or somebody has to go, then I want the person that's working here to have a place to go. I think allowing people the latitude to think about a solution for themselves, and then supporting and challenging it, is a good thing. I think it's critical to personal growth and it's critical to team building and building leadership.

I have an interesting anecdote for you. I was running the domestic development team at Hyatt in the United States. The president had been my predecessor as the president of the development group and my predecessor as the general counsel. I literally followed him up the ladder. He named his managing committee, which consisted of our field operations and corporate people. We had a quarterly managing committee meeting where we talked about all the things affecting the company. I used to sit next to him. There was never a question about who was the smartest guy in the room—it was him. An issue would come up and he would start to express his view on it. I used to kick him under the table and it got to a point where he'd say, "Why are you kicking me?" I'd say, "If you tell people what you think, then they are all going to find a way to jump in line. Don't you want to get their opinions? Maybe we'll take the direction you're thinking, but at least let them express their opinions without you guiding them to the opinion you want to hear." He stopped doing that. I realized it's important to get people to express their perspectives before decisions get made.

I know you reflect on your leadership. You sent the following e-mail to your team after having read Aaron Nurick's book, *The Good Enough Manager* (New York, NY: Routledge, 2011):

Team—
As you can see, this e-mail is directed to virtually all members (direct and indirect) of the H&C team. I am sending this to ask a favor of each of you; it even comes with a present.
*   I recently completed reading "The Good Enough Manager" by Aaron Nurick, a professor of management and psychology at Bentley University in Boston. It resonated with me for several reasons, mostly because it addresses what it means to be a good leader and manager.*
*   Of late, I have been feeling that I may be letting you down in that regard. As I finished this book, I thought about seeking feedback from you—collectively, but individually—on my late feelings of being somewhat lax in my team leadership. Then, I realized that each of you, in turn, may be a leader of your own team or teams in the future, and you might benefit from reading the book, as well. So, here it is ([our EA] will be distributing the book).*
*   My request—I hesitate to make it an "assignment"—is that each of you should, upon reading the book, write down any thoughts you might have that might help me be a better manager and team leader. If that means highlighting areas where I am not doing sufficiently well at being "good enough" (or, I suppose, areas where I am), please do so.*
*   To address my hope that your comments are fully and completely anonymous, I have asked [our EA] to give each of you a pristine thumb drive. Write your comments—in bullet point format without regard and with no clue to your specific role or identity—and save them onto the thumb drive [USB drive]. We will set a place for you to leave the thumb drive with your comments and allow them to be intermingled, so that no one will know whose comments are which.*
*   I have asked [our EA] to assemble the comments for synthesis into one document, then I will set aside one or more of our Stand Up meetings to deal with your comments. I see this as a late September/early October exercise, and I would truly appreciate your help.*
*   This may be the last job in my career, so I want to do it right for its duration. Please help me out. In the meantime, you may get something out of the book, too.*
*   Many thanks.*

What did you learn from that experience and how are you trying to become a better leader using the feedback?
I am going to take you back in time before I address the question. I mentioned that I developed particular leadership observations over some time. I actually wrote about some of them when I had my own consulting firm. I also shared some of those observations with Aaron Nurick. He gave me a copy of this book. It is a 125-page monograph and somewhat academic, but not entirely so. Many of the things Aaron wrote about resonated with me. His observations were strictly from an academic point of view, but our thoughts converged in many places.

I started my own personal study of leadership in 2001. My mother-in-law gave me a biography of John Adams as a Father's Day present. I turned 50 that year. Before I started to read the biography, something clicked: I had never, as an adult, read a biography of George Washington. Why would I read a biography of the second president of the United States before I had read one of the first? I went out and found a biography of George Washington. I love American history. I was a political science major. I read the biography of Washington, moved on to read the biography of Adams, and then decided that, before I turned 60, I would read a biography of every president in order. I realized I was studying several things at the same time—my love of history, my love of politics, and a true study of leadership. How did each of these men rise to become president of the United States? I finished my study of presidents before my 57th birthday. I was reading four, five, six biographies a year. I was so fascinated by the contents of the biographies, the history retold, and the roads each man took to the presidency.

I occasionally go through periods of inward looking. I sat down and wrote the e-mail to my team. I sent the e-mail for two reasons. First, I wanted feedback on my leadership. *I wanted to make sure my team recognized that I was thinking about how I lead. More important, however, I wanted people to reflect on their own leadership. I wanted my team members to realize that, in three to five years, they may become leaders themselves, and not necessarily in this company.* What kind of leaders are they going to be? And so I wanted the book not only to be a reflection on me, but also to stimulate self-reflection. I didn't know my team's reading habits, so it helped that the book was a short read.

We sent out the book. People wrote down their observations. My assistant collected the thumb drives. The vice president of human resources transcribed the files. If she could tell who had written the comments, she cleansed the materials. She put together a report on what she called my "successes" and my "opportunities." We addressed the feedback in a weekly staff meeting about eight weeks later.

Can you highlight one or two things your team members observed?

I divided the feedback into three different buckets: work behaviors, personal behaviors, and temperament. In some cases, people were criticizing others in the department. I was not going to talk about those.

Some people commented that I have a tendency to be very direct. I learned that some of my colleagues take that approach the wrong way, and, hence, this is something I have to be careful of. Another comment indicated I was curt, abrasive, and insensitive. This comment hit me the hardest. I can be curt. I don't think I'm abrasive. I know I'm not insensitive. I care about these people as people as much as the positions they occupy. I don't know whether it was one comment or a series of comments that my colleague put together as one.

The feedback was interesting because I got it in writing. I re-characterized the comments and sent them back to my team to make sure people realized

I had read them. At the end of the day, the vice president of human resources and I decided we were not going to address the feedback in detail. We did not have the kind of in-depth discussion that I originally hoped we would. It would have probably started to reveal who had written what and that was not the purpose of the exercise. But I promised the team I would reflect on the feedback and focus on both the work and personal behaviors—the "opportunities," as we labeled them.

Interestingly, the list of successes was long, and some of the successes were directly contrary to what was listed as an opportunity for improvement. Clearly, not everybody sees me the same way. Some people on my team really like working with me, but obviously there are a few—and I'm not going to try to figure out who—who don't like me so much.

I read through the successes once and haven't gone back to those. I keep looking at the opportunities because that's where people are saying I'm deficient. I think some leaders would ignore the channel of opportunities and focus on the successes. I'm the opposite—focus on the opportunities and ignore the successes. While working for Hyatt, I learned a maxim from Jay Pritzker, one of the great business leaders of the latter half of the 20th century: "Protect the downside and the upside will take care of itself." I applied that maxim to my "successes" and "opportunities."

Which of the biographies of U.S. presidents was most inspiring?

Years ago, I read *Team of Rivals* (New York, NY: Simon & Schuster, 2005). I actually wrote the author, Doris Kearns Goodwin, a fan letter. To this day, it is the best historical book I have ever read. Much has been written about Lincoln's leadership. His leadership style was to pull people together, including his fiercest rivals, listen to them, but then make his own decisions. I realized *Team of Rivals* was a leadership book first and foremost, as well as a wonderful history book. That encouraged me to start thinking about my experiences in corporate life.

Leaders learn to manage paradoxes. I can imagine that, in your industry, you have to be aggressive yet at the same time patient—aggressive in the goals you set for the organization, but patient and understanding that it might take some time before you achieve those objectives. You have to be optimistic about the future, but also realistic given the current economic climate. How did you learn to manage these and other paradoxes in your leadership career?

This is a simplified answer, but I learned it as a child—I watched my parents. I'm a parent. I've been a parent for more than 32 years. There are paradoxes every day when you're raising children. You want your children to go out, to learn, and to be self-confident, but, at the same time, you want to make sure there's a safety net and mom and dad are right there when needed. There's a bit of the parent–child relationship in most organizations. I want my people to be able to fend for themselves and articulate a course of action. You want that for your children, too.

I always believed that, as your children become teens and rebellious, they want to do things a particular way . . . sometimes, the wrong way. And then they start to realize mom and dad weren't so stupid after all! I have adult children and I'm proud of them, each for different reasons. I see what good and bad my wife and I fostered in them. And I think bringing that into the organization is the same thing. Sometimes, you need to tell employees things that are good for them, even if they don't necessarily want to hear it; sometimes, they don't want to do things you need them to do; sometimes, you have to rein them in; and, sometimes, you have to punish people. All of those things are part of leadership and trying to make the proper decisions. "Is this the time I have to be firm? Is this the time I have to be comforting and supportive?" And it's instinctive. I don't think there's an exact score card that tells you when you have to be firm and when you have to be comforting and supportive.

A leader who is only comforting and supportive may sometimes get walked on. And the leader who is the other way creates every possible negative lesson—I had that leader. Neither extreme works. The good leader combines both—he or she is able to bring balance. They understand when they should be somewhat dictatorial and when they can afford to be somewhat of a doormat.

Throughout our conversation, you used the term "good leader" rather than "great leader."

There are too many leaders who try to be perfect. They try to do all the things they think they need to do and be perfect at each. Sometimes, you don't need to be perfect. As the old expression goes, "Don't let perfect be the enemy of good." Good enough is sometimes good enough. I don't know what a great leader is—I haven't seen too many!

You work with talented people. Some of these individuals might have derailed. What have you learned about career derailment? How do people with potential derail a promising leadership career?

They don't continue to learn. As you move up, you will encounter things you have not previously encountered. I don't expect anybody to master a particular accounting principle overnight. But, at some point in time, you have to understand the accounting principle if you're going to take charge of that responsibility. I have seen a lot of people start to delegate or dictate—they don't continue to learn. In my view, if you want to show a subordinate that you care, then learn what he or she does. This is why I advise students to learn what your boss does, what your peers do, and what someone junior to you does. I encourage them to learn the jobs that touch their jobs. For example, if I go to my finance person and start talking about accounting principles affecting us, she knows that I'm paying enough attention that I can discuss it. It's not something I could have discussed five years ago, but, because I've got that responsibility, I need to know what she's doing. Maybe not better than she does, but well enough to make sure she's doing it right and to challenge her on it.

Leadership Themes

- Treat others the way you want to be treated. Leaders need to set an example.
- Fight the battles you can win.
- Always learn about your boss's job, your subordinates' jobs, the job of the person sitting next to you, the job of the person across the desk from you, and so forth. It will make you a well-rounded person and you will understand where your job fits into the bigger organization.

21

If You Have the Illusion That You Can Do Everything Well, God Help You—It Is Going to Be a Disaster

Chaviva Hošek

Chaviva, when did you first realize you were a leader, and what happened to make you realize it?

I have to start by saying that I'm very skeptical of this word "leader," because it seems to me that, in the business community at least, it's often the same as the word for "manager" or "boss." I don't think every manager or boss is a leader, because, if you motivate people because they have to listen to you, because you can hire them or fire them, they'll listen to you up to a point, but that doesn't necessarily make a leader. So I think that this whole concept of leadership is quite subtle. I don't think that people are leaders. I don't think that you can point at someone and say, "That person's a leader," because people act differently in different contexts. If you put me in charge of a hockey team, I would not be a leader. I wouldn't know what to do, and I would not be happy doing it, no matter how much you put me in charge of it. I actually think of leadership not as a quality inside of people; I think of it as a relational quality. It's a relationship between some people and other people, and, unless the relationship endows at least one person with the self-confidence or the capacity to help the others along, it doesn't matter if you designate them as a leader. People will obey when they have no choice but to obey. That's fine, I understand that. But I live in the real world, and that's not leadership.

I began to see that I might be able to move people along in the women's movement, when I was a volunteer—and it's very important that this was a voluntary organization. Nobody had a boss. Nobody could make anybody do anything. The only way you could get anything to happen is if people agreed that they wanted to do it, and enjoyed doing it. Now, "enjoy" is a funny word when you're in an advocacy organization, but, basically, if they were unhappy, they'd leave, or they just wouldn't do what other people wanted them to do. I discovered, in various roles I had in the women's movement, that I sometimes said things that made people nod their heads and say, "Yes, let's do that." So, one of the ways I would kind of define this capacity for leadership, in retrospect, is that when people are struggling to solve a problem, sometimes there is somebody in the room who is able to sum up what everybody is struggling with, and point a way forward that causes almost everyone in the room to nod their heads and say, "Yes." So, that person can become a leader for that project or for that question. It was very much about recognizing a possibility of action together, rather than someone telling someone else what to do. Over time, I discovered that I had this capacity more often than I would have expected.

Eventually, I ended up in various groups here in Canada of like-minded people who, together, identified things we might want to do to make progress. It was very much a shared process; it was colleagueship, there was no boss. On certain topics, certain people took the lead; on other topics, other people took the lead. I had no idea what the tools were for making political change. I actually thought that you voted in elections, and then you waited, and then you were disappointed, and then you voted in another election. I had no idea how much room there was to try and make the world a better place between elections, if I can put it that way. It was a major discovery, not only about what I now would call the nature of shared leadership, but also about what was available inside the political system to push things in the direction one would want to push them. It was in the women's movement that I learned a little bit about what I would now call leadership, but it's because I learned it in a series of voluntary organizations, in which, if someone had tried to be the boss, they wouldn't have survived longer than two days. In a time of significant social change, when all of us were inventing things together as we went along, my view of what it is to move things along in society, to make things better, is very much about pulling people together. I don't really need to be the one pulling everyone together—to go somewhere you want to go together. This has always conditioned my way of working. I'm more comfortable that way, but I also think it's one of the most important ways to actually make change.

I don't think at all that your answer is peculiar. At our school, we talk a lot about the difference between being a boss and a leader or a manager and a leader; they are different.
They are incredibly different, and I think the reason I insist on the distinction is that if you read the management literature, the word "leader" is sprinkled liberally everywhere. It devalues the word. I think that, when you misuse a word, or when you devalue it, then you don't have that word available to identify what you want to talk about. I have certainly noticed this in the women's movement, where we made a lot of progress explaining to society that, though people claimed to be interested in equality, they weren't actually acting to enhance equality. "Equality" is a very powerful word. It must have been really powerful, because, when the anti-feminists came along, they started to use the word equality, and then we had to find another way of expressing what we were trying to communicate. It is really distressing when there isn't an adequate word or set of words to describe what you're trying to get at. It's a free society, people can say what they want to say, but getting the concept and keeping it in mind in a way that is useful to people so they can share the understanding ... when you lose that word, it's much more difficult.

How did you learn to lead? What have been the formative influences on you as a leader?

I think it was just watching other people. It was watching how some people were able to express what needed to happen in a way that made me say, "Yes, let's do that," or watching other people react to them. Being able to see what was convincing, not just to me, but to others. Some of it was beginning to understand strategy, though I didn't know what the word meant at the time. Many people use the word "strategy" when they really mean plan of action. But strategy is not a plan of action. It's where you want to go; how you want to get there; and why you want to go there. That involves analysis. What is the situation we are in? What resources do we have? How can we deploy these resources?

We had no resources. We were a volunteer organization, so we had no money. We had very intelligent, talented, passionate people, and that's it—that's all we had. We shared knowledge, we found things out and brought them together and said, "Maybe if we did this, that would work, or maybe if we did that, that would work." Most of the people I was working with at the time had the benefit of good educations, and therefore a certain amount of self-confidence about their ability to analyze what was going on, and to write, and to express themselves or to help each other express themselves, or to do research to pull together a storyline or a plan that might resonate and make sense.

And, so, what I watched was how things came together. I had many people very much worthy of admiration to watch, to see how they thought—and they were ahead of me. First of all, in understanding Canada and Ontario better than I did. This began for me when I came back to Canada after graduate school. Many of them had contacts I didn't have. So, basically I watched, I listened, I learned, I collaborated as much as I could, and, I have to say, the other thing about it was that it wasn't very personal. You know, the people I was with were not interested in their own personal advancement. They had careers, their life was going the way it was going—it was very clearly a communal effort on behalf of women, not a career-building strategy for any particular woman. For the people I was closest to, we were trying to make the world a better place. *A very old-fashioned idea, but the world still needs to be made a better place. So, mostly I learned by watching and listening, and also, as we tried things that worked and didn't work, the feedback from the world basically taught us something about what to do next.* It helped, of course, that there was turmoil about women's equality essentially all over North America at the same time, and so, if we read and learned about what was going on in other parts of North America, we could both learn good things and bad. We learned a lot from our American sisters, including some things not to do. What was exciting about it was there was no protocol, there was no plan, there was nothing to follow. No one knew how to do any of this; we just tried things out, and kept talking. In that sense, it was intellectually very exciting as well, because there were no clear answers. There were answers in the sense of the kind of society we wanted, which is better than the one we found at the time, but nobody had a plan of action that, if we all followed it, we would get there. *Part of what I learned was flexibility, willingness to try different things, respect for other people's knowledge and other people's ways of thinking about things, and understanding that academic knowledge, which was the kind I had, was a very small sliver of what there was to learn in the world.* In that sense, I think it changed my life for the better in many ways, but, in particular, it showed me how much was to be learned by doing, and not just by reading and thinking.

What role did mistakes play in your learning process? Can you talk about a mistake you made as a leader and what did you learn from that mistake?

I would say that, in my political career, it took me much longer to understand the mistakes I was making. I overvalued intellect and I undervalued politics; even though I had chosen to be an elected person in a political system, I had much, much less understanding of what that really involved. I had been inside the academic culture and I had gone quite a bit outside that culture in the women's movement. Then, when I entered so-called "real" politics, I think I underestimated the lines of force, the degree to which people were contesting purely for power, which I didn't fully understand. I knew the words, but I didn't understand what it really meant. I just didn't understand what it was to be in a power struggle, which is what one is in in an elected system, both inside a caucus and a cabinet and then related to the opposition. I didn't understand all the lines of force there. I made a bunch of mistakes, mostly by not understanding the world I was really in—and I would say I corrected for some of them, but my real learning happened when I got defeated and wasn't in politics anymore, and was able to reflect on what had happened and how not to behave in the future. I would also say that I learned that I should never have run for public office, that I had the wrong temperament for it. But I'm not sorry that I did because I learned a lot of things, and, when I was working with Mr. (Jean) Chrétien, both before and after he was Prime Minister, the fact that I had been elected, the fact that I had been in a Cabinet, the fact that I had had both bad and good things happen really enabled me to do a much better job as a policy advisor than I would ever have been able to do if I hadn't had that experience. No one can tell you what it feels like. I can tell you the words, but the words don't convey what the sensations are. I think that helped in the next stage of my learning. I learned a lot of important lessons, many of them not so much about my own behavior because there are only so many different roles one can play, or there are only so many versions of one's self that one wants to live with. *My view has always been that, in the end, you have to be able to look into the mirror and tolerate the person that you see there.*

You were the president of the National Action Committee on the Status of Women and you said, "It was the harshest political experience I ever had." Can you elaborate on that statement?

The first group I was describing to you, in which I learned a lot about the women's movement, was the Ontario Committee on the Status of Women. The National

Action Committee on the Status of Women was a national organization, a much broader political scope, and so the Communist Party of Canada's Women's Commission was part of the National Action Committee on the Status of Women. So were the Progressive Conservative Party's Women's Commission, rape crisis centers, and the Daycare Centres Association. It was a broad group with much more conflict. It was also national in scope, so the things I learned watching a Cabinet table in Ottawa about the regional stresses and strains in Canada, I learned for the first time in the women's movement. The other thing was that it was really too broad in political spectrum ever to be in internal peace. Some of what was going on there was a fundamental disagreement in how you make political change. So, there were people in the group who believed that you made political change in the streets, and there were people in the group that thought that you made political change by talking with elected people, and by marshalling resources to convince governments to change certain laws to make things better for women. And so, between the left and right splits and the different analyses of how social change happens, it was a very complicated group. The group, or large numbers in the group, didn't wish to have any discipline about how decisions were made inside the organization, and, when decisions were made, were happy to contravene them. There was a tremendous amount of internal struggle; some of it entirely legitimate, in that we disagreed on what to do, and some of it I considered illegitimate, because, once decisions were made according to the rules we agreed to, people would under-mine them anyway, and quite explicitly. It was a war of all against all—what can I say? I learned a great deal, we made some great progress, and it certainly taught me a great deal about Canada. Here was proof that people who, on the surface, would seem to want to get the same results, don't, in fact, want to get the same results—because, of course, we were all in love with different ways of getting those results. Many people's allegiance was more to the way of getting to the result than to the results themselves. It was a very complicated time, and the culture of the organization was not sustainable over the long haul.

As you transitioned to more and more senior roles, what were some of the challenges that you faced, and how did you overcome them?

I would say that almost everywhere I've been since my time as the president of the National Action Committee on the Status of Women, I've had what I thought of as significant responsibility. It certainly felt like a burden, and it scared me. The lessons I learned were about the different cultures and how people worked in those cultures, and how I could adapt myself to the culture I was in in order to do the best possible job. I think of myself as a responsible person. Where people have said, "We expect you to accomplish these things, or to fix these things," then I believe that you have to find a way to do that with the help of others, or to help other people do that, or to be clear about what you can't do. In that sense, I felt respon-sibility in all those jobs. If you start, as I did, doing this work in the voluntary world, one of the discoveries I made early on is that there are people who do what they said they would do, and there are people who don't. If you are one of the people who does what you say you're going to do, it's amazing—they just give you more stuff to do! I've always had a sense of responsibility that way, and I don't think it was because I wasn't paid, I just had a sense of responsibility. For me, the learning was more about how different cultures work; and how people in them make decisions, how they talk, how they interact with each other, how you can make progress together in certain styles in some groups of people and other styles with other groups of people.

I think it really helps that I was an immigrant child. *I always thought that having been an immigrant is one of the best things that has ever happened to me.* I came to Canada when I was six years old, I had two other languages before I learned English, and, in retrospect, I have learned that my move to every new culture has been the same: I walk into a new culture and I think, "How do they do things here? How do they talk to each other? What's the language? How does this move?" Then, I figure out what the rules are, and I figure out a way to work inside those rules. So, I brought a mindset that doesn't assume that I know how to behave. I assume they know how to behave, and I've got to figure out how to fit in. It has actually helped me a lot. I've done it so many times now, it doesn't frighten me anymore. It doesn't mean that I know what to do. It means that I know I'll figure out what to do, and that has been a very great strength for me. I've always felt that if people want to get to more or less the same place, and are coming from a place of goodwill, they'll probably find a way to do it together. But you do have to figure out whether you want to go where everybody else wants to go, or if your aims are very different.

You talk passionately about this sense of responsibility. Where did that come from?

I don't remember not having it. I'm an only child; maybe only children have a sense of responsibility, I don't know. I've always had a sense that you have to do what you say you're going to do, that you have to help something along. Why are we here if we're not here to help something along and make the world a better place? Surely, we didn't arrive here to play golf forever?

You worked with different leaders. What did you learn about working with individuals who had different approaches to lead?

I've been lucky in that I've worked with people that I respected, and I think respect is actually more important than love. I don't think I would have been comfortable for very long working with anyone I didn't respect. If you respect somebody, part of it means that you believe there is something valuable about who they are and what they are trying to accomplish. Mutual respect is a very big part of making anything happen in the world, and it has to be genuine, because people know how you think about them. Everybody knows everything—that's the big secret! Everybody knows everything about how they are actually treated and how people are relating to one another. If you can't be genuine in a respectful relationship with someone, you can't really work with them. In order to do that, you have to have, I think, not just the capacity for respecting other people, but a healthy dose of self-recognition.

If you think everything you yourself do is wonderful, you can't possibly work with people. You have to have capacity for self-criticism—you don't have to tell the world, but you have to have that capacity in order to succeed. And a reasonable sense of your limitations. I don't find working with others difficult because I have a very clear sense of the things I am terrible at, and I've gotten to the point that it doesn't worry me; as long as I can find someone who can do what I can't do, and I can do what they can't do, together we can make something happen. I don't feel defensive about the things I don't know how to do. Frankly, I'm too old to feel defensive about them, but also you just have to make peace with your limitations. If you can find the things you're really good at, and do them as well as you can, and help other people find what they are really good at, together you can make incredible things happen. If you have the illusion that you can do everything well, God help you—it's going to be a disaster.

It seems to me there's an awful lot of people that think they can do everything well?
If you think you need to be able to do everything well, you're out of your mind and you are very insecure. Just find the few things you can do well, and do them, and then let other people do the things they do well, and appreciate what they can do. So, if you're in an organization, as I was, with these incredibly brilliant people from all over the intellectual spectrum, why be defensive? Figure out a way to help them do what they can do best. Get a team of people around you who can do things you can't do, and let them do it. Respect them for doing it, and thank them for doing it. It's amazing what will happen. I think that the people who can't do that are insecure. They need to believe that they are the smartest person in the room.

What have you personally experienced as a barrier to learning and how have you tried to overcome this barrier?
I didn't overcome some of the barriers. What I did was I kept trying to learn. There are some things I find very difficult to do, and, with some of them, I've just cut my losses. I've said, "I can't do this. I'm not good at this—somebody else can do this better. Let them." I've invested in the things that I am good at. I met one of my former students in the political world. He told me something that was very helpful to me. He said, "You know, Chaviva, really you're a teacher. No matter where you are, that's who you are—you're a teacher." Teachers are people who learn things and want to share them. That's what it means. I think that is a basic part of who I am—I'm a teacher. That doesn't mean I know everything I want to know, but I have used the opportunities I've had to learn the things I could really be helpful with, and then try and share them and not be too concerned about the things that I'm really terrible at. Just make sure that someone else knows how to do them and get them done.

I appreciate that. But as a person in a leadership position, what were some of the hardest things for you to learn that actually were part of your role?
In the role of having responsibility in an organization, the hardest thing for me to

learn was not to be so wishful about what other people might be able to do. My impulse is to assume the best, and sometimes I'm disappointed, as we all are. I have often waited too long to figure out something's not going to work. I've often assumed someone's capacity is bigger than I thought it was, not so much intellectual capacity, but the ability to work with others and a willingness to be respectful to others. It turns out, as my mother told me long ago, character is hugely important, it doesn't change very much—that's, for me, the sad thing. I sort of hope that people's characters can in fact evolve. Character evolves, but I don't know how much it really changes. ***Most of my mistakes or problems have been in not taking action quickly enough when I should have known something wasn't going to work. I think I have a tendency to be a little too indulgent sometimes, and that comes from having been a teacher, where you always think your student can do better—but, at a certain point, you're not in that role anymore.*** They are working for you, and so I haven't cut my losses in some cases as quickly as I should have. On the other hand, I don't actually want to be a harsh judge of other people, so I've sometimes paid the price of not judging quickly enough. I would say the other thing is sometimes not recognizing quickly enough when things were going bad in relationships between people—not between me and them, but in the organization. Sometimes, I haven't either known or noticed, or not noticed quickly enough, that relationships are going bad.

How have you learned to deal with setbacks and failures?

I've had many setbacks. But there is not a generic method in addressing these. Mostly, I guess, when things go wrong, I've literally pulled back to figure out what went wrong and what can be done to fix it, if anything. Part of the question is how much in the way of resources—personal, emotional, intellectual, and financial—are you willing to invest in fixing something that's gone wrong versus saying, "That's never going to work. Thank you and goodbye." It's partly an analytical process. It's also partly an emotional process of figuring out what you've done to make this happen, what you could do differently, who is responsible for what happened—not in order to blame anyone, but in order to understand. I was working in the Prime Minister's Office with a wonderful group of people. My method has always been to sit down after an event, both good and bad, and say, "What went right? What went wrong? What could we do to fix what went wrong and go on from there?" I don't believe in blaming things on people, because, for the most part, there is nobody to blame. Things just go wrong. If someone is always making mistakes, you've got a problem, but, for the most part, you really need to analyze what was really going on. What did you think was going on? What did you do that worked? What did you do that didn't work? How do you try and make it possible not to make the same mistake again? How can you learn from it? Mostly, it's about an analysis of what you can learn from the errors, from the things that didn't go right. I think it took a while for some people in the organization I'm currently in to understand that I wasn't looking to figure out whom to blame, I was trying to understand what we learned. There are people whose reaction to every setback is to find someone to blame, and usually someone other than themselves. I don't respect that. The people who are in the blaming business are making sure they never have to look in the mirror. How is that helpful?

You worked in the Prime Minister's Office. How did that experience contribute to your learning to lead?

I had been an elected Member of Parliament. I had been a Cabinet Minister. And I had spent three years working with Mr. Chrétien when we were in opposition working on policy development. The role of director of policy and research in the Prime Minister's Office was an entirely bigger, more stressful role. But I wasn't alone: there was a chief of staff, there was a chief policy advisor. There was a whole group of us who had already worked together when we were in opposition. We liked each other and trusted each other, knew how to work together, and knew everybody's strengths and some of our weaknesses. I would say that Mr. Chrétien was very unusual in that he was not like a boss. He was the kind of person, still is the kind of person, who either trusts you to do your job, in which case he leaves you alone to do it, or doesn't trust you, in which case you don't stay very long. He is, as I've said many times, not the kind of person who picks the flowers up by the roots to see if they are growing. We had an honest relationship. I gathered together a team of the smartest young people I could find who had some subject knowledge. I chose people with different, as they say in French, "*formations*"—a historian, a philosopher, a lawyer, someone who could analyze science. People with different skills and different backgrounds who were intellectually curious and reasonably pragmatic about what could be done in a political environment. They were all young because no one stays in the Prime Minister's Office in that role forever. And we were lucky to get some very talented young people. I assumed, and I turned out to be right, that, if you sent people on an assignment to figure out what was happening between department X and bureaucrat Y on a topic we were all concerned about, and if we sat once a week around a table with everybody sharing what their files were, and if people with completely different ways of thinking and disciplines more or less agreed on what the right path was, the chances were you were right. And so, it was a very open conversation with about 12 or 14 of us talking quite straight about what was really going on, and who was doing what to whom, and where the stresses were, and what the complexities of the issues were, and how you could possibly resolve the conflicts between department A and department B. Then I would tell the Prime Minister what we thought, and he would either agree with me or disagree with me. He would invariably ask me a question I hadn't had the wit to think about, so I always learned something new from him. He always knew more about things than I could ever have imagined because he had been the Minister of every-thing, so he knew an enormous amount, both about Canada and about the Canadian political system. We gave advice, and, as I said, sometimes he accepted it and sometimes he didn't.

What are you learning these days to become an even better leader? Are there any recent "aha" moments?

I've just stepped down from what looks likely to be my last "real" job, so I'm in a reflective mode. I must say that I am worried about the political process, both in Canada and in the rest of the world, because, as we face much more frightening challenges, I think the culture of political decision making is much more polarized and much more angry. I understand some of the anger, but I think some of the anger has been deliberately provoked by certain political operators, who, in my opinion, don't appreciate how dangerous that can be. I worry about that. It's not that people can't disagree, because, on some of these issues, it's not clear to me what the right answers are. I think that it's not at all clear to them what the right answers are either, but they are happy to polarize opinion. I worry a lot more than I did, say, even 10 years ago, about the political culture in the so-called "developed world." My worries are about how we talk to one another about the issues we face. It distresses me that it seems there is less space for people to think together on how to solve problems. There is much more blaming; there's much more, "Who is the culprit?"; there's much more, "Whose fault is this?"; there's much more, "Who do we get to punish?" There are people who deserve punishment, but, for the most part, it's much more complicated than that. If it were simply a matter of finding the five culprits and throwing them off the ship, life would be much simpler. I think the problems that we face are complex, but many of the political tools we bring to them, and, in particular, the way we talk about them, are unadvisedly simple-minded, and therefore destructive. So, I'm more worried about that than I am about whatever I learned about leadership in the roles that I played. I worry that the problems of the human race are huge, and they will not be solved if we just figure out whom to blame and end up calling each other names.

Collaboration seems to be such a dirty word these days. It's the only way to solve anything.

I don't, by collaboration, mean that we should all hold hands and sing together. I think collaboration is necessary. It's not that it's nice, it's necessary. There is no other way. Competition and name-calling and deciding that so and so is to blame may be fun for five minutes, but it's not going to solve our problems. You know, I've been lucky to have spent the past decade in an organization that has been collaborative, the intellectual collaboration of the very best minds; it's a beautiful thing to watch.

You're a passionate advocate for the status of women. What have you learned about women and providing leadership? And, maybe, to what extent their learning to lead journey is different to that of their male counterparts?

It's very hard to make generalizations about this. But let me put it this way: There are cultural constraints both on men and on women, but many more on women about how they are allowed to behave, how they are allowed to speak, and what will be considered acceptable behavior. As a result, many women have had to make their way in the world inside those cultural constraints. They may be able to break some of those assumptions, but, if they break too many of them, other people won't accept them. Among the people who might not accept them are other women. So, they are much more constrained than men are by what the culture allows them to do and say. There are constraints on men, too, but they are not as constraining, if I can put it that way. Insofar as leadership is assumed to be being a boss, I think women bosses have a harder time because they are more resented—both by men and by women. I think that the world is tougher on women than it is on men. The price women pay for errors, or for things not going well, is greater. More men have been able to pick themselves up and keep going than women have. There's much more tendency to take something that's gone wrong and generalize it as something about women in general. When a man does something stupid, you say, "I'm not going to hire him again." When a woman does something stupid, people say, "I'm never going to hire a woman again." How does that make sense? I also think that there are personal styles that men can get away with that women can't. I think it is very much in flux, especially at the moment. I don't believe that women are more naturally team oriented than men. It depends on the women, and depends on the men. I'm wary of making generalizations about who is more like this, and who is more like that, because I think people are very different from each other. One of the things that is pretty obvious to me is that when a woman is put in a position of responsibility, she's watched more closely.

It is also hard for men to identify with women. They may like them, they may respect them, they may be happy working with them, but they don't identify with them. I remember sitting at a Cabinet meeting when Mr. Chrétien was Prime Minister as a perfect example, in which a male Cabinet Minister was extremely upset about a decision that was about to be taken that would damage something he was interested in. He expressed his upset in a certain way, and half the men around the table responded, "He's so upset, we've got to fix this." I realized that, if a female Cabinet Minister had expressed the same thing in the same way, they would have said, "She's not fit for the job, she's too emotional!" A man is allowed to be "emotional," and, in this instance, everybody ran to help him. If a woman were "emotional," they would have said she's not fit for the job. Nobody in the room would have disliked the woman in question, but they wouldn't have identified with her—they identified with their brother, who was upset. If you're male, you're allowed to be upset, and, if you're female, you're not allowed to be upset. This happens constantly, right? The standards are different. I think the world is changing a lot, but I think the standards are different, and figuring out how to thread a path to accomplish what we want to accomplish in an organization, whatever task or responsibility you have, while feeling comfortable in yourself and not getting either the men in the room upset one way or the women in the room upset in another way, is not an easy task.

What advice do you have for women as they embark on their journey of learning to lead?

My advice is not that different for women or for men. *I think you need to find what you really care about and what matters to you. Find out which of your strengths do you want to use, what do you want to accomplish in life, and in what spirit do you want to accomplish it. And then try to be true to that.* Over time, some of those things will change, and, if you can find a way to check on yourself to see if you're still the person you want to be, or you're growing in the direction you want to grow, then you're much better off than if you're just ticking off the steps on a predetermined ladder.

Leadership Themes

- Leaders work with others. They have respect for other people's knowledge and their ways of thinking about things.
- Be true to your values. You have to be able to look into the mirror and tolerate the person that you see there.
- Leaders are adaptable to cultures and situations in order to do the best possible job.

22

There's Credit in Mission Accomplishment—Don't Bring Back Excuses

Lt.G. Russel L. Honoré, USA, Ret.

General Honoré, when did you first realize you were a leader, and what happened to make you realize it?

I was a member of an organization called the 4-H Club. It was a club focused on rural America—kids that were interested in agriculture and leadership were part of the club. We helped in the community. It was one of the largest rural youth organizations in America at the time, other than Boy Scouts and Girl Scouts. I was very active in the 4-H Club because I had some farm animals that I used to show at the livestock shows at middle school and high school. But, a big part of 4-H was about the human dimension—leadership. Every year, I'd go to a two-week camp, and the focus of the camp was not necessarily on what did I join 4-H for—which was to be competitive with my animals—but it was about leadership. By the time I was a freshman in high school, I had been to two camps, which exposed me to organizational skills, creating an agenda, and having meetings that informed people—and, in some cases, I made decisions. By the time I graduated from high school, I had been class president twice and president of the 4-H Club for three of four years in high school. I took on these roles because it appeared no one else wanted them. But soon things went from obligation to an opportunity to be the leader. As president of the 4-H Club, you weren't supposed to be taken down to the principal's office, so there was a certain amount of expected conduct. You didn't break the rules; you lived by the rules and your role model's rules. That's the burden of leadership. Along with that burden came being careful of what you say, what you read, and what you think—because what you read can lead to what you think, and what you think can lead to what you do. There's a relationship there.

Have you always wanted to be a leader?

Those positive experiences in high school set the stage for when I went to college. There was a big difference in leadership experiences between high school and college. I think we go through life in plateaus and, when you get to each plateau, you need to be prepared to start over. The previous experience was good enough to put you in a leadership position, but, when you go into a different environment, you have to re-establish yourself. It's not just about what people say about you—although your reputation goes a long way—it's as much about what you do. Some people are more experienced and better than you at most things. You have to, again, reassert your credibility. I was never a leader in college, other than in the Reserve Officers' Training Corps. That was my niche. I found my space there and in the department of agriculture. Many of the big guys on campus were football players—everybody on campus knew them, as, in high school, everybody had known me. When you go to college, it is a different thing that brings notoriety. You might get to know a lot of people, and most of those came out of the athletic department. I was not in that league in college. By the time I graduated, I was the Commander of Cadets.

You talked about levels of leadership. As you transitioned to more and more senior roles, what were some of the challenges that you faced, and how did you overcome them?
The biggest challenge for me was when I got promoted to General Officer. You're selected for this partly because of how well you've done with the opportunities given to you, but also on your potential for future service at a higher level. I was a hands-on leader. In current-day vernacular, as was used when I was promoted, a lot of folks would say, "He's a micromanager." My defense was, "Don't confuse micromanagement with a heavy emphasis on standards." I didn't see myself as a micromanager, but *I grew up with a burden that, if you see a mistake and don't correct it, you become a part of that mistake.* If I saw a mistake, I'd stop, particularly if it related to safety, talk to the troops about it, and I would give them the opportunity to tell their Commander about it. I had that burden. The other burden involved talking in the vernacular of the troops. Along the way, some senior leaders told me, "You need to get rid of that profanity. One of these days, that's going to catch up with you." I did have a couple of close calls with that because it's a habit—it's a bad habit. But that transition to becoming a General Officer was probably the hardest.

How has your learning to lead been influenced by others? What did people do to help you?
I grew up being around general officers. *I learned that, the more senior you get, the more important it is to focus on the "what" and "why" of what you do, and set a space for your subordinates to figure out "how."* As technology evolves, and as areas of operations change, the "how" can be very different. My strength was always the "how."

So how did you create a climate where people felt like they were really given the opportunity to think about the "how"?
I guess that came to me when I was a division commander in South Korea. Number one, make sure everybody understands what the standards are. That took about six months. In the remaining time, I had to maintain the energy and then retrain new leaders, because we were constantly bringing in new recruits. People are only

there for two years. You're in constant training mode. As soon as you think you've got it right, four or five key leaders leave at the battalion and the brigade level. Battalions are made up of about 800 troops and brigades about 3,000 to 5,000. With those leaders changing every six months, you had to constantly teach. It's kind of like winning the Super Bowl or the Stanley Cup—once you win it, you've got to start all over because your team changes. You've got to remember that. You're in a constant state of teaching and providing opportunity for your subordinates to learn. Once you establish your standards, people know what you think is important based on the environment you're in, and with emphasis on the "what," and the "when" you want it done, and the "why," and constantly allowing people to figure out "how" to do it. All of a sudden, you figure out, "Hey, the way I showed them is pretty good, but this is even better!" I would throw a problem out to my subordinate commanders such as, "I would like one of you to lead this effort to do a product improvement on how we maintain tank engines. Would you like to lead this?" Within a few hours, I got a note back saying, "We'll come and see you; we want to make sure that we understand what you think the problem is with tank engines." From that, they wrote a book that was used within the division, and then used in the Army to improve tank engine life spans. Those were the types of things we would do. The job was to collaborate with our peers and to get the smartest, most experienced people we had in the division to figure out the best way to do a product improvement. They'd come up with a new "how." I think that's where we get the innovation. That's the important lesson I learned about being a senior leader.

What were some of the hardest things to learn in becoming a good or an even better leader?

Patience! Change takes some time, and it takes some people a little longer than others to adapt to change. There's always somebody who didn't get the word, or they got the "what," but they didn't get the "why" and the "when," so you have to be very explicit about that if you have a time expectation to your task. You have to have an appreciation that people have priorities they are trying to achieve, and sometimes it comes from the environment—a reduction of resources. I've lived with a couple of those in the Army. All those could have an impact on everybody. On the other hand, some of my greatest successes were because I wasn't patient with status quo—we had to do stuff now, and not over-study the problem. It was better to do something now and get some forward momentum than to set it out and try to do something perfectly later. The "good enough" sometimes *is* good enough.

I guess this highlights the importance of situational awareness?

Yes. Every decision has a clock on it, depending on the immediacy of the "when." When people's lives are on the line, it's "now." You don't have an option when people's lives or health are concerned. You can't over-study those "now" events. Based on the information we've got, we come up with the best course of action we can, and then constantly look for ways to improve it.

Did you learn that the hard way? How did you gain this insight?

I was fortunate. I had a string of effective leaders from whom I learned, who were different from me. They were patient by their nature. I was fortunate enough to work for some of them. *I was also fortunate to work for a couple of guys that were like me. You know what? I didn't like working for people like me, and that caused me to make adjustments.*

You were a three-star General. What expectations did you put on yourself in the leadership role?

Take care of your people and get the job done. There's no credit for trying. There's credit in mission accomplishment. Don't bring back excuses. Get the job done. Adapt and overcome. Throughout history, it hasn't been the biggest Army that won the battle. Take what you have and accomplish a mission while taking care of your troops. At the end of the day, the true measure of a leader is—does he or she get the mission done? I think people will sometimes forgive your methods, but they'll ask, "Did you get the mission done, and did you stay inside the common decorum of what's accepted by the people?" That's what people expect their leaders to do.

You have taken on significant assignments in disaster planning and relief. You took command of the Joint Task Force Katrina operation, where you led the Department of Defense response to Hurricanes Katrina and Rita in Alabama, Mississippi, and Louisiana. You also supported the planning and response for Hurricanes Floyd (1999), Lilli and Isidore (2002), Isabel (2003), and Charley, Frances, Ivan and Jeanne (2004). Furthermore, you were involved in the military response to the devastating flooding that swept Venezuela in 1999 and Mozambique in 2000. How have you learned to cope with the fact that all eyes are on you during the dark days, and that people expect miracles from you?

I think there will be a lot of people available in dark days to tell people how bad it is—they are all over the place. You've got players and you've got observers. If you're a player, you're either pushing or pulling the event, and you've got to accept that and take responsibility, and then your mission is to keep messages coming out from the other players in perspective. Then, you've got to tell everyone observing, "This is what we're doing. This is our mission, and this is when we hope to have it done by."

I'm a player. By sending me in as a player and as a team captain, understanding I had bosses and rules that I had to play by—I had the governor, the mayor of the city, my commander, and his commander in the Pentagon over me, and they understand the playing field, to use sports as an analogy—you get your job done. Dealing with the media is one of these jobs.

I grew up in a culture where we were discouraged from talking to the media. I understood the importance that you talk to the media, not just for the purpose of talking to the media, but so the troops' families know what you're doing, and the

American people know what you're doing. Talking to media is a medium so the troops' families, wherever they are, know what they are doing and the impact they are making. The observers—the American people, who you represent and who resource you and pay for your boots, health care, and the house you live in—know what you're doing. That's why you talk to the media.

Talking to the media isn't about you, the individual, it's about telling the observers what's going on. It's about telling the players' families what's happening. The leader has to be prepared to play that role, whether he's the leader of a military formation, or a town, or a manufacturing company.

Be visible, put yourself on the line, and take responsibility then?
Take responsibility! Be available. You may not tell all that you know, but you'd better not lie.

Some leaders are not comfortable with taking on responsibility.
True, and, unfortunately, the old proverbial silos kick in: You think, *It's not my job.* Well it is, regardless of what the situation is. It might be saving the livestock because this is the most important thing to people, preventing a field from flooding, or evacuating people after events happen. Whatever it is, you get the mission done. We're not looking for excuses. If you don't do it, somebody else will, or we'll collectively fail.

You have had successes, setbacks, and failures. How did you develop resilience to deal with disappointments?
I think some of the resilience comes from the experience of growing up poor in south Louisiana. You might wonder, "What does that have to do with resiliency?" Well, from that experience, you learn to adapt to the situation—you adapt and overcome. I remember when I was young, we had two televisions—one had sound and one had a picture. Nobody said the picture and the sound had to come on the same one. You adapt. When the antennae got old, you got a little piece of aluminum foil and worked it just right. By the time I got into higher education and went off to some of these experiential learning camps, guess what we were doing? Giving people the experience of, "What do you do when you've got one television with sound and one with a picture? You put them together." And there we were, in some outdoor location with a professor teaching us how to adapt, and I said, "Well, wait a minute, I learned that when I was seven years old!"

When I talk to leaders, they talk a lot about their upbringing and the influence from mom, dad, and their siblings. Has your family in any way shaped your approach to leadership?
I came from a family of 12, so you quickly learned your space and your place. *No one will be as true to you as your brothers and sisters, particularly when you're growing up. They'll be true to you, and they'll tell it like it is. They'll tell you what they see.* That helped me to see where I was in the old proverbial pecking order.

You have your space, and you move up when opportunity comes. You create your opportunities through hard work and good luck; and the harder you work, the luckier you are.

Character is a critical component of good leadership. The military is often seen as an institution that builds character. How can we bring leadership character to the classroom?

By teaching and by looking at some examples of courage and character where they trump ego and self-serving events. I think that's the importance of history. I don't know a good leader who doesn't have a good appreciation of history. For example, I have learned a lot about leadership by studying George Washington and how he, as the commander-in-chief, led the Continental Army in the American Revolution. He gave his soldiers a clear purpose—freedom. This is an important lesson for business leaders: To provide unrelenting focus and purpose. Washington displayed three other characteristics of good leadership. First, lead from the front. Leaders are on the scene to see what is going on and to smell the action. Second, don't be afraid to take on the impossible. And, third, don't be afraid to act when you are being criticized.

You have emphasized the importance of collaboration. When we think of Katrina, so many different parties had to come together and collaborate. What have you learned about collaborating effectively?

The future is going to be about speed and power. Knowledge management and—as I used to tell the folks down in New Orleans—if you ask a question, somebody will know the answer. You've just got to find the person with that answer. Somebody's seen it. Someone will know it. I've just got to find that person. I'm not going to get it by sitting and watching a screen, I'm going to get it by going out there and empowering my commanders to do what they've got to do. Tell them what's expected. Tell them to look for places that make a difference and we'll get it done that way, as opposed to a scripted play. We had a big impact on some events—everything from recovering remains to dealing with pets. A lot of the observers were not happy with the way pets were handled. As soon as we finished the search and rescue, I announced one afternoon we were going out to look for pets. My staff didn't know that I said it on national television. I guess the power of that was, as soon as the interview was over, my secretary called and said, "The phone is ringing off the hook. People are calling, and they are sending e-mails. The computer here will say you have some 15,000 messages backed up. We told them to shut your e-mail off from anyone with a subject line writing to say 'Thank you'." That was the intent, but, while we were doing it, we didn't have the equipment to pick the dogs up—but there were people with money, and with jets, and the next morning, I said, "Our biggest challenge now is getting the equipment," and the following morning I had a 747 land in New Orleans with dog-catching equipment, and all this collaboration is handled under the screen. It just happened—people were talking to each other by computer, "Hey, my son is on that unit, and we've got all this stuff!" Or, "We're a pet store, we've got a neighbor's son in that unit—find out where they are and give us a name and a number." That's the power of open collaboration, as opposed to a commander-controlled system—let us figure out how many of these things they need to eat, and where we're going to put them, and what we're going to do with the animals. Now, you get surprises; when we went to collect the pets, I might think of a pet as a cat and a dog, but we started getting some weird things—things with teeth! Big old lizards, and snakes, iguanas, raccoons, baby tigers—you just don't know, in an open collaborative system, what you'll end up with. It stretches your values of what you think is the world as you know it, and you go with it. That's the power outside of just strict command and control; study the problem, make sure you reduce the risk to an open collaborative system, but there are many different ways to solve a problem.

You retired from the U.S. Army, yet you are still very active and a passionate advocate of the need for good leadership. What are you learning these days to become an even better leader? Are there any recent "aha" moments?

Read more, listen more, and stay engaged. When I went in to be interviewed to be a three-star General, the Secretary of Defense told me—I was 54 at the time – "You're a little old for this job." I said, "I will remind you that McArthur was 72 in South Korea." He rolled back in his seat and said, "My god, I'm 72 now." I said, "The fact that I'm a little older means, hopefully, I'll be a little wiser." I think people expect you to be.

With regard to my transformation from military life to civilian life, it's trying to stay with what you are good at, or what you believe you're good at, and the only way to do that is to be active. The day after retiring from the military, I joined the Red Cross and said, "What I can do for you is I can be a spokesman. I can go out and help you raise money, and I can come to your board meetings." That's what I do, and it's been a very rewarding experience because, at a lot of places where I speak, somebody will see me and say, "We're having a convention in my association, and we'd like you to come speak." The philanthropic piece has been a very rewarding experience. I continue to publish. I continue to speak. I continue to write op eds. Be active in the community where you live. *People often ask me what I miss about being in the military, and what I really miss is the responsibility. In the military, you're held accountable for what you do and what you didn't do.* When you're retired, if you just go sit in the corner and watch television . . . I see that there are better uses of time. Instead of sitting back and being an observer, I still want to play.

What do you see as the biggest leadership challenge of our time?

The challenge for the new leaders is: How are we going to live in a world with nine billion people—with everyone looking for safe food, and water, and clean air? I don't think we're going to solve that problem in the battlefield—we're going to solve that in the classroom. We've got to drive our technology and our innovation toward those three things. Otherwise, we'll just continue to live in a world of conflict.

We are going to have to find solutions. For example, we're going to have to teach computers how to smell and taste. I speak in a lot of MBA classes. More often than not, there will be someone saying, "You can't do that." I respond, "There is no such thing as 'can't.' Sixty years ago, we didn't have a computer. Now get off your ass and go figure it out, because we've got to live globally safe."

And for an American to say, "It's not possible"!

Go do it—solve the problem. Ninety years ago, we didn't have any airplanes, and two brothers figured it out. They took some sheets and some sticks. Now, we fly globally. We have to figure out how to have safe air, safe food, and safe water. This is the new Vietnam. Every generation has something with which to deal. This is the new Second World War for this generation; but there are no buses waiting to pick them up and take them off to war.

Leadership Themes

- I learned that, the more senior you get, the more important it is to focus on the "what" and "why" of what you do, and set a space for your subordinates to figure out "how."
- Assert and re-assert your credibility.
- Collaborate with your peers and get the smartest, most experienced people to figure out the best way to improve performance.
- Every decision has a clock on it. Be prepared to act.
- There's no credit for trying. There's credit in mission accomplishment. Don't bring back excuses.

23

I Constantly Learn Lessons About Letting Go
Robert Bell

Bob, when did you first realize you were a leader, and what happened to make you realize it?
I'm a cancer surgeon, and, when I first came back to Ontario to practice, the standard of care for the tumor type that I treat was far below international standards. I started working to improve the standard of care across Ontario, which involved pulling together a large team. At the end of about two years, the team was in place, and we received funding from the Ministry of Health. My reaction was, "Holy smokes, that was pretty cool!", because our patients benefited dramatically. It was that clinical leadership, change management initiative right at the beginning of my career that made me realize I was a leader.

You were trained as a doctor and cancer surgeon. Now you are the CEO of University Health Network. Did you want to be a leader?
Not particularly, but I've always been a leader. I led a Cub Scouts pack, a Boy Scouts pack, baseball teams, hockey teams, football teams, student council, and more. I fell into those roles without really thinking about them too much.

How did you prepare for the role of leadership at University Health Network? You didn't arrive there one day and say, "I'm the leader—just follow me." What did the process of learning to lead look like?
It was very much experiential learning based on enhancement of clinical care. I encountered a number of change management challenges based on trying to enhance cancer care and orthopedic care. Those experiences, plus mentorship from senior surgeons and hospital administrators around how things work in the hospital environment, were useful. By the time I got to the point where I was ready to bid for the CEO role, I had completed the Advanced Management Program at Harvard and a few leadership courses at the University of Toronto. I had a little bit of formal education beforehand.

What's the best leadership advice you ever received that helped you develop into a better leader?

Probably to look at the drive for quality improvement and change management in our environment and link it to patient outcomes. It's very easy to engage people on health care. However, if you're actually looking at enhancing the quality of the care of patients and your intentions take money out of the system, figure out a way that you can actually align your intentions with patients' quality experience.

Does this always work?

It always works. You need to have a great story.

You were a cancer surgeon, then chair of Clinical Counsel of Cancer Care Ontario, COO, and now CEO at University Health Network. As you transitioned to more and more senior roles, what were some of the challenges that you faced, and how did you overcome them?

I've had some interesting roles. I've been a teacher, scientist, surgeon, and administrator, and all of those jobs were interesting and I was reasonably successful at each of them. *My biggest problem was that each role kept expanding, and, at a certain point, I thought,* Okay, I've got to start dropping things. I can't be successful unless I drop some things. *It was hard to stop doing surgery and tricky to become the CEO.* It was challenging to manage the role so that it fit into the time available to do it.

What changed in terms of the competencies or character required to be effective in the leadership role?

Leaders in the automotive industry sometimes come from finance and other times from production. The best leaders in that industry come from the design world, because they love cars. They build cars and know how to develop cars that are good for consumers. They make consumers want to buy those cars. I'm a product guy. Physician leaders and clinician leaders in health care are passionate about the products they produce. That part of the leadership role—the knowledge about how to design and communicate about products—was already there. I had to develop political skills and learn how to deal with government. It took some time for me to develop those skills.

The health-care system is hard to navigate and, at times, appears to be highly political. How did you learn the political skills required to be effective?

Through experiential learning and trial and error. Fortunately, I had that first successful experience to hold up as an example. We put in place a system for Ontario that was considered a cancer care model. I could validate my role as a leader, and politicians and bureaucrats started coming to me. It was simply experiential learning, and I learned that it was not much different from politics at a hospital. You listen to what people need and figure out how you can help them and how they can help you. You learn to make trade-offs.

Can you please reflect on your leadership? I found out that people around you admire you as a leader. For you, what is the key to good leadership?

The most important thing is that you care about patients. That needs to be authentic. It's like being a product person because you want to design new systems that work for patients, and you want to incorporate the great science into clinical care to create more effective and cost-effective methods. That is my passion. I think people would probably describe me as passionate about that, and eager to develop a leadership team that will do those things. The most important thing for me is the drive and innovation to create new knowledge and systems that help patients. That sense of innovation is the hardest thing to find. If we find a person who has got that, but not the other leadership skills, we'll try to teach him or her those other leadership skills or will surround him or her with people who can help in those areas.

You are leading a research and teaching hospital. It is about innovation and further development—learning is front and center. What are you learning these days to become an even better leader? Are there any recent "aha" moments?

I constantly learn lessons about letting go, even though I thought I understood that five years ago.

Can you please elaborate?

The executive team that I've got around me now is far more liberated to innovate than it has ever been. That is due, in part, to the relationship and trust that has been developed over time, and, in part, because I let the team go. I recognize that it's important to learn what each person values, how each person contributes to the culture, and to make sure each person understands what we're trying to accomplish as a team—and then to back off. I let my team members go, but am there when they need help, or to assist with milestone checks. I've learned to do this progressively.

You mentioned the word "trust," and that word comes up a lot in my interviews with leaders. How do you build trust in your organization and how have you learned to trust others, especially in the political and multi-stakeholder environment in which you operate?

I think it all boils down to the fact that health care inspires our business. It builds our idealism and our vision. There are also a couple of things that inspire our passion. One is that we talk about the Canadian publicly funded health-care systems and the fact that they are the key elements of the social fabric of Canada. I must admit that we're a little bit contrived in saying that the system is under tremendous risk and it's University Health Network's responsibility to demonstrate how it can be sustainable. That element underlies a lot of what we do. There is also research that says our goal and responsibility in the system is to innovate. We have a moral responsibility to innovate, and that's why I come to work at University Health Network. I care about the sustainability of the publicly funded system and about bringing innovation to patient service. Those two things are aspirational and the people in our organization align around that kind of a message. *It starts with trust. If you really believe that people feel as passionate as you do about those things, then you trust them. You realize they are going to make mistakes, but those mistakes will be learning experiences.* In pursuing those two goals, we've also developed some additional goals, such as wanting to have the best people and wanting to treat people the best—but it starts off with the products.

What have you learned about trusting others?

There is trust and I also verify that metrics are there for people so they know what I expect and how my trust of them is related to them meeting my expectations. I put things in a measurable form, which is actually not much different from what we do in health care. In health care, we're used to measuring the success of treatments by measuring some outcome.

You live in a transparent environment. Your actions are public. How did you learn to deal with such transparency and the associated pressures?

In health care, you've got to have accountability or else people will die. Accountability is not a problem. All of our data is on our website. We will evaluate any result to see if it has significance and use it to improve quality. That kind of action is engrained in our culture. Our goal is to record 5,500 incidents per year. This means we want our staff to record 5,500 mistakes. We apologize to patients when we make a mistake. We tell people that we're going to make mistakes, and we also assure them that we're going to tell them what we'll do to fix those mistakes. Our targets are constantly evolving. Our board has a very impassioned quality committee and most of its members are laypeople, but they've learned by asking the right questions. These committee members are smart and they've learned that, if they ask the right questions, even as non-experts, they can actually learn to hold physicians accountable. We have a board that demands accountability, and has done so for years. We have a history and culture of accountability that we're proud of and it's all over our website.

I've seen enough examples in business settings that tell me that taking ownership is difficult, at best. Is "accountability" just a word that we use?

I don't think it is. Our hospital policy says that, if you make a mistake, you must tell the patient and you must apologize. I chair the quality and care committee at the hospital that reviews those 5,500 incidents, and our senior executive team is there at the table, so the highest level of the organization looks at those mistakes. There aren't that many egregious errors, but there are some. We treat tens of thousands of patients a year, so, if an egregious error is made, we'll talk to the patient or the patient's family and say, "We're sorry we made a mistake, but here's what we're doing." Doing that has reduced the number of lawsuits we've had.

What expectations do you put on yourself in the leadership role? What is your commitment to lead?

My biggest commitment is to the executive team. My primary goal is to inspire the people who report to me—I've got 13 direct reports—and to hold them accountable and coach them. I care very much about these people, and that keeps them connected to the organization. A leader should be visible and present on the shop floor, and make a point of regular visits to the shop floor to take care of people and engage them. That's the next layer of leadership. *The primary element of my leadership is to make the 13 people who report to me successful.*

I know what sustains you—I see it quite clearly because you talk very passionately about your leadership at University Health Network—but what drains you?

The hours do. My day starts at 7 a.m. and usually ends at about 9 p.m., in part because there is a huge amount of fundraising involved. I end up at cocktail parties smiling at people and thinking, "What am I doing here?" We've been successful and we bring in C$130 million a year. Fundraising is part of the game, but, sometimes, I can't help but think, "Is this really worth it?" I realize, though, that we're not going to get the financial support unless I'm there.

There is always a cost to leadership. What has been the price of leadership for you?

Leading the hospital is a great job. We have unbelievable people, some who are the most outstanding people in the world. I'm a little tired, but there are probably about 10 or 15 people here who are the best in the world at what they do, and a lot of people who really care about what they do, and that is just outstanding. My wife tells me, "It's not your work, it's your hobby," and she's right. Being around the hospital, driving administrators and driving clinical, is a hobby that I enjoy.

How did you develop resilience to cope with the stress and adversity in this particular environment?

I build off the people on my team. I love to visit the floors at the hospital. I don't know if you have heard the expression "rink rats" that Canadians use to refer to people who love hockey. Rink rats are people who stay on the ice long after they've finished playing hockey, just to skate and shoot the puck because they just love being on the ice. That's how I feel about hospitals; I love hospitals. I love the people who work in the hospital. I get my resiliency from the nurses, the housekeepers, and the people who sell you a coffee at Second Cup. It's a great environment where everyone is energetic and focused on the needs of others. It's very altruistic.

I understand that University Health Network was named one of Canada's "top 100 employers" in 2009 for the sixth consecutive year—is that correct?
Yes, and [Mediacorp Canada] told us it couldn't give us the distinction anymore. We've been told not to apply anymore.

Good leaders learn. They evolve. How has your leadership evolved over time?
Being appreciative matters, and looking for different views is important. If not, you can rapidly get into the process of groupthink. Doctors and nurses think one way, so we need to engage people from the private sector and learn their perspectives on events. Getting different opinions has helped me to grow as a leader. I used to think I knew everything about hospitals!

What were some of the hardest things for you to learn in becoming a good or an even better leader?
That you need to get rid of people who are failing. Since you selected them and mentored them, if they don't deliver, you feel it's a reflection of your selection process. You have to put that feeling aside and you've got to be tough sometimes. Usually, when this happens—and it has only happened three or four times for me—the people are so relieved that you're letting them go because they know they're failing and they know they can't do it. It's usually an act of kindness.

Leaders learn to manage paradoxes. You have to be aggressive, but you also have to be patient. You want to be humble, but, at the same time, you have to be confident. Those leaders with confidence can become arrogant, and, perhaps, reckless. How did you learn to manage those paradoxes in your leadership career and, hence, maintain balance?
Everybody needs somebody to report to, but board members can only hold you accountable for what they know to be important. You've got to guard against the executive that says, "Well, the board can't possibly understand, they're not experts." You've got to make sure the board knows what the issues are, and holds you accountable. We've got a couple of board members that drive me a little crazy, but they are the most valuable board members we've got.

Is that because they keep pushing you and asking you questions?
The most important board members are the ones that keep asking you questions. You can't have enough of those people. Board members who pat you on the back and tell you that you're doing a great job aren't the most important ones. They aren't doing the work of asking questions and trying to figure out where problems might arise.

We have seen that in the lead-up to the financial crisis—board members did not always ask the tough questions.
Yes, nobody asks the right questions, or the CEO is glib and articulate and slaps everybody on the back and says, "Don't worry—trust me." I tell my team members

that they are responsible for providing the board with enough information for the board to hold them accountable. I also tell them that only they know what information the board needs to have. Sometimes, my team members don't want to hear that and they say it's too much detail. When that happens, you've got to say, "No, that's the detail that's important."

What advice do you have for people as they embark on their journey of learning to lead?
I learned to lead from my experience in learning to be a doctor. Doctors are naturally born to be problem solvers. Doctors plan, do, study, and act—it's part of their culture. People put their faith in doctors, so doctors learn to lead people through situations—that part comes naturally. More formal stuff came later, but, for me, that was an excellent foundation for leadership. The clinical foundation for leadership is interesting, and there isn't much written about that.

Leadership Themes

- The role of the leader is always expanding. Leaders can't be successful unless they drop things and let others lead.
- Leaders must be transparent. They will make mistakes and they'll have to explain what they'll do to fix those mistakes.
- Leaders make sure that each person on the team understands what they are trying to accomplish as a team.
- Leaders must "walk the talk." They should be visible and present on the shop floor. They make those who report to them successful.
- Leaders collaborate. They look for different views to avoid groupthink.

24

I Like to Think People Think I Stand for Something

Eileen Mercier

Eileen, when did you first realize you were a leader, and what happened to make you realize it?
I think I'm still figuring it out. Mostly, I think I found myself in situations where there was no other way out than to take charge. I guess that's the closest I could come to it. It's still evolving. I don't think there was any one defining moment.

Did you want to be a leader?
I don't think I ever thought about it that way. My father was particularly demanding and I think he always felt I should be at the top of my class. If I got 95 out of 100, he wanted to know where I lost the five marks. A lot of people might have that story, but I think it shapes your thinking that there is no other place that's good enough. I think that is what starts the ball rolling more than anything else.

How did you learn to lead? You don't wake up one day and proclaim yourself to be a good leader. What experiences did you learn the most from?
I think a lot of it is watching other people, both the good and the bad. You learn a lot from people whom you admire. You admire their style, the way they do things, and the things that they make happen. Whether you realize it or not, I think you become a student of that, and then, when you see something that really doesn't work, you file that away, because you want to avoid those mistakes, if possible. You make enough mistakes on your own and you don't want to repeat other ones from which you should have learned.

Can you talk about one of those role models who provided a lifelong lesson—good or bad?
I was very junior at the TD Bank Group in the early 1970s. The president and chairman of the board was Allen Lambert, and he was famous around the bank for collecting art and Inuit sculptures. One day, I was riding in the elevator with him. I got into the elevator and he was there, and he looked at me and said,

"I'd like you to see something." He took me to the executive floor, where I had never been, and over to a pair of paintings and said, "I just got these, and I was wondering what you think about them?" I like art, although I'm not an artist myself. I told him what I thought and what I saw there. He said, "Fine, thank you. I really appreciate that," then took me back to the elevator and sent me on my way. Having him talk to me and be interested in what such a junior person thought was a huge lesson for me in how to deal with people, engage people, and give them good memories of you.

I read an article about you in *The Globe and Mail* (Toronto, Canada). The article makes the point that you are not afraid of anything. To quote: "For the past 16 years, she had been a blunt and vocal conscience on more than two dozen boards, challenging executives and directors when she believes salaries are exorbitant, financial results opaque, or corporate behavior too risky. It is particularly unique to hear the criticism emanate from the small and self-conscious rank of female directors." ("Eileen Mercier: 'It's all about multitasking,'" 2012.) I have three questions. First, how come you are never afraid? Second, how did you develop the confidence? Third, what have you learned about becoming influential in communication?

I was taught never to be afraid. My Dad used to tell me that he wasn't afraid of anything. He always used to say that you shouldn't be afraid because that was a very important component in getting ahead. I developed confidence from watching other people. When I was at TD Capital in my early days, the bank allowed those who were involved with the different investments to be observers at the board meetings. We were supposed to only sit and listen, but I watched a lot of other people who were contributing and knew that, someday, I would be doing that too. I knew I could do it if I just had a little bit more time to figure out how. I picked up things from watching a lot of very, very good people in those early days. And then, of course, you develop your own style. It's about principles and things that you feel strongly about as being right or wrong, or as making sense or not making sense. It's also about finding a way to get those ideas into the conversation in such a way that people can listen for those things, or, at least, take those things into consideration. You don't win arguments around the board table. It's all about getting the group to come to a decision that is sensible and right. If, too many times, the group doesn't do that, or the group does something that you don't feel happy with, you have to go. I've left a bunch of them because, for one reason or another, it just wasn't working. It could have just as much been about me as somebody else, but, if the chemistry isn't right, you know you can't continue. You have to find a way to become a productive member of the group.

So, what would I have seen you doing in these meetings?

I guess a lot of it revolves around asking questions, because you can ask questions in such a way that you bring out the point that you want to make one way or the other. I guess you have to make sure that the questions get asked, because, if you don't, then maybe nobody will ask them and the point won't get discussed. I spend a lot of time raising issues, asking questions, and then trying to move the discussion in a way that will eventually make for a better decision, or, at least, one that everybody has thought through.

You can't always be at the front of the line. So, what did you learn about followership? I imagine followership might be a challenge for senior leaders, including CEOs?

It's funny you mention that. Imagine a group of CEOs around a table—a bunch of Type A people that don't react well oftentimes to not getting their own way. As a board member, I've only been chair a couple of times, but I've been chair of committees, and so you get a good mixture of people. You have to decide which things are important to you, and which things you think are important to the company, and then work on those things, because you just can't do everything. There are lots of other people who have different skill sets in different areas, and I'm quite happy to let them go forward. One of the hard things to learn about board meetings is that you don't have to have an opinion on everything. There are lots of times when the best course of action is to sit and do nothing, and just listen to others having a conversation. As chairman, that happens more often than not. What you want is for the other people to talk, and you can do a summing up at the end. You have to do a lot of listening to people having conversations and learning something about things that are not your area of expertise.

What were some of the hardest things to learn in becoming a good or an even better leader?

I went through a lot of very difficult times when I was with Abitibi-Price Inc. [now Resolute Forest Products]. There was a time, in 1992, when we were in a deep hole. It was an awful time in the marketplace, and the currency was going against us. We had to sell off a lot of assets. Dealing with that situation was like catching a falling knife. Things were getting away from us and we had to rein them back in and get everybody to work together. We had to work very long hours and work through a lot of very thorny problems. You learn a lot going through an experience like that. If you haven't gone through a very bad corporate experience, I don't know how you'd learn those lessons. From such experiences, you gain a set of skills that you sometimes wish you didn't necessarily have to have, but they are all part of a tool kit that adds up to a sum of experiences. You certainly say to yourself, "I never want to go through one of those again." But, sometimes, you have to deal with the situations you are dealt. I don't know how you get that experience any other way.

What was the best leadership advice you ever received that helped you develop into a better leader?

Someone once told me, "Become very, very good at one thing, and then you will get opportunities to do other things as a result of that and everything else will open up." After receiving that advice, I decided I was going to become the best at analyzing and synthesizing information and then making concrete recommendations.

What have you personally experienced as a barrier to learning and how have you tried to overcome this barrier?

Listening is something we like to think we do well, but probably don't do as well as we should. There are also situations where we think we know a lot and then we later find out there was much more to learn.

What expectations do you put on yourself in the leadership role?

We're our own worst critics. You never quite live up to what you want to be, but you have to think about it and then let it go. You can't dwell on these things, but you are always thinking about what you could have done a little bit better, and how you could have gotten more out of somebody or been more helpful or got a better decision. You never quite get over those things. You always want to do that bit more.

True. But can you talk a little about what you stand for as a leader—the expectations that you put on yourself?

That's a hard one. *I like to think people think I stand for something because I'm not shy about talking about issues, including ethical ones.* I'll give you an example. One of the companies of which I'm on the board has quite a big operation in Brazil. The internal auditors discovered an issue involving a loan. At the audit committee meeting, I asked a follow-up question about the event. Management told us that the perpetrator was still there. This was three or four days after they had found out about the transgression. I asked to get the CEO of that business on the phone. We were about nine hours away from where he was at the time, but I said, "I don't care what the time is, get him on the phone." So, we got him on the phone, and I said, "What are you thinking? What kind of a message is that? This person has to be out of there, and everybody needs to know what happened and why." Management and the committee were shocked, but I just couldn't understand it. Occasionally, somebody has to just say, "Beg your pardon?"

Where do these convictions or principles come from? Is that upbringing?

Partly, but also it's my training. As a chief financial officer, you have to have these principles—you have to stand for something—and people need to understand that you stand for something. You can't always be there, so your staff has to be able to say, "What would she do?" and then do that. They have to know. I used to say to the people who worked for me in corporate finance, "First, you have to understand that investment dealers are the enemy. They are not your friends. They may want to take you to lunch, but they may want you to do something that is in their best interest, not in the best interests of the company." You have to teach them from your hard-won experience to save them from making a mistake, if you can.

What has been your most rewarding experience as a leader and why?

It's watching people develop, particularly watching young people really take off. A lot of times you'd hire them right out of school, or you'd hire very junior people, and now they are senior officers of companies and doing wonderful things. They've gone away from you, but they still stay in touch. You see how far they've come along.

Are you a mentor to these younger people?

I have always tried to mentor, particularly the women, but often young men as well. I also mentored some MBAs as well as young directors and women who would like to become directors. It always gives you a lot of satisfaction to see them succeed.

One of the things I found out is that leadership is about learning to manage paradoxes. Earlier, you said that you have to be principled. At the same time, though, I can imagine situations where you have to be pragmatic. How did you learn to manage those paradoxes in your leadership career?

The pragmatism piece is probably the hardest because it sometimes involves political realities. I think this type of solution is often the most unsatisfying because you realize that there might have been a better answer, or that you may have to wait for one. So, you don't get much satisfaction from those, but you also realize that you know that's just the way of the world. I think the main thing is you have to be able to let go and move on. I don't have the time to spend ruminating over what might have been. It's very unsatisfactory, and I'm too busy.

You received an honorary degree from the Schulich School of Business [York University, Canada] in 2010. You delivered an interesting convocation speech. Discussing reputation, you said, "In business, as in life, in the final analysis, [reputation] is really all you have. Don't lend it to any company or individual that you do not trust. Your reputation must be your first, last, and most important consideration." First, can you elaborate on that statement, and, second, how did you learn the importance of that message?

First, you learn it from your family. But, also, there have been a lot of examples of companies and people that went wrong and how it's impossible to recover from that. *In my mind, as an individual in business, you're selling yourself—a skill set and a reputation—as a package. Anybody can have a skill set, but a reputation is built very carefully, over many years.* If you overstate your academic achievements, somebody somewhere is going to find out, and, with one little thing like that, everything you've ever done is called into question. There are some things you can recover from, but many of these things that we're talking about you can't— you're never the same after that. So, when I was putting that speech together, I asked myself, "What do young people need to hear?" and I thought that message was really important.

In Canada, you were among the very first women on the boards of directors of large organizations. How has being a woman affected the learning process?

Maybe I think differently. *I'm never afraid to speak up on boards. I'm not afraid of confrontation or controversy, and I think a lot of the people who have been on boards for a long time don't like controversy or confrontation in the boardroom. It's just something I've observed, and so often they would look at me and wait for me to ask the question, or say something, because they didn't want to and they knew I would.* I guess it's subtle, but I believe it's there, and I think it's often women who do this.

I didn't want to be treated differently, and so I never wanted to be the token woman. If somebody asked me to be on a board, I would try to find out what they thought I was bringing to it. I'd ask, "What is it that you want from me, and what are you going to give me in return in terms of a learning experience?" If they couldn't articulate well enough what it was they thought I brought, I would be more suspicious that they were just looking for somebody who looked different, and I didn't have any time for that. I've made lots of good board choices and a few that weren't as good, and I've learned from every single one. The same goes for career choices—you make some career choices that are better than others, but no experience is ever wasted.

I was looking for people who really did want a slightly different point of view and, of course, one of the big demand factors in my case was the finance portfolio. If you have a board mostly composed of CEOs, not many of them come up the finance route—very few. They usually come from operations or marketing. To find somebody with a finance background, you have to look elsewhere. I had a valuable network, so I got a lot of calls from people whom I had worked with who had other connections. That was how it started.

But that's an important lesson, too—the networking piece—right?

It's very important. When I counsel people, it's about making sure that you develop these connections early in your career. You shouldn't wait to try to develop them until the point that you need them, because people recommend you based on personal experience. Even if you're going through a search firm, somebody has to speak for you. The people who will speak for you are people who have had some kind of reasonably deep knowledge of your capability in a work setting, and, for that, you need to have spent time with them, and they need to know something about you. You have to get that early because you can't manufacture it later.

We talked about the influence of your Dad. How has your Mom affected your role as a leader?

She was a force of nature. She was a nurse in the 1940s and she was an operating room nurse at the Toronto General Hospital. She was a very capable person and fearless in her own way. I don't think there was a lot of fun involved in being an operating room nurse in the 1940s. They didn't have the equipment that they have today. She quit when the family came along, because that's what you did in that era. Then she nursed the rest of the world—she looked after all the old people in the neighborhood. She died last November, when she was 93. She was a big influence.

This book is about learning to lead. What question did I forget to ask you about the learning process? What did we not touch on?
It's just a journey. When you asked me to do this, I really had to think about it. How I've learned to lead is not something I think about every day. I just go out and do whatever it is I'm doing. At this stage, I'm not likely to change a whole lot, but you can still learn. At the Ontario Teachers' Pension Plan board, we decided we were going to do peer reviews, and we had a facilitator come in and ask us all questions. We each assessed the contribution of everybody else, and then received our own feedback. That's a very humbling experience. Every little wart—everything that you do that people wish you didn't do—was there, along with the few times when people said, "Oh yeah, great job on that." You take for granted all the good stuff, and it's always the little criticisms that come out. There's no question about not continuing to learn, because it's really all there if you're willing to take it in.

Leadership Themes

- Take the time to learn from difficult situations and understand how not to encounter them again.
- Understand the importance of reputation and how it follows you throughout your career.
- Try not to be afraid and let your voice be heard.
- Learn to lead by watching other people, both good and bad.

25

Leaders Tend to Be People of Broad Interests and Knowledge

Purdy Crawford

Purdy, how would you characterize your leadership style or approach to leadership?

When I worked on government committees and with boards of directors in both Canada and the USA, I was exposed to and observed many topnotch business leaders. I observed that there are many brands of leadership, and that leadership styles should differ according to the situation. For instance, stickhandling a merger requires a different leadership approach than fostering excellence in operations.

My leadership style has always involved being open to people. It is critical not only to relate to people, but to also make them relax around you and know they can present their views. A book on Abraham Lincoln, *Team of Rivals: The Political Genius of Abraham Lincoln* (New York, NY: Simon & Schuster, 2005), describes how Lincoln related to people—and it really blew my mind. The book describes how Lincoln brought into his cabinet people who were opposed to him, including three opponents for the Republican nomination, who, for the most part, thought Lincoln was a country bumpkin. However, within eight months to a year, he succeeded in getting these people to look up to him. His rivals were turned into allies because he had the confidence and wisdom to collaborate with the best people. It's a great story. *I have learned that combining the perspectives of people from different backgrounds and with different viewpoints and expectations can be a source of advantage in the marketplace.*

I used to visit the leadership teams of various companies at their offices, and would take people with me and try to get them to ask the teams questions. For example, when I became chief operating officer of Imasco Ltd. in 1985—and later president and chief executive officer (CEO)—I didn't know much about operations. We had a number of holdings, such as Shoppers Drug Mart and Hardee's fast food restaurants, and their operators were reporting to me so I tried to learn about them. I made it my personal challenge to understand Shoppers Drug Mart and I visited the branches. I loved those visits and learned a lot about operations from them.

I think leaders have to make some difficult decisions once in a while. We once owned Peoples Drug Mart in the USA and I had to fire the person running the organization because of poor results. I didn't want to ruin his Christmas, so I waited until after the holidays to do it. Thinking about that sure ruined my Christmas, since I had never done anything like that before. I later had to do more of that.

When I look back over my career, I wish I'd been tougher at times. I find the hardest thing is to come to grips with dealing with a CEO. Openness helps, but it can still be challenging. When you have to fire someone, I find it helpful to keep in mind that doing so is a win–win. When you replace that person with someone better suited to the organization's goals, your company moves on in achieving success, and, likewise, the person fired has an opportunity to get reoriented in terms of a career. When a person is particularly ill suited for a position, it is not necessarily his or her fault. Companies change—sometimes overnight—and long-time employees and managers can find themselves on the outside looking in, in terms of skills and orientation.

What have been the formative influences on you as a leader? What did people do to help you?

I attended the law program at Dalhousie University. One professor, Graham Murray, wasn't very well liked. He'd always annoy his students by ending his lectures saying, "This stuff is horribly complicated, so you'd better do your reading." The material was complicated, and I'd think, "By God, if he can't explain it, I'll figure it out myself!" As a result, I probably studied more than I should have. I've come to admire Graham for motivating me that way. The Law School dean, Horace Reid, was also significant. Graham and Horace had very different teaching styles— Horace was Socratic and Graham was quite different. Bill Lederman, an Oxford-type teacher who later became the first dean of Queen's University [Ontario, Canada] Faculty of Law, also influenced me. I also got to know Archie Cox, a Watergate special prosecutor teaching a seminar in labor law at Harvard, and Louis Loss, who was then the world's foremost leader on security regulation. I remember interacting with them, but I still didn't get the personal involvement that I got at Dalhousie University. Looking back, I think I studied too much and didn't get to see the finer things of Massachusetts or Greater Boston, but I guess you can't have everything.

There was also a lawyer at Osler named Hal Mockridge who was head of the firm and incredibly bright. He went to Princeton and read Greek and Latin. He had a broad-gauge approach. I worked with him a lot. He was never out chasing business. He figured people knew where he was if they needed a lawyer. I learned a lot from him. He had a good understanding of my weaknesses, and, from time to time, pointed them out to me.

Leaders tend to be people of broad interests and knowledge, like Hal. They maintain a broad perspective on business issues by reading widely. When I was on a committee reviewing the Ontario securities laws, I used to look for articles related to the topic and give them to a woman working with me whom I called my "chief of staff." She used to distribute these articles to the other committee members, and called them "Purdy's Picks." This started a tradition, and, today, most lawyers in the firm and a lot of clients and friends get Purdy's Picks. The articles typically included in Purdy's Picks are from *Barron's* newspaper, *Fortune* magazine, the *New York Times*, the *Wall Street Journal, Forbes* magazine, the *Financial Times, Harvard Business Review*, and other business publications. Occasionally, when I'm away in Nova Scotia for the summer and don't get Purdy's Picks out for three or four weeks, I get calls from people asking what happened to it.

I tell the young lawyers at Osler that they'll be better lawyers if they understand business and public policy issues. That's true of business people, too—they shouldn't have a narrow focus.

What was the best leadership advice you ever received that helped you develop into a better leader?

Paul Paré, my predecessor at Imasco, also had a broad-gauge view. He liked to play golf and played better than me. He was a member at Augusta National Golf Club in Georgia. A group of us would golf there together. It was a great experience, but, at times, I was frustrated because I didn't play golf well enough. Paul, on the other hand, didn't get uptight. He used to tell me, "Don't sweat over it." His advice was to be comfortable with your decisions. Think about it and then make a decision and move on. I'm very comfortable with that.

Good leaders must have a substantial degree of self-confidence. Making decisions is a lonely business. Listen to all the advice you can get, but, ultimately, you have to make the decisions. Self-confidence gives you the courage to make decisions and also to make mistakes. *Leadership has never been a risk-free endeavor and, in today's rapidly changing business environment, mistakes are a valuable source of learning.* Leaders who are confident can take instruction as well as criticism from their board members and other people. In my experience, those who have little or no self-confidence tend not to hire good people and are often defensive in the face of constructive criticism.

Part of learning is to be open to information, whether solicited or unsolicited. How difficult was it for you to open yourself up to information that you perhaps did not expect or want to hear?

It was not easy. I didn't react immediately and I'm glad I didn't or I might have done something stupid. I'd wait two or three days, until I was relaxed enough to talk to the source. I'd often find the source to be very helpful. *I have learned that good leaders listen—truly listen—to the people around them, and they see things from a multitude of perspectives.*

I grew up in rural Nova Scotia. My father was a coalminer. My English wasn't always as good as it should have been. I remember some lawyers took me aside once and talked to me about that. It wasn't easy for a lawyer to tell me I'm a "country bumpkin" and had better improve my use of the English language.

I am a great believer in being articulate. I quote people all the time. I think it was the Duke of Wellington, in writing to Napoleon, who said, "I didn't have time to write you a short letter, so I wrote you a long one." I remember arguing a case and the person opposing me stood up and argued for about three hours. As far as I was concerned, there were only three issues to discuss and he didn't have to take so much time. It is easy to ramble on, but it takes real effort and discipline to be succinct. It is a learning process.

Learning requires reflection. Did you reflect on your leadership?

I've prepared speeches on leadership. That process forced me to reflect both on what I've done as a leader and what I've read about leadership. I think if I knew at age 50 what I know now, I would have been a better leader going forward from then. I don't want to minimize what I did as a leader, but there was a learning process involved. This process involved reading a lot, including a lot of biographies, talking to other leaders, and reflecting on leadership when I worked on speeches. I'd be ahead of the curve today if I could go back knowing what I know now.

What is your commitment to the role of leadership?

Whenever I went into a meeting on a new subject, I tried to make sure I knew more than anybody else there. I'd read or work on the weekend and make sure I knew the file forward and backward. I was also good with people. I remember once being on the board of Canadian National Railway. The federal government owned Canadian National Railway and it was getting ready to distribute its ownership to the Canadian public. The company had hired an outside lawyer as general counsel. He explained something to the board and I thought he was dead wrong on this particular issue. I didn't say anything during the meeting, but, instead, spoke with him afterward and gracefully gave him an opportunity to change direction. I didn't want to embarrass him in public because I had had experiences myself where somebody would interrupt me in front of everybody and ask, "Are you sure that's right?" I'm good with people and good with relationships. The ability to relate well to people is of paramount importance. Robert Horton, former CEO of British Petroleum, put it bluntly when he said, "No one will follow a turnip!"

You have always been interested in helping other people to develop as leaders. Do you think talented people these days take the time to reflect on their leadership and critically examine what they could have done better?

I remember in about 2000, when I went back to Osler, I wasn't intending to prac-tice law again, but thought I could help the younger lawyers. I think I did help to some extent, but I was also disappointed because they were so busy doing their own things that they didn't have time to talk about some of the issues involved. I found the most rewarding part of it was when I met regularly with the students and young associates. They would listen. However, when they had a meeting of young partners, only half of them would show up, so I reached them, to some extent, through Purdy's Picks.

How do you see the role of mentoring and leadership development? Is the mentoring piece a significant part of developing as a leader?

I believe it is very important for people in leadership and managerial activities to have one or more advisers or "mentors." Leaders can learn a great deal from their mentors' experience, intelligence, and frankness.

I recruited Brian Levitt for Osler, and he is now co-chair. Brian built the Montreal office, and soon became chair of the TD Bank Group. He was incredibly bright and hardworking, but didn't quite have the people skills that I had. I used to occasionally leave notes on his desk stating my observations and advice. For example, I told him that I thought he reacted too quickly to things that were unfolding. I think a lot of people do that. I always find it better to take a few hours, or even a day or two, to think about an issue. That contemplation period almost always changes your approach somewhat.

What do you think makes for a good mentor? What is required for the mentoring process to work? How would the person benefit from the mentor?

If you're running or operating in a company, it helps to show your mentee how you operate and, later, discuss the events and whether or not you did the right thing. That sort of interchange is what mentoring is all about. It's easier that way, rather than just having a theoretical discussion. That's how I helped to develop some lawyers at Osler. I didn't help them with technical skills as much as I helped them to develop good judgment.

I have seen mentoring relationships fall apart. What are some of the contributing factors to the derailment of these relationships?

Sometimes, people won't listen to you, so you're just wasting your time. For example, I was disappointed, the other day, when I learned some of the younger lawyers at the firm are not reading Purdy's Picks. It seems to me that they are really making a big mistake. Some lawyers tend to get very narrowly focused and think, "I have to understand this and this, so don't bother me with that other stuff." The good lawyers are not like that, and those are the ones that will rise to the top.

You have taken on significant challenges—how have you learned to cope with tension and stress?

Stress can be a good thing. It's tough to cope with, but it makes things happen. Sometimes, stress gets to me and, when it does, it's usually when I'm in the middle of trying to think through what I'm going to say the next day or in a letter or e-mail. But, during the day, when I'm going strong, other people around me might be losing their heads due to stress and blaming me for it, but I don't let stress get to me then.

How did you develop resilience to cope with stress?

I'm not entirely sure, to be honest. It might be my genetic makeup. Stress certainly impacted me more as a young lawyer because I didn't have a lot of confidence and I would worry about things. But, I'd also see people who were getting worked up because they didn't know exactly what they were supposed to be doing in their jobs, and I'd say, "You're lucky—ambiguity is the greatest thing for you! You've got the flexibility to do things."

Part of the reason why I cope well with stress is because I have a broad-gauge view and can see the big picture. I don't see things as only black or white. *It is critical to have a well-rounded view of the world and our place in it. Leaders must be competent in their fields, but they should never believe the sun rises and sets only in their own field of functional expertise.*

What has been your most rewarding experience as a leader and why?

A current example was from the period 2006–2009, when I chaired the committee that had to restructure the frozen asset-backed commercial paper market worth C$35 billion. I was in my mid and late 70s then, so it was quite surprising for me to have one of the top experiences of my career at that age. I didn't realize until it was over that it was such a highlight. It was hard work. I had the direct lines of all of the CEOs at the banks in New York and Canada. I got to know Mark Carney, Governor of the Bank of Canada, and his predecessor, David Dodge, and Finance Minister Jim Flaherty. They all answered the phone very quickly and I was grateful for that. It was hard to deal with the bureaucracy in Ottawa, but Jim Flaherty gave me his cell phone number and I could reach him any time.

If I had really known what was involved, I'm not sure that I would have participated. I was asked to chair a committee to restructure the commercial paper market and I didn't know anything about the paper market. It was all new to me and I thought we might be done in six months!

I never did master the technicalities of it the way some people, such as our financial advisers and some of the lawyers, did. However, that wasn't necessary—my role was to persuade the committee to make decisions. The committee members were all across Canada and we had about 80 meetings within two years. I got along incredibly well with, and gained the confidence of, the committee members and, even more so, the small investors. I remember I had no idea that we had about 2,000 investors of C$200,000, C$80,000, or C$1 million. There were thousands of investors who were retired public servants and retired schoolteachers and I met with them and responded to their e-mails. At first, they thought I was the enemy and they were justifiably upset.

Eventually, I gained their confidence. I'd say that accomplishment related more to leadership than technical know-how, by far.

You talked about how you were able to gain confidence—how did this relate more to leadership? What was it about your approach that, in the end, helped you to gain people's confidence?

I was flexible. If somebody made a point that seemed to make sense, I wouldn't get hard nosed about it. I think people respected my judgment and learned they could rely on me. *Good judgment is widely applauded as common sense, which we all know is not terribly common!*

This book is about learning to lead. What question did I forget to ask you about the learning process? What did we not touch on?

Max DePree, former CEO of Herman Miller, wrote in his book, *Leadership is an Art* (East Lansing, MI: Michigan State University Press, 1987), that leadership is something to be learned over time, not simply by reading books. I found this concept mind opening. Looking back over my career, both in law and business, the one regret I have is that I did not become more involved in the development of leaders. I was late in realizing that it is possible to do that.

During my career, I came across an incredibly bright young star who started his career with a strategic consulting firm. He was doing exceptionally well working in business development. Like all young stars, he was eager to broaden his experience, but, when given the opportunity to work in operations, he simply did not have the emotional intelligence competencies, such as self-awareness, self-regulation, motivation, empathy, and social skills, to do the job effectively, and he refused to acknowledge that he needed help to develop these skills.

In an earlier era, this shortcoming might not even have hit anyone's radar screen. However, this company has a well-educated workforce for whom the price of commitment is personal respect, a sense of inclusion, and opportunities to contribute and grow through shared ideas and goals. In this environment, his lack of emotional intelligence was clearly a barrier to success.

Luckily for him, he is now being put through a leadership development process that can, if he buys into it, help him to identify and overcome his shortcomings in emotional intelligence.

I think leadership skills are both inborn and acquired. There is a role for both nature and nurture. The good news is that people who are committed to enhancing their leadership skills can do so to a great extent. To do so, leaders must create a personalized development plan, or else any efforts are a waste of time.

Leadership Themes

- Combining the perspectives of people from different backgrounds and with different viewpoints and expectations can be a source of advantage in the marketplace.
- Leaders tend to be people of broad interests and knowledge. They maintain a broad perspective on business issues by reading widely.
- Be comfortable with your decision. Think about it and then make the decision and move on.
- Good leaders listen—truly listen—to the people around them. They see things from a multitude of perspectives.
- Don't react too quickly to things that are unfolding. Take a few hours, or even a day, to think about an issue.

26

Trust Is Built on Behavior, Not on What We Say the Values Are

Charles Brindamour

Charles, when did you first realize you were a leader, and what happened to make you realize it?
It might surprise you, but I never thought of myself as a leader. Not too long ago, I first realized that my leadership had an impact. When I look back on what we achieved through having good leaders around in a period of massive volatility, change, and uncertainty, I know leadership has made a difference. We've seen it have an impact on customer satisfaction and employee engagement, and it has made the organization stronger than it was at the start of a period that could have gone totally the other way. I never really thought of myself as a leader before, or early in life. I thought about this question. I tried to remember if I one day thought, "Yeah, I think I'll be a leader." I don't think so.

Did you want to be a leader?
To be honest, I didn't think in these terms. I always wanted to be with the best people around. I joined this company because the people had an incredible reputation. *It wasn't a conscious choice for me to be a leader, but I did choose to be associated with the best, the smartest, the toughest—the winners.* I wanted to thrive within the group, and, maybe, lead the group at one time, but not for the sake of leadership.

You've been at Intact Financial Corporation for more than 20 years and have held numerous positions. You spent significant time in The Netherlands and Romania. You are now the CEO of Intact. How did you prepare for the role of leadership? How did you learn to lead?
I would break it into stages. The first thing for me was to become self-confident, based on achieving things and building things. That's an important part of leadership. Through realization and achievement, I developed self-confidence in my ability, not to lead, but to contribute. The second key stage, in my view, was to build credibility with my peers, the people I lead today, the people on my team, and the rest of the organization. How do you do that? In my case, it was by contributing to what they want to do and build. Credibility is about helping others, in part. It's

about going above expectations. People like to be with you because you give more than what the customer wants. It's about being transparent, open, and honest with your colleagues. I think that was probably the most important point, because, as you rise in the organization, ideally, you don't want to have to gain credibility once you're in the role. You want that credibility to be in place before you are in the role. I think the third key element is to learn from the people with whom you work. It's about retrospection and going back and looking at my predecessors. For example, one of my predecessors was incredibly rigorous. I learned rigor from him, and, to this day, I think about how he would behave in certain situations. Another of my predecessors was incredibly good at putting himself in other people's shoes. I developed by reflecting on the exceptional behavior that I've seen within the organization. I think the fourth thing is just to strive to learn outside of your areas of knowledge and outside of your country. I devoted a lot of time to exposing myself to what else happened in the world.

You talked about things that you've learned from good leaders throughout your career. Have you also learned from bad leaders—such as, "I would definitely not do that"?

Yes, a bit, but nothing compared to what you learn from good leaders. For me, the core learning is more with the people that are around me. I talked about my predecessors in terms of preparing, but I learned from the people I have been working with at large. I think it's spotting the exceptional behavior around you, not just in other leaders, that has been key. I think that I've learned from exposures I had to bad situations for sure. But I was privileged to not be exposed to bad leaders much.

As you transitioned to more and more senior roles, what were some of the challenges that you faced, and how did you overcome them?

I think the most important area of learning, or area you need to be sensitive to as you move up, is the fact that, when you move up one layer, you don't manage the same people, the same profile, and the same level of seniority. As you move to be a senior VP, you manage vice presidents, which is very different from when you were vice president and managing managers, and, in turn, really different from managing employees. It's the adaptation, from step to step, to the fact that, all of a sudden, as you move up, the people reporting to you have different sets of expectations and things that drive them. To adapt, it's important to properly understand what drives the new level of the organization for which you're responsible. When moving into a new role, I'd spend a lot of time on that area so that I could be successful as quickly as possible. Clearly, as you move towards the CEO role, having a good understanding, not only of your operation and company, but also the environment in which you operate—whether it is economic, political, or industry dynamics—and how these things interact, calls for extra effort in terms of reading and reaching out to people who have been exposed to these areas.

Did this require a significant time commitment on your part?

Absolutely. A few months after I became CEO—in January 2008—I decided to block three or four hours every morning, as much as possible, to researching and exposing myself to areas that could influence the business, our strategy, or our employees. I've never done that before in my career. I invested a lot of time then, and still do today. It's a lot of fun.

Learning requires reflection. Do you reflect on your leadership?

I reflect all the time on the impact I have on others. It's introspection and retrospection on the impact you have on others in situations, in meetings, and when we debate projects. *I step back, look at the past year or two, and have this inner dialogue—probably more than I should—on the impact I have on others. I assess whether it was calibrated properly and whether it had the desired impact.* I consider whether or not it was constructive, whether the other party was open to the feedback, and so on. I spend a lot of time—informal time—retrospecting and introspecting on the impact I've had on others, and, therefore, on leadership.

Can you give me a specific example of something that you realized afterwards and said, "I didn't handle that properly, or I could have done things better"?

We foster an environment that's open and honest. It's critical, from my point of view, to get better every day. I don't think people are used to that. Newcomers in the organization have to adapt to the fact that all the questions are on the table. I think sometimes we have to be more sensitive to people's ability to be asked many questions or challenged with intensity. We have a strong desire to get to the bottom of things and that can be intimidating at times.

What were some of the hardest things to learn in becoming a good or an even better leader?

I found it difficult not to dismiss too quickly the things that are counterintuitive or appear illogical to me. I'm getting better at this, but it's difficult to properly weigh things that don't come naturally to you, or that might be counterintuitive. I'm working on this to ensure I don't miss out on those things that I would normally dismiss. For example, we are in an industry where product pricing takes some time and, when you miss on the trends, it can be really painful for a long time. Our organization tends to move fast on areas where trends are emerging. This generally tends to be the right approach for us. However, there are situations in which it makes sense not to act too rapidly and to instead pace yourself, but doing so would be counterintuitive to our culture and the way we operate. A second point, in line with that, is to remember that everybody is different. People have different sets of strengths and, in building the team, you want to create diversity, but also integrate the value of other people's strengths that might not be your strengths. You need to place the proper importance to the strengths that don't come naturally to you, or that might be foreign to you. Good leaders need to build the strongest team possible and this is not easy to do. It's easy to appreciate people who are better than you at things you're good at, but it takes more energy to appreciate people's strength in areas that you have not historically seen as important or in which you don't excel. This is difficult, but hugely important when you want to build a strong team.

What role did mistakes play in your learning process? Can you talk about a mistake you made as a leader and what you learned from that mistake?

Dealing with poor performance is relatively straightforward. People say I've been too patient with average performers.

How did you learn to step out of your comfort zone and take risks? You operate in an industry in which there is a lot of ambiguity and the decisions that you make today may not have an impact until years later?

The fact that we're rigorous and focused on the things we're really good at makes our business simple. We're in one country and have lines of business in which we have a competitive advantage and we know the business cold. That's the characteristic of my team. In my view, that's a precondition for risk taking. Once you build self-confidence, because you outperform your peers on a sustainable basis, the mindset allows you to take risks. As an organization, the self-confidence in what we're doing allows us to step forward. I've learned to take risks because I've been exposed to exceptional entrepreneurs as well, such as family members, when I was younger, or people I admire and have studied outside my organization. We have a few entrepreneurs on our team. I think the self-confidence to build risk came learning from these examples, and the fact that our foundations are really solid.

What have you personally experienced as a barrier to learning and how have you tried to overcome this barrier?

The first barrier to learning is very simple—you learn as you go along, but that only does part of the job. You need to step back and be conscious and disciplined about learning. It's a conscious effort and you need to make time for it. CEOs often sit in meetings 12 hours a day. *You have to see learning as a key element for moving the organization forward and making it prosperous. It's a key responsibility for you as the leader. If you don't make this a priority, you risk the organization becoming complacent. You need to make time for it in an organized fashion.* Another barrier to learning—if you accept the premise that you learn from what's around you—is that you might be fed nice information that's not necessarily real information. A key element for us, which is also a key leadership success factor, is to create an open and honest environment. We have 10,000 employees and we still evaluate our managers on their ability to create an environment where the information flows up. I try to do my utmost to lead by example on that front, and that in itself is a big source of learning. While finding time to do these things appears difficult, it is manageable.

Leaders often talk about their learning during a crisis-like situation, but it appears to me that leaders need to learn throughout the entire business cycle. Can you discuss how you learn during the full business cycle?

You don't want to get to the point where you're learning from a crisis. Learning needs to be done in the good part of the cycle so that you can prepare as much as possible for the worst. I strongly believe that a healthy dose of paranoia in good times is important, because it forces you to anticipate how things can go wrong. You need to be prepared for potential crises. The question becomes, "How do you learn about how things can go wrong?" We do a fair bit of introspection about what our organization has gone through in the tougher part of the cycle, where we dropped the ball in the past, and how we can consciously try to avoid that again going forward. We're working hard to learn from what went wrong in the past. I'm a big student of history as well. In 2007–2008, when things started to go wrong financially, globally, I invested a lot of time reading as much as I could on what happened in the past century to see if I could anticipate how bad things could get, so that we'd be prepared for it. I would say, having gone through that, that preparing for the worst in the good times is critical.

But this approach might be quite difficult for a lot of business leaders—they might say, "There is no crisis, there's no reason for change, everything is going well." Hence, taking the time to learn during good times requires even more discipline?

Absolutely. That's why I said earlier that, to me, learning is a conscious thing. It's not that you step back at the end of the year and wonder, "What have I learned?" You identify at the start of the year what you want to learn. I do that in January. I identify the few areas that I want to learn about or want to improve on and I go at it in an organized fashion during the year. Discipline is very important for learning.

What expectations do you put on yourself in the leadership role?

I think the key element for me, and the folks that I work with, is leading through example. We've clearly identified what values should guide the organization. We chose those values and what they meant word for word. We've identified the key elements that successful leaders should display in behavior. So, what I impose on myself is to lead by example times two on the values and on the leadership success factor. I think this is where you need to impose a standard on yourself that is higher, or much higher, than what you anticipate and expect of others, and you need to lead by example day in and day out. That's pretty much the main thing that I impose on myself.

One of the values is to act with integrity, and part of that is openness and being transparent and accountable. Those are easy words to use, and we use them all the time. Can you talk a little about how you have learned to give meaning to those two words—"transparent" and "accountable"? We're not always rewarded for being open and taking accountability.

I was exposed to extreme openness when I worked in The Netherlands, and, at first, I thought it was a bit odd. In observing the best leaders I've worked with, and in reading about a number of people I admire, open debate is a common factor. It's about weighing the pros and cons by putting everything on the table. You have a problem the moment people feel they cannot put everything on the table. What have we done, other than leading by example, on that front? We've clearly identified it as one of four success factors for our managers. We have a culture and one of the elements you'll see as a value in that culture is respect. ***For me, respect means that you don't lose it on people. This sounds basic, but I think you'd be surprised how often it's forgotten.*** That's key if you want people to speak up, because, the moment you lose it—even if it's only once or twice—the openness will shrink. I ask lots of questions, but I don't lose it. We've made it an important success factor for our leaders. We display it and my communications with the organizational members are very balanced. It's always, "Here's what is going well, here's what is not going well." I talk to my managers every three months. We have 750 managers here and I always conclude with one of their key responsibilities, namely to create an environment for the information to go up, because this is critical for our success. We need, as managers and leaders, the opportunity to improve things. To have this opportunity, the information has to be on the table, but there should not be negative consequences. Not only do you not want to lose it on people, but there should not be negative consequences when the information comes out. It's tough. It's not a lot of fun to hear about the bad stuff, but this makes a difference. It doesn't happen overnight. I think that, when people see that you act on their feedback and you don't lose it when you're being told something that is not pleasant, and when people are thanked and rewarded for their openness, it matters. It also matters that this is part of how our managers are being assessed. It gets engrained in how we're trying to run our business, and leading by example is really important here.

What have you learned about building trust?
Leaders are judged by how they behave and trust is built on behavior, not on what we say the values are. It's how we actually live them that matters, and it's the same thing for brands. I've learned from the person who helped us create the Intact brand. He said, "Keep one thing in mind: Brands are judged by how they behave." As we were about to invest in the brand, I knew we needed to make sure that the experience for clients and brokers would be up to par with the message we're conveying. I think this is true, as well, within the walls of the organization, with employees amongst each other and management with the employees—it's about living the values. It's about behaving the way you describe your organization. That's how I think trust is built. I think trust is built also by accumulating success and by recognizing what has been built.

How have you learned to trust others?
I tried to be with the best—the smartest and the toughest—the people that had the most success. It's easy, when you get in an environment of very strong players, to

trust. That's really important for me. We talked about transparency and openness, and, early in my career, I identified that as a key factor for me to reach out to people and not reach out as much to others when I felt the openness was not there. I think these are really important elements in terms of learning to trust others.

How did you develop resilience—to cope with disappointment, obstacles, setbacks, and not to get demotivated when things are not going your way?

In periods of difficulty, people look at you—your emotions, your face, and what you say—and you have to be conscious of the impact these things have on others. When there are 10,000 people, you have to be conscious of the impact these things have on the whole organization, and, eventually, on the service you're providing to clients and brokers. So, how have I developed resilience? Running has been a big source of energy and a source of reflection, and it has helped me cope with difficult periods. I don't know how much you can develop resilience. I think it's sort of a core attribute that's needed to do the job. Learning to have perspective on things is really important. It's never all black or all white, and having the time and the ability to step back and put things in perspective is important. It's about being in the solution mindset naturally, as a reflex, and having the people around you be in a solution mindset really helps you develop resilience. Despite tough times, you feel empowered, and that's a critical element for resilience. Another element in terms of being resilient is to have a clear sense of priority, particularly in periods of high demand or difficulty. I have a very clear sense of what I need to achieve over a given period of time, whether it is three years, one year, three months, or one week. I have a very clear sense of a few things I need to do, and I think having those anchors in place helps in tough periods. I rarely get overwhelmed by difficult situations as a result. I think this applies individually, and I think it applies to the organization as well—a very clear sense of the key priorities helps you go through periods of turbulence and, therefore, makes you more resilient as a company.

You're leading a successful organization. How difficult has it been to stay true to yourself, and to remain humble and not become overconfident?

In building the team, one of the key elements I'm looking for is authenticity. You can read people, and the more you can create an environment that's open, and the more grounded your team keeps you, the better you'll be. To be quite honest, it has not been that difficult. My wife and my daughters are doing a fantastic job in making sure that I'm true to who they knew 20 years ago, and who they know today. That's really important. Another point is, once you create an open and honest environment, it's very hard to pretend. It's so simple, but I think that's important.

What are you learning these days to become an even better leader? Are there any recent "aha" moments?

I'm focused on learning what worked well for the company we just acquired. I've been 20 years in the same company, so, the more insight I can have in other environments, the more I take. This is a fantastic opportunity for us, so a lot of emphasis is put on learning from the new people that are joining our team. We're also really pushing the culture of the organization to be completely customer driven. We're an insurance company. We're a company that has been built by people who are great at risk selection. But, we're competing in a world where there are new threats and new forms of competition, and a number of them are experts at understanding what's important to our customers. We need to be ahead of the pack on that. We're making great progress, but the big area of focus these days is on what the best organizations do from a customer-orientation point of view. A lot of time is spent on that these days.

Leaders learn to manage paradoxes. Leaders need to be optimistic and realistic. Confident and humble. Aggressive and patient. Intuitive and analytical. And so forth. How did you learn to manage those paradoxes in your leadership career?
One of my predecessor's exceptional behavior was to operate in the gray. He was fundamentally convinced that white and black don't exist, and had this incredible comfort of operating in a gray environment with multiple dimensions. I worked alongside him for many years, and one of the key things I learned from him was that the world was gray, and that the job of a leader—the CEO, in this case—was to see through the gray. When you're the leader of the industry –we're twice the size of number two—the danger of boasting is there because of our track record. One of our key messages to our troops and the staff who are in contact with brokers and customers is, "With leadership, comes humility." We are living a paradox. There are many reasons why we could boast, but we consciously go out of our way to say, "No boasting." We don't talk about our competitors, and humility has taken us where we are today. We need to build on that. Through an open environment, those paradoxes are pretty clear.

Good leaders learn. They mature. How has your leadership evolved over time?
I talked about how, as you grow in the leadership role, your appreciation of other people's strengths that are foreign or counterintuitive to you change. I've evolved a lot from that perspective because I've seen that other ways of doing things actually work. It took time, and maybe I should still be more trusting, but certainly I've learned a lot from that point of view as a leader.

Situational awareness is critical to good leadership. How have you, over time, developed this aspect of leadership so that the signals you pick up are the right signals and, hence, you can make an intelligent decision?
It's critical. You develop situational awareness when you are exposed to crises. But, quite frankly, I cannot say that, over 20 years, I've lived through many crises or difficult situations. I have had some, and I've learned from them. But, in my view, you develop context by studying what others go through. You learn by studying others outside the organization, such as other competitors or organizations in other fields or countries. I spend a lot of time reading about what organizations go

through and I ask myself, "Okay, if the organization had been more customer driven here, would it have made a difference? Would I have made the same call?" I try to gain a sense of context by learning from the context of other organizations. There have been so many extreme situations globally, especially in the past three or four years, and I've tried to learn as much as I could from these periods, as well as those back in time. I read about the Great Depression and the 1970s and so forth. I think I've learned to put things in perspective by looking outside our organization and our industry. I put things in perspective because, when you work with others, people come at things in different ways. Some people have a tendency to panic. Some have a tendency to react too slowly and never be bothered by anything, even when they should be bothered. Some people are in the middle. I try to assess each of these reactions. I analyze the sound bites that are coming out of the organization and weigh all of that and then take action accordingly.

What has been your most rewarding experience as a leader and why?

What's really rewarding for me, because I've been with this group for 20 years and many of my colleagues have been here for a long time, is to come into the office every day and be exposed to these people. Looking back on what has been achieved collectively is incredibly rewarding—more so than I would have thought a while back. The event that was probably the most rewarding for me as a leader was when we really made the most out of the financial crisis in 2008 and 2009. We improved our performance during the crisis. We improved growth, employee engagement, and customer and broker satisfaction in a very, very difficult period. Of everything I've done professionally, I'd say this has been the most rewarding moment, and I would think that many of the people that were along for the journey would feel the same way. Making the most out of a terrible period is incredibly rewarding.

This book is about learning to lead. What question did I forget to ask you about the learning process? What did we not touch on?

I think there's a lot of learning from your life—before the professional part of your life—that shapes you tremendously. I was taught about entrepreneurship by members of my family at an early age. I was taught at a very early age, by my father, the importance of being steady. I was taught about accountability at an early age by being exposed to different family situations and coping with things, good or bad. When I think back in periods of reflection, I go back to the first 20 years, or even part of the first 20 years of my life, and remember them as an important source of learning.

What about school? Any experiences at school or university that you think were really helpful in growing as a leader?

I learned one thing at university that really helped shape our culture and, hence, the influence of leadership today—rigor. School taught me rigor.

Can you define "rigor"?

School was about analysis and depth. It was about efforts to master a subject, a theory, an equation, and so forth. In my mind, in the intellectual context, rigor is about depth and the discipline to go deep. Rigor, operationally speaking, is about execution. It's about being interested in details—some details are really important and others are not important—and having the ability to contextualize which details are important. Being rigorous on these things is important, in my view.

You read a lot. What book was helpful about leadership or how to run an organization?

I've read a fair bit about Winston Churchill. His motto—"Never give in"—is about rigor, passion, and drive. That's a key element that I've retained. That's certainly an example to me.

Leadership Themes

- Leaders must be transparent.
- Leaders bring out the best in others and let them shine.
- Leaders see learning as a key element for moving the organization forward and making it prosperous.
- Leaders must "walk the talk"—they live the values of the organization.

27

You Have to Create Not Only a Network, but Also a System Through Which Information Can Flow

Amit Chakma

Amit, when did you first realize you were a leader, and what happened to make you realize it?

Leadership skills are innate to all of us, but how much we develop those skills is, in large part, determined by the opportunities we have to take on leadership roles, and how readily we embrace those opportunities. As a student, I enjoyed working with others on fundraising, community, and other projects. In playing those roles, you just do what needs to be done and things happen for all sorts of reasons. You always need somebody to take control. While I wouldn't define those as leadership roles, they were early indicators of my desire to work with others.

Standing up for what you believe is right is also a part of developing leadership skills. Let me give you a few examples: As a freshly minted assistant professor, I didn't have the reputation that others did, so students didn't flock to my labs. I asked some of my friends to recommend students, and one very good friend suggested a student to work with me. For me, that recommendation was as good as it gets—a friend and a good scholar who I trusted recommended somebody from his school. When I tried to admit this student, though, the dean of graduate studies would not allow it. I asked, "What else do you need? You trusted me and, through a competition, you hired me. I need a good graduate student for this project, and who is going to be more concerned about the quality of the graduate students— you or me?" He replied, "I'm sorry. We have these rules." I realized that I had picked a big argument. I was trying to do my job. My interest was motivated by my own ambitions—scholarly and career—to get a good graduate student, and the system was standing in my way. At the end of the day, the dean won and I could not admit that student. Over time, I have attracted some great students, but I have also learned the lesson that, to effect change, you need to be a part of the decision-making process.

As you expand your enterprise, you run into more of these difficulties. I recall being assigned to a lab course that involved running a large set of experiments. I liked it, so I took on the project happily. There were five professors, including me, assigned to that particular course for five experiments. These were large experiments and the students couldn't make them work because the equipment they were using didn't function properly, so, as a result, the data were inaccurate. Since the students were not able to analyze the data in order to write good reports, they all resorted to cheating. I told the students, "I'm going to fix this. The equipment is not functioning properly, and I don't know when it will be replaced because it's a large investment, so your purpose is not to get the anticipated data. You're going to be recording the data and you're going to tell me what's wrong with them. I'm going to test you on the spot as you're running the experiment." I did this very successfully. I also started questioning what those other professors were doing. They were paying very little attention to the lab—they were remaining in their offices, where students would have to go to see them. I went to see the head of the department and said, "I want you to assign me all five experiments and I want five teaching assistants. I'm going to run the lab. I'm going to be in the lab from one experiment to the next, but I want these four people out." The department head replied, "We have rules and people have to have the minimum workload." I argued, "This is not really a serious workload." These are examples where I said, "Boy, this is not right—this needs to change."

So, how do you change things? You change things by participating in committee activities and by challenging the status quo. When you take a proactive role, people notice that you are willing to take things on and they ask you to do more. That's, essentially, how I got involved in administration. It was by necessity, not necessarily by design.

Did you want to be a leader?

No. My intuitive feeling is that people who think they know what they want to be, and then plan a rigid career path, by and large don't achieve what they set out to do because life is unpredictable. I never planned my career. That doesn't mean that I don't think about what I'm going to do next. When I was provost at Waterloo and completing my first term, I had to think about whether or not I wanted to do a second term. The decision point came when I knew that, because of the time required to do my administrative duties, I was quickly losing my research edge. If I agreed to a second term, essentially, I'd be kissing goodbye to my research activities. I would be doing work I enjoyed, but I would not be at the forefront of the field. In accepting a second term, I knew that I would be looking at an administrative career for the rest of my life. If I returned to the classroom today, I would not be a top scholar or researcher, but I believe that, with all the experience I have gained, I would be a better teacher. Once I step down from this role, I may actually go into my faculty and teach.

In rapid succession, you went from a professor to the dean of engineering, vice president, academic, and provost—and now the president of Western University. How did you learn to lead?

I learned by doing and by observing others. Mentors come into play. Those of us in academia or in a professorial role have had mentors, such as PhD supervisors or other professors. I think the role of mentorship becomes part of our DNA because of our supervisory roles. I was fortunate enough to have a large number of wonderful people who taught me, either directly or indirectly. Human beings observe, and teachers observe more than others. I just like to learn about people. I find it fascinating to observe how people behave. I find negotiations fascinating, whether it's me at the table or I am observing others.

As one grows into senior roles with more responsibility, learning shifts from your own experiences toward what you have seen others do. Early on, you're learning mostly by doing, reading, or observing. I read a lot about universities after I became provost. Whenever I visit a country, I try to learn about the history of a particular university. I once had a fascinating conversation with the then president of the University of Amsterdam. I was at Waterloo and a group of Dutch university presidents were visiting Canada. After I described what Waterloo was all about, the president of the University of Amsterdam made a fascinating observation about Dutch universities. He pointed out that Waterloo has maintained close contact with its community and is supported by that community. He added that Dutch universities started out having strong linkages with their communities, but, as they grew older, acquired reputations, became more global, and also became more detached from their local communities. I thought that was a fascinating observation, and I began researching the history of some of those universities. When I'm looking at Western, I'm always mindful of the lesson I learned from that research. Historically, the community of London has supported Western, but, as the university grew larger, older, and more prestigious, it lost some of that support. I'm now trying to rebuild some bridges with the community.

As a leader, I also benefited from having some great mentors. The most significant mentor I had in my professional life was David Johnston, former president of Waterloo University. David never directly taught me, but he is a great storyteller and I learned lessons from his stories. I also learned by watching him in action. I remember inviting David to my house to meet my mother, and, unbeknown to me, he had asked my brother, "How do you show respect to your mother?" My brother had no clue why he was asking, and just thought it was one of those cultural questions. He replied, "We touch my mother's feet from time to time." On meeting my mother, without missing a beat, David touched my mother's feet. That was a heartfelt moment for me, and, more importantly, a learning moment. I was touched by the fact that David went out of his way to show his respect. My mother was only a little older than David, but he was not concerned about status or age—he just embraced the culture.

As you transitioned to more and more senior roles, what were some of the challenges that you faced, and how did you overcome them?

The higher you go, the more you have to rely on people. I learned that long before I was a university president. I learned that as dean. Although running a small faculty is completely different to running a university, the basic elements are the same. You have to keep your eyes wide open and learn just as quickly. That requires a certain skill set. As educators and as students, we actually have those skills, and you work at honing and broadening them throughout your career. That's a big challenge, but I've been blessed because of my personal life experience. I landed in Algeria at the age of 18 without knowing a single word of French or Arabic. I was faced with a culture that was totally foreign to me and food that I didn't like—including couscous and baguettes. I felt completely out of place there. If I had had money, or my parents could have afforded it, I would have returned home because it was so tough. Since I didn't have either of those options, I had to adjust to all sorts of changes, including cultural changes.

I have been privileged with the opportunity to live in many different places. Those experiences have helped me to develop a natural ability to open up and adjust to changes. As difficult as it was, I eventually fitted in while in Algeria. When I moved from Algeria to Vancouver [British Columbia], and then to Sherbrooke [Quebec], and finally to Calgary [Alberta], I also learned to adjust and to feel at home. It took me some time, admittedly, but I learned to embrace putting on my cowboy boots and my cowboy hat, going to the Stampede and yelling, "Yahoo!" I never thought I would leave Calgary. Then I went to Regina [Saskatchewan], and you might think, "Calgary, Regina—same thing." They are not the same. So, I had to adjust in Regina, too. I eventually felt at home in Regina, to the extent that, when I now visit there, it is as if I'm back at home because I still have so many friends there. My most recent move, prior to London [Ontario], was Kitchener-Waterloo [Ontario]. I don't think there is anybody there who wouldn't recognize me as part of the Kitchener-Waterloo community. While London is also a new city for me, I feel very comfortable here. London feels like my home. *All these moves have taught me that it's not just your education or the skill sets you have, but also your life experiences that shape you.*

Learning requires reflection. Do you reflect on your leadership?

Being a professor is a privilege, and the most significant thing that happened in my professional life was when the University of Calgary offered me a tenure-track position as a professor, and I am ever so grateful to that wonderful institution for giving me that break. After my first appointment in 1988, I could pick and choose what I wanted to do. This is beneficial because, when you're doing something you chose to do, you are motivated and you like what you're doing so you do your best. That is an important aspect of professorship versus being in some other professions. In most other professions, leaders, no matter how senior they are, don't always get to do what they want. Such people, as leaders, may have more say or negotiating power, but they don't have the kind of freedom that I enjoyed as a professor. Anything I have done since was something I wanted to do. At some point, you realize that you have a privileged role. I realized that even when I was an assistant professor—I thought, "Boy, I'm teaching!" The magnitude of what I was doing really hit me when I visited various chemical plants. I was in Fort McMurray, in Syncrude Canada's dining hall, when I heard someone ask, "Dr. Chakma, how are you?" Someone I had taught remembered me. I realized then that I had helped to shape the lives of those engineers. Incidents like that made me realize that I was privileged to have had the role I had. With that privilege comes responsibility, though. I always want to do my best. As I took on progressively senior roles, that conviction became even stronger.

I love every moment of my work at Western, but I also carry a heavy burden on my shoulders. I often look at the history of this university and how far it has come since its founding in 1878. During that time, there have only been nine presidents before me, so I feel very privileged to be leading this university. Sometimes that fact is overpowering so I tell myself, "My community—the Western University community—placed its trust in me." I don't look at what I do as my job, but as my mission. The community has given me an opportunity—a privilege—that only nine other individuals have had over the last 134 years. That makes me realize I must do everything I can, to the best of my ability, to advance the ideals and the mission of the institution. Having that conviction is important. *I think we want our leaders to have a sense of mission and personal commitment.*

Earlier you talked a little bit about the burden of the presidency, or being in leadership positions. What do you fear the most about the role of leadership and how do you overcome these fears?

I'm not afraid to fail, because of the scholar in me. I'm an experimentalist. In my lab, I failed all the time because I was exploring, and things don't always work out as you planned. It's in my psyche that failure is part of the game. I recognize that there will be people who will criticize me. From that point of view, I'm a risk taker—a calculated risk taker—perhaps even an entrepreneur, but an entrepreneur who is not going to take on so much risk that the institution would have to pay a price.

I recognize, however, that I have limitations. The longer you play the kind of role that I play, the more you understand your limitations. I remember once being at a meeting between the presidents from Canada's 15 largest research-intensive universities and 21 German university presidents. While there, I bumped into an old friend from my days at the University of British Columbia. He had been a postdoctoral scholar while I was a PhD student. He's now president of the Technical University of Dresden. Our other colleagues who have tried to form partnerships with Germany generally find such relationship building to be rather challenging, because of the cultural gaps, but here I had a personal friend who is leading a major university in Germany and who is willing to work with us. It was a great opportunity, except that it would mean nothing if no one else besides the presidents from Western and Dresden took an interest in developing a partnership. In my world, you see lots of opportunities yet only a fraction of those can be implemented because of the realities. As a result, you tend to become a bit conservative.

Here's another example from Western. I believe this university is way behind in terms of embracing online learning. We should be doing more and the students are demanding it, yet I haven't done much about it because I have not had champions to lead the effort. I am also still learning what needs to be done and hearing from people who have different views. Eventually, we will tackle this initiative.

As a leader, I also sometimes think that I am accepting too many obstacles and not advancing the mission of the institution fast enough. My second concern is that perhaps I'm too slow because I want to carry my colleagues with me. When I reflect on my time at Waterloo, I say, "I should have done things a lot faster. I took too long with that." I took two years to come up with the academic plan! I worry about how long things take, because it's my role to lead, but I don't want to move so fast that I find myself alone. I have to find the right balance. So far, I have been able to garner the support of my colleagues, but I often ask, "Am I pushing fast enough?" I'll never know. I may be pushing some people too hard, or in too many directions, and others not hard enough.

I hear that quite often—that there is that balance. Sometimes, people push too hard and end up losing their colleagues, and sometimes they finally take the initiative head on and people ask them, "Well, why did you wait so long?" How do you feel about that?
I ask my colleagues all the time, "Are we aiming high enough?" because there is no bar. I wonder what our capacity is, or if we are ambitious enough, or am I pushing the provost and the deans hard enough, and are our aspirations high enough? I don't have precise answers to those questions.

What have you personally experienced as a barrier to learning and how have you tried to overcome this barrier?
There have been a few, so let me tell you about one thing that I did not even know was a barrier for me. At the University of Waterloo, we had a great chair of the board of governors who once suggested that I should take some professional lessons in public speaking and crisis management. I said, "That would be interesting," and so I signed up for one-on-one coaching in Toronto. In session one, I was told I was going to be tested on what to do in a difficult situation—when things had gone wrong from a public relations point of view—and you're going to be facing a hostile press with no preparation. My coach told me that point number one is you have to listen very carefully. He asked me, "How good of a listener do you think you are?" I replied, "I think I'm very good." He said, "I'm going to test you. I'm going to say things to you, and you are going to give me 100 percent of your attention." We then talked for five or ten minutes, and then he stopped and said, "You're not a good listener at all!" I asked, "Why do you say that? I can tell you everything you told me." He replied, "That's not the point, you're distracted. Your BlackBerry was vibrating. I could tell that you were thinking about your BlackBerry and you weren't giving me your full attention." He also gave me examples to demonstrate how preconceived biases are critical in

communications. For instance, think of a troublesome faculty colleague—someone who is highly predictable. He or she may have some good ideas, or some important messages to deliver, but, if you're preconditioned, you're thinking, "This is what this person is going to say," and you're not really hearing their ideas. I still understand that listening can be a barrier, and it's not just because of the attention you must give, it's also because people have different styles of expressing themselves.

Forging trust is critical for a leader. What have you learned about building trust?

Bring it down to the human level. When you know me as a person and I know you as a person and we're sitting here facing each other, it would be difficult to contemplate you as a monster, even if somebody tried to portray you as such. On the other hand, if you don't know me and enough evidence is presented about me in a particular way, it will impact the impression you form of me. *You need to bring things down to a personal level to build trust.*

To earn trust, people need to believe what you say. When I stand up at senate to say something, I have to be genuine. *I can't try to sugarcoat a difficult situation because these intelligent people will see through it.* You have to demonstrate through your actions. If I say research is important, but I don't give a damn about chasing a Canada research chair, I will lose the trust of the research community. If I say internationalization is important, yet, for a year and a half, we don't have any visible progress, people will start to wonder, "Is it just talk?" Now, we are doing something about internationalization. *Earning trust can be a long process and you can lose it in no time. If you make one mistake, it can be gone. Trust is absolutely important, because the more trusted relationships you have, the more things you can do.*

You're a very public figure. What does accountability mean to you and how have you learned to be accountable?

I cannot hide behind things. At the end of the day, I am accountable. My first accountability is to our students. If the quality of this institution goes down under my watch, I have not done my job. I should be held accountable for the success rate of our students, the financial wellbeing of the institution, and more. I remember one time at Waterloo, Bill Gates was coming to visit. We had a few projects in the works, and, to accommodate Bill Gates' visit, some of the processes got moved forward and short-circuited. For instance, an agreement with Microsoft Canada about the use of several computer programs in the curriculum was settled in a bit of a rush and announced in mid August, at a time when key faculty and committees were away from campus. This led to an allegation that Microsoft was "buying" its way into the classrooms. There was a firestorm of protest as soon as the agreement was announced. I was a freshly minted provost at Waterloo, having arrived eight months before the planned Gates visit. I was on my summer holiday, travelling in

Quebec, and out of cell phone range. When I arrived in Quebec City, and my BlackBerry buzzed, I learned a crisis was unfolding at Waterloo. I returned to campus, but it was challenging to get to the bottom of who did what. The crisis was spiraling out of control.

When I finally figured out what happened, I sat down with the president and said, "This is what we are going to do," and the president agreed. We called a meeting and we apologized. We said, "As president and provost, we take full responsibility. My preliminary findings of this are that it is probably a case of a premature announcement, nothing more than that, but I'm going to need more time to investigate, and I will report to senate." Even though I had no role in causing the crisis, it was nevertheless important that I took charge in that situation in a public and dramatic manner.

Situational awareness is critical to good leadership. How have you, over time, developed this aspect of leadership so that the signals you pick up are the right signals, and, hence, you can make an intelligent decision?
It's an ongoing and never-ending process because things change and you rely on networks. In my role, information is not always accessible. You have to have the right metric and you have to have thoughtful people. University presidents don't have to have all the concrete information, but, rather, a good sense of what could happen and anticipate changes. For example, we can't wait for a provincial budget to be tabled, and then, based on what is tabled, come up with a fiscal plan. If we were to do that, then we would not have a budget until well into our own fiscal year. More importantly, we would not be able to have a multi-year budget plan. As a university president, you have to anticipate some of those things. Your metric is the best way of getting helpful information, and this works for presidents, political leaders, and business leaders. That's one level. The next level is staff support, because you don't have time. We have staff at various levels, such as public relations and government relations, and we rely on them. We also rely on colleagues. I'm fortunate enough to have colleagues with strong connections, so, from time to time, when a colleague comes back from Ottawa, we'll sit down and that colleague will give me his or her sense of things. It's an ongoing and difficult process. There are some complex matters that, no matter how you try, you'll never get absolutely right.

As you progress more and more, the amount of complexity you have to deal with increases dramatically. I think life as an assistant professor is pretty straightforward; things are quite different as a university president. How have you learned to be comfortable with a great amount of uncertainty, and to live with a knot in your stomach?
The answer is trust. You have to trust people. You simply don't have the capacity to know everything. *You have to trust and have good judgment of people, number one. Number two is you have to create not only a network, but also a*

system through which information can flow. People will let you know something if they think you need to know it, and it takes some time for people to become comfortable with what information is needed. I rely on my colleagues, and I try to reach out to people as much as possible so that they will feel that they have access to me. They are all wonderful members of this institution, and, if they feel I should know something, they'll write to me. It's not a perfect system, but that's what it is.

You told me that you are a straight shooter and that you can be quite candid or blunt in conversations. What did you learn over the years to do this effectively, because not everybody will respond well to that?

This is an interesting question. First, I describe the Western community as my family. I tell our communications people, "You have to give me the freedom to speak my mind when I'm within the family." I have to have the ability to speak to the Western community freely, and have the capacity to take things back, because I'm a member of the family. I can ask for forgiveness, and people will forgive me because they know I may be wrong sometimes.

Second, I am careful when dealing with individuals, because some people can't take harsh criticism coming from somebody who is close to them, or someone they admire, or with whom they have a close working relationship. Criticism has to be delivered in a very delicate manner. I criticize my direct reports indirectly. For instance, if a colleague gets into trouble for using e-mail too frequently for sensitive matters, I might change my practice and not respond to e-mails anymore. This sends the message that, if you have something serious to tell me, you should set up a meeting.

I'm not usually blunt in my direct conversations, though I can be when something terrible happens—you have no choice. For example, if a senior member of my team were to get caught in an academic misconduct situation, I'd try to be as polite as I can be, but I'd say, "I need you to write me a letter of resignation. I'm sorry, but there is no other choice." Even in public, I try to be straightforward, but I'm careful about how I say things. For example, I recall once that an individual was being a bit difficult at a senate meeting. He was taking too much time to make his point, so I challenged him. At the end of the senate meeting, I reached out to him. He was relatively young, and was trying, unsuccessfully, to get a motion through senate. I told him, "Look, if this is your objective, you have to get the senators to vote with you. The approach you're taking is annoying everybody, and nobody is going to vote with you. Next time you do it, be polite and respectful of people's time, because people are busy." He actually took this advice well.

It goes back to building trust. As a leader, it's important to be honest with people, but, for communication to be effective, how you deliver your message can be as important as what you say.

Leadership Themes

- Leaders need to build trust by bringing things down to a human level.
- Leaders need to build a network of people they can trust.
- How leaders deliver their message is important.

28

Coming From a Long Line of Leaders, I Was Raised to Be a Leader

Jody Wilson-Raybould (Puglaas)

Jody, when did you first realize that you were a leader and what happened to make you realize it?

I live in a small First Nations community—Cape Mudge on Quadra Island, British Columbia, Canada—and we are part of the Musgamagw Tsawataineuk and Laich-kwil-tach peoples of northern Vancouver Island, the Kwak'wala-speaking people. I am a citizen and a council member for We Wai Kai nation. Our community's population is just over 1,000 people. I was raised to always believe in myself—to know who I am and where I come from—and that has guided me throughout the course of my life.

Coming from a long line of leaders, I was raised to be a leader. I was raised to use my skills to improve the lives of our people. And, so, throughout the course of my life, there has been a series of different steps that I have taken—all of which were with the intention to gain the experiences, knowledge, and skills in order to give back to our community.

There has been an increasing sense of responsibility in my leadership. I am a lawyer and was a crown prosecutor. I ran to be a commissioner for the British Columbia Treaty Commission, the independent organization responsible for facilitating treaty negotiations among the governments of Canada and British Columbia and First Nations in British Columbia. The chiefs of British Columbia involved in these negotiations elected me to this position. I am also on the council in my home community. But none of these positions carry as high a level of responsibility as I feel right now as the regional chief of the British Columbia Assembly of First Nations (BCAFN)—the organization that represents the 203 chiefs of British Columbia.

You were raised to lead. Can you please elaborate on that?

I have been fortunate to grow up in a small community where all of my family was around. I was raised by a very loving family. I come from a long line of activists and people who work in our community to try and improve the quality of life for others.

We are a matrilineal society, which means that descent is traced through the mother and our maternal ancestors. Power and inheritance flows through the mother's line. My grandmother—Pugladee was her name—ensured that I knew our culture, our values, the laws of our big house, and how to conduct oneself as a leader. She raised me to know who I am and where I come from—and to recognize the rights and responsibilities that my people have in Canada. Both my grandmother and my father advocated for and pursued those rights. They were activists. And it was in that context that I was raised. My father—Bill Wilson—dealt with Prime Minister Pierre Trudeau. I watched their meetings on television when I was in sixth grade. He fought for the entrenchment of our rights into the Constitution of Canada.

We live in a communitarian culture. *Everybody has a role to play in making our communities work well. The roles are very different, but equally important in terms of ensuring the community functions the way it should. I was chosen to push the boundaries and move the goal posts in terms of advancing and implementing our aboriginal title and rights, including treaty rights.*

I never questioned my role or where I would go. I never questioned that I would go to university and study law, because it was just something that was already determined. It was a foregone conclusion. My family raised me to know that I had something to give back and to contribute. I should mention that I believe that leadership comes in many different forms, and not just necessarily from being elected to an office.

Your traditional name is Puglaas. It means "woman born to noble people." What is the story behind your name?

The naming goes back to our big house culture and how things are passed down from generation to generation. We are a matrilineal society, as I have mentioned, and we have hereditary chiefs. Hereditary chiefs—always men—are identified from the time they are born and they are groomed for leadership. My dad is a hereditary chief of the Eagle clan. His name is Hemas Kla-Lee-Lee-Kla, which means "number one amongst the Eagles, the chief that is always there to help." He was given that name in a potlatch, which is our traditional institution of government. We still practice our potlatch. It is here where our names are passed down or given; where laws are made; disputes settled; people are married; where possessions are redistributed; and so forth.

My grandmother's name was Pugladee, or Ethel. Her name means "a good host"—a name that was given to my older sister, Kory, the same time I was given my name. She gave me the name "Puglaas" in a naming potlatch at Gilford Island when I was five years old.

The name came with expectations?

For sure. There's a hierarchy in names. With positions and names come a lot of responsibilities and obligations—and, in particular, for my dad, who still is our hereditary chief and will be until he transfers his name to somebody.

Women, for the most part, are taking on the important and often informal leadership roles in our communities. In addition to many women now being elected as chief or to the council under the Indian Act, women are directing much of the change that is happening in our communities as we transition and move beyond our recent colonial past and rebuild our Nations. The women are speaking—as they always have—behind the hereditary chiefs in terms of what needs to be done.

You were first elected regional chief of the BCAFN in 2009. How did you end up in this role?

The regional chief of the BCAFN provides the political leadership and strategic direction for the organization. However, the BCAFN is not a government. Its membership includes the 203 First Nations in our province. The 203 chiefs that represent the First Nations vote every three years for the position. I was first elected in 2009, and re-elected in November of 2012.

The role is a challenging one. I feel honored and privileged to be in this role and to have the support of our chiefs. The role allows me to work with our First Nations to assist them moving forward in whatever their priorities are. *Is the position something that I sought to achieve, in terms of a title? No. As with all of the different positions that I have held, an opportunity presented itself at some point in time.* I was encouraged to run.

Putting your name on the ballot is a big step. What made you decide to do it?

The first time I ran for a position that I was elected to by the chiefs was when I ran to be a commissioner for the British Columbia Treaty Commission. This was in 2003. At that time, I was on staff at the Treaty Commission as an advisor. A vacancy came up for one of the First Nations-appointed people to be a commissioner for the Treaty Commission. I had been with the Treaty Commission for nine months. I liked being on staff. But I also realized I could contribute more to the dialogue between government and First Nations in this particular role.

It was a political contest and I was reluctant to enter the race. I do not really like politics. I had a good friend, Jack Weisgerber, who used to be the Minister of Aboriginal Affairs in British Columbia and was then a Treaty commissioner. I was reflecting on whether I should run. He told me, "Jody, stop being a chicken and just do it." I put my name forward—and, I tell you, it was the scariest thing that I have ever done. I made a speech in front of the chiefs during the all candidates election forum. I was about to introduce myself and I actually forgot my name and where I came from!

I put my name up for regional chief for the same reason I ran to be a commissioner—to be able to use the office to improve the quality of life for our people. Just before 2009, when I ran for regional chief, I ran for the first time in my home community to be on the council. I did so because my community, like most First Nations communities in Canada, is undergoing a huge transition. We are in the process of taking back control of our lives. We are in a period of nation building and nation rebuilding. We want to rebuild our economies. We need social development. We are addressing some fundamental questions. How do we select our governing bodies? How is our government accountable to our people? What is the policy that guides our law making? And how do our traditions get respected while meeting the needs of modern government and the market economy? Moving beyond the Indian Act implies significant change on the ground in First Nations communities. My community is no exception. I ran to be on the council because I felt that being on the council would give me an opportunity to assist my community in the transition, and to help empower more of our citizens to make decisions for themselves in what is, for many, a scary time of change. This process of radical change and transition from our colonial past has to be led by our people to be legitimate and have a chance of success.

I saw what was lacking in this country in terms of allowing First Nations communities to govern themselves when they are ready, willing, and able to do so. I knew what was needed in my community to help support people to move beyond the Indian Act. And, hence, I looked at the office of the regional chief. I saw the office as something that could link up all of the First Nations in British Columbia together to share information and our stories. I did not see that happening. I believe in celebrating success where success is being shown. I thought that this office could show what communities are doing in a really substantive way to improve their current conditions. There are tremendous successes that First Nations are having and I wanted to celebrate that. In fact, the motto for my re-election campaign was, "Building on Our Success." Some First Nations leaders said, "What are you talking about? Why are you always focusing on success when we have such devastating poverty in our communities?" I am a positive person and want to celebrate the successes we have achieved. I know there will be more. Success begets success.

So, that is the reason why I ran for regional chief. *I do not run for anything unless I think that there is an opportunity to actually accomplish change, or that there is something I can contribute.* It is really important for leaders—whether you are the chief or somebody who is advocating social change—to be mindful of the ultimate goal, which is to figure out some way to improve our community.

You indicated that the role comes with a lot of responsibilities and obligations. Is there anything that you fear about your role as regional chief?

My leadership skills have been tested with the increase in responsibilities for the positions that I held. The role of regional chief is a 24/7 job. I never had gray hair, but now I have lots of them! The role comes with stress and anxiety—but no fear.

We are trying to move away from the Indian Act towards self-government. We are trying to dig ourselves out of the history of colonialism, but its legacy is profound. There is often a sense of powerlessness and apathy in communities. Some of the citizens in my community are afraid to move beyond the status quo because of fear of the unknown and the relationship we have with the Government of Canada. There is an overwhelming belief that change is challenging, if not impossible. Some leaders I spoke to have said to me that we have not accomplished anything in over 20 years. People are afraid and reluctant to vote for self-governance because they do not trust band government and the federal government. And some people cannot see beyond their daily reality. There is real desperation. People need hope. The office needs to create optimism and hope. Leadership in First Nations is not about acting like the colonial master, but, rather, empowering the spirit of the colonized to be their own master.

We are developing materials to help people and communities make the transition. For example, we put together a governance toolkit, including a guide to community engagement. This toolkit also offers a confidential and internal self-assessment on how the governing body and administration are operating and how they can become more effective. There are other resources that can assist communities to re-establish their nations and re-establish their institutions of government. So, I do have hope that things are changing! In fact, I know they are. And I speak to people about this. I tell them stories about what our communities are doing—there is real change.

But sometimes you think . . . God . . . is it worth all the hard work? The social and political challenges are real and significant. I thought I would never be surprised by anything anymore, but I am continuously surprised. But, of course, it is worth the effort. *Challenging the status quo and long-held beliefs among your constituency may not always be seen as politically wise, but it is absolutely necessary if we are to create the space for social change and find solutions to seemingly insurmountable problems in moving beyond our colonial past.* I met a young woman at one of our community engagement sessions. She is from an isolated community and she took a boat to attend the session. She had a copy of our governance toolkit, which she had printed off the Internet, and wanted to be a part of the change in her community. You know then that you are not alone, and meeting her reinforced my belief that the opportunities that come with the role of regional chief are awesome.

I have also learned that people listen to what I have to say now, and, sometimes, I've found that people take what I have to say as being the way things are or should be. I am conscious of the things that I say, and I make sure that, as I always do when I put something out there, my thoughts are well thought out. I see my role as providing people with information in order to formulate their own opinion and determine what course of action to take. *With leadership comes the responsibility to be really conscious of what you say and do. People look up to you. They look for advice or guidance. They look for support. You have young people who want to become involved and may look to you as being a mentor or a leadership example. You have a huge responsibility, so don't say or do thoughtless things.*

We have to try to empower our citizens. They are the only ones who are going to create the change. They are the ones who have to step up and lead the social change movement. We have to ensure that we change our current situation and get rid of the Indian Act.

The role of regional chief comes with a lot of stress. A lot is being asked of you in the current context. How do you develop resilience?

My family has always been supportive. I'm a pretty outgoing person and like to develop relationships where I can. Humor is also very important. I surround myself with positive people who want a lot of the same things that I do. Furthermore, I live in my home community and it is the place in this world that I absolutely love. My husband Tim and I make a point of getting home at least once a week. I can drive there in about 3.5 hours from Vancouver with a couple of ferry rides. It is important to be part of a community. I do things like mowing my lawn or chopping wood. I love being there. It's that place away from everything else. Of course, you can never turn your work off completely because of your BlackBerry. But, by being in the community, you put yourself in a different situation and gain that grounding again. We have a communitarian culture and have a high standard of supporting one another. For example, my mum lights the fire in our house when we go home so it is warm when we arrive. The woodpile will be full because my neighbor went out and chopped some wood for us so we can continue to throw wood on the fire, even when my husband is not around to go out "wooding" with the guys. Our grass will be mowed. Likewise, I am a lawyer by training, so, if my neighbors have a problem, I will write a letter for them. We cook for one another. And so on. We recognize where our strengths are and how we can work together. This is one of my core principles in leadership.

The Crown–First Nations Gathering took place in Ottawa on January 24, 2012. The audience included Prime Minister Stephen Harper, Governor General David Johnston, and members of Cabinet. You delivered a hard-hitting speech on unlocking the potential of First Nations economies. Was that a transformative moment for you as a leader?

Yes, I think it was. I am confident in my knowledge and skills, but you always have some anxiety when you are presented with an opportunity, but also a responsibility. The anxiety comes from the unknown, and what things could be.

In this case, I was given the opportunity to meet the Prime Minister and to speak to him directly in front of a captive audience. I really never thought I would ever have that opportunity. And I thought that, if I am given the opportunity, then I better say something meaningful and I better put my views out there. To take full advantage of it.

I will always challenge things that I do not think are right or I put forward my own opinion on things. I certainly do not back down. I know that is a perception that a lot of people have of me. I was brought up that way. Not backing down, however, does not mean not being receptive to new ideas—quite the contrary. What it does mean is not being afraid of tackling the tough issues and not backing down—despite the potential political consequences.

I have also learned that it is important for a leader to be grounded. Change is happening in our communities. People participate in conversations involving self-governance initiatives and ways to improve the quality of life at different levels—at the national and provincial levels, and in their local communities. I am a citizen and a council member. I am also the regional chief. I sit on the Executive Committee of the Assembly of First Nations. But the most important conversation is the one that takes place back home in my community. Any leader should have the ability to speak the same there as they do in front of the Prime Minister, and say the exact same things. You cannot have one message for one audience and another for a different one. I am driven by my own principles and have a plan based upon a shared vision for our nations.

Do you take the time to reflect on leadership?
I do not sit down at the end of every day at midnight and consciously think about what I've done. I think about other leaders—their motivations and how they get things done or not done. There are some political leaders who are leading, I think, because they like the proverbial crown or the status that comes with the position. They want a position just for the sake of getting the position, and that is where everything seems to end.

I reflect on my own leadership skills and how I approach my roles. I work as hard as I can. I base my decisions and how I conduct myself on a set of principles. I seek to engage with people and empower them to make their own decisions. I also realize there are different styles of leadership, and that people approach issues in different ways and yet are equally successful.

Recent events surrounding "Idle No More"—the social media-based "grass-roots" indigenous protest movement—have caused me to reflect on my leadership. Our citizens have to be "idle no more," both to challenge the Government of Canada, but also their own government and leadership. For those of us that have been anything but idle, this is exciting. Our job as leaders now is how to embrace the call for change and help direct the energy of protest into the empowerment of our citizens to actually undertake the work needed in community to rebuild.

In particular, one recent event made me reflect: A controversial working meeting between the Prime Minister and a delegation of First Nations leaders, coordinated by the Assembly of First Nations. First Nations leaders became deeply divided over the circumstances of that meeting, and, hence, whether or not to attend the meeting. There were a lot of protests. A number of the regional chiefs did not attend the meeting.

As for myself, I never even considered not going. We need to create the space for our citizens to rebuild. We may have major challenges with the federal government, but Stephen Harper is still the Prime Minister. My grandmother would have been very disappointed if I passed up an opportunity to speak to him. There was no question I was going to go. I would have gone even if the national chief hadn't gone.

Some people were looking at me, and others even shouting at us, in condemnation for going to the meeting. They did not understand why. But it was something I had to do. My leadership was challenged by other leaders across the country, but not challenged by the leadership here in British Columbia. I kept in communication via email, phone calls, and conferences calls with my constituents. And none of the British Columbia chiefs told me not to go. Instead, they provided their advice, support, and prayers.

This meeting and the events surrounding it brought to the forefront all of the challenges we have in terms of our differences in regions, and how we address issues with the federal government.

If, ultimately, I was politically defeated because I stuck to my principles in trying to support social change, I can live with that. What I could not live with is not trying; the stakes for our people are too high and the personal sacrifices of political leadership demand it.

You have a significant challenge indeed. British Columbia is home to more than 200 Indian Act bands in Canada. That is about one-third of all bands.

It is challenging, indeed. Some of the other regions have 45 or 64 chiefs. It is a lot easier to communicate when the numbers are smaller. It is more difficult if you want to sit down face to face with people. I took the time to visit the majority of communities across British Columbia and develop a relationship with almost every chief. I get great satisfaction and benefits (in terms of knowledge) from that.

I have two BlackBerries. We bring chiefs together for assemblies to have conversations. We also have assemblies at the national level, and a lot of the British Columbia chiefs attend those. I send out regular e-mails with updates on what is happening at the provincial and national level, and distribute a detailed quarterly report.

I am an open person. The chiefs know that they can pick up the phone and connect with me. I learned that people like to be heard or have someone to listen to them. As a person in a leadership position, you have to appreciate open communication and dialogue.

There is the realization among most of our leadership in British Columbia that we're stronger when we work together. I know that fostering collaboration is one of my strengths in my current role as a leader. I know that our communities are doing many different things, and that they are really looking for that link with other communities and they have found it—not because of me, but because of us all working together.

As you transitioned to more and more senior roles, what were some of the challenges that you faced, and how did you deal with them?

I'm a bit of a control freak, and I know this is a personal challenge. I love to sit down and do a lot of the writing. I love policy. But I have to release that control. I have recognized that, in order to be successful in this role, you have to surround yourself with people who share the same goals and perspectives. They have skills that may be better than the skills that you have; you should learn to take advantage of that. Letting go of the control factor has actually opened up a lot of doors for me, in terms of bringing in people who can move the work forward more quickly than if it were just me.

As part of the Executive Committee of the Assembly of First Nations, I was given the portfolio in governance, which I relish. Since that time, I've had additional portfolios or responsibilities placed on me. Recently, I gave one up because there's no way that I could have done all of the work. But it was challenging to do so!

What role did mistakes play in your learning process? Can you talk about a mistake you made as a leader and what you learned from that mistake?
I was elected to the office of regional chief in 2009. There is always politics—some of it negative. Initially, I tried to separate myself from people who, in my opinion, played negative politics. I was responsible for appointing people to positions and committees, and didn't appoint some of the naysayers. Some of the people whom I could have originally appointed are now close allies of mine. We worked through a lot of challenges. So, never underestimate the ability of people to change—including yourself.

You talked about the influence of your family in becoming a leader. What did other people do to help you to learn to lead?
I had a number of people who have helped me in my development as a leader. I had teachers in high school that were supportive and who took an interest in me. I sometimes would get into trouble. I was a rebel and got suspended from school. One teacher thought I needed more focus and he brought me into this leadership class—we worked on public speaking and working together. We talked earlier about my colleagues at the British Columbia Treaty Commission and their influence in my development. My sister and I have been close our entire lives and she has always been honest with me. She certainly does not agree with everything I do, but she is entirely supportive. I get support and advice from my amazing and much-loved husband Tim, who is always there for me. We are a team. He also works with a number of First Nations and First Nation organizations—so we share the same work and passions. And, in my role as regional chief, I have gotten to know former Prime Minister Paul Martin. He just fell into my world. I consider him a mentor. He takes a genuine interest in me as a person and gives me advice. He has a passion for the well-being of First Nations. And I have great colleagues whom I work with and I value their advice, even though I do not take it all the time! Also, my hereditary chiefs and elders have always been there, and, in particular, hereditary chief Robert Joseph and my elder advisor at the BCAFN, whose wisdom and gentle counsel I seek on a regular basis.

If you had some general advice to give to people about becoming a better leader, what would it be?
I would tell people that what has been able to keep me grounded and to continue moving forward is to be confident in who I am and know where I come from. I would encourage leaders to approach every person with openness and recognition that they have something to contribute. You should value other people's opinions and what they are doing and not to judge. Be open to being challenged. Be open to

sharing information and supporting people. You have to be able to sift through lots of information in a short period of time. And be who you are, no matter what circumstance you are in or who you are meeting with. Be yourself, and stick to what you believe in and the plan that you have.

Your father told Prime Minister Pierre Trudeau that you and your sister Kory deserve the chance to be Prime Minister.
Do I want to be the Prime Minister? I don't think in terms of advancement in that way. I've been asked to run for the position of national chief. In my mind, the greatest thing that I can ever do is to be home in my community and be there all the time—and, if opportunity presents itself, take on a great leadership role. I certainly have planned out a lot, but I also take things one day at a time. I think that the world or the universe unfolds as it should. I really look forward to the opportunities that will present themselves when my current term as regional chief is done.

Leadership Themes

- With leadership comes the responsibility to be really conscious of what you say and do. People look up to you. They look for advice or guidance. They look for support. You have young people who want to become involved and may look to you as being a mentor or a leadership example. You have a huge responsibility. Don't say or do thoughtless things.
- Learn to take advantage of people who have skills that may be better than the skills that you have. Collaborate.
- Approach every person with openness and the recognition that they have something to contribute.
- Be open to being challenged.
- Be who you are, no matter what circumstances you are in or who you are meeting with.

29

Reach for the Stars—But Keep Your Feet Firmly Planted on the Ground

Gautam Thapar

Gautam, when did you first realize you were a leader, and what happened to make you realize it?

I don't think I realized I was a leader, to be honest. I spent nine years in boarding school. Sport is a big part of one's success in most boarding schools. I played almost every sport. At school and in university, I was captain of some sports teams. I soon discovered people were willing to follow. This led me to consider, "If I have the capacity to lead, am I interested in doing it?" I had no strong feeling about being a leader any more than I had any feelings about entering the corporate world. I didn't plan it.

Did you want to be a leader? Where did your ambition come from?

I don't think I always had the ambition to be a leader. *My upbringing, my education, and the environment in which I grew up—there were manifest inequities—contributed to me aspiring to the role of leadership.* For example, I often thought about why the inequities existed and what I could do personally to try and even these out. Typically, in a lot of families, the eldest inherits the family possessions and business. I always wondered why. Just because of a certain accident of fate? That was not good enough for me. I have always been unwilling to accept a lot of the rules or unspoken rules that encourage people to just silently fall into line. From my time at school, I challenged that mindset. *I was never willing to conform and accept the status quo—not at school and not in business. Not in a manner in which I wanted to ever create any upheaval, but in a manner to say that, "I personally, as an individual, am unwilling to accept that this is the only way it's going to be."* If I have the power to change it through my own actions and achievements, I will. If I don't have the power to change it, I will move on and do something else.

I think leadership always develops in a context. It doesn't just happen. Which brings me to another point: I think, in the Western world, there is a problem in that you have a system today that grooms you through education for success. For example, I go to the best high school, then to an Ivy league institution, and then secure a nice job in a top bank. In that entire stream, I have never had any failure.

So, the first time I'm confronted with failure, I don't know what to do. Here, in this part of the world [India], where the social systems are very different, the environment is very different, the challenges are very different, and you have to learn early that, ultimately, leadership is about how to deal with failure. It's perhaps more important than learning how to deal with success.

You were trained as an engineer in the United States. You did not have formal business education. You came back to India and became a successful business leader. What have been the formative influences on you as a leader? What did people do to help you? What experiences did you learn the most from? Was there any particular experience that supercharged your learning to lead?

I had a mentor. His name was Brij Mohan Bakshi. He was the best mentor I ever had. Mr. Bakshi was a vice president and worked for my uncle. He was very important for my development. I was a management trainee, one year out of training and working here. I wasn't directly in the line of succession. I was just another family member. He was looking after a problematic business. He called me "son" all the time. He told me, "Son, my office door is always open. Even if you see somebody in my room, don't hesitate—just walk in and sit down. Just listen, observe, and ask questions if you have to. Don't interrupt the discussions, because you may not know what is going on. But, ask questions afterwards and listen to what I have to tell you." I always had questions, and, in our subsequent conversations, many things were discussed. Many nuances concerning leadership came out. He would be sitting in his chair and discussing something with somebody whom I did not know. The person would leave and Mr. Bakshi would ask me, point blank: "So, what do you think of that?" He would listen and then tell me, "That person is a complete scam artist." He would explain, in detail, that the person said this, and said that, but he knew that it was not correct. So, there was a lot of learning on the ability to gauge people. But, at the end of the day, what are you learning? You are leading people. You are not leading machines, you are leading people. From him, I learned to read people and understand them, and to gauge whether a person is actually telling you what he thinks you want to hear as opposed to what he should be telling you and what you need to hear. I spent three years with Mr. Bakshi. I rose very quickly through the organizational ranks because a lot of what he said was not difficult for me to put into practice. *I have learned that, if you have people with good leadership potential in your organization, give them a couple of years with your key leaders. Let them be in an environment with high exposure, and where there are no secrets and hidden agendas. Then watch how they develop. Those three years with Mr. Bakshi were worth 10 years of leadership training at any organization.*

If you reflect on those discussions, what was the best leadership advice you received that helped you develop into a better leader?

He always told me to reach for the stars, but keep my feet firmly planted on the ground. Similarly, "Avantha" means to move forward, but with your feet firmly on the ground. The first time he gave me that advice, I wondered what he was talking about. How can I reach for the stars? *But I understood he was telling me I should remove the word "impossible" from my vocabulary. It was a good lesson, because, when you deal with people, they are often limited by a lack of imagination or experience. As a leader, your challenge is to make sure you expand people's horizons and ask them questions that make the impossible possible.* I don't have the word "impossible" in my vocabulary. None of my people come into my office and tell me things are not possible. My point is I am sure there is a way of doing things. We just need to think. The more we think, the more likely we will find a way of doing it. We have done a number of things in the group over the last 15 years that people thought were impossible. It's not always productive to be like that because you may continue to push an agenda that, ultimately, doesn't work. I can confidently say we do not give up on something easily until we have exhausted every possibility. The willingness to keep pushing on a problem builds resilience. People see that the chairman of the business is not someone who is ready, at the first sign of a problem, to get stuck. So, it really builds resilience in people and they get inspired.

What were some of the hardest things to learn in becoming a good or an even better leader?

I have not mastered everything. I think leaders need to be very introspective. You need to understand yourself more or better than anyone else. By understanding yourself, you understand how to be better. I have many weaknesses and a few strengths, and the biggest frustration is trying to overcome those weaknesses by trying to do things differently and not succeeding. I display my strength. I delegate. I try to hire good people, and I trust them—but I keep pushing them. I am a long-time owner of my business. My time horizon is not 2 or 3 years, it's 20 or 30 years, and, hence, I can be patient—I am very patient. But I keep pushing and pushing until I get the result I want. I'm not in a hurry. And, if the people who work for me are driven to do things in a shorter period of time, that's good because it benefits us. But, personally, if you don't take the time to introspect and you don't have a certain amount of humility, then I think it's very difficult to be a balanced leader. I think you will have spurts of leadership and burn out.

As you transitioned into more and more senior roles, what were some of the challenges that you faced, and how did you overcome them?

It was a difficult balance because being a part of a family and having the name creates both a hurdle and opportunity. The name obviously opens doors. The hurdle is that people are always comparing you against other family members. And you don't always come out looking better in comparison. This you know, but selling people your ideas and your vision, and not taking the line that, because you have a certain last name things should happen, helps a lot.

Fifteen to twenty years ago, I was still asked to deliver numbers and deliver performance. It was a monthly, weekly, and daily affair. Over the last seven years, my work has been much more strategic. We created the Avantha name. We made the transition from a collection of different businesses doing their own thing to a more tightly run group, with similar systems and processes. We have been at that for the past five years and, in my view, will be at it for the next twenty years. We are growing and adding new businesses. We are exiting certain businesses. We are looking at which countries are opening up. Where are the opportunities for tomorrow? The changes have been significant these past five years.

The ability to sell your concept to people, to sell your ideas, and to delegate and support people were some of the things that posed a challenge to me. It was challenging as I transitioned to the role of CEO and chairman—from actually running a business to having other people to actually do the operations—and, for me, to conduct the orchestra rather than playing a particular instrument. That was the bigger challenge; to try and get all the individual companies to start playing the same tune. This was not a unified group per se. I had to be patient and demonstrate a willingness to continue to work on creating a coherent organization. I found success breeds success. If you have been successful, your credibility goes up and that credibility impacts people willing to join you.

In a country such as India, with its hierarchical structure, success can be a problem because people look at you as if you are some kind of a superhuman person. Success adds an aura of awe, which makes it difficult to foster candor and establish relationships. People don't necessarily see you only as their boss, but also as a very successful person. Each success adds another layer of complication and, in my opinion, very often a barrier between an individual and his or her direct boss. This barrier is not easy to overcome.

You have said that learning to deal with ambiguity is a huge pressure. But it is a huge learning, too. What have you learned about leadership and ambiguity?

I am pretty direct. If I don't like something, I'll express that opinion. I'm not always politically correct in that sense. I observed problems our businesses were facing when I made the transition from management to leadership. I think clarity and directness helped because there was only one person out there that was absolutely clear on what we needed to do and equally clear about expressing it and not fearful about the consequences. *If you have the courage of your convictions, and have proven you can deliver, I don't think you should ever hesitate to speak your mind on issues. In difficult times, that's what the organization needs. You need clear thinking, clear direction, and a willingness to say, "Hey, you know, this is what we need to be doing."* But, there may always be other views out there and one should accept that. Adopt those better views. Don't be afraid to express those views. I wasn't.

I read somewhere that, when you joined the organization, you moved from being an "outsider" to an insider. You stated that outsiders "get to hear and

see a lot more" and that what remains hidden "can be quite debilitating from a decision-making point of view." [Ghosh, S. Manner of decision making needs to be removed from firm's owner. 02/18/2011, livemint.com] You are now an insider. You discussed the importance of candor. How do you get candor from your colleagues? If there is bad news, you want to hear it now—and uncluttered. Those are easy things to say. Actually getting that from your employees and your colleagues can be very challenging. So, how do you create a climate where people give this kind of candid information to you?

Maybe it is human nature or maybe it is in the organizational structure, but people always trip up. That's my experience with my direct reports. People tell me the bad news, but inevitably they will slip up somewhere by omitting something. As long as they tell me the truth, there isn't a problem. But, if a senior person slips up, it is far more embarrassing than for someone junior. Over the years, the people who work with me—whether they are younger, my age, or older—have learned that I will give them a long rope. But the day anyone hides something from me, they are psychologically on the defensive string. Earning back trust and credibility is then their job. And that's the way it works.

Am I going to take away or discard the 95 things that I've heard? The answer is "no." I also have to make my point again that candor and honesty are critically important to me. Otherwise, how do I use my judgment? The moment you slip up, the onus is on you to win back the trust.

Do you think there is a difference in candor between North Americans, Europeans, and Indians? The Dutch can be brutally candid. North Americans are more concerned about political correctness. Where does India land?

People in India shake their heads and you don't know whether they mean yes or no. In the hierarchical nature of our society, nobody wants to be the bearer of bad news. I wear two hats—I am the owner and CEO. Ultimately, much more than a CEO, I have the power to decide whether I sell a business, keep a business, fund a business, or don't fund a business. You always have to keep in mind that people are not just looking at you as the CEO or chairman of the group, but also as the owner. You have to allow for some conversation to draw from them what they want to tell you. People will come into the room to say something, but often are reticent, which is part of our culture, to actually say what they wanted. I have to help them relax and then draw it out of them. Inevitably, it comes out. Such delays are due to the nature of Indians.

You lead organizations, sit on a number of boards, and are also involved in the sports, cultural, and educational sectors. I'm sure that you've seen talented people whose careers derailed. How do people with potential derail a promising leadership career?

Hubris! If you start believing that you are God's gift to management and that you know everything there is to know—sorry, you don't. I have witnessed ordinary people doing extraordinary things without the benefit of an MBA or without the benefit of any formal education. ***If you don't have a certain amount of humility and introspection, you are at risk of derailment.*** Just look at the last six months, one year, two years, three years, ten years, or fifteen years—there are so-called "icons" of management and business leadership whose corpses litter the road of downfall. ***I have one firm rule. A business leader should be sacked if he or she writes a management book while still in office. The first thing you should do is say, "Thank you very much and bye; we need to get the next person in here." This is because I think that person has now reached a point where they start believing in their own stuff.*** An organization is not static—it's a dynamic, living thing. No leader can believe he or she knows everything there is to know about the job today, tomorrow, and the day after.

What are you learning these days to become an even better leader? Are there any recent "aha" moments?

I think the biggest lesson for me, these past two or three years, is that I need to speed up my decision making. At times, I've been a little bit too willing to let matters take their own course, often assuming things will fall into place over time. I realized that, while you can let matters take their own course, you also need to be constantly pushing, driving, and directing to get them into place. I think there are activities we could and should have done earlier, but did not because of my "let it happen when it happens" approach. I think people still want to be lead in certain ways. People may not necessarily like to be told what to do, but they certainly like to be asked to do certain things.

The second lesson centers around the cost of renewal. You have to constantly challenge yourself and remind yourself that you've not yet reached the goal. This is a challenge because, as you get older, both your risk appetite and energy levels drop. It's easy to sit back and say, "Hey, I've done it. I headed something that was bankrupt and created a $4- or $5-billion global business. I can sit back and relax." You can never sit back. You constantly have to look at renewal. This is something I work on a lot.

A third thing I've learned is, very often, circumstances do dictate events. You often hear people say they were in the right place at the right time. ***I don't think being in the right place at the right time is enough. Being in the right place in the right time and understanding the opportunity for what it is is the most difficult part. Just being there doesn't mean it's going to happen.*** So, from a passive position, being at the right place at the right time, to an active position of being there at the right place at the right time is fine, but one needs to understand that pro-activeness is very important. Hence, if you talk about renewal, you have to talk about how pro-active you are going to be. The opportunities are enormous. We have a limited amount of resources. We need to focus on how we can get better and what we can do differently.

You said something interesting about leadership. Leadership is about the desire for power. And power cannot be granted; it has to be taken. Power

sometimes has a negative connotation. Can you elaborate on the meaning of the statement?

My definition of "power" is the power to change. Those individuals who aspire to lead need to acquire the power to change things—the power to influence and drive initiatives forward. But they also need to want that power. The very nature of change implies that few people, if any, like change. It is a hugely difficult task to bring change to an organization. We are all comfortable in the cocoons we've built. We enjoy stability. We like to know people and what to expect from them, and so forth. If you want to have the power to change, you're going to have to take it. You have to use whatever tools you have and want it enough to go out and take that power and make a difference. You can't take it by being passive. It is not power in the sense of life and death, or the power of a chainsaw. It's the realization that, if you want to lead, you must appreciate and understand that leadership is about change. It is not about continuity. If that's the case, then let the previous person carry on. Why did you need to get rid of him or her? Ultimately, you must realize that, if you want to be a leader and you believe the statement that "the buck stops here," then it's about change. No one is going to come and give it to you. Why should they? If I'm doing a good job, do I really want to give it up to you?

I see what motivates you and what sustains you as a leader. What drains you?

People who make the same mistakes over and over again drain me. People who stick to old routines or approaches, even when everybody around them wants to change, drain me. People not seeing the better way of doing things drains me. Dishonesty drains me. We talk a lot about integrity. *We tend to use the word "integrity" in a financial context. But, to me, intellectual integrity is equally important. If you have knowledge about something, are you always sharing it with people?* Typically, it would be in the best interest of the organization to do so. Most people don't because the instinct is to keep things to themselves so they can show themselves in a better light. Inevitably, it comes out that people have been hoarding information. I find that draining because the organization is losing by people not sharing. Everybody is losing. That kind of behavior really drains me.

No leader is perfect. We all make mistakes. Has there been one of those moments where you stared into the abyss? What made you turn around? And what concrete lessons did you learn from the experience?

I think you always need to be willing to say, "Hey, I made a mistake and I need to fix it." That is not easy. We have been at the abyss before, and we've come out of it. For example, in 1996, we were bankrupt. We were running out of cash. We had 15 or 16 months of cash left. It was a complete mess—performance was deteriorating month after month. But I was not responsible for bringing us there. There was a lesson for me there, even though I was not the person responsible for the crisis. I was the person who said we don't ever want to go back to that situation again. Now, we are a lot more frugal and we plan a little better.

Here's a great example. In 2006, in India, we had a compound growth rate of 8.0–8.5 percent and low cost of capital, hence giving us opportunities to do interesting things. Now, in 2012, growth has dropped to 6 percent or lower and the cost of capital in the last two years has shot through the roof. Our businesses are leveraged and in position for the next opportunity, and the next one—even when growth is slowing down. So, are we in a position where we can ride the situation out? The answer is "yes." Fifteen years ago, we could not just ride it out. Management transitions have happened, business transitions have happened, as well as the global economic situation. Thus, in three years, things have gone 180 degrees in the other direction. I think that's a good test to put yourself through. It is a great question. Are we in a position to manage those developments? Do we have the appropriate systems and processes in place? Do we have the resilience? If the answer is "yes," carry on. If the answer is "no," quickly put on the brakes and start slowing down. You learn in the process that certain decisions need to be accelerated and certain decisions cannot be emotional. You learn and the environment and circumstances play a large role in your development as a leader.

Leadership Themes

- Leadership is about how to deal with failure. It's perhaps more important than learning how to deal with success.
- Constantly challenge yourself, and remind yourself that you've not yet reached the goal. This is a challenge because, as you get older, both your risk appetite and energy levels drop.
- Don't be too complacent and assume that things will fall into place over time. Lead!

30

There Are Two Things in Life You Should Not Let Go—Your Values and Your Family

Umran Beba

Umran, when did you first realize you were a leader, and what happened to make you realize it?

In my school years, in Turkey, I was into folk dancing. My interest in folk dancing started in primary school and continued in high school and my time in university. I became very involved with the folklore club, but my involvement went beyond just practicing and performing. I was part of the team that coordinated activities, and, by the end of high school, I was the president of the club. We had performances in school, but we also participated in competitions outside of the school. Among other things, my job included recruiting people to the club. I also needed to put together a managing team, set a performance agenda, obtain funding from our school management, engage in outside fundraising, enter the dancing teams into competitions, put a communication plan in place, and so on. The team and I had to demonstrate that the club was adding value to the student membership. This was my first experience in leadership. Of course, I continued with folk dancing when I went to university; and, again, I became president of the club. We had about 200 members. And although we were a small organization, I understood the responsibilities of leadership and the importance of delivering results. Again, I was involved in many aspects of leading people: Deciding on an agenda, making sure that the various subcommittees—dance, music, costumes, and the like—operated as they should, communicating with the leadership of the school and external bodies, sorting out the politics of running the club, moderating conflict between individuals, and so on. I learned a lot from this experience. I received a rector award for my academic achievements and social contributions to student life at the end of my time at university. Providing direction to the club and collaborating with others to achieve great results was really rewarding. And at that point I thought, "This is leadership, right?"

Did you want to be a leader?

I don't think that I had the ambition to be a leader. But, as you go through these kinds of experiences, leadership feels natural and then you start thinking about the concept of leadership. I like to be involved with people, achieve results with people, succeed as a team, and deal with barriers to success. I brought the passion, which is critical in achieving results. You accept some challenges along the way, but, at the end, you celebrate the successes. It was a natural experience for me. I felt positive about the idea of leadership and started to consider future possibilities.

What have been the formative influences on you as a leader? What did people do to help you? What experiences did you learn the most from? Was there any particular experience that supercharged your learning to lead?
I was trained as an industrial engineer. I reflected on what I wanted to do after my university education—to be an engineer or do something different. I decided to pursue an MBA degree because I had an interest in marketing. My thesis was on consumer trends. I was really interested in managing a brand. Hence, I was excited when I got a job at Colgate-Palmolive as junior brand manager. I learned a lot about managing a brand and interacting with the different functions in the organization and external agencies. I was able to use my experiences from school and the folklore club. Then, in time, I started to have people reporting to me, and, eventually, I moved from the junior level to marketing director.

I transitioned to the PepsiCo Frito-Lay organization. I spent a year in marketing and then I was asked to move to the human resources (HR) function. I thought the move would be a great experience—I like to share what I do and enjoy teaching. I wanted to be involved with training and development. This was a significant lateral move. Again, I worked with different functions in the organization, learned what it took to lead a large team, did a lot of listening, and worked with people at different levels—from the frontline to general management. I had to find a balance between the interests of the organization and those of the employees. I was in HR for about three years. Then, I moved to sales.

These jobs and transitions were a great preparation for the job of general manager. I was trained to do three things. First, to manage brands. Second, to manage people and people-related agendas; this also involved addressing conflict. Third, to manage the field and motivate sales teams to deliver results. The three distinct roles—marketing, HR, and sales—offered various experiences that helped me to understand the big picture required for being a general manager. I knew the different parts of the organization and how they related to one another. Still, there were some functions that I didn't have much experience with. Hence, I needed to understand people's capabilities and provide the support so that they could deliver the results we wanted to achieve. You need to trust people and their skills.

The next step was to move into more regional roles, where I had to manage several countries and cultures. In my current job, as president of PepsiCo Asia Pacific, I lead 23 markets and 21 nationalities. I learned that there are many building blocks of success. First, I had exposure to different parts of the business. *You must be open to new experiences and willing to stretch in order to develop as a leader.* Second, you must learn to trust people who have skills that you don't have and empower them to deliver on your agenda. Third, you must be able to put together, and lead, a diverse team. You must be comfortable with—and, indeed, appreciate—individual differences in delivering results. You learn these insights as you move through different roles.

Is there any particular experience that supercharged your learning to lead?
Three general experiences have helped my learning. They have also underpinned my leadership values: Passion, determination to achieve, listening and empathy, respect and trust, providing support and asking for support, and perseverance. First, I moved into HR. This was a significant transition, as it required me to develop a new skill set. For example, I needed to improve my listening skills and work hard on understanding people around me. This is important when you move into a new role, but is particularly relevant to the HR function. Also, I came from Istanbul to Hong Kong. I had to develop an understanding of this place: I had to learn about the people and the opinion leaders, understand the past, and get a better handle on the challenges and current opportunities that we faced as an organization. I had to develop patience—to listen first and not to jump to conclusions.

Second, having lived in Turkey for many years, I had a lot of crisis experience. For example, we had instances of devaluation and inflation. You can imagine our profit-and-loss statements—they went up and down. We had a large earthquake and, as a result, our plant was shut down. We had to rebuild the plant in a few months, which required the support of a lot of stakeholders. You learn a lot about yourself in crisis situations. For example, over time, you learn to remain calm and be grounded.

Third, I worked with people from different cultures. For example, in one of my earlier positions, I managed five countries: Turkey, Jordan, Lebanon, Syria, and Iraq. This was a diverse set of countries and each had its unique challenges. You have to deal with different cultures, languages, and religions—and still deliver results. The problem was that I could not visit some of these countries. Airports were closed because of political and safety-related issues—political unrest, bombs, wars, and so forth. You have to learn to manage from a distance.

You were born and raised in Turkey. Is there anything in your Turkish upbringing that has helped you in becoming a good or an even better leader?
I thought about that question a lot prior to coming to Hong Kong to lead the Asia Pacific division. Turkey is not exactly Europe, or the Middle East, or Asia, but we definitely have some aspects of the European style and flair. There are bonds with European history and values. This helped me when I worked in southeast Europe—in the Balkans and Greece. The same applies to the Middle East and Asia—there are elements of an integrated culture. So, these common bonds with history and values helped me a lot. I was able to adapt quickly to the cultures in which I had to work and the people I had to work with.

Your industry is a lot about people and building relationships. What have you learned about building trust and learning to trust others?
As I mentioned earlier, respect and trust are important leadership values for me. These values really come from my late father. He had this very deep trust in my

sister and me. He always said, "If you want to do it, do it—because I know you will do your very best. I trust you." This value was important in my upbringing. It gave me a lot of confidence, but, at the same time, it came with responsibility. I took on that responsibility and perhaps matured a bit faster than others. I started to feel the responsibility—it was real.

In business, I try to be positive. I start with trust. And I hope that people will reciprocate that trust and not take advantage. There are certain things I don't tolerate. For example, trust is damaged when people misrepresent facts for personal benefits; when people make promises, but don't deliver; and when people say something in a room, and then say something different in the room next door. Therefore, if I observe these things in a business relationship or in my team, then I think it's better to address the issue head on and challenge the person. You need trust to build relationships, and, if there is little or no trust, then it is difficult to build strong and lasting relationships.

Some people prove, through their behavior, that they are not worthy of your trust. I don't want to deal with those people in my everyday life because their behavior puts a lot of pressure on me and my values. *Our values get tested from time to time. You should not be afraid to make a decision. If you feel that a relationship is not working, then you should not procrastinate in terminating that relationship.*

As you transitioned to more and more senior roles, what were some of the challenges that you faced, and how did you overcome them?
I have a couple of observations. First, as you move into more senior roles, you start to have different functions reporting to you. You may not be a technical expert in all of these areas, and, hence, you have to learn to trust other people. Second, I needed to discipline myself to balance my time across the different functions. It would be tempting to spend a lot of time with the marketing people because of my background and interests. But that would not sit well with the operations or manufacturing people. Third, it is critical to always keep in mind the big picture—to understand the challenges inside and outside the organization, to formulate a series of opportunities, and to set a vision with the involvement of the team. It must be clear to the group where we want to go and what objectives to shoot for. Fourth, you need to prioritize continuously. *I think as you transition into bigger and bigger leadership roles, everybody wants to do everything and yet resources are limited. You have to be realistic about what you can handle—as a person and as an organization.*

I imagine that you often deal with ill-defined and ambiguous problems. The information required to make decisions might not be available or is incomplete. How did you learn to deal with ambiguous situations and make decisions based on imperfect information?
This is a good question. The information that is available when you operate, for example, in the emerging markets can be limited. I dealt with Syria and Iraq. Later, it was the Balkans. And now we are working in Myanmar (Burma). You often don't

have a lot of information—you may not be able to get the information you would like to have available because the place is not safe or you don't have agencies on the ground that you can trust. Hence, in such cases, you learn to listen to people who have different perspectives, and then come to a conclusion. I like to involve people in the decision process before I arrive at a conclusion—team members, functional experts, or my manager. You realize that someone might have gone through a particular experience that is relevant to the problem you are trying to solve. And, sometimes, no such experience is available. Hence, the decision and its execution may not always be perfect. But you learn not to be unhappy about that. Those of us who have children will understand that insight well. The white dress that you like so much will get dirty when you play with your children—there will definitely be some stains on the dress and you might have difficulties getting those out. This doesn't make you happy, right? In business, you may be very unhappy because critical information is missing or it turns out that you cannot trust the people on the ground. I think you have to try to get the best from the people, or from the information that is available, and then make the best possible decision. There is always risk embedded in making decisions.

How did you develop resilience? How did you learn to deal with obstacles and setbacks and remain focused?

I have learned to operate under high-pressure situations—to stay calm and address the challenges. Some of this I believe comes from my DNA, but the rest was developed through experience. You reflect on what worked well for you and what did not. Being a good observer is also important.

The year 2001 was an interesting year for me. I was pregnant and expecting my first child. I was also appointed to the role of general manager of the business in Turkey. We had a significant economic downturn happen. The announcement of my promotion was in January, the crisis happened in February, I was officially in charge in March, and I delivered the baby in May. As you can appreciate, I had to deal with a very unique series of events. My manager was around, and he supported me in any way he could during this transition. I was working from home during my maternity leave—and I was connected to the business.

So many things were changing. This was, of course, not the first time that we had an economic downturn—these things happen in a developing market. But it turned out that this was a very deep downturn. We did our best to deal with this setback. We did not attain the objectives outlined in our business plan. But what can you do? You have to live with it. Nobody is very happy with a performance like that. But you realize it was not because of you or your inability to lead. This was an external event that impacted the business, and the team and I had to work through this in the best way possible. You develop bitter feelings, but you do your best. And what I have seen is that, during those extraordinarily difficult situations, people work even harder than they normally do. Everyone is trying to keep the business going. I think what I have learned is to be happy with the end result, whatever is the outcome. We all know we gave it our best. And we should try to focus on what we can control, as opposed to what we cannot control. We went back to basics and tried to make the business simpler. As I mentioned before, I went through a number of these crisis situations. You learn lessons from each crisis.

Has your learning to lead been influenced by other individuals? For example, have you had the benefit of a mentor?

You have different role models, mentors, and sponsors during the different stages of your life and career. My father imparted to me the values of respect and trust. My mother instilled the determination for achievement—she was always encouraging me to do even better in school and my education. So, my parents have been very important in formulating my values.

I think, during the school years, there are always a number of teachers who will guide you. Also, for example, I worked as a research executive in my first job. The owner of the company was a woman. She built the company from scratch. She was an entrepreneur. She became an important mentor to me. I still see her. She was my witness in the wedding ceremony. We built a strong relationship. She has been very influential in my career.

I had good role models and bad role models. I think that it is important to also learn from the negative role models, because you don't want to act or operate like them. There could be a problem around their level of openness and trust. I have seen people who are driving too much their own personal agenda. You don't want to be like that. You want to perform, but also wait for the right moment to go for the next job—that is, when you are ready for the next step in your career.

My current manager is a great mentor and sponsor. The relationship between mentorship and sponsorship is an important one. As you are showing progression in your career, just the mentorship is not enough. You also need people in the organization who are willing to sponsor you. You need people who believe in you and who can mention your name at the right time.

What were some of the hardest things to learn in becoming a good or an even better leader?

I think, throughout the years, you work with people who have different styles and characteristics, dictated by their cultures, nationalities, religions, and so forth. But, even within your own national background or culture, you see differences in styles or approaches toward life and work. *Good leaders learn to understand and appreciate those differences, and try to create synergies in the team and deliver great results. The bottom line is that we have to achieve results. You don't want to be losing energy and time with unnecessary conflict. But adults do not always act in mature ways, and, hence, they have issues in working together.* You find yourself moderating conflict situations. This is always a challenge and it can create a lot of frustration, both within oneself and with others on the team. People expect their leader to solve the conflict. This can be draining. The difficult part is that, sometimes, you have to dismiss people because they are not adding positive contributions to the team.

You have to make sure that you have a well-integrated and operating team whose members understand one another. For example, I like to do a number of developmental exercises in the teams that I lead. I like to spend time on understanding our personalities and how we can work together even better. We have to address our individual differences somehow. And we better do this in the beginning of the team's evolution, rather than when things derail.

There is always a cost to leadership. What has been the price of leadership for you?

Becoming a leader puts a lot of responsibility on your shoulders. For example, you have to do the right things for the business and deliver results; you have to do the right things for the people and their communities; you have to be a role model for others; and you have to balance your work and personal life. This balancing act can be a real challenge. You often have to make sacrifices in your personal life. This is the case, in particular, as you start to take on leadership roles with bigger and bigger responsibilities. I travel a lot. I work and have meetings sometimes on the weekend. You are not always available. You always wish you could spend more time with the family and the children.

What have you personally experienced as a barrier to learning and how have you tried to overcome this barrier?

I have taken on different roles and operated in different functions. I was always open to the opportunities and challenges that people gave me. But my current assignment as president of PepsiCo Asia Pacific was the first assignment out of my home country. I had grown as a leader. About two and a half years ago, the organization indicated that this was the right time to make the transition to the Asia Pacific region. They communicated that I was capable in taking on the role. I was, of course, very pleased with the decision. But, to tell you the truth, for many years I wasn't open to relocating to a different country. I did a lot of traveling for work and visited a lot of places. *Moving to a different country offers big learning opportunities for a child, adult, or business leader. I moved at a later stage in my life. I think being open to relocation earlier in your life may have benefits. You develop great perspectives on life.*

Can you talk about a mistake that you made as a leader, and what you learned from that mistake?

I worked with some leaders for many years—sometimes seven or eight years. You know each other well and I learned from all the people I worked with. But there are moments that you feel you're not on the same track. For example, you realize you are not sharing the same values. That, I believe, should be the moment of separation. I appreciate the efforts that people made to my development as a leader. But there was a moment where I had to say, "This doesn't work. I cannot be in this camp." There were a few instances where the facts were misrepresented, and I was not given the full picture. That's the moment you have to make a decision on your loyalty to that relationship. This is a tough decision. People expect loyalty. There was a moment in one of the relationships where I had to say, "I'm not in this camp." That was not a popular decision. I separated our ways. I stuck with what I thought was the right place—the right values. You have to learn to deal with separations. I was not happy at the moment that happened, but you feel relieved when you have made the decision.

You have to make these difficult decisions, because you don't want to end up in the wrong place. You may end up in a position that will make you unhappy. Sometimes, these things happen because people don't question things enough—they just move with the flow. This was an important lesson and I learned it the hard way: You can't go with the flow and be happy and satisfied all the time. *Sometimes, there are moments where you have to stick with what you believe in. You may feel alone for a while. But I think, at the end, you will be happier than had you not made that decision to separate.* There are two things in life you should not let go—your values and your family. These two will make you stronger at the end of the day.

I agree. And I am reminded of what a friend of mine once told me: "You better figure out your values and what you stand for—otherwise, people will do it for you."

You have to think about your personal values. I attended two training programs in 2006 or 2007. These programs were important to my development. One program was called the Authentic Woman Leader and the other one was Leading with Purpose. Both were about the importance of being an authentic leader. I enjoyed reading the book *True North: Discover Your Authentic Leadership* (San Francisco, CA: Wiley, 2007) by Bill George. The book examines authentic leadership in clear and simple language. I have read this book often. I reflected a lot on my leadership and identified my values. I feel that the six values I referred to earlier are the right set of values for me. You need those kinds of programs and deep reflections. They help you to see who you are—your core and your moral compass. The match of company values and personal values is critical. I am lucky to work in a company where I can stay authentic.

There will always be difficult situations as you grow into new roles. You have to deliver results, and there will be a lot of pressures—financial pressure, senior management pressure, peer pressure, external pressure from NGOs and the government, and so forth. I think, in those moments, you'll always see that your values play a role in making decisions. *You can never start too early to reflect on your leadership style and your values and how they drive your decision making. Think about your legacy. What am I doing? And why am I doing it?*

I could see that some people—younger people—roll their eyes and believe all the talk about values is soft. "Reflection? Values? Legacy?" What would you say to those people, the next generation of business leaders?

This week, my son asked me a number of questions. He is 11 years old. He came home from school and asked me what my strongest value is. Maybe things are changing a little in the education system?

It is really important to question yourself and what you are doing, in particular at an early age. Why do you want to get this education? Why do you want to start in this company? What is attractive to you? What do you stand for? You need to have some basic reasons to do things in life. Why do you want to get an education abroad? Why do you want to study art, science, or politics? Why do you want to work in a summer camp?

I think those experiences are related, somehow, to you as a human being—your personality, your values, your basic motivations in life. So, I suggest we start a little earlier to question those things. Maybe it will build a better or more satisfactory career, rather than jumping from place to place or job to job. I think that, especially in the first 5 years in their career, people need to find out what is the right thing for them to do for the next 10, 15, or 20 years.

You have passion for women and leadership. You are a frequent speaker at conferences and meetings. During one of your presentations, you stated that: "In general, women need to improve on networking, getting a mentor, being assertive, and taking credit for success." Can you elaborate on that statement?

First of all, research shows that there are differences between the male and female characteristics of leadership. These differences are driven by biology, the brain, hormones, the way you are brought up in the family, the socialization patterns, and so forth. For example, we are brought up to behave in a certain way—be respectful, do not be too competitive, and do not fight. It is a big thing when girls fight. But when boys compete and have a fight on the playground or the soccer field, then, typically, the next day they will be friends and be happy. It is the same in the business world—you can have a vigorous debate, but, the next day, you will still continue to do what you were doing. So, these socialization patterns somehow bring into the leadership of women some positives, but also some restrictions. The positives include empathy, listening skills, understanding others, compassion, the concern for the environmental and social matters, working as a team, collaborating, and sharing success. On the other hand, networking does not come naturally to us.

Women often believe that, if you do the work and deliver results, then somebody will notice and you reap the benefits. This is not always how things work. The reality in the business world is that many women need networking and support. For example, women sometimes do not have time to network and foster relationships. Some women may need to go home at the end of the day—they don't have time for a dinner or a reception to network. As a result, women need mentors or sponsors who can provide them with exposure that will help them in their career.

Then, in a meeting, for example, women will wait for the right moment to share their opinion or insights. But, if someone just voiced your opinion, then you don't want to articulate that again—it would be a repetition. You don't want to show off. You don't want to contribute just for the sake of contributing. The point is that you can't be too modest—you have to be more assertive. You have to raise your voice.

Another example. Women often share the success of a project—"It is our project and we succeeded together because of great teamwork." For men, it is a little easier to say, "These are my results on the project that I initiated."

I believe these differences are real, and that women need to address these issues in their own ways. We don't want to replicate male leadership characteristics. Women need to find ways to network and get credit for their success. For example, they can take the initiative and schedule a lunch meeting—meet with people and talk about what you are doing. Each person—man or woman—has to find his or her own way of doing things.

What expectations do you put on yourself in the leadership role?

It's always important to set a vision, because everything you do to create results should link to that. At PepsiCo, we believe in "performance with purpose." The "purpose" piece is important for leaders—it can be developing people, it can be working with the communities, it can be creating value for the shareholders. The point is that performance is not only about the numbers. If everything is around numbers, then, after a point, work and life get meaningless. You have to bring some meaning to the numbers game, because you create numbers for what? You add value to the world—to the economy, to the community, to the people around you, and so forth. So, we have to find our satisfiers. You can derive satisfaction from the promotion of a person you mentored. You bring clean water to a village in one of the places you do business. You receive an award for most improved performance. Yes—it is about performance, but you should also find your purpose.

What sustains you as a leader? And what drains you?

I am motivated by creating a positive impact in the economy, communities, and in the lives of people. *Corporate politics, people who over-promise and under-deliver, and people who are focused too much on their own priorities, rather than on delivering results, drain me.*

You are a visible leader. You work for a world-class company. You have achieved personal success. You have made the lists of the most powerful women in business. How do you remain humble?

I learned a lot about being humble from reading *True North*. I took the advice from the book—have people around you who can tell you that you are a little off the mark. It is important to have family and friends around you who observe you, and, if you begin to demonstrate some strange behaviors, they will call you on it. We should always be open to feedback.

I should also mention that I come from a middle class family. My father was working in a government office for many years. He comes from a village background. He focused a lot on the importance of education. I got a great education, and, as a result, I started to work at an early age. I had summer jobs at the age of 13, just to earn my own money that I could spend. I think these experiences probably made me mature a little earlier than most people.

My background in folk dancing also helped. You deal with a lot of different people and perspectives. I was confronted with the differences in people's lives at an early stage.

All those experiences help me to stay grounded. *I never forget where I am coming from and how I built my success. And, in the end, when I go home, I am a mother and wife.*

What are you learning these days to become an even better leader? Are there any recent "aha" moments?

Yes. I participated in a lot of meetings in the last couple of years—for example, the World Economic Forum in Davos, the *Economist* meeting, the *Financial Times* meeting, and the Asia-Pacific Economic Cooperation meeting in Vladivostok. In these meetings, you participate in panels and debates, you listen, and you read. For example, the World Economic Forum encourages business leaders to think about broader matters, such as the impact of climate change on business. At these meetings, you force yourself to go beyond your own business circles. I meet people who have a different background, and I keep those contacts—these meetings offer great opportunities to network. I travel a lot and so I have time to read and reflect on the discussions that took place. For example, I have four specific observations from the most recent meeting in Davos: Complexity is increasing; trust is declining; connectivity is increasing; and, despite the doom and gloom, opportunities still exist.

The "legacy" piece is important to me—what are we delivering to our employees, customers, and communities? We spend a lot of time thinking about creating shared value. As a company, we cannot operate in isolation. And we cannot focus on creating shareholder value alone. There are a number of societal issues nowadays that any leader has to be aware of. You must appreciate the societal impact of what you do. So, when you attend those meetings, such as the World Economic Forum, you start to think about new models of leadership. And one of my conclusions coming out of recent meetings is that the concern for positive societal impact is becoming more important. Leaders, therefore, have to learn to manage multi-stakeholder relations—NGOs, governments, other businesses, and so forth.

I also realized that you need to be ready for a crisis at any time. And, when they occur, leaders must be able to create high-impact solutions within a short time-frame. For example, last year, we had six natural disasters in this geographic area. How do you stay cool headed and warm hearted as a leader under such conditions?

Based on the challenges that I see, a new model of leadership is needed. First, as business leaders, we must show a genuine concern for positive societal impact. Second, we must be able to manage multi-stakeholder relations and create high-impact solutions. Third, we must always be ready for a crisis to unfold and move into fast action planning mode. Fourth, we must learn to use the power of diversity. Fifth, there is a real need for transparency and authentic communication.

Leadership Themes

- Be open to new experiences and willing to stretch in order to develop as a leader.
- Learn to trust people who have skills that you don't have and empower them to deliver on your agenda.
- You must be able to put together, and lead, a diverse team. Appreciate individual differences in delivering results.
- You learn lessons from each crisis.
- It is important to have family and friends around you who observe you, and, if you begin to demonstrate some strange behaviors, they will call you on it. Always be open to feedback.

31

If You Are Not Creative in Getting Solutions and You Limit Your Expectations and Outcomes, You Are Not Going to Change the World

Antoni Cimolino

Antoni, when did you first realize you were a leader, and what happened to make you realize it?

Some time in high school, when I was working in the theater and producing, writing, and directing plays, I realized, to lead this forward, I had to take great responsibility. I was more interested in it than some of the others, and I realized I had to serve as a kind of leader and coordinator, and provide the impetus. I also wanted to teach things I had learned, so, on some level, there was a desire to share.

You ended up as general director of the Stratford Festival. Did you want to be a leader?

I wouldn't position it exactly like that, but the question is valid. It wasn't so much that I felt I had to lead others, just that I was so damn interested in what everybody else was doing. I have been a debater, public speaker, and an actor, and, in each of those roles, you're a strong individual contributor to the outcome. In the theater, I found myself so drawn to what people were doing when they were building costumes, or the role of the director in putting together music, interpreting the play, helping others understand it, and bringing together a great team. I find that very fulfilling. It's not that I liked being a contributor less; it's just that I loved working with others more.

How did you learn to lead? What have been the formative influences on you as a leader?

Developing empathy and being able to understand the position of another person is very important to the theater, and I learned it when I was young. I found myself having strong opinions, but also being able to sense where other people were coming from and understanding that to find a middle ground and resolve issues. Over time, that ability contributed towards me being able to understand and advance their interests more than my own. That was very important. In addition, I learned from the different plays of Shakespeare. You spend the year doing *Henry V* and that play has a lesson in leadership. When you're working on a play, you listen to what is being said and what situations confront the leader, and also how the leader goes about building support, finding the right thing to do, and getting people on board. It has been a great gift to work on *King Lear*, where something goes wrong, or on "the Scottish play," where power is misused. There are different mediations on power, and, from more than 30 years in theater, I've had the pleasure of hearing those mediations very often and they've been instructive.

Was there any particular experience that supercharged your learning to lead?

I had a very difficult situation a number of years ago. I tried to change the structure of the festival and invited individuals to take part. Everybody came to the table with the best will in the world, but it didn't work. There were many reasons why it didn't work, and we didn't see eye to eye on why that was the case, but, nevertheless, it was a significant kind of failure. That affected me profoundly. It made me wonder why I was doing what I was doing, and how I could better serve the Stratford Festival that I love. It changed me. I found myself getting right back to the most prime instincts as to what made me tick, what made me happy, and how I related to others. It made me more humble and direct with people. It also taught me that I have to constantly look at the courage of my convictions and whether or not a person is modest or strident in character. There are times when the entity that we serve demands we do what's right and move forward. It made me more connected to the reason I do things, and also more courageous. It was a hard lesson to learn, but I think I'm in a better place because of it. It was very much a crucible. It was very difficult, but I feel significantly stronger now because of it.

What did people do to help you develop as a leader? Are there examples of people who have been instrumental in your development?

I've been fortunate because I've been given opportunities. For example, when I was first allowed to become a director here at the festival, I was asked by the former artistic director to serve. David Williams served as an assistant director with a very famous and gifted director from England, and that was a great opportunity. *I don't know if I quite recognized it as such at the time, but I look back and realize people took a chance on me.* That was also the case when I was asked to step up and do more work in terms of production. I don't think all of us realized how important we can be to young people in helping them to find that right opportunity, and preparing them for that opportunity. Rather than going for the tried and true, which is maybe the responsible and safe thing to do, it's important once in a while to just take a risk and follow your gut. You're not doing people favors if you set them up to fail. I think that ability to take a chance was something with which I was blessed and I'm now trying in this role to make sure to encourage young people to look for such opportunities.

What specifically do you do to help young people to become better, or to become the future leaders in the arts community?

There are a number of things we can do to help the next generation. First, express interest in them. You need to stop and say, "Look, I'd like to see your work. I'd like to understand what you do better," and ask your colleagues about who is showing talent and a real gift. For the senior leader in the organization to cut through the ranks and talk to someone several levels down who shows promise is a major empowerment and gift to that young person. It comes with responsibilities, too. You can't just give someone an opportunity and walk away. There is an ongoing responsibility to be there as an ear and source of advice. There is also a responsibility to be very frank and honest. *You have put those young people in positions where they could sail and fly, or they could have a very scarring experience that could set them back several years in their development. It's very important for leaders to take responsibility for the opportunities they've provided to young people and to ensure those people are successful.*

Several years ago, you told me that you benefited greatly from the board of governors in learning to lead. I think the quote you used at that time was, "None of us should be too proud to admit their ignorance. You need to be open to learning." Can you elaborate on that statement?
As a not-for-profit organization, we're blessed to have a larger board because its role is larger than simply governance—it's also to help out, raise funds, and reach into various communities in a big geographic area. It's an international group. We've got some very accomplished people there. Today, my day started with one of the board members calling me to talk about a certain situation, and I said, "Look, there are elements of the future where you could help so much and the committee that you're chairing will be central to that work." It's important to ask them for advice and input at an early stage, not when it's all done. *There is something very powerful about allowing people to make a contribution. Then, people buy in and feel not only included, but a sense of responsibility. They become invested in the outcome.* Asking for help, advice, and consulting is a great chance to build directional support. It's a much better approach than the more dictatorial "This is where we're going, you can either get on or get off" approach. With a dictatorial approach, there are many reasons for people to not bother. You want to find reasons for them to really care.

You gave a presentation at the Ivey Business School and argued that leadership is a central theme in many of Shakespeare's plays. Have you learned specific lessons from plays that you've tried to make your own?
Yes. The plays repeatedly look at how a person or a leader finds a real sense of meshing and finds fulfillment. They also examine the two bodies of the king— there is the leader as the corporation or as the state, which is the formal role, and there is also a personal role. Those two roles have to be balanced. King Lear, for instance, in renouncing the trappings of state, loses himself because he has always thought of himself as that function. We meet leaders like that, who think they are the corporation or the government because they've been doing it so long. In fact, they're not. They must remember that they are serving a greater cause, not themselves, and they are not the cause themselves. King Lear, in finally realizing that he

is just a human being like everybody else, gains a soul and an understanding of how to help and serve others. These plays tell you about finding the essence in yourself, both as a person and in serving the common good.

What were some of the hardest things to learn in becoming a good or an even better leader?

One of the most striking things I've learned over time is how people will surprise you. You can think carefully about all of the variables, and then somebody comes at you with a unique point of view that surprises you, despite how carefully you thought it out. This is testament to the world as a whole. Always be aware that such a curveball might come your way. You can't anticipate every single curveball. If you try to, you'll spend all your time as a nervous mess. The questions are, "How well can you listen?" and "How well can you take a deep breath and go back to the bigger picture?" You need to become comfortable to say, "Right . . . I want to go from here to there, and this new input means I have to modify my plan." I've learned a lot about responsiveness. You need to take a deep breath and not be flustered when you're in a situation where everything you worked on is now in question. You've got to just take a step back and tell yourself, "You know we will get there and this is how we're going to get there."

What role did mistakes play in your learning process? Can you talk about a mistake you made as a leader, and what you learned from that mistake?

When I was younger, I was much more prescriptive as to outcome. I would say to myself, "Right, I need to go from here to there, and that's what I need, and you're going to do the following things to get from here to there." The problem with that is it removes the role of the contribution of others, to a certain degree. It removes their ability to make a creative contribution to the process, and it assumes that you, as the leader, have the entire outcome already mapped out. That might be the case, but it doesn't mean it's the best solution. The solution could be a hell of a lot better than what you had in mind, so removing that arrogance is very important. Removing the dictatorial element of leadership, in my view, is very important. Removing the prescription is also important. *You need to effectively articulate not only the vision of what you see, and excite people around it, but you have to make sure there is enough room in that picture for them to add their own painting, color, and shapes. Their contributions might improve it, and then you will be surprised at how good it is.* Here's the thing—you can still take credit for it.

True—but it can't all be "kumbaya," right? There will be situations where you will need to be directive and say, "Listen, we've talked about this enough, we need to commit to a decision, and this is what we are going to do."

Sometimes, there are times when leaders must say, "You know, I've heard what you've had to say, and here is where we need to go, and here's why I think we need to go there." In those cases, leaders should show you that they have really listened. They should also articulate a response that is cogent, comprehensive, and persuasive. You want people to say, "Okay, maybe he's seeing something I'm not, but he has listed a lot of good reasons why we should go in that direction." When there is an openness about the decision-making process, you find people gradually learning and beginning to understand where you are trying to go. You've shown them that there is respect for what they brought to the table, and that you've decided you're going to take some parts of it—not all of it—and go in a different direction. People get that. What they want is clarity, decisiveness, and to be shown respect for what they brought to the table. That doesn't stop the need or the desire for the leader to lead.

We learn from good leaders. You talked about people who helped you throughout your career. What did you learn from bad leaders? You must have encountered bad examples of leadership that provided lessons?

We all have personality foibles. We have times when maybe we aren't inspiring people the way we should, or paying attention to details the way we should, or giving the right reasons for decisions. It's not like you have to go searching for them, just look carefully. *There's something to be learned every day, both by looking in the mirror at yourself and by looking at the people around you.* You can't be critical, but, rather, say, "That person does the following things fantastically well, but here's one area where he or she might be better." Helping somebody else is very difficult, so, usually, it is better to start with yourself. A lot also depends on the relationship you have with others. If you're trying to help a subordinate and you do it in a nurturing way, you can help others to improve. I think it touches very close to the bone for a lot of us, because leadership is a manifestation of our own inner being. It's a delicate thing, but it demands constant observation.

You have stepped out of your comfort zone on several occasions and taken on progressively more challenging leadership roles at the festival. Where does your confidence come from?

There are times when you've got to step into the unknown, even at personal cost, and say, "You know, the thing I love—this entity, the theater—is asking me to do the following thing and I don't know whether I'm going to succeed." You have to take a deep breath and trust that, between the decision and the ultimate event, you will have time to think, to gather a great team together, and move forward. It's good to have this wonderful statement about the blessings that flow to anybody who commits to a course of action, but, once you make the decision, it's like the whole universe comes forward to provide opportunities for you to strengthen and build on that decision. Making the decision is hard, but you've got to have faith that, if you feel it's the right direction, no matter how hard it's going to be to get from here to there, you will have time to put the practical steps in place to get all of the details straightened out. I think it's important to move forward; otherwise, we can see corporations and entities—rather than making the right move at the right time—play it safe. Suddenly, in a year's time, they look like dinosaurs. It comes down to having courage at the right moment. Sometimes, you need to make decisions even when you don't have all of the answers to your questions.

You've made several leadership transitions at the Stratford Festival. Leadership transitions can be challenging to manage. What have you learned about managing those transitions that, over time, allowed you to do them more effectively?

Transitions are surprisingly hard because, even if you know where you want to go, people around you might not see the logic in your vision. They may not understand your role in that vision. When someone is moving into a significantly different role, it's always amazing how people will put that person into a box, the box of what that person was before. For instance, I'm an artist who became an administrator while continuing to be an artist, but, when I stepped back into a solely artistic role, I was amazed that people were one step behind. When I became an administrator, people said, "He can't do that, he's an artist." When I later went back to being an artist, people said, "Well, he's an administrator." We should not be surprised at the degree of drag that's in the world around us in terms of transitions. A leader has to see through other people's eyes and understand that others are not going to see the vision immediately. You have to communicate it and understand that people may not immediately get it. You need to press ahead if you believe in it, and not be surprised at the amount of effort that requires. You've got to keep pressing forward, and examining it as a whole; otherwise, you're not going to make a change.

You speak passionately about the importance of collaboration—that theater is a collaborative enterprise. Was this insight an epiphany or learned over time?

I realized over time that the theater, especially, is a collaborative art form. When we're young, most of us are so driven by our own needs, egos, and desires. We want to be stars of our own movies. *The great gift for me was to realize there are many people here, each carrying a different piece of the jigsaw puzzle to the table, and, if you really want to make it work, each person plays a part. I learned that over time, and it was huge because I then realized that, by enlisting people's support and getting them to really want to come to the table, we would ultimately have a much better product—a better play—at the end of day.* Even when the team gets together and creates a beautiful play, it is still not a success until you have hundreds of people coming together every night to watch and respond to it. They might respond in hushed silence as they watch the horrible things happen, or by laughing as they watch the delightful things happen. That's when you really, truly have a successful event. I think that's true with every product—you need a great team to put it together.

You have to deal with a lot of stakeholders. The opportunity for conflict is quite high. What have you learned about dealing with conflict and sharp differences?

As we serve a cause, we have particular views. It's important to realize we hold those views and to understand that others have different views and that could potentially lead to conflict. If you represent a direction for the future that you really believe in and that you've communicated, there will still be people who disagree with you. You still have a responsibility to advance the agenda that you believe is so critically important to the future. To minimize the friction, you need to do it respectfully, but not step back from what you know is right because there are people who disagree. For individuals who work with organizations that have a mission apart from simply driving shareholder value, things can become very heated. All you can do is be true to your own convictions, and be clear about that so no one is surprised, and then move ahead.

The current economic climate offers challenges to the Stratford Festival. I suspect, therefore, that your leadership is about managing paradoxes—you have to be optimistic yet, at the same time, realistic; to be aggressive yet patient; deliberate and decisive. How did you learn to manage those paradoxes in your leadership career?

It's important to always be ambitious and to always be trying to shoot the lights out. At the same time, you need to put together the best plan you can. If you rely solely on limiting risk, then you're probably not doing what you need to do in terms of excellence, moving things forward, and finding the solution. You need to put the problem on the table and say, "It's got to be fantastic, so how do we get there?" The question "How do we get there?" is very important. I still keep learning this lesson. If you're not creative in getting solutions, and you limit your expectations and outcomes, you're not going to change the world. You may not come up with a product that people really want to see. There is something about a hard-fought victory. It's the best victory.

You are familiar with the "Leadership on Trial" project. We talk about the importance of commitment to the leadership role, and that doing the hard work of leadership always comes at a cost. What has been the price of leadership for you?

Leadership takes time. It is consuming. I will have one hour to have dinner with my wife on a day that starts early in the morning and ends at midnight. Sometimes, during that hour, as was the case on my birthday recently, I will still be looking at notes for a speech I have to give. My daughter came to me a number of years ago, and, although we get along great, she said, "You were absent a lot when I was a little kid." I didn't feel that way—I felt like I was there all the time. Clearly, that wasn't her view though. The commitment to making change, serving something you believe in, and working along with others requires a lot of time. A leader isn't alone in this. There are many jobs that require that kind of giving. Finding balance is critically important overall, but I would say I was consumed with the theater and making plays. Something had to give. If you like reading a lot of books just for personal interest, or you like to go to a cottage, do sports, or other personal hobbies, then you're probably not going to be able to lead in quite the same way. Things have to give sometimes, but leaders still have to find balance and make time for those few things, such as family, that are very important.

What are you learning these days to become an even better leader? Are there any recent "aha" moments?

Leaders need to be galvanizing and inspirational, as well as resourceful and flexible. It takes a combination of skills and a strong central nervous system to be able to do that. I'm always amazed at how things change and surprise me. Sometimes, if you've got one big problem on your desk, it can become all consuming, but, when you've got 10 big problems on your desk, there is something relaxing about that. You say to yourself, "I've got to solve all of these, so take a breath!" When you have that ongoing situation, you realize you've got to just breathe, move through it, and work through it. It's very important for leaders to simply allow themselves to get in the flow. If you keep thinking, observing, and breathing, you're going to be okay.

I think it's fair to say that, in your interactions with the board, you've learned a lot from business leaders that helped you develop as a leader. Let's flip perspective. What would be the one leadership lesson from the theater that you believe business leaders can benefit from a great deal?

That's a really good question. Having worked with a lot of very accomplished business leaders, I've been struck by their intelligence and passion, and also that the most whole thinkers usually have been the best overall leaders. When I look at what the very best artists do, there is a sense of profound thirst for excellence, a real drive to understand yourself and the material you're interpreting in a very, *very* deep way. The very best artists applaud people who are able to overcome smallness and go to the heart of something important. They have a thirst for excellence and an ability to put ego second to the need to do something right and beautifully. I wish I saw that a little bit more in the business world. I see very effective people, and I see people care about others, but to have this very strong need to drive at something . . . that is exceptional and rare. It's not that it's not out there, just rare.

This book is about learning to lead. What question did I forget to ask you about the learning process? What did we not touch on?

Why we want to lead is important. We need to ask that of ourselves and our situation more regularly. There may be a whole bunch of reasons—we want to advance in the ranks, we see ourselves in the important chair, or there can be compensation issues. Since leadership comes at such a great cost to our family, ourselves, or the corporation or entity that we serve, at the day's end, we should be asking ourselves why we want to lead and what we hope to do in leading. If we did that more regularly, we'd be much more effective. We might even be happier.

Okay, Antoni, why do you want to lead the Stratford Festival?

I want to move the Stratford Festival more into the heart of our society. I feel it is here to serve an important role in helping us to understand ourselves and the world around us better. On a very basic level, Stratford is here as an escape. On a more profound level, it's here as a restorative place where you come to understand things, feel things, laugh and cry, and go back home and treat everybody a little bit better.

Leadership Themes

- There is something very powerful about allowing people to make a contribution. People buy in and feel not only included, but a sense of responsibility. They become invested in the outcome.
- Take a chance on people. Encourage young people to look for opportunities.
- There are times when you've got to step into the unknown, even at personal cost. You have to take a deep breath and trust that, between the decision and the ultimate event, you will have time to think, gather a great team together, and move forward.
- A leader has to see through other people's eyes and understand that others are not going to see the vision immediately.

32

If You Are Not Working for People Who Inspire You, Who Are You Working for?

Sukhinder Singh Cassidy

Sukhinder, when did you first realize you were a leader, and what happened to make you realize it?

It's an interesting question—it depends on whether you are talking about leadership in the most general sense, or just professionally. Personally, I would say it was very early—public school, high school? ***I figured out I was a leader because I was always the person who was taking on more than I needed to.*** I was always intense, expending more energy doing something than other people were willing to do. I don't know when I started stepping into positions of responsibility. As long as I can remember, I was always the person who was trying extra hard; and when the assignment was X, I did X plus Y plus Z—not because anyone told me to, I just did it. I remember when I was in second or third grade, and we had to do a science fair project. My father sat down with me and we built a model of the human eye. He built most of it, but he got me engaged and my project was way beyond anyone else's. I was the person who went the extra mile, but it certainly was promoted by my father.

Professionally, there were several different moments. My first job was as an investment banker at Merrill Lynch. On one of my first assignments, the managing director realized that, although I was an analyst, I was operating at the associate level. He pulled me aside to work directly with him on an initial public offering while the other analysts were relegated to the more tedious jobs. Then, I worked at British Sky Broadcasting, where my first project was on debt ratings. I worked next to a superstar analyst working for the chief financial officer (CFO). He was annoyed with me, and even though we are good friends, I think he felt like I was trying to show him up since I had just arrived and put so much effort in to everything. I told him, "I can't help it! That's just who I am."

Another moment that comes to mind happened a few years later. I had always been successful in whatever job I was in, but I had never managed people. While working in business development at my second start-up, Junglee, we were acquired by Amazon. They had launched an effort to get third-party merchants on the Amazon site, and I was chosen from the group to be the person negotiating the third-party deals. I went from being a peer with my colleagues to managing them.

I remember feeling guilty. I was the same age, so why was I the manager? That was the first time in my professional life that I realized I was a leader, leading other people who didn't necessarily think I should be leading them. What made me so qualified?

Where did the "eager beaver" orientation come from? Was it always there, even when you were a little child, or was it your dad who was encouraging and pushing you?

I believe in people being genetically wired. Even without the enormous influence of my father, I was always intense. My mom says that, at the age of five, I was mature for my age. She looks at my daughter now and says, "She's a little you—who would believe she's a five year old? She acts like an eight year old!" In kindergarten, my Mom sent me off to school telling them that I already knew "all this stuff." They didn't believe her, but, two weeks later, they said, "Your daughter knows all this stuff—let's send her to first grade!" And so, I think it was always me. But my father was the wind in my sails. He was a doctor, but he loved running his own business. He loved science, he loved art—he loved everything. He had such intellectual curiosity, and, at every opportunity, he encouraged us. He saw fertile ground and stimulated my sense of possibility.

What have been the formative influences on you as a leader? What did people do to help you? What experiences did you learn the most from? Was there any particular experience that supercharged your learning to lead?

There are quite a few people that I learned from. Clearly, one of the most formative experiences was as a co-founder in my first opportunity to build a company. I've always felt that, every time I've been put in a leadership position, I've been unqualified for the job. I fundamentally believe that. When I was still only 28 or 29 years old, I wanted to start a company. Through my network, four engineers approached me when I was at Amazon because they heard that I was good at business development. They had built some technology and invited me to be the business founder. I found myself leading Yodlee, helping to hire the chief executive officer (CEO) and raise the venture capital. *But I believe that you will learn to be a leader simply by doing it. If you're feeling very comfortable where you are, and somebody offers you a job and you don't know if you can do it, take it.* From that time forward, when offered the chance to run groups, such as Asia Pacific and Latin America operations at Google, even though I didn't have the qualifications, I accepted the challenge, and, just by stepping in and doing it, I was able to move to the next level. *I firmly believe that you learn to lead by taking advantage of opportunities when they are presented to you, and rising to meet the challenge.* Another experience that comes to mind is the opportunity I was given to lead large groups of high-powered people at Google. It is one thing to lead a set of people who are younger and less qualified than you. It's a whole other challenge to lead people who are just as experienced as you are and who could rightly be in your job. When I was responsible for building the infrastructure for Google in Asia Pacific and Latin America, and providing leadership to the regional leaders, I felt like I was running 18 separate fiefdoms where the people we were hiring were the equivalent of CEOs in their countries. At the regional level, the leaders we were hiring were heads of large divisions at companies such as HSBC or Yahoo. *What I learned is that, at some point, you have to stop apologizing for being the leader, and start acting like one.* At the same time, you have to harness all of these big personalities and get them to work together. I learned to appreciate when it is important to lead from behind, and when to lead from the front.

What were some of the hardest things to learn in becoming a good or an even better leader?

As I mentioned earlier, when I was put in a position of leadership for the first time, I felt guilty that I was the youngest in the group and the leader. However, at some point, I felt that I had earned my stripes and was able to shed that feeling. Now that I had a body of work and accomplishment to feel good about, I could go out into the world in a more confident way, feeling less apologetic for being in that role.

I also struggle with a combination of letting go, not taking things so personally, and managing within diverse agendas; when these elements converge, it is even more difficult. And I don't know why it is, but I believe that, for a woman in a leadership position, everything feels like a personal failure if you don't get it all done.

I confronted these issues when I was running Google in Asia Pacific, including China. This area was quite controversial and somebody in the organization was lobbying politically regarding China. After learning about this from my boss, I was very emotional and upset: I felt like a failure. My instinct, when I was younger, would have been along the lines of, "What can I do right now to change this?" but now I knew that I had done everything I could, and that, even if the situation didn't work out the way I wanted, it was not about my failure; it was not that I was not good at my job. I had to learn not to take this as a personal affront. Although I felt that the way the situation was handled was unethical, I trusted that my body of work would speak for itself, and decided not to play the game—it was not who I was. In the end, nothing changed and my position/views prevailed, but I had to let go of the outcome along the way.

Through this experience, I also came to realize that, the more senior you get in an organization, the more diverse the agenda set is of people around you. It's no longer just about the merit of your argument; it's also about managing all of these diverse agendas. *I learned that, sometimes, it is better to let things unfold than to push your own specific agenda, to learn when you should continue to push and when you should let go and throttle back. You can't control the whole outcome, only the effort you put into it.*

I don't think that this reaction is woman specific—I would be furious as well.

I think women have a harder time sometimes letting go, realizing that that the situation is a reflection of a set of circumstances that maybe could have been foreseen, but it doesn't mean that you are inherently a bad person or a bad leader. Women, I think, will internalize some of these things more than men.

You've made several transitions in your career. Leadership transitions can be challenging to manage. What have you learned about managing those transitions that, over time, allowed you to do them more effectively?
I have learned a number of things. First, particularly as I've taken on more senior roles, I've been able to access more resources to help me think about leadership. I have, as an example, an executive coach I am very close to. For my last two transitions, out of Google into Accel, and out of Accel into Polyvore and then into JOYUS, he has been a great help for me.

The second thing is that I'm very definite about managing transitions with support. Always having somebody who can reflect back to me. But it is important to remember that, in any transitional scenario, people need both professional and personal support. We all like to think that our spouses are meant to be perfect people who give us support in every sphere, but you can't be everything to all people. For me, it's most important that my husband provide some perspective, cover on the home front, and be a great partner in the other areas of my life, with an understanding of what I'm going through for work. But expecting him to be my coach and psychologist when he has his own set of worries puts a lot of strain on a relationship.

The third lesson about managing transitions has always been to listen to my gut. I have tried to manage transitions by moving in the direction of the things that make up my purpose in life, and what I think is my unique contribution to the world, in sync with my business purpose. *I fundamentally believe that part of why I am a business leader is because it's how I'm meant to give back to the world. I believe my contributions to the world will be in this arena and that's why I have the skill set I have.* Particularly as I hit a very senior point in Google, and I had accomplished a lot, I started measuring transitions differently. I asked myself what it is I think I'm meant to give, and still meant to create, and contribute to. Earlier in my career, my transitions were about learning and the need for another challenge or another accomplishment. The last three transitions have been about giving something back to the world in an area I'm passionate about. It's important to align your authentic self with your work.

We learn from success; but we also learn a lot from mistakes. Has there been one of those moments where you stared into the abyss? What made you turn around? And what concrete lessons did you learn from the experience?
Your trademark strength is often your vice. What are my trademark strengths? My trademark strength is I lead from drive, I lead from passion, and I lead from a lot of energy output. The good news is you attract people and you can thrust forward. The bad news is I am always acting with urgency. I can't even help it. One of the key things for me is how to throttle my energy. Let's talk about one of the more critical decisions I made—the decision to go to Polyvore after leaving Google. I wanted to start a women's commerce company, or to run one, and I was excited about

it—making women feel good is a great mission and I think we can do it through
e-commerce. Polyvore had been pitching me for two years to join them as CEO,
and had first approached me when I was with Google. I met the founder, an incredibly smart engineer, and we were intellectually well matched. He's everything I like
and know in terms of being smart, capable, and just like the partners I had at Yodlee
and Google. I was very attracted to the company and its business model, but I felt
like I hadn't seen enough. They kept in touch with me, and I did a strategy session
with them for a day after I left Google that they found very useful. Then, I had my
second child. My husband wanted me to take maternity leave, but I had been out
of the market for nine months and I was ready to go back. I had known Polyvore
for two years and I loved the business model, so, when the board came back to me
three months after I'd had the baby and said, once again, that I was their first
choice, I thought, "Okay, we are well matched, I'm ready to go, this must be fate."
Within six months, I left the company and the founder and I parted ways. Our
value systems and how we want to run a company were completely different. The
whole thing unfolded very quickly. After two years of knowing a company, I joined
them and, by September of the next year, we're done. My first CEO job! How could
this happen to me? I knew the founder, I knew the company. When I play it back,
one of the things that stands out to me is my sense of urgency—that it has to be
now. Even though there were differences between the founder and me stylistically,
I felt that we were so well matched IQ wise that it would work. But of course it's not
always about IQ—it's about EQ.

For me, this was a convergence of two lessons. Number one was about a sense of
urgency. The good side of that urgency is needed in a start-up environment and it's
been so successful for me, but, in this case, acting urgently and with impatience
failed me—I should have taken more steps to lay the foundation for my values prior
to joining. Number two was the triumph of IQ over EQ. For the first part of my
career, it was all about IQ. It's not that I don't have EQ, but, if you are really good
at what you do, IQ is enough. However, leadership is as much about EQ as it is
about IQ, especially with the founder—CEO dynamic, which is like a marriage. I
was so overconfident that IQ would prevail, that our intellectual parity was all that
was needed for a good marriage. That was not the case. I should have given myself
more time to observe that. But patience is one of the hardest things for me to learn.

**You're a role model to many individuals. You have served as a mentor. How
do people with potential derail a promising leadership career?**
One thing that derails people is an inordinate focus on what they can't control
versus what they can control. *Lots of things are out of your control, and I've always
struggled with being obsessive about what is in my control.* But, for some people,
there are 10 reasons why 10 other people aren't allowing them to get their job done.
That's when you have to tell them to forget what other people are doing to them
and understand what they are doing themselves.

Another way to derail a leadership career is to always be the victim. I've
managed people who, no matter how smart, are always the victim; something is

always being done to them. I would say I'm probably the opposite extreme, always wondering what I could do better.

The third way to derail a leadership career is to allow big talent to be destroyed by big ego. I don't lack confidence and I am sure there are people who would say I've always been a handful to manage. I've also managed people who are incredibly talented, are very aware of how talented they are, and, to some degree, are very ego driven. Such people risk derailing teams, if they manage for their own agenda rather than the company's agenda. The important thing to manage is that balance between being confident and managing one's own agenda. If somebody is really good at what they do, you will take their arrogance or their selfishness and you'll manage it, but you are always walking a fine line between whether their first agenda is themselves or is it moving the organization forward? People don't want to follow people who are all about themselves, and, at some point, that all comes back to you somehow.

There is always a cost to leadership. What has been the price of leadership for you?

For me, the price of leadership has been that my mind is never at rest. My mind is naturally always going, but then there is the added responsibility of having to worry not just about yourself but about a company, a set of people who are depending on you to get them to where they need to be for their careers, their lives, and their ambitions. Not to mention your children and your spouse. I am always worried, and it would be nice to be able to shed that worry. But I think that is the burden of a leader. For me, I can experience the joy of 80 percent of leadership, but I know that last 20 percent for me is really hard, which is about letting go. Even letting go for a day, or an hour, or even a moment—to be able to say, "It's okay if I don't think about something 24/7. That doesn't mean it's going to be a less good outcome. It may be a better outcome."

What are you learning these days to become an even better leader? Are there any recent "aha" moments?

What I have learned over the past ten years, and particularly the last seven years as I became more senior at Google, is that I am much more intense than I ever thought. I don't think of myself as that intense, but, after years of taking part in 360s, coaching sessions, and reflections, I began to understand that I am a true outlier in this respect. And, having realized this, I need to understand what my challenge is. Can I hold back? When you're leading a company or a group of 2,000 people, there are many people to expend your energy on. You can multiply your bandwidth a thousand-fold. The biggest challenge for me at JOYUS is that I could create work for 100 people right now, but we have only 27. We have to decide what to focus on. There is only so much people can do.

My intensity, to me, is optimism; my intensity, for some people, is pressure. I think, when you're in a start-up, it's about throttling your energy further. There are only so many messages people can take in at once—even if I can hold them all in my head. They are all exported to the same finite amount of resources, and so you have to prioritize, stay focused—I think that's probably been the biggest lesson in leadership coming back to a small company.

I recently attended an event where Rahm Emanuel talked about the upcoming U.S. presidential election. He said that, when all is said and done, what people want in a president and CEO is someone who conveys three things: Strength, confidence, and optimism. For me, energy and intensity equals optimism. My job as a leader is to make sure that my intensity is conveyed to you as optimism.

You presented to MBA students. The title of the presentation was "Note to self: What have I learned the last 12 years." Can you elaborate on the following insight: "Heads up versus heads down—when politics matter."

You get to a certain point in your career driven firstly by merit. The goal in the first half of your career, to the extent that you want to be in a leadership position, is to lead from what you know and be the best that you can possibly be at whatever is your functional area of expertise. That gets you quite a long way; it's what you build your reputation on and it's what gets you into your first leadership role. But, at some point, as your world becomes more complex, and you move to a more senior role, it becomes a combination of how good you are at what you do, and how good you are at helping other people achieve what they want to achieve, or convincing them that what they want to achieve intersects with what you want to achieve. You have to lift your head up and spend more time understanding the other stakeholders.

And: "The organizational chart is a pendulum; don't worry what side you're on."

People think that power in an organization swings through the organizational chart. I think it swings through proximity to people, and who they feel is giving them the most value. A tangible example of this occurred at Google when we were running Asia Pacific and Latin America operations. Like many organizations, we would swing through a functional organization chart and a regional organization chart, so where is the center of power in an international organization? Is it with a country or is it with a function, such as marketing or product development, which has historically had all of the expertise needed to make something successful? At Google, there would be times when the organizational chart swung functional, and there were times when it swung regional. People would always worry about who reported to them, and my observation, particularly to people in the region, was to be helpful to the person in North America, be helpful to the person sitting next to you, and that, at the end of the day, the organizational chart may swing from one person to another, but, ultimately, it is the people who give value and who can help get the job done better who will succeed. If you're one of those people, you have power.

Stop worrying about the organizational chart—the chart will move. It will always move. The people who you influence and who you add value for are the constant in your career.

And: "Everything you do as a leader is analyzed, accept it."

I'm the founder of JOYUS and, even if it is only 27 people, everything I do is analyzed much more deeply than I think about it. If I cancel a meeting, somebody thinks, "Does she not want to meet with me?" and I think, "I have to pick up my daughter at 5:30—it's her last day of school and I want to be there." If I leave a meeting early, people think, "Is she not interested in the topic?", and I think, "I've got to go to the bathroom." There are always points at which people are looking for signals about what you're thinking. Your job is to be cognizant of that, and be aware that, whether you like it or not, people do want to be led or, in being led, they are always looking for some telltale signal as to which way the wind is blowing. Anything you do has an implication for your organization.

And the last one: "Delegation versus detail—the importance of operating range."

This is the number one thing I look for in leaders. When you talk about scaling companies at any level, I look for people who can fly at 50,000, at 50, and at 5 feet. I say that because, at any point in time, your organization needs something from you. Part of being a great leader is having the judgment to discern what that is, and I don't think that changes when a company gets bigger. Let's take a very concrete example—Google is obviously one of the biggest and most successful companies in the world. The company is exceptionally data driven. It's great to say, "We should pursue a particular strategy." But the command of the details is essential. Where is the data that supports that strategy? If you're a leader, your job is to understand that as much as it is to provide a grand vision. I believe that is true even more so in Silicon Valley, which has such a data-driven culture, where command of the details and the data is essential to give you credibility at the vision level.

I also believe it's important, in all companies, to understand what your teams need from you. There are times they need you to be the evangelist and identify vision, but there are other times when your job as a leader is to provide the unique insight into what, at first glance, seems to be going well, but in fact may not be. It's your job to know when to go to the next level of detail with your teams to help them problem solve or, if you're not getting the right answer and you don't understand something, to understand it enough to have command of your business and to help your team have command of their business. *I'm a believer that there are times when you absolutely need to know the smallest detail of your business, and there are other times you need to let others run with it because you need to be operating at a higher level.* Steve Jobs is the perfect example of that. He could operate at the most visionary level, but his obsession with the details of his product didn't stop when Apple got big—it continued and, if anything, intensified.

I fundamentally believe that, at every level of any size of company, operating range is hugely important.

Good leaders learn. They mature. How has your leadership evolved over time?

I believe that I have become better at trusting that things will unfold as they are meant to, as opposed to me driving something to a conclusion. More and more often, although not always, I feel much more able to admit that we've done everything we can; that I'm going to sit with it and let it unfold how it's meant to unfold, and trust that there is a reason for everything.

There is also trusting people that they will do the right thing. How did you learn to trust others?

My presumption is that I can hold you accountable and that you can be trusted, because you were good enough for me to hire, and that's what I look for when I hire; a set of presumed competencies. I've always been the kind of person who presumes these competencies do exist as opposed to presuming they don't. I then sit back and observe who starts managing: Managing the situation, managing me. My best people, they manage me. They are telling me what they need, and then I can give it back to them and we both go away happy—they feel like they have lots of latitude and I feel like they are driving.

What I do, and this is part of my own operating range, is to fly at 50,000 feet for the first weeks after hiring someone. I meet with somebody when they first arrive to watch what they do. I think that everybody gets better once they have been in a situation for three or four weeks and have sized up the situation. Then, I drop down to 50 feet after about 3 months, maybe even 60 days. Sometimes, I don't have to drop to 50 feet because they've already started to manage me. But if they're not managing me by that time, I start managing them. My leadership style is you manage me, or I'll manage you—what would you prefer? I would prefer that you manage me, and the best folks do manage me, meaning they know exactly where they want to get to and what help they need from me. But they are always creatively moving themselves forward.

I am naturally trusting, but you have to go through a period where you really earn my trust or you don't. If you haven't earned my trust, I'm going to start to actively manage you. And then you *may* earn my trust, but we're now in a back and forth process where you're going to need to earn it. There's always room to earn, but there are those who earn and those who don't earn, and then there are those who operate for a period where I'm deciding whether I can trust them or not. That's my style—it gives people a lot of latitude at the beginning.

What, specifically, do you do to help young people to become better, or to become the future leaders?

I've always said, if you can do something for somebody, do it. If somebody asks me to share my belief system, I'm always happy to do it. I just presented at

Stanford for their Entrepreneurship Leadership series—400 engineers attend the lecture, but it goes out to thousands of people online. I like the ability to help in a leveraged way.

But you can only spend time with so many people, and that is one thing nobody can give you back—time. I pick one or two entrepreneurs a year and one or two CEOs who I want to work with, and I sit on their boards and I advise them. I would rather go deep with three or four people and feel like I've had an impact on their career. I currently sit on two start-up boards and on a public company board with a CEO I just love. I want to help him. I spent the last six months advising the Twitter CEO and CFO because I love what they are doing and I love them as individuals, and, if I can be helpful in accelerating their success, I will.

My network of people I've worked with is pretty extensive now, so I spend a lot of time on coffee dates with people who have worked with me in some capacity or another who are thinking about their next move. I try to give back to the people who are already in my network, and I guess that's my point. I'd rather have more of an impact on people who are already in my network, or deeply helpful to three or four others, than be of marginal impact to more people. This is my thesis on networking too: It's nice to have a broad network, but so what? I'd rather feel that there is a set of people to whom I've contributed something meaningful.

This book is about learning to lead. What question did I forget to ask you about the learning process? What did we not touch on?

We did not talk about how leadership has been influenced by role models. I think everybody has role models on learning to lead. *Look for role models in the people who are closest to you and around you. If you can't find one, ask yourself if you're working for the right person. If you're not working for people who inspire you, who are you working for? Who are you working with? How are you spending your time? I think people should be moving toward working with people who give them energy and inspire them.* If I don't do that for people at JOYUS, they should go find someone else to work with because I've failed them as a leader, or my own leadership style isn't working for them.

My career has been influenced by four people. My first mentor was Ram Shriram, the original investor in Google who was my boss at Junglee, the company that was sold to Amazon. Then he was my boss at Amazon. He was also an investor at Yodlee. He's a strategist extraordinaire, and, from him, I learned a lot of competencies around business development.

Then, at Google, I worked with Omid Kordestani. He is considered, by some, to be the business founder of Google—he was employee number 13 or 14 and was the person who built the company's revenue model, taking them from $0 to $26 billion before he left. He was my boss, and he is the opposite of me. Where I am the person charging up the hill, he is the charismatic, diplomacy filled leader who is the wind behind your back, sitting in the background and just letting you do your thing. He can amass a team that can charge up the most amazing hills, and you ask yourself,

"How does he do that?" From him, I learned diplomacy and how to let other people run.

Bill Campbell, a coach to many executives in Silicon Valley, spent a lot of time with me. He is a former football coach, more of a command-and-control kind of CEO, but he leads with a lot of empathy and heart. For him, it is not just about writing the best code in Silicon Valley, it's about how you lead. In Silicon Valley, you don't have a lot of people talking about how you lead. They're talking about creating a brilliant product, and that is very different. Bill supports a leadership style that centers on leading from the heart; that it is okay to show up as your authentic self and lead with what works for you. For me, it was very much an endorsement that it is okay to come to work as a leader who is not just fully packaged as a professional, perfect entity, but as somebody who leads from their own personal passion.

Finally, David Lesser, my executive coach, has been the reflection back to me over the last five years of everything I've said I wanted to do, holding me true to that mirror at every single point in time. "This is what you said when you left Google, this is what you said was important. You said you wanted to be a better leader." I trust that he knows what drives me, and he's been through enough difficult situations with me that he knows what doesn't work.

I didn't go out into the world looking for my role model, I just went out into the world looking for people who inspired me, and that's where my role models are.

Leadership Themes

- You learn to lead by taking advantage of opportunities when they are presented to you and rising to meet the challenge.
- Learn when it is important to lead from behind, and when to lead from the front.
- Know when to let things unfold and when to push your own specific agenda.
- Learn that you can't control the whole outcome, just the effort you put in.
- Manage major transitions with support. Always have someone who can comment on your decisions.
- Learn how to manage your energy.
- Don't let ego destroy your talent.
- Stop worrying about the organizational chart, and try to add real value to the person next to you.
- Everything you do as a leader is analyzed—accept it.

33

The More I Learn, the More Exciting My Life Is and the More Opportunities That I See

Dennis ("Chip") Wilson

Chip, when did you first realize you were a leader, and what happened to make you realize it?

In my suburb community of many, many children, I was the oldest one of a large group of people. I was ten and everyone else would have been nine or eight. And, so, if I wanted to have fun, then it was about organizing the children for games, such as prison tag or kick the can.

Your question is a tough one. I'm not even sure that leaders think of themselves as leaders. I believe in a phrase that Werner Erhard shared with me: "A leader is someone whom everyone forgets." This means that, if the leader has done a great job, then no one knows the leader did the job. I see leadership as enrolling others, getting others excited, and making others believe that they were the ones that actually had whatever it took to get the project done.

I was the first born and, hence, the oldest male in my family. My parents divorced. Perhaps I became the pseudo-father in the family. So, that was another way my leadership started to develop.

Of course, I also watched my father and looked up to him. He was a director of a camp—Camp Kiwanis. He was a teacher. He was a quarterback of the football team when he was young. He was the athlete of the year in high school. He had the athletic ability to be a leader and the right kind of a personality, and he had a real love for teaching.

These experiences enabled me to develop the ability to have teaching be part of leadership. It wasn't just a matter of enrolling children and playing kick the can or prison tag. It may have been about teaching them the game and how to play it better. From a selfish point of view, doing so was in my best interests because it would make the game more fun for me.

What have been the formative influences on you as a leader? What experiences did you learn the most from? Was there any particular experience that supercharged your learning to lead?

I think the biggest experience for me centers around a company that I founded in 1979/1980—Westbeach Snowboard Ltd. The company was a Vancouver-based skate-and-surf clothing designer and retailer. I believe we had about C$10 million dollars in sales. But, in 1997, we ran out of money. The combined effects of increased competition and the collapse of the Japanese yen caused sales to drop significantly. Japan was a big market for us. It represented 30 percent of our business. I was maybe 36 years old at that time.

I sold Westbeach to a private equity firm for C$15 million dollars, which I thought was phenomenal given that we made no profit. What became apparent to me is that I had a company for 15 years that hadn't made any money. It had great brand value, but no profit.

The people that came in from private equity were great. I had no problems with what they did, such as putting in more controls. But I remember being in Hong Kong and getting a fax conveying that I had been removed as CEO and that they had decided to put in their own CEO. I did the predictable. I complained. I jumped up and down. I called my lawyers. And then, you know, I just settled down and started to reflect.

The real insight is that the private equity people formed a board of directors. I had never had any experience with a board of directors before. The directors were older, more experienced men who were interested in giving back their knowledge in life and to mentor and to teach. And I think what I really learned about leadership from this experience is that there comes a point for a leader when the important thing is to get out of the way.

Entrepreneurs are leaders. They get things going, and, when they see an opening in the market, they take advantage of it. They put the right people in place, and set up the right structure and processes for making the company successful and ensuring that success is sustainable.

It is very unusual to have an entrepreneur who knows how to do it all. So, having a strong board of directors is essential. *I learned to train and mentor those under me to be better than me—and then, simply, get out of the way.*

Were you able to transfer the lessons learned at Westbeach Snowboard Ltd. to the next company you founded—Lululemon, in 1998?

Definitely! I started Lululemon and got it to C$100 million dollars. I recognized that the company was incredibly profitable and that I needed a world-class human resources (HR) person and a world-class chief financial officer (CFO). But I didn't know how to hire those people. I didn't even know what questions to ask them. A lightbulb went off for me and I thought, "I've been in this situation before. I need a world-class board of directors." I had a world-class company here, and I needed a world-class board of directors to help me hire world-class people.

I wanted to win the USA, but was determined not to become another casualty like so many Canadian companies. Hence, *I brought in the board of directors who helped me to hire the next level of management that I needed. It was really a matter of getting my ego out of the way.*

Sure enough, my board of directors helped me get a world-class management team. Then we hired a chief executive officer (CEO). I got out of the way of being the final decision maker. I became chief innovation and branding officer. That worked really well for a while. But, then, there was a point when we realized that the CEO—Christine Day—had been in the company long enough. Christine, the former president of Starbucks in Asia, flexed her muscles. She had learned enough and she said, "It's my turn now to really run the company. It's very difficult for me to run the company because people see two leaders who, at times, communicate conflicting directions." And I went, "Okay, I get it." So I left management.

I recognized that I had not been following my own advice: I hadn't gotten out of the way quick enough. I recognized I wasn't doing a very good job as an employee of the company, and I wasn't doing a very good job as the chairman of the board. Lululemon had gone from a C$1 billion- to about a $10 billion-dollar market capitalization in a short period of time. I realized I had a board of directors that was excellent for a C$3 million-dollar market capitalization company, but not for a C$10 billion-dollar company. I did not have a global board of directors. "Okay," I thought. "I get it." I should have moved myself to the side sooner. I should have allowed people underneath me to grow and fulfill their ambitions and realize their dreams. I should have recognized that, as the chairman of the board, my job was to build a global board of directors that was ahead of the company rather than behind.

You talked about ego. In the midst of all of the success at Lululemon over these past years, how difficult has it been for you to stay true to yourself?

I think, to some extent, staying true to myself has become easier for me. What really helped was taking a lot of training and development courses through Landmark Education. Those courses deal a lot with communication, leadership, and integrity as the basis for success. It helped me to understand that I was doing so many things in my life to protect my ego; to look good. That was really working against me.

My ego told me I needed people to pat me on the back and tell me that I had done a good job. All those things that, as an undeveloped young person, felt really great, really important, and made me feel good inside. I realized that type of personality works against me being part of a successful company that's going from hundreds to thousands of people. In other words, if it's all about me getting all the glory, then I can't get quality people to work under me. And so, by taking these courses, I realized it's about everyone else, not about me.

What were some of the hardest things to learn in becoming a good or an even better leader?

Getting out of the way and understanding that it's not about me. It's a bridge to cross. It's called "giving without expectation." In other words, I need to provide for everyone else in my company through mentoring, and profit sharing, and making available phenomenal training and development. For example, I understand that, at Starbucks, people had to prove themselves and then management provided them with training and development opportunities. My approach was to give people training without them having to prove to me that they deserved it. In other words, I just come from a point of view that it's up to me to make people great. And then they can produce. But that's a very small part of the whole picture of giving without expectation of return. I think, as a young person, especially an entrepreneur, I was in survival mode. I worked 18 hours a day, 7 days a week, and was trying to feed myself and my family. I was trying to make the mortgage payments. The last thing that came to mind was actually putting other people in my company before me. People who hadn't worked the same hours as I did and who did not have the ideas I had. *When I switched from thinking about me first, and started thinking about what I can do for other people before me, I think that was the monumental shift in my success as a leader.*

Entrepreneurs and leaders learn to manage paradoxes. Leaders need to be optimistic and realistic. Confident and humble. Aggressive and patient. Intuitive and analytical. And so forth. How did you learn to manage those paradoxes in your leadership career?

That's a great question. I had an interesting thing happen to me when I was 10 years old. I was a competitive swimmer, and a very mediocre one. But I was about to turn 11 and move out of the 10-and-under age group. My dad came to the end of the pool and said to me, "Why don't you just try for once going full out, right from the very start, and not holding anything back." In other words, I should not go slow at the beginning and then sprint at the end of the race to look good. He said, "Why don't you just go full out, and, if you collapse in the third length, and have to walk to the end of the pool, that's just fine. Just do something nobody's ever done before." So I went, "Okay. That's great." Ten year olds are very much influenced by their father, and so I did that. I broke a Canadian record by seven seconds! No one could believe it. People had me redo the race. So, the interesting thing about this episode is not that I was a great swimmer. But I developed a winning formula, and that is to give 100 percent and hold absolutely nothing back or I'll never be successful. What did that mean for a 10 year old? It meant that I never held anything back in whatever I did in my life. Ninety-nine percent of people actually operate the other way. They hold back. They give maybe 85 percent. They miss the insight that the additional 15 percent can make them very successful. How would you live the rest of your life if you had put the 15 percent in and made it work? I believe most people in the world have some event like that swimming event, and have probably failed at some point in their childhood. They may have developed a winning formula that centered around, "Okay. I'm going to go for it, but I'm going to hold something back. That way, if I am in the middle of the race, and fail, then I can at least make it to the edge of the pool and not drown."

So, that's how I led my business and personal life. I would bet the farm in every circumstance. What happened was that the odds of life kept catching up to me, and, once every three years, I'd lose everything and have to start over again.

The beautiful thing with the board of directors is risk control. And I only started making money once I started surrounding myself with people that could actually temper my desire to bet the farm. I was so sure of myself. And I was so sure of the future that nobody else could see.

I think good leaders are transparent and candid in conversations. What have you learned to do this effectively, and have people listen to you and not become defensive? What have you learned about becoming influential in communication?

I always remember the story about me being at Dome Petroleum when I was 22 or maybe 25 years old. I was getting in the elevator with the chairman and the CEO. At the time, Dome Petroleum was a C$20 billion-dollar company. Its headquarters was in Calgary. We were getting to the bottom of the elevator, and he hadn't said anything to me or even acknowledged me. I was completely petrified. What I got from that event is how people are around me. So, in those kinds of situations, I make myself completely vulnerable. I have to tell stories about my youth and my failures. "Okay. When I was in your situation, I did it this way and I totally messed up. I was wrong, but now I've figured out that this is the way to go." I try to use a lot of context—the reasons why I'm saying things come from my errors and mistakes. It's like learned knowledge.

What have you learned about building and leading successful teams? You're the chairman of the board. What have you learned about leading teams effectively?

I recognize that, if I want to create a future that otherwise would not have existed, I can state what that future is. But I have to be in communication with my team to find out what comes up for them, emotionally, when I say it. When I'm talking about the big picture, and I'm trying to create a future that would otherwise not exist, and I have somebody in my project team whose mind is thinking about something small and insignificant that is stopping them from listening, then that person is subconsciously undermining the project, because he or she doesn't know how to get around something he or she is unwilling to admit to. So, at Lululemon, we call this "creating a clearing" for people. After the future's been set out, what do people think of? What may stop the project? What may get in the way? In most cases, when a future is being created, I'd say 80 percent of people have been through the experience—or a similar experience—before and failed. They are unwilling to try again or try it from a different angle. I believe most people come from a point of being fearful, and the only way the conversation can move forward is to let people state their fears, and then their minds are clear to create a future.

You live in a fishbowl. You're a well-known person. Your actions and decisions are very public. People may second-guess every action and every

decision. How did you learn to deal with transparency and the associated pressures?

What come to my mind are analysts and people from the press. I've had a lifetime of being a person that started things that nobody thought were possible, even ridiculous. If you look back at my career—surfing, skateboarding, snowboarding, and yoga—the places I'm heading next are 10 years ahead of other people's thinking. Your question is interesting. When I actually hear people say that it can't be done or that's not the right way to do it, it actually has me believe even more.

Why is that?

Everyone has their own expertise. People who are analysts are analysts because they haven't started their own business or they have never run a business. And yet they are analyzing other people's businesses. Unless you are actually in the business, there are 10,000 nuances inside of a business that you could never explain to an analyst or a newspaper person. To actually spend any time thinking seriously about a comment that they have said is often wasted time on my part. It's even more interesting now, because what I'm seeing in the digital world is that somebody can make a lie about me or a lie about Lululemon. It's there digitally, and then it becomes "true" because the next person to write an article searches on the Internet, finds a quote or a statement by somebody, and then uses that as the basis for the next truth. If I lived in a world where I believed what people are writing or saying who aren't actually in the company, then I wouldn't be able to operate effectively.

There is always a cost to leadership. What has been the price of leadership for you?

There's been no price. I'd say that actually it works the very opposite. Brian Tracy wrote a book on the psychology of achievement (New York, NY: Simon & Schuster, 1993). He writes about the law of attraction. *The greater I make myself in life, the greater I become as a person of success and integrity, then the more people will come into my life who are the same way. The more I learn, the more exciting my life is, and the more opportunities that I see.* There is nothing in leadership or success that would be a negative in any way.

What has been your most rewarding experience as a leader and why?

I think my most rewarding experience was probably when we went public as a company. I had no contractual obligation to do it, but I gave 10 percent of my shares away to my staff that had worked with me for nothing from the start—for very little money, for nothing but a dream. Many of them became multimillionaires. That was rewarding for me to see.

I found this interesting quote of yours. When you received the University of Victoria's Distinguished Entrepreneur of the Year award, you said the

following: "When I first think about it, what comes to mind is 'I've been so lucky.' But then, I grab ahold of myself, realize it took me 30 years of mistakes to get here, and possibly deserve what I've got." Can you talk a little bit about the importance of mistakes in your learning to lead?

I have operated from the position of wanting to be 50 years old and being set for life. In other words, I have seen that, even at a very young age, somehow it intuitively came to me that, at the age of 50, I wanted to be healthy. I don't want to have to be doing manual labor. I don't want to have to be working 18 hours a day. I want to have total choice about the life I want to live. Once that happens, then the ability to have a long life has increased exponentially.

When I was 24, I was on my own and it didn't matter how I spent money. It didn't matter what risks I took, as long as, at the age of 50, it all came together. Maybe that is part of being a leader, too: I had a very long-term vision, even as a young boy. As a leader, I like to look long term and never trade short-term gain for long-term pain.

Learning is never ending. What are you learning these days to become an even better leader? Are there any recent "aha" moments?

There are great people on my board of directors. And, as I mentioned earlier, they don't have to work and they don't have to be on our board. They all have learned a lot in life and they want to give back. But, they are not willing to give back to a company that doesn't have integrity, or has a lot of ego issues with their CEO or the chairman. What gives them their juice in life is giving back and learning. So, it's my job to develop my company, and to continue to push the boundaries in business so that I can continue to create great profits and continue to attract great leaders or directors. If I do that, then I am surrounding myself with people that I can learn from. And, at the end of the day, selfishly, I think all my leadership really has to affect my ability to lead my family—my wife and my children—into a future where communication is the basis for success. My motivation behind continuing to run a great company is to surround myself with great people and to pass that on to my children in order for them to continue to make a better world for other people.

Good leaders learn. They mature. How has your leadership evolved over time? How are you different today than, say, 25 years ago?

If I look back to when I was 25, I was working with a bunch of 16 year olds who knew nothing, and I didn't know anything. It was really a collaborative event where no one pretended to know anything. When I turned 30, and I was working with 16 year olds in the surf, skate, and snowboarding business, it became more a style of telling them what to do. It probably was a combination of telling and enrolling. And I'd say that was my weak point in life. In my 40s, I was dealing with 23- or 24-year-old women, because I have moved from surfing and skateboarding into a woman's business. All my employees were young, because I didn't have any money to pay anybody with experience. It was really about being a leader. It was about creating a future for people that they can't see, but which I can. It goes back to getting 10 percent of that stock when I went public because I wasn't able to pay them much at the very beginning. Enrolling and having them be part of the decision making, and always showing them the monthly financials, and articulating where we were going, and how we were progressing, so they were really deeply in it, became important. Now, in my 50s, the company has exploded. I am hiring and surrounding myself with people that are 45 to 55 years old who actually know more than I do in their area of expertise. I'm a generalist who knows how to put it all together, but definitely don't have the expertise of the CFO or the HR person. So, it comes back to creating a future that wouldn't have existed without doing a clearing, finding out what the problems are, and then moving things forward. Enrolling people and then constantly thinking what their self-interest is in order to continue to motivate them. And now, of course, it's entirely different. I'm 57 and the business has turned into something where I can't tell anyone how to do anything in the company. I have to be happy with the results of mentoring and teaching people, and actually letting them make their own mistakes at some levels. So, it is an evolution.

What advice do you have for people as they embark on their journey of learning to lead?
Continue to believe in what your vision is and do not let other people tell you it can't be done. I think that's critical. I'd be telling people about leadership. I'd say the most important thing is to do three things: to read *Good to Great: Why Some Companies Make the Leap … and Others Don't* by Jim Collins (New York, NY: HarperBusiness); to listen to the CD called *The Psychology of Achievement* by Brian Tracy (Chicago, IL: Nightingale-Conant, 1984); and then to take the Landmark Forum personal development course delivered by Landmark Education.

The book is about learning to lead. What question did I forget to ask you about the learning process? What did we not touch on?
I'd like to leave you with this thought: "Nothing in leadership is done perfectly." As a leader, no matter how something turns out, I'm always very introspective as to what I did right, what I did wrong, and what I could have done differently. Don't get wrapped up in emotions. I'm actually quite interested in the game of it—it's a game to continually get better at things. I find I become better having that mindset or frame. It's a little bit like when I'm playing squash and I'm behind in the game; if I let my emotions get in the way, and I try harder through emotions, I almost inevitably lose. Whereas, if I look at it as a game, and how I can get even better at it, and calm down, then I find my ability to operate is exponentially better.

Leadership Themes

- Get out of the way and understand that it's not about you, the leader. It's a bridge to cross. It's called "giving without expectation."
- Leadership involves the desire to continually get better at things. Don't get wrapped up in emotions.
- Never trade short-term gain for long-term pain.
- Continue to believe in what your vision is and do not let other people tell you it can't be done.

34

There Is No Individual Who is Ever Bigger Than the Team

George Cope

George, when did you first realize you were a leader, and what happened to make you realize it?

I recognized I had leadership skills during my early sports and school activities. I was the captain of basketball teams and also the student council president of my high school. You certainly need a set of skills to lead people in situations like that, but I was not thinking of the word "leadership" then.

Those early successes in sports and school built confidence, and it's absolutely critical for a leader to have confidence. I gained confidence when people in authority positions I respected confirmed that I was moving in the right direction, which I believe set the stage for my eventual leadership in business.

When did you first realize, "Wow . . . this is serious . . . now I am leading"?

I first realized that leadership came with a set of responsibilities when I was student council president. An interesting anecdote from my last year at high school illustrates this well. In a game of basketball, an opposing player took a very cheap shot at me. It got pretty heated and, in the end, we were suspended. I remember thinking after the game, "I can't be suspended, I'm the student council president." My actions were wrong—I should have walked away from the incident. I had responsibilities to the team and to the school. This was an "aha" moment—I was in a leadership role, not just a guy on a basketball team.

Basketball played an important role in your life. I found a quote from you about your entire career coming back to basketball. Can you elaborate on that statement?

I played with two or three people who ended up impacting my entire career, as did my coach. For example, the father of a fellow player named Gord Simmonds hired me to help lead a wireless distribution company called BrookTel in the early 1980s. We built it into a market leader before selling it to Bell Canada. Then, we created Clearnet Communications Inc., also with the support of the Simmonds family, which became the most successful wireless start-up in North American history. And Gord's brother Bob Simmonds, whose technological prowess was instrumental in building Clearnet, now serves on the board of Bell Canada Enterprises Inc. (BCE). Without the relationship developed through sports, my entire career would have been completely different.

Another one of the guys on the basketball team—Wade Oosterman—is now president of Bell Mobility and Bell's chief brand officer. Wade was involved with every business I helped build, including BrookTel, Clearnet Communications, and Telus. My entire career links back to this small but very talented group of people.

Did you want to be a leader?

I never thought, specifically, that I wanted to lead, but I knew I loved to compete. The competitive dynamic of business is actually what attracted me to leadership roles. In public companies, you get to keep score; you track performance, just as you do in sports. I found that concept inspiring: "Can I build a team that can beat other teams?"

As I got a little older, I recognized that leadership came with a long list of responsibilities. This became real when we created companies such as BrookTel and Clearnet Communications. In the case of Clearnet, we were raising significant amounts of money and quickly grew our employee team to 2,000 people. The responsibilities associated with the leadership role grew quickly, as our organizations grew.

At BCE, you took a 130-year-old company and fundamentally changed its cost structure and culture. You nursed it back to a strong company. What prepared you for the leadership role at BCE? How did you learn to lead? What have been the formative influences on you as a leader? What did people do to help you? What experiences did you learn the most from? Was there any particular experience that supercharged your learning to lead?

When I was 23 years old, no one thought wireless was going anywhere. But I was lucky enough to be working directly in that space and realized the opportunity. We were successful in building a wireless company called BrookTel, and later sold it to Bell Cellular, now known as Bell Mobility. I was 25 years old then, and, overnight, became president of a subsidiary of Bell. I learned how boards operate and closely watched the behavior of people in leadership roles. I gained valuable insights into the business world and leadership concepts at a young age. This was an important learning experience and provided a good grounding in an important part of the telecommunications industry.

Later, I was one of the builders of Clearnet Communications. This experience really supercharged my leadership learning at a young age. I was in my early 30s when I became president of Clearnet in 1987. We took the company public in 1994, and raised almost C$4 billion in capital in less than 6 years. I remember doing road shows around the world trying to raise money to start the company. Some people said we were too young. Today, people say, "I want you to be young and look like the guys from Facebook"! But, back then, the world was quite different.

It really was a great experience because I came to understand that, as a leader, you need skills well beyond your own to build something successful. *I learned, early on, the importance of building a team of people with skill sets unlike your own. At first, you resist the idea because the people aren't like you; they don't have the same approach, or set of experiences. But then you recognize that's exactly what's required to achieve success.* You have to add complementary strengths to your own if you want to be successful—you can't build an organization with sheer passion alone.

In 2000, we sold Clearnet to Telus for C$6.6 billion, and I joined Telus as head of its wireless unit. Working at Telus was really important to me. The CEO is a very bright man. We were of similar age and had a very good working relationship. And he lived up to the Telus–Clearnet partnership, enabling the wireless team to focus its expertise on building a new and competitive national mobile business.

Telus was much larger than Clearnet Communications, where most of the team was concentrated in a few locations. So, a question emerged: How do you assume the leadership role when you cannot necessarily be physically present as your corporation has locations across the country? At a small company, you walk around and shake hands, you talk to people in the cafeteria. That, of course, is not practical when you get into companies as large as Telus or BCE. Hence, I learned the importance of communicating in different ways using various channels, while ensuring consistency of the message. This is important in increasing understanding and confidence across the organization. Telus really helped me to appreciate the challenges of leadership in large organizations.

Bell is quite unique in Canada. Generally, if our competitors do something big, it's going to make page B-1 of *The Globe and Mail* (Toronto, Canada). If we do the exact same thing, it'll be on A-1. That's a great benefit of being Bell. It's also the great challenge of being Bell. When it's good, it's very, very good, but, when it's not good, it can be very, very bad. I don't think people understand the true impact of the brand until they are here. I certainly didn't.

Clearnet was an entrepreneurial company. Canadians saw BCE in a different light. This was a much bigger company and bureaucratic. Some would argue there was little urgency in the company and that mediocre performance was accepted. What did you learn at Clearnet Communications that you were able to implement at BCE and help make it a better or stronger organization?

Bell is one of the top Canadian brands. To drive that brand forward in a fast-changing industry is a great responsibility. My friend and colleague Wade Oosterman would say there's no canvas in Canada as fun and interesting as Bell. I so feel like an explorer in this industry right now. What is the future of Internet protocol television? What is the next thing Apple or Google is going to dream up? How big is wireless really going to be? How can we take advantage of these opportunities? Bell is a most exciting place to be and the constant change is key to that.

When I arrived at Bell, we started to put together a transition plan. I wanted to give a consistent message of change and opportunity to 55,000 people. It was important to build confidence in a better future for Bell, and enable execution of a marketplace strategy to achieve it. The company had a history of saying it wanted to be efficient, but it really never addressed the various management layers that had built up over decades. The frontline people were asked to do more, and then the frontline would be cut. Service levels would go down. But the layers of management remained extreme. I learned we actually had 11 layers here, from my office all the way to the customer. Bell is a big company by Canadian standards, but I doubt even many global organizations have 11 layers. So, we took three levels of management out in six weeks. It was probably the most radical restructuring ever done in Canada.

There were board members who asked all the right questions about what we were doing—they wanted to ensure the glue would hold. And people asked in hindsight, "How did you know the transformation would work?" Our answer was that we knew we would be 10 percent wrong, but also that we were going to be 90 percent right. And we would fix the 10 percent. Since that time, we've taken out double the amount in management as we did in that original transformation. We had formulated a clear strategy and people were not allowed to spend time on things that weren't relevant to the strategy. It was focus, focus, and focus—and it's worked.

Has your learning to lead been influenced by other individuals? For example, have you had the benefit of a mentor?

I have had important leaders throughout my life. For example, I had a great leader who coached me at high school and who instilled confidence in me. He told me I could do whatever I wanted to do. He told me I could play university sports. When you are in a small Ontario town of about 3,500 people, that's not really what your head is thinking. His confidence in me mattered.

Gord and Bob's father—David Simmonds—was very influential. He put a 23-year-old kid in charge of a division called BrookTel. He said, "You have a business degree . . . now, go run this." Not many people would take such a chance on a young kid. David was one of my mentors: He taught me a lot about the industry and running a successful business, and he built my confidence.

I don't think I could have successfully executed in these leadership roles without the counsel of my wife all the way through. We've been together since we were both 23. It is important to have a different perspective, someone to ensure you always broaden your thinking in a given situation. She has no other agenda but to think about what might be the right thing for the organization and for whatever strategy you are pursuing in the leadership role. I firmly believe my leadership results would not have been as successful without her involvement.

I also learned from my parents. My dad was very important. He influenced me in terms of my willingness to take risks.

Lastly, I have learned from my teams. The leadership team has to make major decisions, but the leader always makes the final decision. One thing I have learned over the years is that collecting everybody's views can be pretty powerful. When the company wins, the team wins.

But the leader has to take responsibility; when the outcome is disappointing, the leader must take ownership. For example, I insisted that I be the one out there in public when our original bid to purchase Astral Media Inc. fell through, not the head of our media division. It was my duty to explain what happened and what we'd do to move forward. Happily, we're now back to the Canadian Radio-television and Telecommunications Commission (CRTC) with a new proposal to join Astral with Bell Media.

For many people, those words are easy to use, but much harder to live by. How did you become comfortable taking accountability and be so transparent about it?

I think a big part of it is having a good track record, and the confidence that results from it. It's about calling more strikes than balls, a record of getting it more right than wrong. The other part is reflection. You develop a set of beliefs about what is the right thing to do. And this comes from experiences in both business and life. People learn to do what they believe is the right thing to do.

What was the best leadership advice you ever received that helped you develop into a better leader?

I can't think of an epiphany. But I think it became evident to me through fostering relationships with people that teams drive everything in business. A team builds a company. The most important thing in a leadership role is to absolutely trust the people with whom you're working. *One of the most important parts of my career has been never having a direct executive report quit—ever. And, to me, that is the result of my desire to build strong and unified teams.*

Actually, one line that resonates the most in all my years in business, and I still use it, came from David Simmonds: "calculated negligence." This phrase means, *if you're going to be successful, you have to know what not to do, even if they are things that other people see as being important. You have to differentiate between what is most important and what you can actually risk letting become a problem.* In other words, an outside consultant might say, "That problem needs to be fixed now!" And I would agree—but also point out it's number 977 on the list of the top 4,000 things to do. If you don't have that barometer, that perspective on what really matters, it's really hard to lead. I think the transition from the entrepreneurial start-ups to running BCE has been successful thanks to an ability to understand what falls into the category of calculated negligence. I have used that term throughout my entire career.

What have you learned about building trust and learning to trust others?

Once you know you have a person's trust and vice versa, you can give him or her so much more because you're both working in the same direction. But, if you think someone is working against the team, or not fully committed to it, it will not work. It does not matter how skilled these people are—their skills do not matter if they're not working in the same direction.

People who work for me now, or who have worked for me in the past, will tell you it's a lot tougher to work with me once you have that trust. I'm harder on them than ever before because my expectations of them go up. My team members will probably tell you that it is great once you have established trust with me, but—wow—the accountability gets even higher because I have put everything into that relationship. The only way you build these types of companies—Clearnet, or Telus, or BCE—is through delegation. But trust is required before you can effectively delegate.

What were some of the hardest things to learn in becoming a good or an even better leader?

Being "on" all the time is tough. I'll give an example. A few years ago, my assistant, who has been working for me for a long time told me, "People say you're really grumpy these days and you're not smiling in the elevator." Maybe that morning my wife and I didn't get along or the kids were late for school. Who knows? But leaders are always on. You have to acknowledge the fact that you might be at a coffee shop and, in that room of 20 people, 2 might be your employees. Although they may never come up and say hello to you, they will observe your behavior with the person across the counter. *As a leader, you cannot behave at less than your best, even if you're having a tough day. You'll be judged, and rightly so—you're the leader.*

What have you personally experienced as a barrier to learning, and how have you tried to overcome this barrier?

Time is a barrier. We all have busy lives. I was president of a company at an early age and things never really slowed down for me. My wife and I also raised a family. Hence, I never really had the time to head back to an academic institution to refresh or listen to other people's perspectives in that type of environment. But I would say that my experiences in business, and the associated wins and losses, have enabled me to be educated in a way that now allows me to give back. I do enjoy talking to business school classes, gaining the perspective of the next generation of leaders while offering them the benefit of my own experiences.

Learning requires reflection. Do you reflect on your leadership?

I think sometimes you catch yourself. For example, you might realize you've been hard on people in ways that are completely unrepresentative of the way one should lead. So, you reflect on that and think, "Is that constructive or am I actually demoralizing people?"

It's important for leaders to reflect often on their behavior. Your behavior becomes the permission for other behaviors in the company. I firmly believe that, if you start to cross the line in any negative way, everyone else is going to cross the line. You have to recognize this.

How did you develop resilience? You have to cope with stress and obstacles. How did you learn to deal with obstacles and setbacks and remain focused on the day-to-day activities?

Your timing of the interview is ironic because we're in the midst of one of those interesting times. We had our annual dinner with our senior vice presidents just after the CRTC's original Astral decision. I knew the dinner conversation shouldn't just focus on that. Despite our collective disappointment in the CRTC decision, the company is having some incredible successes from an operational point of view. So, I let the conversation on Astral go for a while, knowing that's what people wanted to talk about. When my turn came, we switched focus and discussed the developments that are especially positive and exciting for the company. Now, of course, we'll be heading back to the CRTC with our second proposal to acquire Astral, and that's also positive and exciting news.

I really just focus on the results and the long-term strategy required to deliver them. That has helped me and the team to see things in perspective.

What are you learning these days to become an even better leader? Are there any recent "aha" moments?

This is quite straightforward—*you need to be careful what the world is telling you about other people, especially in the new world of social media. You need to actually sit down with people and listen to them.* This past year, I've developed a lot of new business relationships. For example, we partnered with our number one competitor on the acquisition of Maple Leaf Sports and Entertainment (MLSE). It was very important for me to determine whether the CEO was someone we could work with. We met, got to know each other as people, and realized that, while we and our companies must compete fiercely in the market every day, we could indeed work together on this project. You may have impressions of people from the media, or from other information sources, but I've learned not to pre-judge people. Go and talk to them, get to know them directly.

Good leaders learn. They mature. How has your leadership evolved over time?

As we discussed, I was very fortunate to have had some early successes in sports, school, and, later, my business career. I was high school student council president, captain of the basketball team, and, later, had the opportunity to attend the renowned Ivey Business School at Western University, where I also played varsity basketball. People might say I was on a successful path early on. But you can get narrow in your focus. Arrogance can build, particularly when you are young. You may come to believe that you know it all. *The piece that I'm convinced comes only with age is wisdom. You're able to reflect on what it takes to be a better leader and a better person. I think that is the biggest fundamental difference that time and experience brings.* And I think people who have worked with me for many years would say that, too. The intensity with which I conduct business has not changed, but my broader thinking about what success means has. And I think that makes me a better leader.

What advice do you have for people as they embark on their journey of learning to lead?

First, I tell young leaders to embrace people who aren't like them. If you're going to be a leader, you cannot surround yourself with people like you. If you do, your perspective will be narrow. The Ivey HBA degree is a great degree. But you need a range of talent. I have seen people with arts degrees move into sales roles at Bell. Engineers moving into marketing. Business people working in creative and design roles. They all bring a broader perspective. As a leader, you have to attract and be willing to open up to broader perspectives and recognize diverse skill sets.

Second, if you can't delegate as a leader, you're done. People ask me, "How did Clearnet Communications grow from 3 people to 25, to 50, to 100, to 1,000, and to 2,000 so quickly? How is it that you can go home at night with that level of intense growth?" The answer: You have to be able to delegate to a team you trust. That's been fundamental in building the team that's transforming Bell.

Third, I tell people to build an ability to turn it off. I can go to my cottage on a Friday and just enjoy the weekend. I tell my assistant, who has worked for me forever, that it's not likely Bell is going to burn down. So, unless an important and urgent issue that we need to deal with emerges, please don't connect with me. My wife would say I can compartmentalize things. I can leave work and go to a bunch of Toronto Raptor games with my sons or watch my daughter compete in swimming. And I don't feel that I need to be doing work when I'm with them. Some people can't do that, but I know I would burn out if I did not have that skill.

You work with talented people. Some of these individuals might have derailed. What have you learned about career derailment?

Sometimes, we promote an individual who is not yet ready for a new position. They may think they're ready—no one ever says, "I don't think I'm ready for that position"—but you can derail people's careers by over-promoting them. It's your fault, but, at the end of the day, it's the other person who may lose their job as a result of your decision. I have made that mistake from time to time, and am wary of promoting people too early. It can be a painful experience for a person when it happens.

How do people with potential derail a promising leadership career?

Not wanting to play their positions.

What does that mean?

Sometimes, people are constantly challenging their roles. They don't actually do the job they're supposed to do. When I first got to Bell, it was quite a culture shock. People believed that, if they were in a job for more than 12 or 18 months, they were limiting their careers. I interviewed vice presidents and they said, "I've been in the job for 14 months and I'm looking for a new role at the company." They wanted to be fast tracked, to move from job to job as evidence they were progressing. I responded by saying, "In your first year in a role, the company loses money on you. The second year, we break even. The third year, the company may make money. And, in your fourth year . . . please come see me." Suddenly, no one was talking about their next roles!

I kept wondering, "Don't you want to see your projects through? How can I know if you're good if you're not making any money by your third year? How can you know?" People can push too hard at their own agenda, and that can make it hard to view them as part of the team.

As you know, I am a sports junkie and I find it interesting that the Edmonton Oilers won the Stanley Cup after Wayne Gretzky left, but Wayne Gretzky never won the Stanley Cup again after he left. That was a profound lesson for me. Gretzky is the best hockey player the world has ever seen, but he never won the cup without that team. There's no individual who's ever bigger than the team. It's always about the team.

Leadership Themes

- Leadership comes with a long list of responsibilities.
- You learn a lot about leadership by watching the behavior of people in leadership roles.
- You must add complementary strengths to your own if you want to be successful as a leader.
- The leader takes responsibility when the outcome is disappointing.
- Trust is required before you can effectively delegate.
- You cannot behave at less than your best, even if you're having a challenging day.
- Beware of arrogance. Reflect on what it takes to be a better leader and a better person. Wisdom comes with time and experience.

35

I Went Into Public Life Because I Felt That Was the Place That I Could Make the Biggest Contribution

The Right Honourable Paul Martin

Mr. Martin, when did you first realize you were a leader and what happened to make you realize it? What particular gift did you have?

I don't know if there ever was a moment that I suddenly realized "I'm a leader." "When did you first realize it? What particular gift did you have?" These are perplexing questions you ask. I never woke up and said, "I must become a leader." The assumption in your question is that one decides one is a leader, and then one goes out and seeks something to lead. That is not the way I believe things occur. As you grow up, there are certain things that you want to see happen. *What has been a consistent theme throughout my life is that I wanted to get things done—and, essentially, the only way I could do it was to take the initiative, but it never crossed my mind that this was leadership. The question was more, "How do I accomplish what I want to do?"* My first step was always to gather a group of people around me who shared that view, and shared my desire to make it happen. I don't think you realize this makes you a leader. It simply makes you somebody who has a commitment to do something.

For example, when I was a kid, and I wanted to play baseball in the spring, I was always the guy who would call a bunch of friends and form a team. But I don't think I ever had a lightening strike hit me and say, "Genghis Khan, here I come." In business, politics, or academia, opportunities present themselves. Some people take advantage of these opportunities, whereas others don't. I guess I did. In the case of baseball, I wasn't very good, and, if I had waited for people to call me, I don't think they ever would have!

You never had a desire to be a leader or a person of influence? You had a strong role model. Your father was a well-known politician.

I am not trying to be cute . . . but no. I had a strong social conscience, which I had inherited from my father. This social conscience also reflected the times in which I lived. The first great movement in which I participated was the civil rights marches in the state of Michigan. I grew up in Windsor. I was not a leader in the civil rights movement, but I gathered a lot of my friends and said, "We're going to Detroit and Flint Michigan. We're going to march." The other great issue to me was the development of the Third World. This issue was salient when I was in university—and still is. My intention was to go to Africa and work for the benefit of the Third World. But I was not thinking "leadership."

You became a successful business leader and Canada's 21st Prime Minister. What have been the formative influences on you as a leader? What did people do to help you? What critical experiences did you learn the most from?

The single greatest influence in my life was my father. He had been born into a very poor family, and had polio at a young age. He was the first one in his family to go to university. He had been a member of the Canadian delegation to the last meeting of the League of Nations in the late 1930s, and then again to the first meeting of the United Nations at the end of the Second World War. The two main interests in his life were the building of Canada's social infrastructure and international affairs.

I went into business by accident. I studied law because I had always thought I was going to become a lawyer. Midway through my first year of law school, I realized I didn't want to be a lawyer, but it never crossed my mind to leave law school—to get an MBA for instance, as my two sons with MBAs constantly remind me. And then, one day, I met Maurice Strong. Maurice is many things. He was Canada's first environmentalist; he was a successful entrepreneur in the oil and gas business; he had a strong social conscience; he was the first head of Canada's International Development Agency; and he was one of the very few Canadians to have done what many Americans and British business people had done—to make the transition back and forth from business to government and from government to business.

I ran into him after I graduated from law school, and he said to me, "What do you want to do?" I said to him, "I want to go to Africa. I want to work in Third-World development." He looked at me and said, "You're absolutely right. You're just what Africa needs—another fresh-faced lawyer." Then he said, "If you really want to help in development, what you need to do is understand the economy. You need to develop an interest in business." I said, "How in the world do I do that? I don't know anyone in business."

Maurice was the president of Power Corporation of Canada at the time, one of the country's most powerful holding companies. He said, "Come and work for me as my executive assistant. You can do that job for a couple of years, learn about business, and then you can go to Africa." And so it went—I began to work for Maurice Strong.

When Maurice left Power Corporation, he was succeeded by Bill Turner. Bill was a brilliant businessman. He provided me with many opportunities to learn and develop as a business executive. Power Corporation had made a number of investments in a series of smaller companies that were not doing so well, and none of the senior executives wanted to touch them. Bill said to me, "Let's see what you can do with these." I was 27 years old and knew little about business. My job was to either fix them up or sell them. In most cases, one way or another, I was successful.

From this experience, I learned the importance of listening. When you go into a company that is in trouble, you had better learn what the company is all about before you open your mouth. Ask questions, and, if you listen long enough and if you talk to enough people, the course of action that is required will eventually come to you. And it will come to you quickly.

I was a "fireman." People have asked me—how could someone with so little experience be given that kind of opportunity? The answer is I was a *pre* baby boomer. This was probably the luckiest generation ever because, quite simply, we were in short supply.

Eventually, Bill Turner departed to run Consolidated Bathurst, a major pulp and paper company, which was a subsidiary of Power Corporation. He asked me to join him, primarily to look after a group of U.S. tissue mills that were in trouble, which I did.

Subsequently, Paul Desmarais—who, by this time, had obtained control of Power Corporation—asked me to come back to Power Corporation and to become president of Canada Steamship Lines (CSL), which, while not in trouble, was having difficulties.

As with his predecessors, I learned enormously from Paul Desmarais—the importance of people, for instance. One of his greatest talents was to understand not where things were, but where they were going. It was he who sent me to Japan very early on, and who supported my interest in China.

So, let me go back to the first question you asked. *I did not seek, in any of these instances, to become the leader of these companies. In each case, Maurice Strong, Bill Turner, and Paul Desmarais gave me a chance, which I grasped.* To say that I was influenced by what they had each done in life would be an understatement.

I learned different skills from each of them, but there was a common and critical element they all shared: integrity. They were people of character. None of them would have succeeded if it had not been for their values. This is fundamental. I don't believe that integrity and character are the soft tissue of business. I believe they are very much part of the hard construct of business.

You said that one of the lessons that you learned from Paul Desmarais was to figure out where things are going. How would one learn that?

Most of us understand the need to try and figure out where the world is going. Some people are better at this than others, and I don't think any of us has the magic answer to the exact timing that certain events will materialize. Anybody who tells you that they get the timing right every time is just not telling the truth. But back to your question: The skill doesn't just lie in being able to look ahead. The real issue comes from having the grasp of where things are going, and not blinding yourself to what's afoot because you have an investment in the status quo. I have seen too many instances where business leaders have such an investment in their comfort zone that they refuse to accept the emerging realities.

Did you want to be a business leader?

I wanted to be a business owner! I had built up valuable experience at Power Corporation and Consolidated Bathurst. I learned that I had a knack for business and I loved it. I was also a father, with a young family, and putting bread on the table was important. But I also knew that Sheila—my wife—would back me up if I decided to risk it all.

I never regarded Maurice Strong, Bill Turner, or Paul Desmarais as bosses. They were, of course, but I was given complete carte blanche in everything I did at Power Corporation, Consolidated Bathurst, and Canada Steamship Lines. However, as time went on, I wanted to have my own business. I knew that sooner or later I was going to leave Power Corporation, raise money, and buy a company. I never made a conscious decision to become an entrepreneur in my early career. I didn't think about leadership or titles—I just wanted to own my own show.

Then, several years after becoming President of Canada Steamship Lines, the opportunity to buy the company from Power Corporation presented itself. I found a partner in my friend Laurence ("Ladi") Pathy, the owner of Fednav Limited, the largest ocean shipping company in Canada. I put everything I had into the purchase and we borrowed C$150 million. We bought the company in 1981. It was the largest leveraged buyout ever done in Canada at the time. We did it on a handshake. Indeed, it was only six years later that we put everything down in writing.

The day we signed the deal was the day interest rates hit their peak, at 22 percent. We had calculated the interest rates at 20 percent, and experts were predicting they were going as high as 30 percent. We would have been in trouble if that had happened. Fortunately, as some of us expected, they fell to 14 percent. We took a heck of a chance and we succeeded. We took another chance, too, and started a new shipbuilding program, borrowing more money to do so because we wanted to take our specialized self-unloading vessels deep sea. Until then, Canada Steamship Lines was limited to the Great Lakes. Today, the company is the largest self-unloading shipping company in the world. I bought Ladi out in 1987, and we remain close friends to this day. I could never have done the deal without him.

You were a successful business executive. You were the owner of a business. Why did you make the switch to politics?

As mentioned earlier, my initial interest in going into business was to learn about the economy so that I could go to the Third World and make a difference. I stayed in business because I liked it and because I had to support a young family. But the underlying desire to make a change in the Third World was always there.

Once we had Canada Steamship Lines in good shape and I had bought Ladi's shares, the time had come when I had to fish or cut bait. There was a level of young management coming up that was capable of taking the company further, and, indeed, they did a tremendous job when I handed them the reins. Canada Steamship Lines prospered. I no longer had an excuse not to go to Africa. I looked at myself in the mirror and I said, "You're either going to do this or you're not."

So I left the business, but ... I didn't go to Africa. I was older and I had always believed that, through government, you can do the most good, and I still believe that very much today. I suppose this is the result of growing up in a family where my father had dedicated his life to the public service. The fact is you can do more good in five minutes in government than you can do in five months anywhere else. In my case, I suspect I proved this when I became a governor of the World Bank.

You have both a business and a political background. What did you learn from both?

People often think that the differences between business and politics are significant. They are considerable, but not as considerable as people think. For example, business leaders like to think that they plan long term and they criticize the short-term electoral cycle in government. But the fact is, for most public companies, the shareholder is king, and when the king is a hedge fund, there is not a lot of long-term vision. One of the strengths of Canada Steamship Lines is its ability to look long term, and that is why we never considered taking the company public.

The electoral cycle rules too many governments, which is unfortunate. But I can tell you that the people who go into government with the right motivation don't go in just to win elections. Elections are important, they give you the legitimacy required to do what is needed, but good policy normally goes beyond the electoral cycle if it is to have an important impact. Doing what is needed is why one goes into government. It's about conviction. For example, the 1995 budget led to the elimination of the deficit, but there were four years when I was not the most popular person in Canada. At the time, I thought that doing what needed to be done meant that I was going to have a relatively short political career. In summary, successful government does have a different time frame than business, but it's not always the time frame people think.

I have the greatest amount of respect for business people. A successful business is the framework around which the economy is built—the economy that pays for the great social programs people need. On the other hand, while it should, business doesn't always have the broader perspective that recognizes the needs in the longer term of all members of society. This is the prime business of government—it can be a balancing act, but it is one that is imperative if society is to thrive.

Leaders always live in a fishbowl, so your actions and decisions are public. People might second-guess every action and decision. How did you learn to deal with such transparency and the associated pressures?

When I left politics, a close friend who had been a very successful provincial premier told me that: "One of the greatest benefits of being out of politics occurs in the morning, when you go to pick up your newspaper and you don't shudder just before you read the headlines."

There is some truth in that, but the fact is you don't have a lot of time to dwell on headlines when you are in office. Actually, you're so busy that you don't have a lot of time to worry about the criticisms directed at you. I missed most news broadcasts. I didn't read most of the papers I read today. I was heavily reliant upon people telling me what was being said, and half the time they didn't tell me about the nastiness. This does not mean that I didn't know about the criticism or that I was immune to it. I just had too much to do to think about it.

There are two kinds of criticism. First, the uninformed that just rolled off me, which was good because they also tend to be the most vicious. The second were the legitimate criticisms, those with merit. I would worry about these because, once you decide on what has to be done, you have to carry it through. That being said, you also have to deal with the inevitable flaws in the course of action chosen. For example, I believe that a key role of government is to advance the state of human knowledge. Basic science is the foundation of progress. I cut research and development in the 1995 budget. I reinstated the funding five years later. But we did some real damage with those cuts, and I was worried that the funding cuts we made in research and development might never be reinstated if we were defeated in the next election. The criticism that was leveled against me on those issues really got to me. I felt I was cutting in an area that is one of the most fundamental functions of government. This was the reason, once the deficit was eliminated, we created the Canadian Foundation for Innovation, which guaranteed that basic research would never again be subject to the whims of the economic cycle.

In any event, criticism was not among my worries. I don't want this to sound like it didn't get to me, but I went into public life to do certain things and I was going to do them. For instance, as mentioned, I received a lot of criticism at the time of the deficit fight. But I knew that I only had one shot at eliminating the deficit, and, if it succeeded, it would pay dividends for generations to come. It was the right thing for the country. Why else did I go into public life?

To be honest, when I was a kid, attacks directed at my father bothered me far more than criticism directed at me. They bothered Sheila and our sons much more than they did me. I think it's actually a natural thing that personal criticism bothers you a lot less than it bothers those who are close to you. In any event, I knew that criticism was part of the ball game.

For you, what were some of the hardest things to learn in learning to lead?

One of the hardest things for me was speaking publicly. I really had to work at it. A politician has to be able to communicate a vision. My father was a tremendous speaker. I was not. Bill Clinton's speeches grab people because they are based on telling stories. Take a look at the average business speech: "Ladies and gentlemen, I'm going to give you 20 minutes worth of statistics." I had spent most my life in business, and, for the first few months or years in politics, I must have been a guaranteed sleeping pill for most people.

When I first went into public life, I didn't have a storehouse of political experience, despite being my father's son. But after you spend some amount of time in politics, you begin to understand the importance of stories. So, what did I learn? I learned to tell stories that connect with people.

The issue of gay marriage was an example of this. In 1999, parliament voted the traditional definition of marriage as the law of the land. The vast majority of members of parliament voted this way, including me. To be honest, I did not think there was any other definition. I just didn't think about it. I should have. But, over time, the courts ruled that the exclusion of same-sex couples from the definition of marriage violated the Canadian Charter of Rights and Freedoms. For me, the Charter of Rights is the single most important piece of legislation in the country. As a result, I began to work on introducing legislation that would include same-sex marriage in the definition. This was a very emotionally charged issue. When I spoke to Canadians who opposed gay marriage, I had first to establish some common ground. I spoke about the Charter of Rights, but, more importantly, I explained to people my own personal evolution on the issue, and, to do this, I told the following story, which was decisive in my case.

I have a close friend whose daughter I know. One day, he told me that his daughter had been the most wonderful little girl in the world. However, she started to have some problems when she was 13, and people told him they were just "the problems of a 13 year old." However, the problems got progressively worse. By the time she was 16 years old, she was almost suicidal. Her parents were beside themselves with worry. Her parents didn't know what the problem was, but neither did she. Then, she met another girl and, all of a sudden, they knew what the problem was. Of course, her parents loved her and supported her. She was happy at last. She got her PhD and now she's living in California with her partner.

My message to people was simple. I would ask them: "Are you going to say to me that we should stand in the way of that girl's happiness?"

Let me give you another example. This one is about my commitment to aboriginal issues. Most Canadians do not understand just how bad living conditions are on many of Canada's northern reserves. Most Canadians have never been on a reserve and the recitation of statistics cannot convey the depth of the tragedy. To convey it, this is a story I tell.

I was a governor of the World Bank as finance minister, and I was to meet with the president of an African country and his cabinet. They wanted a significant loan. The World Bank was holding up the process because they did not think previous grants had been properly spent. I arrived in Africa the day before the meeting, and an NGO took me up to a village about 5 hours' drive by truck from the capital. The situation in that village was just awful. I met with the president the next day. He expressed the need for the loan. And so I said to him in front of his cabinet, "Mr. President, I have to tell you something. Yesterday, I visited a village where you claim to have rectified the terrible conditions in which people were living, using your last grant from the World Bank to do so. The truth is you haven't spent a penny there. How can you tolerate what is simply the greatest degradation of human beings I have ever seen?" The president and his cabinet were stunned.

Then his executive assistant leaned over and whispered something in his ear. The president allowed the young man to speak: "Mr. Martin," he said, "I am a graduate of a Canadian University. Thanks to that Canadian University, I was able to get a summer job working on one of your northern reserves. Mr. Martin, you have seen nothing in my country that is as bad as some of the things I saw on that reserve." He named one I had been to and I knew he was right. There was nothing I could say. You tell that story to Canadians and they come to understand the importance of aboriginal issues.

Prime Minister Jean Chrétien kicked you out of his cabinet. The expression you use is: "I got quit." What led up to the conflict with Prime Minister Chrétien, and what leadership lesson did you learn?

The genesis of my differences with Mr. Chrétien occurred over the battles of the deficit. My fear was that a financial crisis would occur somewhere in the world, as they inevitably do, and would drive our interest rates through the roof, making it virtually impossible for us to deal with the deficit. It would have been crippling. At the time, 36 cents of every dollar was being spent on servicing the national debt. It was the government's largest single expenditure. My fear was that our interest rates would go up at the next crisis, making our debt problem unsustainable.

The Prime Minister and I had a continuing disagreement over this. First, to be fair, we disagreed because he had to keep his cabinet together; and when the Minister of Finance is cutting the living heck out of everybody's spending, it's not easy to hold the team together. However, we also disagreed because he felt that I was going too hard at eliminating the deficit, and that I should go a lot slower. He felt addressing the deficit could be stretched out over a much longer period of time. I believed the deficit was a ticking time bomb and that I had less than two years in which to act. Emotions were quite intense. I never threatened to resign, and I never would have threatened to resign. But it also meant that he was going to have to fire me or support me because I wasn't backing down. The Prime Minister supported me and I give him full credit for doing so.

Canadians were the real heroes in all of this and so were my colleagues who had to bear the brunt of the hits. It was not an easy time for any minister. I benefited, too, from tremendous public servants in the Department of Finance, who were able to work closely with their colleagues in other departments as well as their provincial counterparts.

You asked what I learned. I certainly learned the benefit of cooperation. Not long after the 1995 budget, we discussed how to address the pending crisis of the Canada Pension Plan, which was a joint federal and provincial responsibility. It had been ignored for two decades because both levels of government refused to face up to the issue. ***Leaders reach out when they want to get something done. They collaborate.*** In the case of the deficit, we had to reach out to the Canadian people. In the case of the Canada Pension Plan, I had to reach out to my colleagues who were the provincial finance ministers—and they responded. The Canada

Pension Plan is now the most actuarially sound national pension plan of any industrialized country.

Young leaders may be involved in a clash of wills or philosophies. What advice do you have for them?

First of all, you have to be pragmatic; and pragmatic means you don't get hung up on the little things, the kinds of issues that don't really go to the heart of the problem. Pragmatism demonstrates goodwill. If it can get you to the ultimate answer, then do it. On the other hand, you cannot compromise on the ultimate goal. You cannot give up on the basic issue that is driving you, which, as in the previous question, was then the elimination of the deficit. In that case, I was prepared to let my political career go down the drain.

This was a matter of principle?

Yes! Look at Spain or Italy today and you will understand why I wanted so strongly to prevent a crisis. *Leadership is about making tough choices. Leaders need to have the courage of their convictions. They need to be decisive.* Would I have resigned? No. I was going to do the 1995 budget. Was I prepared to be fired? Absolutely . . . because I felt so strongly that I was right. You cannot argue with the arithmetic of compound interest.

You don't go into public life to get your name in the papers. Most of the time, you don't really want to read the story. This goes back to our earlier conversation. I went into public life because I felt that was the place that I could make the biggest contribution. If I couldn't make the contribution, why would I want to be there?

Do you think finance ministers have a challenge to become good leaders? In the UK, Gordon Brown served as Chancellor of the Exchequer before he became Prime Minister. He had a difficult time. Bernard Landry in Quebec struggled, and so did Ernie Eves in Ontario. These are three examples of high-profile finance ministers who did not fare well as leaders of the cabinet.

I understand why you ask the question. But I don't think my challenges in the role of Prime Minister had anything to do with being a finance minister. In my case, I inherited the sponsorship issue.

Leadership matters. Leaders influence the lives of individuals. This is a significant responsibility. Was there anything about the role of leadership that you feared?

You talk about leadership. I talk about conviction. I don't think you can talk leadership unless you talk about conviction—about getting certain things done. I became Prime Minister with a number of clear objectives. One of the criticisms directed at me was that I tried to do too many things. I don't buy that criticism. I'd been in government a long time, so I knew exactly what I wanted to do; the Kelowna Accord, the national childcare program, same-sex marriage, to elevate the G20 from the finance ministers to the leadership level, to rebuild the military, to establish the oceans as the global commons and deal with the issue of over-fishing, Arctic sovereignty, plus a host of other initiatives. ***People accused me of being too ambitious. You must be selective, but you can never be too ambitious as a leader.*** In any event, the fact is I got most of our program underway. Unfortunately, the new government's priority was scorched earth.

You asked about fear. At no point in my life did the kind of fear that you talk about ever occur. When I became Prime Minister, I had been in government for 10 years, so, all things considered, it was a straightforward transition. I had been there. I understood what was at stake and the responsibilities that come with the role.

If you have some general advice to give to people who suddenly find themselves in a leadership position, what would it be?

First, you must demonstrate integrity; you cannot fake it. Second, you must have conviction, a clear vision of where you want to go, and, as I will point out later, the ability to communicate that vision. Third, when you are at a meeting, listen. Truly listen to the others at the table before you speak. ***If you are the leader, you can speak any time you want. So, stay quiet and let everybody else speak their piece, and you may learn something. Remember, it is you who will draw the conclusions.*** Fourth, reward those who challenge you! They are inevitably your best people. Remember, again, the final decision will be yours. Fifth, you are going to make mistakes. Indeed, succeeding is often a question of minimizing the number of mistakes you make—but you are going to make them, so learn from them. Remember as well that others will also make mistakes. Do not hold it against them or you will destroy their initiative and that of everyone else who watches it happen. Sixth, do not give up. There are few instant successes. Success requires a lot of work. Sometimes, the results of your decisions aren't seen for a decade. Take a long-term perspective. For example, my commitment to the G20 started years ago and continues today. I'm not in office anymore, but I'm actively involved with think tanks around the world that are pushing the G20 initiative and just keep pushing. Finally, good communication in all of its aspects is crucial. It begins with understanding the other person's point of view. Your people will buy into the direction you set if they think you have given them a fair hearing, and if you take the time to explain to them the "whys" of your decision. That's what team building is all about. This was as true for me when I was in government as it was in business. We would never have eliminated the deficit if we hadn't spent a year openly discussing the issues with Canadians across the country before acting. This is true for me now as well when I think about the issues in which I am involved. For instance, the issues of indigenous rights in Canada are trampled on every day. Canadians are a fair people. They would never let the federal government underfund the education of small children, who only want the same chances at life as others, if we did a better job of explaining the issues. If you want to discuss this any further, give me a call!

Leadership Themes

- Leaders want to get things done. They take initiative.
- Ask questions, and, if you listen long enough and if you talk to enough people, the course of action that is required will eventually come to you.
- Expand your comfort zone and learn to accept the emerging realities.
- Leaders need to bring conviction to their role and be prepared to make difficult decisions.
- Do not give up. There are few instant successes.
- Leaders understand the importance of being a good storyteller.

36

Reflections on the Interviews

Even though the 31 leaders I interviewed for this book came from various different cultures, backgrounds, and fields of endeavor, I noticed that many of them were shaped by similar experiences along their paths to leadership. These experiences often influenced them in the same way. Many leaders consequently shared the same perspectives about what it takes to lead others. Overall, I believe the leaders I interviewed have a lot in common.

In the next chapter, I will elaborate on how these leaders learned to lead, the central question I want to address in this book. Then, in the final chapter, I will conclude with their insights about their (ongoing) leadership careers. Each leader volunteered many leadership lessons learned during their leadership career. Rather than having these insights buried in the various interviews, I made them explicit because they are valuable insights that can be of benefit to both the current and next generation of leaders.

But, for now, allow me to share with you the other interesting things these leaders told me about their lives, the people who influenced them, and how they became leaders. Although I have met many other leaders before these interviews, and have studied leadership for a number of years, I was surprised by just how much the leaders I interviewed over the past year have in common. I was equally surprised by the types of experiences and perceptions they share. Here are eight high-level observations gleaned from my reflections on the interviews.

1. Few Leaders Set Out to Become Leaders

> "It wasn't a conscious choice for me to be a leader, but I did choose to be associated with the best, the smartest, the toughest—the winners. I wanted to thrive within the group, and, maybe, lead the group at one time, but not for the sake of leadership."
>
> Charles Brindamour

First, very few of the leaders I interviewed had long held a deep desire or ambition to become a leader. It was remarkable to me that many of them had trouble recalling the first time they realized they were leaders. Leadership was simply not at the top of their minds when they began their careers. They really hadn't thought about it all that much. George Cope said, "I recognized I had leadership skills during my early sports and school activities. I was the captain of basketball teams and also the student council president of my high school. You certainly need a set of skills to lead people in situations like that, but I don't think I was thinking of the word 'leadership' then." People are generally more reflective when they're older.

What the leaders did remember, however, is that, even when they were very young, they wanted to excel and to make a positive difference. They enjoyed taking charge and getting things done with others. And, once they tasted the fulfillment that comes with leadership success, they took on additional responsibilities. These led to more formal leadership roles that deepened their commitment to excel. But, as the former prime minister of Canada, Paul Martin, said, "I don't think I ever had a lightning strike hit me and say, 'Genghis Khan, here I come!'"

In other words, it wasn't as if they woke up one day, decided that they were leaders, and then went in search of projects or jobs that they could lead. Instead, when opportunities to lead came up, they took advantage of these opportunities. Many of the leaders told me that their leadership was the culmination of a lot of experiences that gradually shaped them as a leader.

For some of the leaders I interviewed, these opportunities came fairly early in their career. For example, Linda Hasenfratz worked in or with almost all the departments of Linamar before she became CEO. Michael McCain and Umran Beba had similar experiences. For others, the opportunity to demonstrate leadership potential or leadership came later. That was the case for Mike Harris, who told me there weren't many opportunities to lead in the home or in his father's business.

As Steve Snyder recalled, when I asked him about the moment when he decided to become a leader, "I was very performance driven and I think what happened was that I became a leader by default." For many of the leaders I interviewed, there simply wasn't any grand vision. Gautam Thapar said, "I soon discovered people were willing to follow. This led me to consider, "If I have the capacity to lead, am I interested in doing it?" I had no strong feelings about being a leader any more than I had any feelings about entering the corporate world. I didn't plan it." Others, such as Eileen Mercier, were suddenly thrust into leadership challenges: "I found myself in situations where there was no other way out than to take charge." Overall, however, it was clear that all the leaders I interviewed did have the capacity to lead, even if they didn't know it. As Lieutenant General (Ret.) Russel Honoré said, "You have players and you have observers. I was a player."

2. Leaders Usually Exhibit Leadership Qualities Early on in Their Lives

"I firmly believe that you learn to lead by taking advantage of opportunities when they are presented to you and rising to meet the challenge."

Sukhinder Singh Cassidy

Early on in their careers, there were signs that the leaders I interviewed were "players" who would eventually become leaders. When they were young, many were the captains of their sports teams or elected representatives of the student councils at their high schools. Some recalled leading others as members of agricultural clubs or the Boy Scouts. Others went to military academies or were part of the Reserve Officers' Training Corps, which gave them early opportunities to lead.

Still others talked about when they volunteered to help out a charity or advance a cause. These experiences, in particular, provided a good training ground for leadership because such roles didn't come with power or authority. Chaviva Hošek explained, "The only way you could get anything done was through persuading people to join you in achieving a goal and taking on the tasks needed to reach that goal. And, when these followers were on board, the next challenge was to ensure they enjoyed being part of this work."

For some leaders, their family experiences deeply shaped their capacity for leadership as well. As Michael McCain recalled, "I was exposed to the family business and talked business from a very early age—as far as I can remember. Business was discussed around the dinner table. We visited the plants as soon as I was able to walk."

However, in all cases, these future leaders seized opportunities. Unlike people who never recognize an opportunity, or those who reject them, many of the leaders I interviewed spoke about seeing an opportunity, taking advantage of it to lead, and then learning from the experience. As Lieutenant General (Ret.) Russel Honoré said, "You're selected for this [leadership role] partly because of how well you've done with the opportunities given to you, but also because of your potential for future service at a higher level."

Learning from the leadership experience is vital to becoming a more effective leader. Some people create roadblocks for themselves that prevent them from moving forward in their leadership career. They blame others for the mistakes that happen. They don't reflect on the experience, and, as a result, they don't learn and grow from it. They also don't come up with new ideas. Often, they're afraid of the "what ifs."

The leaders I interviewed are different. They are naturally introspective, courageous, and open to new possibilities. Gautam Thapar remarked, "I don't think being in the right place at the right time is enough. Being in the right place at the right time and understanding the opportunity for what it is is the most difficult part. Just by being there doesn't mean it is going to happen."

3. The Desire to Lead is Often Inspired by One Person

"I remember my first mentor—Mr. Vaghul. He was the one who invested in my first research project. Nobody would touch it because it was seen as a project with a very high risk. I knew him as a man with a strong set of values and principles."

Kiran Mazumdar-Shaw

Most leaders talked about a single person who showed an interest in them or who communicated confidence in their potential to lead. This person provided advice, opened doors, and gambled that they would succeed. For many of the leaders I spoke to, this mentor, boss, or colleague made a profound difference on their lives. As Mike Harris said, "He [David Doney] clearly saw something in me that I didn't know was there." Paul Martin went into business by accident—he met Maurice Strong. George Cope reflected on his coach at school, saying: "He told me I could do whatever I wanted to do. He told me I could play university sports. But, when you are in a small town, that's not really what your head is thinking. His confidence in me mattered." Even years later, the leaders were grateful for this person's support. As Antoni Cimolino observed, "I have been fortunate because I have been given opportunities. I don't know if I quite recognized it as such at the time, but I look back and realize people took a chance on me."

The leaders also described how they felt when leaders they knew and admired did or did not show interest in them. In both cases, these encounters influenced their concept of good leadership. For example, Eileen Mercier told me, "One day, I was riding the elevator with the president and chairman of the board. He took me to the executive floor. . . . Having him talk to me and be interested in what such a junior person thought was a huge lesson for me in how to deal with people, engage people, and give them good memories of you." By contrast, Chip Wilson had the following experience: "I was getting in the elevator with the chairman and CEO. . . . We were getting to the bottom of the elevator and he hadn't said anything to me or even acknowledged me. . . . What I got from that event is how people are around me."

Several of the leaders also spoke at length about the role that their parents played in inspiring them to become a leader. Through their support and discipline, their parents taught them about the importance of a strong set of values and high standards of excellence. Equally important, their parents were role models for leadership. For example, Paul Martin spoke about his strong social conscience and how his father, Paul Joseph James Martin, largely influenced his values. Paul Martin Sr. devoted 33 years of his life to serve as a Member of Parliament and as a Cabinet Minister in four liberal governments. He was instrumental in bringing a publicly funded universal health insurance system, or "Medicare," to Canada.

Sukhinder Singh Cassidy also recalled the deep influence of her father: "My father was the wind in my sails. He had such intellectual curiosity, and, at every opportunity, he encouraged us. He saw fertile ground and stimulated my sense of possibility." Cassie Campbell-Pascall, the former captain of the Canadian women's ice hockey team, said her mother taught her several important life lessons: "I learned that you treat people the way you would like to be treated. A girl got a penalty on me. I was very upset about it and I hit her as she was on her way to the penalty box. Mom took my skates away when I met her in the arena lobby. It was a quick message— treat people properly on and off the ice." And, for several leaders, their relationships with all the members of their family set them on the path to leadership. As Carol Stephenson said, "There was a mantra in the family: 'You can do anything you want if you put your mind to it. And, if you choose to do it, do it well.'"

4. We All Have a Choice

"It is important to always be ambitious and to always be trying to shoot the lights out. The question 'How do we get there?' is important. If you are not creative in getting solutions, and you limit your expectations and outcomes, you're not going to change the world."

                                                                    Antoni Cimolino

During the interviews, the leaders often spoke about the fact that leadership is about making choices, particularly about deciding about the standards we set for ourselves. As Carol Stephenson said, "I have such high standards for myself that I do roll up my sleeves and I do work hard. I'm not satisfied unless I think that I have achieved what is possible for me to achieve." Arkadi Kuhlmann remarked, "There's always more work to do. I never relaxed when I was young. I never relaxed when I was old. Why would you somehow expect me to relax now?" And Barbara Stymiest recalled a lesson from her father: "The fundamental message my dad taught me is to be committed and show the people you care. As a leader, you need to roll up your sleeves and work shoulder to shoulder with others."

Many of the leaders I spoke to further suggested that we make these choices every single day. John Furlong said, "We can choose to make the effort or not. Much of the time, I think we ignore what needs to be done and accept less than the very best." He believes that making the latter choice often exacerbates the problem of poor leadership and the challenges that an organization faces.

However, many of the leaders also suggested that it's critical to concentrate on the things you can control. You can control your effort, the goals that you set, and your persistence in achieving results. Some people handicap their potential by obsessing about things they cannot control. Coaching legend John Wooden once said, "Do not let what you can't do interfere with what you can do." Umran Beba echoed that sentiment: "We should try to focus on what we can control, as opposed to what we cannot control. I think what I have learned is to be happy with the end result, whatever is the outcome. We all know we gave it our best."

In particular, taking control of your learning and development as a leader was very important for many of the leaders I spoke to. Michael Shindler left one position to accept another simply because he felt he wasn't growing in his career anymore: "I realized it was time for me to move on because, at the end of the day, you are only as good as your environment allows you to be. You take responsibility for your own learning."

These conversations during my interviews with the leaders reminded me of Benjamin Franklin and his list of the 13 virtues that he felt every person should strive for in their lives. Franklin deliberately incorporated each of these virtues into his life. He selected one virtue at a time, set a goal for when he would achieve it, and monitored his behavior to assess his progress. Once that virtue was engrained in the way he lived, he moved on to the next virtue. Franklin chose to set high standards and to take the steps to improve as a leader. He took ownership of his own development.

5. Be Yourself

"Just be yourself. People who struggle with leadership are often trying to be something they are not. People will see if you're not authentic. They know if you're not comfortable in your own skin. If people don't know who you truly are, they aren't going to trust you."

Rahul Bhardwaj

The leaders all spoke a great deal about the importance of just being yourself and of authentic leadership. Many told me that they felt there is nothing wrong with a unique leadership style. Cassie Campbell-Pascall said, "I haven't met one leader who is perfect. You are not going to be the perfect leader to everybody, but that doesn't mean you're not a good leader. Listen and learn. But don't try to be perfect. Stick to your own leadership style." Jody Wilson-Raybould articulated, "Be who you are, no matter what circumstances you are in, or who you are meeting with. Be yourself and stick to what you believe in." Many of the leaders also urge aspiring leaders to think about their impact on others, and to develop a clear and consistent leadership brand. As Umran Beba said, "You can never start too early to reflect on your leadership style, your values, and how they drive your decision making. Think about your legacy. What am I doing? And why am I doing it?"

It's just as crucial to always remember that people follow different leaders for different reasons. Steve Snyder argued that leadership style has really very little to do with success. As he observed, employees at General Electric would do things for Bill Blundell and Jack Welch for totally different reasons, but they were equally committed to, equally devoted to, and equally trusted these CEOs, despite their very different styles. Linda Hasenfratz shared a similar observation: "I learned a lot from our president and chief operating officer. His leadership style is different to my father's, but equally successful and impactful."

Nevertheless, good leaders do not differ on substance. For example, they formulate a compelling vision. They set high expectations. They understand people. They lead by example. And they are not too proud to admit their ignorance and, consequently, to surround themselves with smart people.

It is important for leaders to know what they stand for. There will be moments where they have to stick with what they believe in. Peter Aceto, CEO of ING DIRECT Canada, shared an interesting metaphor to illustrate the work of leadership with the students in one of my courses. He pointed out that most people think a sailboat moves because the wind blows into the sails, essentially pushing the boat. But that's not how sailing works. If the wind in the sails was all that mattered, the boat would simply go in the direction of the wind, but soon it would tip over and sink.

In reality, sailboats have a keel on their underside, which helps to create lift by displacing water in the direction opposite from the wind. Although the keel has a much smaller surface area than the sails, the density of the water allows it to initiate a force strong enough to ensure the sailboat has equilibrium. In other words, the keel keeps the boat from capsizing and, together with the rudder, it enables the captain to move the boat forward in the desired direction. Peter Aceto believes that what's below the surface of leadership—a leader's principles, their style, and their authenticity—is just as important as the events and actions above the surface.

6. Commitment is Essential to Effective Leadership

"You have to constantly think things through. You don't want to have regrets. You can't take shortcuts with people or in situations. That's where the danger is."

Arkadi Kuhlmann

All the leaders spoke about the commitment it takes to lead—the hard work necessary to provide effective leadership and to be prepared to lead others. The need to be fully ready to lead is especially salient today, in our complex and rapidly changing world. You cannot turn leadership off. You are a leader all of the time, and, at times, that can be a burden. As Rahul Bhardwaj said, "It creates a bit of an island."

Nevertheless, each leader I spoke to clearly embraced the responsibility of leadership. For example, Mike Harris observed, "You are the leader and, at the end of the day, the final arbiter of what you're going to do, where you're going to go, and how you're going to get there. That, in itself, is scary and drives you to understand, study, research, and read about the implications of the decision you have to make." Linda Hasenfratz spoke about her commitment: "There is always the weight of knowing that 17,000 families are relying on my leadership and my team's leadership to make the right decisions. That's a lot of responsibility."

However, some leaders also spoke about the times when they realized that they no longer wanted to lead. Their aspirations changed. They no longer felt fully engaged in their work. And, consequently, they weren't willing to continue in their current leadership role. Carol Stephenson recalled that, "Boredom closes your mind to new learning. You may think you have seen all the cycles and know what to expect every time. I knew what people were going to say before they said it. I was bored, and that wasn't good because, once you think you know everything and everybody, you quit listening or you jump over steps that you should, in fact, take. Make a change."

For many of the leaders, recognizing when you need to make a change is vital. Knowing when to leave and do something different is one of the hardest things for a leader to do. Carol Stephenson said, "Self-awareness is important . . . It is important to know yourself well enough to realize when it is time to go." Steve Snyder explained that he always uses the "feel good" barometer: "If you got a call on Sunday night saying you got to come into the office because there is a problem, you can either say, 'Yes, let's go,' or you can think, 'Aww, crap.' Once you say, 'Aww, crap,' then it is time for you to leave as the CEO. I realized I was becoming more aware that there was something else out there for me to do, and I decided to start planning for my departure."

I believe Pope Benedict XVI displayed remarkable courage when he announced his resignation as leader of the Roman Catholic Church. As he wrote, "Strength of mind and body are necessary, strength which, in the last few months, has deteriorated in me to the extent that I have had to recognize my incapacity to adequately fulfill the ministry entrusted to me." Pope Benedict showed good judgment. He understood it was time for him to retire.

7. The Price of Leadership is Always High

> "The price of leadership has been that my mind is never at rest. My mind is naturally always going, but then there is the added responsibility of having to worry not just about yourself, but about a company, a set of people who are depending on you to get them where they need to be for their career, their lives, and their ambitions."
>
> Sukhinder Singh Cassidy

The commitment to lead naturally comes with sacrifice. As Sir Winston Churchill once said, "The price of greatness is responsibility." Many of the leaders I interviewed spoke about the burdens of leadership. Many travel a great deal and work on weekends. Some have received threats because of the decisions they made. Others noted that not everybody looks up to them or agrees with their actions.

Yet, for many of the leaders I talked to, their responsibilities as leaders were more important than their own personal considerations. When he accepted the challenge to turn the fortunes of General Motors around in 2010, Daniel Akerson recalled, "It would be a radical change to my life, late in my career, in an industry that I had experienced only by way of my board service. So why did I take it? Well, as the old adage goes, 'If not me, who? If not now, when?' I took the job, in large part, for non-financial reasons, out of a sense of duty and service to our nation. General Motors is an iconic company, it's important to America. I'd rather be part of the solution than the problem; I did not want to be an observer to the demise of an entire sector of our economy."

Many also spoke about how their work affected their families. As the CEO of the Vancouver Organizing Committee for the 2010 Olympic and Paralympic Winter Games, John Furlong recalled, "The project lasted for about 14 years, from beginning to end. I realized the project would take everything I had to give. But it was far more than that. It never went away—it lived on your pillow. It woke up on your pillow. As a dad, I was missing in action for a long time. It had an enormous impact on my family."

Some leaders told me how the personal costs associated with leadership encouraged them to reflect on their leadership and to reconsider why they wanted to lead. As Antoni Cimolino said, "Since leadership comes at such a great cost to our family, ourselves, or the corporation or entity that we serve, at the day's end, we should be asking ourselves why we want to lead and what we hope to do in leading. If we did that more regularly, we'd be much more effective. We might even be happier."

Because of the personal challenges associated with leadership, many leaders noted the importance of resilience. Leaders routinely deal with obstacles and setbacks. So, it's critical to find ways to cope and to bounce back when things don't go as planned. As Michael McCain said, "There are a lot of personal and professional obstacles that life will dish out to any of us at any time. And developing resilience as a skill is important in life." President Barack Obama's resilience, for example, helped him to win the election for his second term in office. He rebounded from the dramatic 2010 congressional election losses, as well as his poor showing in the first presidential debate with Mitt Romney. He proved that he could handle setbacks.

Many of the leaders also spoke to me about how they relied on their networks to help them through the tough times. For example, Michael McCain told me, "Several people from my graduating class are still friends and colleagues today. The network is an extraordinary source of strength—both personally and professionally—through an entire lifetime." Most of the leaders established their networks when they were young and kept these relationships strong. As Eileen Mercier said, "It's about making sure that you develop these connections early in your career. You shouldn't wait to try to develop them until the point that you need them."

8. It can be Dangerous to Underestimate Some Leaders

"I have had a lifetime of being a person who started things that nobody thought were possible, even ridiculous. If you look back at my career, the places I'm heading next are 10 years ahead of other people's thinking."

Chip Wilson

Finally, over the course of some of the 31 interviews I conducted, I learned that some leaders who others initially underestimate, can turn out to be lethal in their effectiveness. For example, John Furlong offered a great vision for the 2010 Vancouver Olympic Games. Nobody believed that he could pull it off. Yet, they were hugely successful, with Canadian athletes "owning the podium" more times than in any other previous Winter Games, and a renewed sense of patriotism among Canadians that endured well beyond the 14 days of sports. He reflected on his leadership challenge: "The biggest challenge has always been the same—the feelings of being underestimated or seen as not as good as you think you are—because there is no proof, no reason for someone to take a chance on you."

People dismissed Mike Harris at first, too. He was an unknown and came from a small town in northern Ontario. He built a network of supporters. He laid out a compelling vision for a better future. And he became Premier of Ontario, winning two elections in landslides, enabling him to fulfill his "Common Sense Revolution." Abraham Lincoln and Margaret Thatcher, too, were underestimated as political leaders. But they had developed the confidence to lead.

Much is made these days of Justin Trudeau running for the leader of the Liberal party. He has been criticized and ridiculed. People think he is a lightweight and not like his father. They say he has not been tested, that he is high on bold vision, but lacks substance and details. Others, including the former prime minister of Canada Brian Mulroney, warn against underestimating Trudeau's political capabilities: "People who trivialize his achievements and hold out little hope for his prospects ought to be very careful ... Life doesn't work that way. And there are always surprises in political life. And he's capable of delivering a major one if they underestimate him." (CBC News, 2012)

There are numerous examples of people who were underestimated as leaders. There are also leaders who arrived with high expectations, but, in the end, failed to live up to those expectations.

The leaders interviewed for this book also agreed that their leadership was the culmination of numerous experiences that shaped them as a person and as a leader. Who we are as individuals is a function of both nature and nurture. There was broad consensus that people who are committed to enhancing their leadership competencies and character can do so through various pathways. As Amit Chakma told me: "Leadership skills are innate to all of us, but how much we develop those skills is, in a large part, determined by the opportunities we have to take on leadership roles, and how readily we embrace those opportunities." Leaders evolve along maturation pathways that tend to differ from one leader to another. I will focus on these pathways to becoming a leader—or a better leader—in the next chapter.

References

Bacharach, S. (2012) Why he won: A lesson in what people really want in a leader. *Inc.* [online], November 7, 2012. Retrieved from http://www.inc.com/samuel-bacharach/why-obama-won.html

CBC News. (2012) Justin Trudeau shouldn't be underestimated, Mulroney says. CBC.ca article [online], October 3, 2012. Retrieved from http://www.cbc.ca/news/politics/story/2012/10/03/calgary-justin-trudeau-liberal-leadership.html

37

Conclusions on Learning to Lead

In the 31 interviews with leaders from different industries, sectors, countries, and in various stages of their careers, my goal was to understand how people learn to lead. I wanted to see how volatile, complex situations shape the perceptions and beliefs of leaders. I was also interested in whether leaders look at routine, everyday experiences in a distinctive way. And I was curious about their role models and other influences. By answering the question of "how good leaders learn," and not simply "what makes a good leader," I hoped to discover important insights into how management educators and organizations alike can help people to become good leaders. Equally important, I wanted to show the next generation of leaders as well as current leaders some of the paths they can take to develop or enhance the leadership qualities vital to their continuing success.

Not surprisingly, all of the leaders I interviewed for this book agreed that good leadership can be learned. Many of the leaders started down the path to leadership when they were very young. For example, Carol Stephenson told me: "I don't think there was a defining moment where suddenly I woke up one day and decided I was a leader. I think it was the culmination of a lot of experiences that gradually shaped me as a leader. Those experiences started in childhood." Many leaders also shared the importance of recognizing and seizing opportunities to grow as a leader.

It was equally clear that many leaders believe that learning to lead is an ongoing process. You cannot wait for a major disaster or a significant promotion to learn about leadership. As Antoni Cimolino said: "There is something to be learned every day, both by looking in the mirror at yourself and by looking at the people around you."

As I outlined in Chapter 3, there are no silver bullets or a single pathway forward to becoming a leader. The fact is that different leaders learn to lead along different pathways. The experiences and careers of the leaders interviewed for this book are diverse and wide ranging. Nevertheless, the journeys of these leaders share several elements in common.

Largely because of my work in executive development, I initially proposed six pathways for learning to lead. These can be summarized as:

1. performing, or excelling in a role;
2. risking, or taking chances to lead and to learn;
3. stretching, or going beyond your own personal comfort zone;
4. learning, or taking the time to reflect on past events to discern the lessons they offer;
5. self-awareness, or deliberately seeking to know your personal strengths and weaknesses; and
6. trusting, or relying on your abilities and those of others to build a reputation of being trustworthy.

I used these pathways to guide me in formulating a series of open-ended questions for the interviews. But, once completed, the interviews revealed four additional and clearly identifiable pathways:

7. adapting, or the ability to act in different situations in the appropriate way;
8. mentoring, or learning from other leaders and role models to develop as a leader;
9. observing, or watching others and yourself to better understand events and situations; and
10. integrating, or having the capacity to see and understand the "big picture."

Figure 37.1 illustrates these ten pathways.

The following are detailed explanations of each of these 10 pathways, together with observations from the leaders I interviewed about how these pathways helped

Figure 37.1 Ten pathways towards becoming a better leader.

them to learn to lead or to lead more effectively. I also highlight the implications of each pathway for learning to lead, and offer advice to the next generation of leaders on how they can learn to become good leaders.

1. Performing

> "You have to win. There's no way around this—you can't be a leader if you're not scoring points, winning pennants, making profits . . . You can call yourself a leader. You can act like a leader. You can be the appointed leader. You can be given the opportunity to lead—you can do all those things—but, I'm sorry, at the end of the day, if you don't get the goal . . . you are not a leader. So, practicing leadership is quite different to being a leader, and being a leader means you've got confidence in yourself as a leader, and you can only get that if you get a track record."
>
> Arkadi Kuhlmann

To be a leader, you must prove that you can perform at a high level. Superior performance demonstrates your leadership potential. It serves as the platform from which leaders can grow and develop. As Robert Bell told me: "Fortunately, I had that first successful experience to hold up as an example. We put in place a system for Ontario that was considered a cancer care model. I could validate my role as a leader and politicians and bureaucrats started coming to me."

Executives and managers assign leadership opportunities to certain employees because they believe these employees have potential. As these employees excel in new roles and develop a good track record, they gain self-confidence in their abilities to lead others. As George Cope observed: "It's about calling more strikes than balls, a record of getting it more right than wrong."

Arkadi Kuhlmann also believes that, as you advance into more and more senior roles, the more and more your performance is scrutinized and judged by others: "As I got into executive roles, the only reason why I ever got a promotion or opportunity was because, when I got an opportunity, I delivered. And that takes hard work." Lieutenant General (Ret.) Russel Honoré echoed that belief: "There's no credit for trying. There's credit in mission accomplishment. Don't bring back excuses. Get the job done. Adapt and overcome."

Leadership comes with growing responsibilities and expectations for results. As a leader, you must be secure, confident, and unafraid to take on new challenges, even if that, inevitably, means that you will make mistakes. This takes courage. Cassie Campbell-Pascall observed: "People are often afraid to be leaders. They may fear criticism or doing something wrong. I think fear stops people from stepping up in the dressing room and just saying whatever they feel needs to be said. People are afraid of the repercussions. I'm a big believer that, if you don't want to be criticized, then say nothing, do nothing, and be nothing."

To perform at the high level required of any good leader, the implications are clear. Aspiring leaders, and those who want to learn to lead better, have to answer some tough questions: Do you understand the mission, vision, values, and strategy of the organization? Do you take ownership of these drivers of organizational success? Do you understand your strengths, weaknesses, and blind spots? Have you committed to a personal development plan to enhance your future performance? Are you receiving ongoing feedback on your performance and the coaching necessary to improve your performance? Are you open to unsolicited feedback? Do you feel you have the resources to overcome obstacles to performance and get the job done? Do you take initiative in your quest for personal and organizational excellence? Do you have the confidence to lead and take on the challenging assignments? Are you prepared to deal with disappointments and failure? If you can answer "yes" to most of these questions, then you are likely to be a high performer.

2. Risking

> "I did not seek, in any of these instances, to become the leader of these companies. In each case, Maurice Strong, Bill Turner, and Paul Desmarais gave me a chance, which I grasped. That I was influenced by what they had each done in life would be an understatement."
>
> Paul Martin

Leaders learn by recognizing and seizing opportunities to learn, and then rising to meet the challenge. For example, Rahul Bhardwaj reflected: "People saw that I had the capabilities to contribute to city-building activities, and to advance that through some sort of leadership role. Those people opened the door and I stepped through, delivered, added value, and created something. Then other doors start opening and the pattern continues."

Similarly, Elyse Allan reflected on her transition from General Electric to the Toronto Board of Trade: "I gained important insights into the intersection of business, government, and the community. I learned how much you can get done when you have a compelling vision and the ability to articulate that vision in different ways that motivate different constituencies all around the same vision. People had spoken to me about the power of grassroots organizations and how impactful they can be. However, this was the first time I saw how that really worked."

Leaders push to get the experiences that will help them to develop their competencies—people, organizational, business and strategic—and their character. They may fail at times, but that does not discourage them from reflecting on their mistakes, setting goals for improvement, and then trying again. As John Cheh said: "In each case, starting a new job, taking on a new role, not without some fear or trepidation, I tried to overcome that, to learn and to perform."

But, pushing yourself is challenging and the process of learning to lead can be daunting. Some people are too insecure to put themselves "on the line." Michael Harris said: "I think going into the unknown is always scary. Kids are nervous the first time they stand up in front of the class to speak. Putting your name on the ballot is a little risky. How is this all going to be received? But, generally, what you learn from this is that there may be things unknown to you, but, if you have enough confidence in yourself and in your ability to learn, then you ought not to be afraid of it. So, every time I went into something new, there was a certain apprehension. Usually, it's the fear of the unknown."

Kiran Mazumdar-Shaw added: "I think the biggest enemy of anybody is insecurity. These insecurities are often unfounded fears. People have a fear of the unknown. They lose confidence. It could be because of a personal tragedy; it could be an emotional disappointment; or it could be a failure on some project."

Volunteering for the tough and sometimes unpleasant assignments, putting your name on the election ballot, or making the switch from one sector to another are critical to learning. Steve Snyder shared his views on the importance of these experiences at the beginning of his career: "Don't underestimate the value of your early career moves. You can't make up lost time. If you don't get your experiences by 35, 38, or 40, you're probably not going to get them. Those early years are really critical."

What are the implications for those who aspire to be in leadership roles? Taking risks is an essential part of learning to lead. Expose yourself to more complex or complicated situations. Readily accept new roles. Commit to new files. Carol Stephenson, for example, never said "no" to an opportunity without thinking about it. Each opportunity has the potential to develop one's competencies, character, and commitment in profound ways. Be mindful of the opportunities presented to you and the potential learning that will certainly come from taking advantage of these opportunities.

3. Stretching

> "In fact, if you're not making mistakes, you're probably not pushing yourself hard enough. If you're not making mistakes, you're not really creating many learning opportunities. You gain confidence when you make mistakes and manage to move on and learn from them."
> Rahul Bhardwaj

Leaders stretch. They have a personal plan and are committed to mastering the critical dimensions of leadership—competencies, character, and commitment—that will make them better leaders. They are never complacent. As John Furlong's father asked of him: "Are you prepared to step out of the crowd, be a little bit more vulnerable, risk a little bit more humiliation, and do more than the people around you? If you're prepared to be [that person], you have a fighting chance to be an inspired human being."

Leaders are willing to step out of their comfort zone. They do things that others are reluctant to do. Umran Beba told me: "I had exposure to different parts of the business. You must be open to new experiences and willing to stretch in order to develop as a leader." She stretched herself by moving from functional roles, such as human resources, marketing, and sales, to regional roles where she had to manage several countries and cultures. When people stretch, they can achieve remarkable results and learn from the experience. As Arkadi Kuhlmann shared: "Those moments stay with you. My belief is that, the tougher your challenge is, the better you rise to the occasion."

For Michael McCain, the stretching started at the beginning of his career in business. As he explained to me, he found himself in the middle of a transformative bottom-up restructuring during one of his first leadership roles. He was sent to the United States to run a struggling business, and it wasn't an easy or simple assignment. In his words: "These kinds of experiences are certainly interesting and instructive."

This same sentiment was shared by Eileen Mercier as she reflected on her time at Abitibi-Price Inc.: "There was a time, in 1992, when we were in a deep hole. It was an awful time in the marketplace, and the currency was going against us. We had to sell off a lot of assets. Dealing with that situation was like catching a falling knife. Things were getting away from us and we had to rein them back in and get everybody to work together. We had to work very long hours and work through a lot of very thorny problems. You learn a lot going through an experience like that. If you haven't gone through a very bad corporate experience, I don't know how you'd learn those lessons. From such experiences, you gain a set of skills that you sometimes wish you didn't necessarily have to have, but they are all part of a tool kit that adds up to a sum of experiences."

Many of the leaders I interviewed for this book shared their "crucibles," a term coined by Warren Bennis and Robert Thomas to describe the "intense, often traumatic, always unplanned experiences that transform leaders" by teaching them critical lessons about leadership (Bennis & Thomas, 2002). Many leaders told me they never really knew their limitations until they had to give everything they had to meet the pressing, sometimes dangerous, challenges facing them. People who never fail probably haven't tested their limits. Unless you have faced hardships as a leader, it can be argued that you haven't learned nearly as much as a leader who has lived through a crucible experience.

In our interview together, Umran Beba lamented on her initial reluctance to stretch: "But, to tell you the truth, for many years I wasn't open to relocating to a different country. I did a lot of traveling for work and visited a lot of places. Moving to a different country offers big learning opportunities for a child, adult, or business leader. I moved at a later stage in my life. I think being open to relocation earlier in your life may have benefits. You develop great perspectives on life."

There are two important implications of stretching as a pathway for learning how to lead. First, to become a good leader, you must develop the willingness and confidence to step out of your comfort zone. Stretch early and stretch often in your leadership career. Stretching teaches you lessons you typically don't pick up in business school. And don't be afraid to fail! People who have never failed probably don't have the courage to fully explore their leadership capabilities. As such, they miss out on the critical pathway to developing the competencies, character, and commitment necessary to becoming a good leader. Failure also teaches you to stay humble—to remain open to the perspectives of others and all opportunities to learn.

Second, by accepting stretch assignments, leaders come to appreciate that leadership is a choice—a courageous choice. Stanley McChrystal, a retired United States Army General, and commander of the U.S. Forces in Afghanistan, said that:

"Leadership is not a talent or a gift. Leadership is not complex, but it is really hard" (McChrystal, 2012). We learn a lot about what it means to lead, and what it takes to become a better leader, through our willingness to stretch. Be aware of opportunities to stretch, and appreciate these opportunities for what they truly are—a chance to learn to become the best leader you can be!

4. Learning

> "If you don't take the time to introspect and you don't have a certain amount of humility, then I think it's very difficult to be a balanced leader. I think you will have spurts of leadership and burn out."
>
> Gautam Thapar

Good leaders take the time to continually learn and refine their leadership skills. They step back and reflect on their successes and failures. They are never complacent about learning, whether it's their own learning or the learning of the team or organization they lead. And, often, good leaders are candid about their own limitations and what they need to do to become better leaders. As Cassie Campbell-Pascall said: "I was captain of the team, but I still had so much to learn and so many great people to learn from by listening to them. You can learn so much from people around you. You need to listen, though. You should never think you're the best you can be. You can always be better, so you should continue to learn about being a better leader."

The importance of learning, even at the top of the organization, was eloquently captured by Charles Brindamour: "You need to step back and be conscious and disciplined about learning. It's a conscious effort and you need to make time for it. CEOs often sit in meetings 12 hours a day. You have to see learning as a key element for moving the organization forward and making it prosperous. It's a key responsibility for you as the leader. If you don't make this a priority, you risk the organization becoming complacent. You need to make time for it in an organized fashion."

Making time for learning, however, is easier said than done. Arkadi Kuhlmann put it this way: "You need to learn quickly from mistakes. It's amazing to me how many people won't do the postmortem. They'll do the homework and they'll do the exercise, but they won't take enough time to reflect on whether that could have gone differently and how that could have been done. I learned very quickly from my mentors that the postmortem is where the value is—good, bad, or indifferent. It's funny. As a society, we do this with sports. We will argue for hours about why a goal was scored, or not scored, and how an individual played, and so on. In business, and even in family situations, we just won't do those kinds of postmortems. We don't do them enough. We get the results and just move on."

Often, the reason—or the excuse—for not taking the time to reflect on experiences is the constant demands on the leader's time. It's like you're on a treadmill without an "off" button. But that reflection is essential. As Chaviva Hošek said:

"My real learning happened when I got defeated and wasn't in politics anymore." We all make mistakes—minor and major—and we can all learn from our mistakes through reflection.

It's equally important to be receptive to the feedback of others, no matter how humbling that feedback can be. As Narayana Murthy observed during our interview: "The biggest challenge a leader has is to create channels for feedback, and keep them open at all points of time so that he or she can get the much needed feedback on where they went wrong . . . We must remember that the day a leader closes those feedback channels is the day when hubris sets in and a leader's downfall starts. I have seen prime ministers and presidents of countries lose their office when they closed the feedback channel. Therefore, an important lesson I have learned is to keep all my channels of feedback open and to create an environment where nobody is afraid of coming and expressing their disagreement with my policies."

Eileen Mercier told me about the 360-degree review process she experienced as a member of the board for the Ontario Teachers' Pension Plan: "Going through the experience was a humbling experience. Every little wart—everything that you do that people wish you didn't do—was there, along with the few times when people said, 'Oh yeah, great job on that.' You take for granted all the good stuff, and it's always the little criticisms that come out. There's no question about not continuing to learn, because it's really all there if you're willing to take it in."

Of course, for real learning to occur when something fails, it's vital to objectively look at what happened. What went wrong, what you could have done differently, and all the other valuable lessons you can take away from the experience. Again, it's not easy to recognize when you fail. It's even more difficult to accept responsibility for the failure. That's why good leaders acknowledge their mistakes, accept accountability, and actively try to learn from their mistakes. They don't blame others, which is the natural tendency of most people. As Chaviva Hošek told me: "The people who are in the blaming business are making sure they never have to look in the mirror. How is that helpful?" Once leaders reflect on their mistakes, they act on the often powerful lessons they learned. Good leaders make learning the bedrock of their development.

In fact, some of the leaders I interviewed talked about their frustration with people who couldn't seem to learn. As Gautam Thapar said: "People who make the same mistakes over and over again drain me. People who stick to old routines or approaches, even when everybody around them wants to change, drain me. People not seeing the better way of doing things drains me."

The thoughts about learning articulated by the leaders I interviewed offer two compelling lessons. First, if you want to lead effectively, you must be disciplined in taking time to reflect on your leadership. Get off the treadmill. Consult with people around you that you trust. Ask them what happened and what could have been better managed.

Second, take accountability and responsibility for your own learning. Michael Shindler took the time to write down some of his ideas about leadership. He then reached out to his friend, Aaron Nurick, who is a professor at Bentley University.

In his words: "I wanted feedback on whether the things I observed in businesses and wrote about made sense." In effect, he documented what he learned. The lesson? Write down the specific lessons you learn and commit to achieving goals for your behavioral improvement. Include these lessons in your personal development plan. Shindler took things a step further when he sent a leadership book and a memo to his team asking for feedback on his leadership. He addressed the feedback in a weekly staff meeting eight weeks later. This exercise was developmental.

Mark Zuckerberg took these lessons to heart when he realized that he needed to be a leader, and not just another tech guru, if Facebook was going to be a great company. He hired an executive coach and worked on his weaknesses. He strived to identify and hone the skills essential to running a fast-growing company. He met with, and learned from, successful leaders in his industry. He matured as a leader. And that's because he made learning a priority.

5. Self-awareness

> "I reflect all the time on the impact I have on others. It's introspection and retrospection on the impact you have on others in situations, in meetings, when we debate projects, and on the impact I have on others over a period of time. I step back, look at the past year or two, and have this inner dialogue—probably more than I should—on the impact I have on others. I assess whether it was calibrated properly and whether it had the desired impact."
>
> Charles Brindamour

Good leaders are self-aware. They understand what motivates them and what drains them. They can tell you about their strengths and weaknesses. They are aware of their blind spots. They understand the impact their behavior has on the environment, and the impact the environment has on them. They take time to calibrate their perceptions and feelings. They are mindful of their thoughts, values, motives, and emotions.

Gautam Thapar told me: "I think leaders need to be very introspective. You need to understand yourself more or better than anyone else. By understanding yourself, you understand how to be better. I have many weaknesses and a few strengths, and the biggest frustration is trying to overcome those weaknesses by trying to do things differently and not succeeding."

It's vital to remember that the "perfect leader" doesn't exist. We all have our limitations and blind spots that, if left uncorrected, could become our Achilles heel. John Cheh realized he could be too impatient. Jody Wilson-Raybould understood that she had to let go of her desire to control things as she progressed in her leadership career. Steve Snyder and Michael McCain wondered whether someone can be too outspoken.

The leaders I interviewed also spoke about how easy it is to lose your perspective. For example, Cassie Campbell-Pascall told me: "I was a young assistant captain and pretty immature. Maybe I thought I was a little better than I actually was. A lot of new things were coming at women's hockey at that Olympics—things we'd never experienced before. I allowed my head to swell a little bit. My leadership got away from my foundation. I didn't reach out to people and ask for help or lean on people as I had done before in my career. I realized that you can quickly become a different person if you allow it to happen."

Overall, developing self-awareness can be tough. Our emotions often get in the way. Chip Wilson told me about the time he was dismissed at Westbeach Snowboard Ltd.: "The people that came in from private equity were really great. I had no problems with what they did, such as putting in more controls. But I remember being in Hong Kong and getting a fax conveying that I had been removed as CEO and that they had decided to put in their own CEO. I did the predictable. I complained. I jumped up and down. I called my lawyers. And then, you know, I just settled down and started to reflect."

As Michael McCain told me, the root of leadership development is self-awareness. To enhance their self-awareness, leaders can rely on self-testing and inventories such as StrengthsFinder, the Leadership Wheel, and the Myers–Briggs Type Indicator assessment. When used properly, such tools facilitate reflection and foster self-awareness. To deepen self-awareness, it's also important for leaders to remain open to feedback, even when that feedback challenges your decisions and actions.

More importantly, leaders should continually strive to learn from their decisions and actions through reflection. Purdy Crawford, for example, found that, when he was asked to deliver speeches about leadership, the "process forced me to reflect both on what I've done as a leader and what I've read about leadership."

Warren Buffett has an interesting routine to increase his self-awareness. He writes down his reasons for making an investment decision as well as the anticipated results. Once the decision is implemented and in play, several months or years later, he reads his initial thoughts about a decision and compares the actual results with what he expected. Explicitly, Warren Buffett assesses the outcomes of every decision he makes.

6. Trusting

> "To earn trust, people need to believe what you say. Earning trust can be a long process, and you can lose it in no time. If you make one mistake, it can be gone. Trust is absolutely important because, the more trusted relationships you have, the more things you can do."
> Amit Chakma

The leaders I interviewed often discussed the importance of trust from three distinct perspectives: The need to trust yourself, to trust others, and to be seen as worthy of trust.

First, they talked about the necessity of trusting yourself to make and then execute well-considered decisions. Self-trust is critical for dealing with the curveballs that life dishes out. As Rahul Bhardwaj observed: "It's remarkable—even people who are very successful hold themselves back. So, I think what I learned recently, and it's an ongoing thing, is to push myself more and to let that come out more. We need to give ourselves permission to really think big." Paul Martin also told me: "People accused me of being too ambitious. You must be selective, but you can never be too ambitious as a leader." Leaders can't hold back, because good leadership is committed leadership. And, to be a committed leader, you must have confidence in your competencies and believe that you have the character to lead.

Second, leaders need to learn to trust others. Leaders must be prepared to cede control to others, because they cannot possibly be in control of all activities. Several of the leaders I interviewed explained that, from the outset, they approach every new relationship with someone with trust. They hope this trust is reciprocated. But, when that trust is breached—for example, when an employee misrepresents facts, hides information, does not deliver on commitments, or engages in excessive political behaviors—then the onus is on that employee to re-establish their trustworthiness and credibility.

George Cope firmly believes that even people with the best skills cannot perform effectively if they do not share a commitment to the organization's goals, or if they lack the appropriate character. He also underscored the importance of trusting others in becoming a good leader. As he said: "If you can't delegate as a leader, you're done. People ask me, 'How did Clearnet Communications grow from 3 people to 25, to 50, to 100, to 1,000, and to 2,000 so quickly? How is it that you can go home at night with that level of intense growth?' The answer: You have to be able to delegate to a team you trust. That's been fundamental in building the team that's transforming Bell."

But Cope's trust in people comes with a cost. Again, in his words: "People who work for me now, or who have worked for me in the past, will tell you it's a lot tougher to work with me once you have that trust. I'm harder on them than ever before because my expectations of them go up. My team members will probably tell you that it is great once you have established trust with me, but—wow—the accountability gets even higher, because I have put everything into that relationship. The only way you build these types of companies—Clearnet, or Telus, or BCE—is through delegation. But trust is required before you can effectively delegate."

Third, it is critical for leaders to be perceived as trustworthy. To be effective, leaders need to ensure that their followers trust them to do the right thing. As Chaviva Hošek said, leadership is not an inherent quality: "Fundamentally, leadership is a relationship between some people and other people, and, unless the relationship endows at least one person with the self-confidence or the capacity to help the others along, it doesn't matter if you designate them as a leader. People will obey when they have no choice but to obey. That's fine, I understand that. But I live in the real world, and that's not leadership."

Daniel Akerson focused on communications as a way to build trust. He told me: "I try to be open and honest in my communications, and I encourage those who work with me to respond in kind. That requires a bilateral relationship built in trust. Subordinates will only trust in that relationship if they feel I will listen and respond in a measured and constructive manner."

Good leaders understand that they will never get the results they set out to achieve without trust. Trust determines, to a large extent, whether the leader will be effective in his or her role and whether people will feel good about his or her leadership. Elyse Allan explained that the underpinning of influence is trust. Trust must be earned. It does not come with the position you hold.

David Horsager, author of the book *The Trust Edge: How Top Leaders Gain Faster Results, Deeper Relationships, and a Stronger Bottom Line* (2010), outlined eight ways to build trust, many of which were embraced by the leaders interviewed for the book. Each of the following provides excellent advice to aspiring leaders:

- Provide clarity in your communication and action: People trust the clear, and mistrust or distrust the ambiguous.
- Show compassion: People put faith in those who care beyond themselves.
- Demonstrate character: People notice those who do what is right ahead of what is easy.
- Showcase your contribution: Few things build trust quicker than actual results.
- Model your competence: People have confidence in those who stay fresh, relevant, and capable.
- Develop connections: People want to follow and be around friends—and having friends is all about building connections.
- Demonstrate commitment: People believe in those who stand through adversity.
- Be consistent in your actions: In every area of life, it's the little things—done consistently—that make the big difference.

7. Adapting

"I have been privileged with the opportunity to live in many different places. Those experiences have helped me to develop a natural ability to open up and adjust to changes."

Umran Beba

Leadership does not happen in a vacuum. Leadership is contextual. And the context in which leaders lead is ever changing, sometimes rapidly and unexpectedly. Good leaders recognize the relevant issues in different situations and match their leadership approach to each situation's specific demands. This is critical. No one leadership approach or behavior is effective in all situations. It's like golf—you need a driver for the tee-off, a nine-iron for chipping, and a putter on the greens. Just like there isn't a single golf club that's best for every shot, there is no single leadership approach that is appropriate under all circumstances. Good leaders are open to new experiences, and, over time, they master a repertoire of behavioral approaches to lead under divergent situations.

Several leaders spoke specifically about how they had to change as they advanced in their leadership career. Marshall Goldsmith's book *What Got You Here Won't*

Get You There (2007) underscores this need to adapt as you climb the corporate ladder. His thesis is that there are several workplace habits that often keep successful leaders from taking the next step in their careers. These habits may have contributed to the leader's success in a middle management role, where you're usually expected to be a "doer." But, as leaders move up in an organization, they have to concentrate more on leading and less on doing. In other words, leaders always have to figure out what's required—in terms of competencies, character, and commitment—to be successful in the new role.

Lieutenant General (Ret.) Russel Honoré described this learning as follows: "I think we go through life in plateaus, and, when you get to each plateau, you need to be prepared to start over. The previous experience was good enough to put you in a leadership position, but, when you go into a different environment, you have to re-establish yourself."

Charles Brindamour addressed the fact that, as leaders move up in the organization, they manage different people—employees versus managers versus vice presidents versus senior vice presidents—and, therefore, leaders often have to change their management style. In his words: "It's the adaptation from step to step . . . All of a sudden, as you move up, the people reporting to you have different sets of expectations and things that drive them. To adapt, it's important to properly understand what drives the new level of the organization for which you're responsible. When moving into a new role, I'd spend a lot of time on that area so that I could be successful as quickly as possible."

Many of the leaders also spoke about how their upbringing and early experiences in life enabled them to adapt quickly to new environments. For example, Chaviva Hošek explained that being an immigrant is one of the best things that has ever happened to her. She always asked a number of questions when she moved to every new culture. How do they do things here? How do they talk to each other? How do they interact? She said: "I figure out what the rules are and I figure out a way to work inside those rules. So, I brought a mindset that doesn't assume that I know how to behave. I assume they know how to behave, and I've got to figure out how to fit in. It has actually helped me a lot." By approaching each new position with an open mind, humility, and respect for others, Hošek was able to quickly figure out what to do and how to make a valuable contribution to her team and the organization.

In addition, leaders must be aware that different people expect different things. A leader needs to understand the context in which events take place, how others may react, and how to respond appropriately. Carol Stephenson shared a compelling story about the time when she was the CEO of Lucent Technologies Canada and the company went through a downturn. The workforce, which included many younger professionals, was anxious. Stephenson had led other companies during downturns in the past, and, in reflecting on these experiences, she decided to present the facts to try to put people's minds at ease. As she recalled: "That presentation was the worst thing I could have done. What I forgot was to pay attention to the emotional cycles that people have to go through. I hadn't allowed for the anger and grief to happen. I was into remedies and solutions, and so it was a terrible misjudgment on my part in terms of reading the situation and how people might be feeling." The employees were quite upset with her, but she recovered. And, in the process, she learned a valuable lesson: Your knowledge is useful, but you have to know when to apply that knowledge.

Good leaders are able to adapt to different situations. They know that they often have to change their management styles as they advance in the organization or take on new challenges. And they are able to grasp the essence of situations by analyzing what others do and what drives their behavior. To become a good leader, in other words, you must become contextually aware and adaptable.

8. Mentoring

"I was always open to learning from people, either directly, by observing them, or by asking for their opinions on my challenges. I would also call people. I still have people today that I call my 'thought partners' who are very important to me. They have helped me immensely to think through the really tough stuff."

Barbara Stymiest

Most of the leaders I interviewed talked about how they had benefited from the guidance of mentors—individuals who helped them to learn and develop as a leader. Research shows that good mentorship can affect a leader's career in many positive ways. Mentors provide a sounding board for leaders. They help leaders reflect on their motivations and aspirations. Mentors share their experiences in handling challenges and help leaders to build their confidence. They also model appropriate behaviors. They provide candid feedback on a leader's performance, offer career advice, and help leaders to formulate developmental goals. Overall, a good mentor helps a leader to become more effective.

Michael McCain said that dozens of people, in different ways, have played an extraordinary role in helping him to learn to lead. Paul Martin credited four specific people for his success in learning to lead. Carol Stephenson also spoke about a vice president who was a formative influence in her leadership journey: "He never gave up on me; he was like a dog with a bone. He was instrumental in arranging a transfer that was totally out of my comfort zone. I really had to rise to the challenge. He moved me into a regulatory job, which was populated with lawyers. There was absolutely no room for being shy, no room for not doing the job really, really well because so much depended on it."

Gautam Thapar similarly credited his mentor for his success: "I rose very quickly through the organizational ranks because a lot of what he said was not difficult for me to put into practice. I have learned that, if you have people with good leadership potential in your organization, give them a couple of years with your key leaders. Let them be in an environment with high exposure and where there are no secrets and hidden agendas. Then watch how they develop. Those three years with Mr. Bakshi were worth 10 years of leadership training at any organization." The leaders I interviewed shared many inspiring stories with me about the leaders who mentored them.

Many of the more senior leaders I interviewed now mentor the next generation of leaders. Antoni Cimolino spoke passionately about the responsibilities of leaders to show an interest in people and serve as a mentor: "For the senior leader in the organization to cut through the ranks and talk to someone several levels down who shows promise is a major empowerment and gift to that young person. It comes with responsibilities, too. You can't just give someone an opportunity and walk away. There is an ongoing responsibility to be there as an ear and source of advice. There is also a responsibility to be very frank and honest. You have put those young people in positions where they could sail and fly, or they could have a very scarring experience that could set them back several years in their development. It's very important for leaders to take responsibility for the opportunities they've provided to young people and to ensure those people are successful."

Although mentoring can be a very useful tool in learning to lead, however, it is difficult to foster effective mentoring relationships. My colleague, Jeffrey Gandz, believes there are several reasons for this. First, it takes time to develop a good mentoring relationship, and senior leaders tend to be busy. Although many leaders appreciate the importance of coaching and mentoring others, they don't see these as urgent responsibilities. Second, providing candid feedback can sometimes prove confrontational. Since most people don't like conflict, they are reluctant to engage in difficult conversations. Third, issues such as character are often perceived as "soft" and subjective, and many people are uncomfortable in bringing up these topics in developmental conversations. Fourth, giving feedback means getting feedback in return, and sometimes that reciprocal feedback is not appreciated. Fifth, a talented person may be in a pivotal role and the leader may not want to risk upsetting or distracting that person with candid feedback and advice.

Sheryl Sandberg, the chief operating officer (COO) of Facebook, offers a sixth challenge in her recent book *Lean in* (2013). She points out that talented women in the early stages of their careers can benefit immensely from the mentorship of older, more experienced male leaders. But men tend to be quite nervous about mentoring a younger woman. For example, two men discussing business over a drink or dinner doesn't raise any eyebrows. But when a man and a woman do the same thing, it looks like they're on a date.

For aspiring leaders, the implications are clear. Find a mentor—or multiple mentors—and invest time in nurturing the relationship to ensure that you foster the trust and mutual respect so essential to candid conversations. Be humble, listen to your mentor, and acknowledge their advice. Remember, however, that you don't necessarily have to take the advice of your mentor. Many of the leaders I interviewed spoke about the importance of developing your authentic self. Avoid becoming a clone of your mentor. And don't just use your mentor when you are in trouble. Regularly meet with your mentor, no matter how busy you are. Lastly, remember that the best mentoring relationships are a two-way street. What unique value do you bring to the mentoring relationship?

9. Observing

> "You learn a lot from people who you admire. You admire their style, the way they do things, and the things that they make happen. Whether you realize it or not, I think you become a student of that, and then, when you see something that really doesn't work, you kind of file that one away as well, because you want to avoid those mistakes if possible. You make enough mistakes on your own and you don't want to repeat other ones from which you should have learned."
>
> Eileen Mercier

Leaders learn a great deal by observing others, how they react to different situations, what they say or don't say, and how they treat other people. As Albert Bandura concluded in developing his theory of social learning: "Learning would be exceedingly laborious, not to mention hazardous, if people had to rely solely on the efforts of their own actions to inform them what to do. Fortunately, most human behavior is learned observationally through modeling: From observing others, one forms an idea of how new behaviors are performed, and, on later occasions, this coded information serves as a guide for action" (1977: p. 22).

Most of the leaders I interviewed told me that they learn about leadership by watching the behavior of other leaders. They observe how others handle challenging situations. They reflect on the behaviors of others, mindful of the consequences of these behaviors. They learn from the mistakes of other leaders. And they learn from their successes as well, modeling the effective behaviors they observe and practicing these behaviors until they are mastered.

As Purdy Crawford said: "When I worked on government committees and with boards of directors in both Canada and the USA, I was exposed to and observed many topnotch business leaders. I observed that there are many brands of leadership, and that leadership styles should differ according to the situation."

Being observant is important to learning when you are young. As George Cope told me: "We were successful in building a wireless company called BrookTel and later sold it to Bell Cellular, now known as Bell Mobility. I was 25 years old then, and overnight became president of a subsidiary of Bell. I learned how boards operate and closely watched the behavior of people in leadership roles. I gained valuable insights into the business world and leadership concepts at a really young age. This was an important learning experience and provided a good grounding in an important part of the telecommunications industry."

It's also essential to continue observing others throughout your career. As Michael Shindler said: "Over the past 30 years, I have held several jobs, and this gave me an opportunity to observe the leadership at each. I was able to take experiences and compare different bosses and their leadership. I learned from those experiences and observations—small, bite-sized pieces. I try to teach my children that negative lessons sometimes are much more valuable than the positive ones."

Several leaders talked to me about their fathers and how their fathers influenced their leadership style. For example, Michael McCain told me that his father was action oriented, decisive, and unfailingly honest: "He was one of the most transparent people. You never doubted what was on his mind. Never! He told you exactly, to a fault maybe, what was on his mind. He was genetically hardwired to behave that way. He couldn't behave any other way. It was just not possible for him to be anything but transparent. I think I happen to be the same way—perhaps through genetics or exposure to my father."

The next generation of leaders should think about their own role models in a deliberate way. What do you admire in a leader? How can you model the behavior of these leaders for your own personal success and for the success of the people you work with? Sukhinder Singh Cassidy offered this valuable advice for finding good role models: "I think everybody has role models on learning to lead. Look for role models in the people who are closest to you and around you. If you can't find one, ask yourself if you're working for the right person. If you're not working for people who inspire you, who are you working for? Who are you working with? I think people should be moving toward working with people who give them energy and inspire them."

10. Integrating

> "I learned an important lesson from these transitions: Always learn about your boss's job, your subordinates' jobs, the job of the person sitting next to you, the job of the person across the desk from you, and so forth. This is important because I believe it will make you a well-rounded person and you will understand where your job fits into the bigger organization."
>
> Michael Shindler

As they advance in their careers, leaders will likely go through distinct changes in their roles or functions. Good leaders are promoted, often moving from one area of the organization to another. They may lead a major change initiative in their own department, which has an impact on all departments within the enterprise. Some leaders start their own companies to capture a new business opportunity. Others are "intrapreneurs," who establish new lines of business or undertake a major change initiative within their organizations. These experiences help leaders to see and appreciate the bigger picture. And this capacity to understand the whole and how its parts are integrated is critical to good leadership.

Good leaders recognize the unique value offered by each business function and how these functions relate to one another in creating value for the organization. They know that the solution to any major problems will only work if it is integrated across different functions. They understand that the greatest product ever won't fly unless it is marketed to the right customers and supported by superior customer service.

To gain this deeper understanding, leaders devote extra effort to reading about what's happening within their own enterprises, within their sectors, and within business and society in general. They reach out to people who have been and continue to be exposed to responsibilities and challenges similar to their own. Leaders tend to be people of broad interests and knowledge. They are comfortable with opposing perspectives and know how to reconcile these differences in opinion or perspective.

Over time, good leaders absorb how their organization works and the dynamics of the environment in which it operates—economic, political, societal, or industrial—and the interrelationships among these dynamics. They gain an integrated and holistic perspective. For example, when Barbara Stymiest became the CEO of the Toronto Stock Exchange in 1999, she quickly learned about many areas new to her, including government relations, branding, and media relations. She reflected on her experience: "As you get more senior and experienced, your thinking becomes more integrated. You start to see problems in multiple dimensions because you now have experience in all those multiple dimensions. I could think about things more broadly, and get different perspectives, and integrate my thinking to produce better outcomes. Experience got me to that point. I've been working for 35 years and, boy, if I knew 20 or 30 years ago what I know now—not just in terms of technical stuff—I would have been better at doing my jobs then."

Purdy Crawford reflected on his time as COO and CEO at Imasco Ltd. By his own admission, he did not know much about operations. But he understood that, in order to run the organization well, he needed to become intimately familiar with this critical part of the business. Consequently, he visited the branches to learn as much as he could about operations. It made him a better leader because he was able to integrate his learning about operations with the other functions of the organization.

Carol Stephenson often speaks to the importance of developing peripheral vision. I asked her about the advice she would give to the next generation leaders. She told me that leaders should develop their ability to look beyond the organization they're leading, and to look beyond the country in which their organization is based. In her words: "Scan the world, be global, look outside your industry. Here at the school, I like to call it 'cross-enterprise leadership.' I would say the more experience I gain, and the more things I've been exposed to, the more I understand the importance of cross-enterprise leadership. It's so important to have that peripheral vision that goes beyond your own little piece of the action or your own little piece of the world. I learned it over time, but I think the earlier you can learn it as a leader, the better you're going to be as a leader."

And Elyse Allan talked about her support for liberal arts education: "It teaches the ability to think across disciplines, and to manage complexity. That approach has a great deal of relevance to leadership today. Successful leaders today will be able to understand interdisciplinary complexities, work with multiple stakeholders, and solicit broadly for ideas to solve problems."

Those who aspire to become better leaders or more mature leaders should seek to broaden their knowledge through a diversity of experiences and successes. They should develop interests in multiple areas, and never stop learning about emerging trends that affect business and society. In this way, they gain a rich breadth of perspectives on business and world issues. Often, promising leadership careers are derailed because leaders develop tunnel vision. It's like looking at the world through a periscope, where you can only see what is in front of you, not what's to the sides or behind you. When you don't see the bigger picture, you limit your ability to integrate information from different experiences or functional areas. This capacity to see the whole, and to understand how its parts are integrated, is essential to making good decisions. When you consistently make good decisions, you develop superior judgment. And that is the essence of leadership.

I believe that all of the leaders I interviewed, at some point in their careers or to varying degrees, used these 10 pathways to help them learn to lead. From our conversations, I know that all of them feel compelled to perform and produce results. I also sensed that many relished taking a risk, knowing that the bigger the risk, the more rewards it would bring. They liked stretching their boundaries, pushing themselves forward to test their abilities. They weren't afraid to make mistakes, or to seek feedback, because they saw these as opportunities to learn and improve.

They also seemed self-aware, with a deep understanding of their motivations, likes, and dislikes. They appreciate the importance of trust. They know how to adapt to different circumstances, cognizant of the fact that "one size does not fit all" in every situation. Each leader also told me about their mentors, and how much they valued their advice and guidance. They shared with me how they learned by observing others in action. They spoke to the importance of looking at your entire organization, how its different parts fit together, and its place in the world.

And although I didn't ask this question during these interviews, many of the leaders told me that they really enjoyed learning. In fact, it was clear to me that these leaders are passionate about learning, even if they didn't overtly express that passion. Overall, I believe that their drive to excel through learning is what makes them good leaders.

References

Bandura, A. (1977). *Social learning theory*. Englewood Cliffs, NJ: Prentice-Hall.

Bennis, W. G. & Thomas, R. J. (2002). Crucibles of leadership. *Harvard Business Review*, Sep., 80(9), 39–45.

DeLong, T. J., Gabarro, J., & Lees, R. J. (2008). Why mentoring matters in a hypercompetitive world? *Harvard Business Review*, Jan., 86(1), 115–121.

Eby, L. T. (2011). Mentoring. In S. Zedeck (Ed.), *APA handbook of industrial and organizational psychology, Vol. 2: Selecting and developing members for the organization* (pp. 505–525). Washington, D.C.: American Psychological Association.

Goldsmith, M. & Reiter, M. (2007). *What got you here won't get you there: How successful people become even more successful*. New York, NY: Hyperion.

Horsager, D. (2010). *The trust edge: How top leaders gain faster results, deeper relationships, and a stronger bottom line*. Minneapolis, MN: Summerside Press.

McGirt, E. (2012). "Boy CEO" Mark Zuckerberg's two smartest projects were growing Facebook and growing up. *Fast Company* [online], March 19, 2012. Retrieved from http://www.fastcompany.com/1822794/boy-ceo-mark-zuckerbergs-two-smartest-projects-were-growing-facebook-and-growing

McChrystal, S. (2012). *Leadership is a choice* [video file]. Retrieved from http://www.youtube.com/watch?v=p7DzQWjXKFI

Sandberg, S. (2013). *Lean in: Women, work, and the will to lead*. Toronto, Ontario: Random House.

38

Leadership Insights for the Next Generation of Leaders

During the 31 interviews, the leaders not only shared their experiences about how they learned to lead, they told me about the many hard lessons they learned about leadership during their careers. Some made potentially disastrous mistakes or bad decisions. Others faced huge challenges and met them head on. And, of course, many learned from the good times and from their ordinary, everyday encounters with other people. The chapters featuring my interviews with the leaders offer many tangible insights, and I urge young people, the next generation of leaders, to read each one to gain a profound understanding of what it takes to lead.

In this final chapter, however, I want to highlight 15 leadership lessons that came up time and time again during the course of these interviews. Some of these lessons are not new, but they vividly underscore what good leaders do, how they act, and how they gain influence and respect. These are the lessons that I believe aspiring leaders should know about, reflect on, and practice to become better leaders.

1. Lead by Example

For most of the leaders I interviewed, leadership isn't simply a title, such as CEO, or captain, or chief, or principal. Rather, leadership is a responsibility that comes with many expectations. The leaders discovered firsthand that they set the tone for whatever happens in the organization—good and bad. As such, each one strived to lead by example—to show other individuals, the teams they work with, and people within the entire organization what they have to do to be successful. George Cope observed: "Your behavior becomes the permission for other behaviors in the company. I firmly believe that, if you start to cross the line in any negative way, everyone else is going to cross the line." Many of the leaders also told me that leading by example is powerful. As John Furlong said: "People will do anything for you if they see a good example to follow."

Leading by example means understanding what is expected of you and being prepared to live up to these expectations. The leaders were reminded of what's expected of them early on and throughout their careers. For example, Barbara

Stymiest said: "For most of my career, I was the first person in the office because I heard my dad's voice telling me that I had to work harder than anyone else. The fundamental lesson that my dad taught me is to be committed and show people you care."

I was especially touched to learn that Narayana Murthy helps out on the home front by regularly cleaning the bathrooms in his house. He isn't just looking to make his wife happy, he's willing to get his hands dirty doing a job that he doesn't have to do. Learning from Gandhi, he takes on tasks widely considered beneath his station as a reminder that all contributions to society should be valued.

2. Remember that Respect is Earned

Leadership is about earning respect. It is not about commanding or demanding. Respect allows you to get things done through others. John Furlong told me about the advice his father gave him: "Live a good life. Don't take it if it is not yours. If you break it, fix it. Don't say bad things about other people. Lead with dignity. Learn how to win with class and lose with grace. Make me proud." He remembered that advice in the months leading up to and during the Olympics. In his words: "If we can live up to this . . . Canadians will be there for us when we need them the most." For him, his challenge was about earning respect. He was clear in his mind how to do that.

Kiran Mazumdar-Shaw also talked about the lessons her father taught about respect: "Never look down upon any profession. It is important how we conduct ourselves in life, and add value." By the same token, Steve Snyder believes that he has to earn his job every single day. He always tries to do better. As he says: "You should be coming in with the attitude that you have to earn your job and employees' respect every single day. Once you no longer have that attitude, I'm not sure if you're delivering your best performance."

There are many ways a leader earns the respect needed to lead effectively. A person earns respect by being consistent in their words and deeds. They are honest, transparent, and candid. They get the job done, and done well. And they acknowl-edge the contributions of others. They are interested in people. They help others out and they share their knowledge with others.

3. Protect Your Reputation

Warren Buffett once said: "It takes 20 years to build a reputation and 5 minutes to ruin it. If you think about that, you'll do things differently." To be effective, good leaders are vigilant about protecting their reputations. As Eileen Mercier told me, "In business, as in life, in the final analysis [your reputation] is really all you have. Don't lend it to any company or individual that you do not trust. Your reputation must be your first, last, and most important consideration."

Many of the leaders I interviewed were also very conscious of the fact that it takes a long time to nurture a good reputation. Eileen Mercier observed: "As an individual in business, you're selling yourself as a package. Anybody can have a skill set, but a reputation is built very carefully over many years." In other words, reputation has a lot to do with addressing failure, with persistently building a record of performance. And most people tend to forget that your reputation precedes you. It does not follow you. Kiran Mazumdar-Shaw said: "The first two years of my business life were spent creating credibility and a belief that what I was trying to do was worthwhile. I think I went through a number of failures in doing that, but I carried on."

It is equally important to remember the difference between character and reputation. Charles Brindamour told me: "Leaders are judged by how they behave and trust is built on your behavior, not on what we say the values are. It's how we actually live them that matters." As Abraham Lincoln wrote: "Character is like a tree and reputation is like a shadow. The shadow is what we think of it; the tree is the real thing." In other words, a leader's character is what a leader truly is and a leader's reputation is how other people perceive the leader. As such, a person's reputation is open to interpretation.

Leaders with a good reputation gain the support and commitment of their followers. And that's vital to any leader's effectiveness. As Canadian football legend Michael "Pinball" Clemons once told me: "If you are leading and nobody else is following, you are just taking a walk."

4. People Watch You—All the Time

It's vital for leaders to remember that that they are being watched—constantly. And people have high standards for their leaders. For many of the leaders I spoke to, this is often a huge burden that they cannot escape. For example, Arkadi Kuhlmann said that: "Life is a blackboard that you cannot erase. Everything counts. There is no such a thing as time out." And Carol Stephenson said: "You are being watched for what tone you set in the organization." Many leaders stated that it can be draining to be "on" 24/7. George Cope told me: "As a leader, you cannot behave at less than your best, even if you're having a tough day. You'll be judged, and rightly so—you're the leader." Jody Wilson-Raybould reflected on her leadership: "With leadership comes the responsibility to be really conscious of what you say and do. People look up to you. They look for advice or guidance. They look for support. You have young people who want to become involved and may look to you as being a mentor or a leadership example. You have a huge responsibility, so don't say or do thoughtless things."

Good leaders also appreciate the fact that their words and actions have a profound impact on their audiences. They understand that every action they take and every syllable they utter will be dissected and parsed for meaning. In the age of around-the-clock media coverage, they must assume they are "live" at all times. As

Kiran Mazumdar-Shaw told me: "Any little wrongdoing is magnified. People can pull you down really fast. One little wrong step and you will be crucified."

Remember Republican presidential candidate Mitt Romney? He learned this lesson the hard way when he suggested that 47 percent of the population is made up of people who believe they are "victims" and are "dependent on government." Remember the former CEO of British Petroleum (BP), Tony Hayward? In the aftermath of the massive oil spill in the Gulf of Mexico caused by his company, he insensitively said, "There's no one who wants this thing over more than I do, I'd like my life back."

Whether running for office or running a business, leadership is always on trial.

5. Be There!

Good leaders lead from the front, when things are going well and when things are not going well. They are personally engaged. A few years ago, Rudy Giuliani, the former mayor of New York, came to the Ivey Business School to give a presentation on his perspectives of the aftermath of the September 11, 2001 terrorist attacks on the World Trade Center. One lesson he shared with the students resonates with me to this day. He said: "Weddings are optional, but funerals are mandatory." He attended more than 200 funerals of firefighters in the weeks that followed the terrorist attacks. He visited with thousands of city employees and reached out to the families of victims. Giuliani believes, as his father told him: "Be there for your people, and they'll be there for you." Lieutenant General (Ret.) Russel Honoré echoed that sentiment in our interview. He said: "Leaders are on the scene to see what is going on and to smell the action. Don't be afraid to take on the impossible. Don't be afraid to act when you are criticized."

In challenging times, good leaders have the confidence to lead. They are visible and they communicate. They put their leadership on the line. Michael McCain took center stage during the 2003 listeriosis crisis at Maple Leaf Foods, earning accolades for his courage and leadership. Four years later, XL Foods Inc. was at the center of the largest beef recall in Canadian history after E. coli bacteria were discovered in one of its facilities. Not a single leader from XL Foods stepped forward to take responsibility for telling people what happened and what the company was doing to correct it. I doubt Canadians can list the names of the co-CEOs of XL Foods.

By contrast, the leaders I interviewed wanted to be there for their people. For example, Robert Bell, the president and CEO of University Health Network, told me: "I care very much about my people. That keeps them connected to the organization. A leader should be visible and present on the shop floor, and make a point of regular visits to the shop floor to take care of people and engage them." Often during the interviews, it became very clear to me that many leaders feel a deep connection with their employees. As Robert Bell shared: "I am a rink rat. I love to visit the floors at the hospital. I love hospitals. I love the people who work in the hospital. I get my resiliency from the nurses, the housekeepers, and the people who sell you a coffee at Second Cup."

6. Act with Courage, Do with Confidence

Good leaders are action oriented. They are exceptionally well prepared for action. They push and push until initiatives are realized. They don't hold back. As Chip Wilson related: "I developed a winning formula. And that is to give 100 percent and hold absolutely nothing back or you'll never be successful. Ninety-nine percent of people actually operate the other way—they hold back. They give maybe 85 percent. They miss that additional 15 percent that can make them very successful."

Good leaders are also courageous. They act in a way that is consistent with their values, even when acting with these values in mind can cost them. Gautam Thapar told me: "If you have the courage of your convictions and have proved you can deliver, I don't think you should ever hesitate to speak your mind on issues. In difficult times, that's what the organization needs. You need clear thinking, clear direction, and a willingness to say, 'This is what we need to be doing.'"

Good leaders have the confidence to act largely because they have developed a solid record of performance. As Purdy Crawford said during our interview: "Good leaders must have a substantial degree of self-confidence. Making decisions is a lonely business. Listen to all the advice you can get, but, ultimately, you have to make the decisions. Self-confidence gives you the courage to make decisions and also to make mistakes. Leadership has never been a risk-free endeavor." And the best leaders learn from their mistakes as well. "Most of my mistakes or problems have been in not taking action quickly enough when I should have known something was not going to work. I think I was a little too indulgent sometimes," Chaviva Hošek told me.

However, many of the leaders I spoke to also told me of the dangers of becoming overconfident and arrogant. As Gautam Thapar observed: "The biggest derailer of talent in organizations? Hubris! If you start believing that you are God's gift to management and that you know everything there is to know—sorry, you don't. If you don't have a certain amount of humility and introspection, you are at risk of derailment."

7. Have a Conviction

We need leaders of conviction. They have drive. They are determined, tenacious, and resilient. They do not run by poll numbers, nor are they interested in participating in a popularity contest—they bring conviction. Paul Martin believed the deficit was a ticking time bomb, and that he had less than two years in which to act.

He took an aggressive approach in cutting the deficit. Emotions were intense—in both the cabinet and across Canada. He knew he would not make many friends. But leadership is about making tough choices. He felt his approach in dealing with the crippling deficit was the right thing to do for the country, and he was prepared to be fired for it. Jody Wilson-Raybould, the regional chief of the British Columbia Assembly of First Nations, has a strong conviction concerning self-government for First Nations. Michael McCain demonstrated his conviction in addressing the listeriosis crisis head on. Daniel Akerson showed conviction in leading General Motors back to being a respectable company. And John Furlong passionately believed that the Olympics would build a stronger Canada. These five leaders don't compromise easily because they strongly believe in their ideas. But leaders can never overdo their convictions—there is always the risk of demagoguery.

8. Communicate, Communicate, Communicate

Good leaders are excellent communicators. They are articulate, sincere, and authentic. They focus on a few core messages that are clear and succinct. And good leaders are not afraid to show their emotions. People can relate to their personal stories. I was moved several times, during the interviews, by the stories the leaders shared with me, such as why Paul Martin decided to support same sex marriage, why Narayana Murthy routinely cleans the lavatories in his house, and how John Furlong felt when his father died. Good leaders connect with their audiences. They understand that old adage of Theodore Roosevelt: "Nobody cares how much you know, until they know how much you care."

We know that poor communications can ruin a leader's career. Tony Hayward's performance during the BP crisis, as I noted earlier in the chapter, was ridiculed. He lost his job. Remember Mel Lastman, the former mayor of Toronto? His tenure was marked by a series of unfortunate remarks. During the SARS crisis, for example, he tried to repair Toronto's reputation through an interview on CNN. The results were disastrous. Michael Ignatieff, the former leader of the Liberal Party of Canada, turned people off. He never had the common touch. Communication, however, is a skill that can be developed. Take Mark Zuckerberg, the CEO of Facebook, for example. He has markedly improved his communication skills.

All in all, a leader's ability to communicate can make or break a career. As Mike Harris said: "It is not good enough to be right. People have to buy into your vision and ideas. It takes time to bring people along with you." And, as Michael McCain of Maple Leaf Foods believes: "An idea that seems so profound in your own mind is really worthless unless you communicate it well. If you cannot communicate your thoughts, your leadership will be diminished."

The leaders I interviewed often spoke at length about how candor is so integral to good communications. Without candor, critical information is not shared. Ideas are not voiced. There isn't the effective debate so vital to developing sound solutions. In short, candor denied is potential unrealized. As Daniel Akerson told me: "You have to be honest in your communication, your feedback. If you accept mediocrity, over time that becomes a hallmark of the organization, and the organization 'dumbs down'."

9. Be Open—Listen with Intent

Many of the leaders I interviewed told me that the most important lesson they learned on their leadership journey was to listen. Everyone can hear, but do we actually listen to what others have to say? Do we reflect on their views or consider their advice? As Ferio Pugliese, the president of WestJet Encore and executive vice president of WestJet Airlines, once told me: "It takes courage to stand up and speak. But, it also takes courage to sit down and listen." And the benefits of listening are clear. As Robert Bell said: "Getting different opinions has helped me grow as a leader. If not, you rapidly get into groupthink."

The business world and government is full of people who did not listen or were not engaged enough in their daily dealings with others in their organizations to pick up signals that bad things were happening—or about to happen—in their department or business. In their book *Predictable Surprises: The Disasters You Should Have Seen Coming, and How to Prevent Them* (2004), Max Bazerman and Michael Watkins illustrate this reality with a number of case studies showing how bad things happen when leaders don't listen. For example, they highlight the collapse of Enron and Arthur Andersen as well as the failed merger of General Electric and Honeywell.

By contrast, good leaders inherently know how important it is to learn to listen with purpose. As Cassie Campbell-Pascall, said, "I became a better listener over the years, and that was important for me to become a more mature leader . . . I wanted to know what I had to say to certain individuals prior to a big game to help them elevate their game. I would simply ask them questions and listen to their answers."

10. Build a Great Team

George Cope said, in his 2012 convocation address to students of the Ivey Business School, that, "The ultimate key to success is mastering the skill of fostering strong professional teams." Like all good leaders, he knows that he can't get his job done on his own. He needs the support and commitment of others to ensure the success of Bell Canada Enterprises, so he works diligently to build and nurture relationships with others. In doing so, he observed: "Teams drive everything in business. A team builds a company. The most important thing in a leadership role is to absolutely trust the people with whom you're working. One of the most important parts of my career has been never having a direct executive report quit—ever. And, to me, that is the result of my desire to build strong and unified teams."

George Cope also believes that no single individual is bigger or more important than the team. Good leaders understand the strengths and weaknesses of the people on their teams. As Umran Beba said: "You work with people who have different styles and characteristics dictated by their cultures, nationalities, religions, and so forth. Good leaders learn to understand and appreciate those differences, and try to create synergies in the team and deliver great results." People may come at you with a unique point of view that surprises you.

Above all, good leaders understand how important it is to share success. When success is about the leader getting all the glory, then he or she can't get quality people to work under him or her. Cassie Campbell-Pascall spoke to me about the leadership exhibited by Hockey Hall of Fame member, Steve Yzerman: "If an article was written about him, he always tried to bring in his teammates and make it about the team." Campbell-Pascall strived to ensure that her teammates knew how important their contributions were to the team's success. She made it a point to tell me that successful teams are comprised of leaders who understand that, some-times, they can follow the lead of other team members. Good leaders don't feel the need to lead all of the time.

11. Don't Try to Be the Smartest Person

Several leaders I interviewed talked about the "curse" of leadership, or the fact that many people assume the leader is the smartest person in the room. In some cultures and organizations, people see their leaders as demi-gods, with the answers to every question and the solutions to any challenge. Good leaders, however, recognize that they don't have all the answers. Instead, they try to create opportunities that enable other people to solve challenges or present new ideas. Antoni Cimolino, the artistic director of the Stratford Festival of Canada, told me that he considered it a gift to be working with "so many great people." Each of the people he works with at the Stratford Festival brings a different piece of the jigsaw puzzle to the table. He found that, by enlisting their support and giving them a voice in making creative deci-sions, his team would ultimately build a much better product—a better play—at the end of the day. He said: "One of the most striking things I've learned over time is how people will surprise you. You can think carefully about all of the variables, and then somebody comes at you with a unique point of view that surprises you, despite how carefully you thought it out."

Barbara Stymiest also discovered the value of listening in her first leadership positions: "I learned very early on, from chairing many meetings of both executive leadership teams and the board, that, when you're in a defined leadership role, you never state your point of view first, or else there will be a natural tendency for people to jump in and support your view. To create openness and allow construc-tive debate, it's better to say, 'I may have a view, but I don't know the answer and

I want to consider all the elements,' and have processes where you can have the dialogue happen in an open, constructive, non-challenging way."

Wade Oosterman, the president of Bell Mobility and Bell Residential Services as well as chief brand officer of Bell Canada Enterprises, when reflecting on his career with Clearnet, coined the phrase "positional authority disrespect." It meant that he and the other founders of Clearnet did not care who came up with an idea. Just because your title was more senior did not mean that your ideas were better. Every person's voice was equal and everyone's input was equally valued.

It takes confidence to admit that an idea of a junior person is better than yours. As Mike Harris said: "Leadership is about being comfortable having smarter people working for you. Your goal, as a leader, is to get the best out of all of them to take you where you want to go." Many of the leaders I interviewed told me about how important it was to solicit the opinions of their people. For example, Gautam Thapar said: "It is critical not only to relate to people, but to also make them relax around you and know they can present their views. People will come into the room to say something, but are often reticent. I have to help them relax and then draw it out of them." And Charles Brindamour added that this is a skill his company values in every manager: "We still evaluate our managers on their ability to create an environment where the information flows up."

Some of the leaders I interviewed also expressed frustration with people who think they have all the answers. For example, Michael Shindler shared this experience: "There was never a question about who was the smartest guy in the room—it was he. An issue would come up and he would start to express his view on it. I kicked him under the table. He asked, 'Why are you kicking me?' [I replied], 'If you tell people what you think, then they are all going to find a way to jump in line. Don't you want to get their opinions?'"

As Michael McCain told me: "Some of the smartest people I know really have the biggest blocks around learning because they are overconfident in what they already know. They don't have the humility to learn. They are too proud to admit their ignorance."

12. Let Go

Many of the leaders I spoke to also talked about the challenges of letting go and stepping away. As leaders progress in their careers, they take on additional responsibilities. And, at some point, they have to trust others, delegate, and let go of initiatives they started. As Robert Bell told me: "My biggest problem was that each role kept expanding, and, at a certain point, I thought, 'Okay, I've got to start dropping things. I can't be successful unless I drop things'." He also reflected on his most recent learning: "I constantly learn lessons about letting go, even though I thought I understood that 5 years ago."

Letting go is not an easy thing to do. As Linda Hasenfratz, the CEO of Linamar Corporation, told me: "I grew up from the floor. Not only am I familiar with the action there, but I loved it! It is hard to step away and let someone else take that on. We continue to evolve as a company, and it's hard to hand over the reins and rely on people to be accountable. It's hard to give people the tools and information they need and then hold them accountable to meet goals."

Nevertheless, relinquishing authority and giving employees more autonomy is absolutely essential to effective performance. Chip Wilson said: "There comes a point for a leader when the important thing is to get out of the way. I learned to train and mentor those under me to be better." Lieutenant General (Ret.) Russel Honoré also spoke about how this changes the leader's role: "I learned that, the more senior you get, the more important it is to focus on the 'what' and 'why' of what you do, and set a space for your subordinates to figure out the 'how'."

13. Stay Humble

Many of the leaders spoke to me about the dangers of becoming overly confident. When you're a leader, you can quickly fall into the trap of thinking that you have all the answers. As Cassie Campbell-Pascall said: "It is easy how leadership can get away from one's foundation. I allowed my head to swell a little bit. It is tempting to think that you are a little better than you actually are." When you're a leader, avoiding the tendency to become arrogant is critical because arrogance will undermine your leadership effectiveness. Many people ruin their promising careers because they don't have humility. For example, boards eventually lose patience with CEOs or directors with closed minds or who are invariably contemptuous of the views of others.

Often, leaders can become arrogant because their followers can't, or are afraid to, tell them the truth. Others go along with anything the leader says because they look up to the leader. Kanina Blanchard, until recently the regional director at the Ontario Ministry of the Environment, cautioned against a leader looking for approval or compliance instead of the truth. She said: "I would challenge anyone to think back to the best friend they ever had, whether a member of their family, a former colleague, a friend in school—someone who told you the truth about yourself. You remember that person because they had the courage to tell you what you needed to hear. Of course, you had to be open to hearing the truth, too. As a leader, don't surround yourself only with people who will tell you what you want to hear. You need the courage to go back to your mother, your spouse, your sister, or whomever, and say: 'What am I really like?' or 'How do you think I'd react in this situation?' You have to open yourself up."

Many leaders also told me that, without humility, it's impossible to learn from others or from your own mistakes. People should be mindful of their mistakes or near mistakes, admit to them, and then try to fix them. But, as Arkadi Kuhlmann said: "It is so easy to get the ego involved—it sneaks up on people and they don't even realize it." Humility helps a leader to remain open minded. It makes a leader pause to reflect on events or decisions, to learn from them, and do better the next time.

In addition, many leaders shared a sense of gratitude toward the people who told them the truth and helped them to make better, more informed decisions. As Kiran Mazumdar-Shaw said: "People that mind don't matter, and people that matter don't mind. Don't expect to be treated in a special way; just give your best."

I recently had the good fortune to meet Sami Jo Small, a hockey goalie who was a member of the 2002 Canadian Olympic women's ice hockey team. Her motto is: "In life, you don't always get to choose the role you play, but you do get to choose how you play it." Sami Jo trained for years. She made sacrifices. And when the coaches told her she would not play in the final game of the Olympics for the gold medal, she was devastated, disappointed, and angry. But, she quickly realized she had two options. One, she could feel sorry for herself, or, two, she could be there for the team. She chose to cheer the team on. She played this role to the best of her abilities. She had an impact.

For many of us—in sports, in business, in government—life doesn't always turn out the way we want. Be humble. Be gracious. As Michael "Pinball" Clemons explained to my students: "I am my greatest challenge." In other words, the greatest challenge for any leader is not the people who disagree with your vision and direction. "I count him greater he who overcomes himself than he who overcomes his enemy." Clemons believes that leaders must take control of their destinies by understanding their weaknesses and striving to improve. And, at the core, that requires humility.

14. Never Stop Learning

All of the leaders I interviewed for this book are people with a strong curiosity. They are avidly interested in learning about and understanding new developments, both in their own field of expertise and in that of others. They seek to have a broad perspective on business issues. As Purdy Crawford explained to me, it's critical to have a well-rounded view of the world and our place in it. Leaders must be competent in their fields, but they should never believe the sun rises and sets only in their own field of functional expertise. He started the "Purdy's Picks" tradition to help facilitate a broad-gauge approach in the up-and-coming leaders at his law firm.

Many of the leaders I interviewed also make the time to keep informed. When Charles Brindamour became the CEO of Intact, for example, he blocked three to four hours in his calendar almost every morning so he could devote time to researching areas that could influence his business, his company's strategy, and the employees who work for him. This helped him to develop the multiple perspectives on events and situations that foster effective leadership. As he shared: "Learning to have perspective on things is really important. It's never all black or white, and having the time and ability to step back and put things in perspective is important."

It is equally critical to look beyond where you live and do business, too, especially in today's global business environment. Several of the leaders spoke to me about the new and exciting developments underway in other countries and how they might affect Canadian companies. They clearly recognized these as both challenges and opportunities. As Barbara Stymiest told me: "My challenge the last 25 years has been to continue to inform myself in a rich way about what is going on in the world. Understand the details and complexity."

15. Learn to Be Patient

One of the hardest things for leaders to learn is patience. That's because they are action-oriented people. They want to get things done . . . now! But, as Steve Snyder believes, sometimes leaders have to slow things down because they deal with people—people who have faults that need to be addressed if you want them to be effective. For example, some people are set in their ways and reluctant to change. Others act purely out of self-interest. By developing patience, leaders can suspend their immediate judgment of other people and situations. They gain more time to analyze what's going on and what people are really thinking. They make more considered, more effective decisions.

As Linda Hasenfratz told me: "The 'do things today, not tomorrow' approach was instilled in me from a very young age. I learned over time that not every decision should be made quickly. You will need to make some decisions quickly. But you should be more thoughtful about other decisions. For example, if the consequence of a decision is something that might have an impact for years, then you should spend some time thinking about that decision. Gather more data. Evaluate a couple of different scenarios."

With patience, leaders also become better listeners and develop stronger relationships with others. There's a tendency among some leaders to jump right in, when they watch others completing a task, and say: "This is the wrong way to do it!" But, as I learned from Michael "Pinball" Clemons, leaders need to know when to use their voice and to appreciate the fact that their voice can be "annoying rather than anointing." There's nothing wrong with making suggestions, but a leader has to be careful not to turn them into imperatives. Telling doesn't inspire better performance. It doesn't help people to accept ownership of their jobs.

This same thought was echoed by Antoni Cimolino. He knows from intimate experience that theater is a collaborative art form. So, he openly invites people—writers, casting directors, actors, set designers—to participate in the vision for a play. He wants their ideas. He takes their ideas seriously and tries them out. He believes his role, as director, is to help other people to see the possibilities that will make the play better. By inviting and openly discussing their contributions from the beginning, he knows that all the members of his team feel like they "own" the production. As a result, "the play holds together." In his experience, when a director behaves autocratically, the play falls apart over time. It gets twisted and lost.

Patience, of course, goes hand in hand with determined perseverance. Leaders must work tirelessly toward the goal they hope to reach, but also patiently, without immediately expecting a positive outcome. This is a paradox that leaders need to learn to balance: To be assertive yet patient at the same time. Consider Michael

McCain and the listeriosis crisis at Maple Leaf Foods. He and his team were aggressive in handling the crisis, but patient in understanding that it would take years to restore full consumer confidence in their company's brands.

Leaders also learn to deal with frustration. They understand that they may not succeed at the first try. And, certainly, patience is required for learning to lead. Ben Affleck, when accepting his Oscar for "Best Film," said it best: "You have to work harder than you think you possibly can, you can't hold grudges . . . and it doesn't matter if you get knocked down in life, because it is going to happen . . . all that matters is that you are gonna get up."

Reference

Bazerman, M. H. & Watkins, M. (2004). *Predictable surprises: The disasters you should have seen coming, and how to prevent them.* Boston, MA: Harvard Business School Press.

Index

Note: Page numbers in *italic figures* refer to illustrations.

acceptance, gaining, as an outsider 112
accountability: accepting 167, 310, 343;
    challenges in learning to take 91–2; virtues of
    a business leader 10, *10*, 11
action-orientation 159, 359; finding it hard to
    learn patience 366
adaptability, contextual part of leadership 83,
    347
adaptation, to new work environments
    238–9
adapting, pathway to becoming a better leader
    347–9
afraid *see* fear
Akerson, Daniel xii-xiii 24–5, 55–62, 333, 346,
    360, 361
alignment: getting everybody on board 75;
    leaders aligned with their organisation 87
Allan, Elyse xiii 21, 44–54, 339, 347, 353
ambiguity, dealing with 49–50, 161
analysis, of a situation 187
approval, leader looking for 364
aptitude, for leadership 17
arrogance, will undermine leadership 364
aspiring leaders, tough questions for 338–9
assumptions: about other people 192; not
    digging deeper 121
authenticity, team-building 233
authentic leadership 87, 88, 272
authority, relinquishing 135, 152, 364
autonomy, giving employees 135, 152, 364
"Avantha" 258-9, 260
awareness *see* self-awareness; situational
    awareness

balance: being assertive, yet patient 366–7;
    between managing and leading 90; critically
    important 283–4; balancing, work and
    personal life 159, 271

BCAFN *see* British Columbia Assembly of First
    Nations
BCE *see* Bell Canada Enterprises Inc.
Beba, Umran xiii-xiv 21, 265–76, 327, 331, 340,
    341, 362
behavior: how we conduct ourselves 173, 356;
    important for leaders to reflect on 311–12;
    standards of acceptable 6, 9; trust built on,
    not on what we say 232, 357; watching people
    in leadership roles 351, 355
Bell Canada Enterprises Inc. (BCE) 306, 307,
    361, 363
Bell Mobility 307, 351, 363
Bell, Robert xiv 205–11, 338, 358–9, 361, 363
Be There!, good leaders lead from the front
    358–9
"be yourself" 64, 331–2
Bhardwaj, Rahul xiv-xv 20, 85–95, 331, 332,
    339, 345
bigger picture: coping with stress by seeing the
    224; seeing the 12, 180, 352, 354
Biocon 168–75
Blackberry, Chairman of the Board 75
Blanchard, Kanina 364
board of directors, essential for entrepreneurs
    298, 303
board meetings, challenging executives and
    directors 213–14
board membership: most important are those
    asking questions 210–11; no experience is
    ever wasted 217
boredom, as a barrier to learning 100–1
BP *see* British Petroleum
brands: great challenge of being Bell 308; judged
    by how they behave 232
Brindamour, Charles xv 21–2, 227–36, 342, 344,
    348, 357, 363, 365
British Columbia Assembly of First Nations

(BCAFN), regional chief of the 247, 249–56, 360

British Petroleum (BP) 358, 360

burnout, build ability to turn it off, or risk 313

business cycle, learning during the full 231

business relationships, sitting down and listening to people 312

buy-in, looking for 136

"calculated negligence", knowing what not to do 310

Campbell-Pascall, Cassie xvi 24, 63–71, 329, 331, 338, 342, 344–5, 361, 362, 364

Canada Steamship Lines (CSL) 317–19

candor: bringing, to a relationship 76–7, 140–1; GE known for a culture of 50–1; getting, from colleagues 261; potential unrealized 360–1; tools that help to deliver 163–4

capabilities, assessing 41

care: commitment, show you 81, 356; leadership behaviors 131; Theodore Roosevelt's adage 360

career, taking control over your 137

career decisions, influenced by balance of life 48

career derailment 183; risk of 261-2, 359

career moves, value of early 138, 140

Cassidy, Sukhinder Singh see Singh Cassidy, Sukhinder

Chakma, Amit xvi-xvii 237–46, 335, 345

challenges: addressing the 133, 170, 269; "I am my greatest challenge" 365; stepping up to 118–19, 122

change: the "Common Sense Revolution" in Ontario 110–12; enjoying 150; leadership through 75–6; power to 251, 263; resistance to "drains me" 263

change-resistance gene, a barrier to learning 165, 363

changes, in leadership role or function 352

character: a big part of success 120; in context of financial crisis 6–7; dimensions of 10; integral to effective leadership 7–9, 317; values, virtues and traits 2–3, 2, 8–9

character development 12–15

Cheh, John xvii 149–56, 339, 344

choices, leadership about 323, 330, 360

Cimolino, Antoni xvii-xviii 277–85, 329, 333, 336, 350, 362, 366

circumstances, leaders made by 35

clarity: on key issues 139; what the organization needs 260

cognitive abilities, required for leadership 19

collaborative leadership 88, 93, 170; only way to solve anything 194; power of open 202–3; skilled, dedicated professionals as a team 75, 76–7; virtues of a business leader 10, 10, 11

colleagueship, shared leadership 186

collective leadership 85

comfort zone: investment in 317; stepping out of 27, 91, 97, 108, 150, 340, 341

commitment: aspiration, engagement and sacrifice 2–3, 2; critical to leadership success 57, 98, 99, 332–3; of employees and leader 125; knowing when to step aside 101; sense of mission, and 241; show you care 81, 356; to do something 315; to make executive team successful 209; to work 124-5

committees, chairing 214

communicating: in a large, widespread organisation 308; a tough message 66

communication 59, 60, 83, 96, 97, 99–100; by telling stories 320–2, 360; in a crisis situation 79–80; delivering your message 138–9, 245; importance of feedback channels 37; leadership diminished without 68, 360; listening and responding constructively 61, 324, 346; in the political world 109, 113; poor, ruining careers 358, 360; preconceived biases critical in 243

communication skills, acquired through Ivey experience 158–9

community: engagement in 143; investing in your 172

community interest, more important that personal 35

community involvement: importance of 138; supporting education 153

community service 146–7

community volunteers, getting them to work together 147

compass see moral compass

competencies: attributes of a good leader 56–7; gaining new 97–8; opportunities with potential to develop one's 340; pillars of good leadership 2–3, 2; recognizing those required in next career stage 46

complacency, killer to organizational success 61

complexities: exposing oneself to 89; understanding interdisciplinary 50

confidence: in ability to achieve change 111; act with courage, do with 359; gaining, when you make mistakes 89; grown from life time's experiences 99–100, 115–16, 306; without over-confidence 77–8; in yourself as leader 123, 339–40 see also self-confidence

confrontation, in the boardroom 217

connection, with employees 358–9

consistency, with leadership style 139–40

context: gaining a sense of 235; need for, to make sound decisions 83

contextual leadership 83, 347

contribution of others, leaving room for the 280

control: being obsessive about what is in my 290; letting go of the control factor 255

conviction: about getting things done 323–4; have a 359–60; and self-belief 110–11
convictions, courage of your 260, 359
Cope, George xviii 306–14, 327, 329, 338, 346, 351, 355, 357, 361–2
cost of leadership 32, 51, 333; finding a balance 283–4; negative reactions to policies 114
counterintuitive, response to something 229, 234
courage: act with, do with confidence 359; having, at the right moment 281–2; lead in turbulent times 103; taking on new challenges takes 338; to tell you what you needed to hear 364; transparency requiring 163; virtues of a business leader 10, *10*, 11
Crawford, Purdy xviii-xix 219–26, 351, 353, 359, 365
credibility: building 132–3, 168–9, 357; earning, as an outsider 112; with peers 227–8; reasserting, in changing environments 198
crises, preparation for potential 231, 375
crisis, learning from a 263–4
crisis-like situations: anticipation and preparedness for 52; communicating in 133
crisis management: and leadership in good times 60; when GM filed for bankruptcy 134
criticism: constructive 45; dealing with 70–1; uninformed and legitimate 320
critics, we are our own worst 215
cross-enterprise leadership 103
cultural constraints, on both women and men 194-5
cultures: experiencing diverse, in Middle East 267; working with people in different 189–90

debate, creating open and constructive 77, 362
decision making: in ambiguous situations 162; in challenging situations 79–80, 141–2; democratically 42; learning from 44–5; not all made the same way 53; requiring self-confidence 223; speeding up 104, 262; transition to more senior roles 109
decision-making process: focus of teaching method at Ivey 158; openness about the 281
decisions: not every decision should be quick 132, 366; regretted 32; unpopular 114 *see also* strategic decisions
decisiveness, just getting things done 159
dedication, to achieve greatness 18
defensiveness, dealing with 164
delegate, or you're done 313, 346
delegating: getting out of the way 298, 299, 364; hard to hand over the reins 135, 364; trust required before 311, 346; as your responsibilities increase 166
delegation versus detail, importance of operating range 293–4

delivering, having a track record of 137
derailing careers: by over-promoting people 313; ways to derail a promising leadership career 290–1
dialogue: importance of 254; learning through 79 *see also* communication
dictatorial element, of leadership, removing 280
different strengths, recognising, in people 229–30
dignity, lead with 30, 356
directness: tools that help to deliver 163–4; what the organization needs 260
disappointments, dealing with 29–30
discussions, with friends and peers 87–8
diversity, handling, in community work 147
doing everything well, an illusion 191
doubt, eliminating 126
drive: leaders of conviction have 359; virtues of a business leader *10*, 11, 12
duty, understanding the concept of 57–8

education: appreciation of leadership through 86; continuous learning 153
effective leadership 24
effectiveness, assessing your impact and interaction with team 49
effort: focus on the 93; making the 33–4; putting so much into everything 286
ego: big talent destroyed by big 291; getting my ego out of the way 298, 299; getting in the way 82; so easy for the ego to get involved 123, 365; suppressing one's 37–8
emerging realities, refusing to accept 317
emotional intelligence: leaders have 158, 160, 161–2; shortcomings in 225
emotions, don't get wrapped up in 304
empathy, developing 277
empowering others, to create collaborative leadership 88
environment: creating an open and honest 228, 230; understanding the one in which you operate 228–9, 365
equality: every person's voice equal 363; need for another way of expressing 186
ethical leadership 25
events *see* life events
example: leading by 26–7, 41–2, 355–6; learning by 231
excel, aspiration to 149
executive coach, supportive in transitions 289
expectations: go up when you have trust in others 311; leaders prepared to live up to 355–6; put on yourself 200
experience: as a barrier to learning 165, 363; learning from 4, 19, 32–3, 64, 364; learning from other leaders' actions and 45;

multidisciplinary 132; of turning round a troubled business 160–1
experiences: bad corporate 214; rewarding 59, 69–70, 94, 127, 166, 224, 235, 302; wide variety of, at GE 138
experiential learning: based on enhancement of clinical care 205; developing political skills 206–7

failure: accept the consequences of 167; dealing with 120, 192–3, 258, 264; fear of 70–1, 173–4, 241–2, 341; need to get rid of people who are failing 210; understanding how to manage 20; willingness to fail 168, 341
failure is temporary, giving up is permanent 169
failures: leaders learning more from 158; loss of public trust 4–5
family: impact of leadership commitment on 32, 82, 333; "keeps you grounded" 82
family influence 38, 44–6, 63–4, 98, 99, 328
family time, missed 82
fast tracking, staff wanting to move from job to job 313-4
fathers, influencing leadership style 351–2
father's expectations 212, 213
fear: of being crucified for an error 173–4; of letting people down 120; taught never to be afraid 213; of the unknown 108; when taking on a new role 149
fear of failure see failure
fears: let people state their 301; that can drain a leader 93; unfounded 174
feedback: constructive 45, 82; creating channels for 36–7, 343; encouraging 103, 136; from people affected by political decisions 115; in a mentoring relationship 350; unsolicited 104; value of 12–14, 13, 37, 140–1, 144
females see women
financial crisis: failings of character 7–8; Leadership on Trial project 1–2, 6–7
"first 100 days" plan, transition to a more senior role 97–8
flexibility: 187-8
flexible approach, gained people's confidence 225
focus: being selective about what you learn 124; don't shift your 174; implementing an initiative 140; on results and long-term strategy 312
followership 157, 158, 167; gaining 162
following, learn to follow before you can lead 58
formative influence, in terms of leadership development 96–7
friends, who can be a sounding board 103
frustration, learning to deal with 367
Furlong, John xix-xx 24, 26–34, 330, 333, 340, 355–6, 360

future: figuring out where things are going 317; setting out the 301
future leaders, supporting 295

General Electric (GE), Canada: being part of the GE system 137–8; working with 44–6, 47–54, 339
generalist, who knows how to put it all together 304
General Motors: filing for bankruptcy 133–4; reclamation and restoration of 57–8, 59, 360
getting out of the way 298, 299, 364
give 100 per cent, and hold nothing back 300, 359
giving back to the world, as a business leader 289
"giving without expectation" 299–300
global business environment, critical to be informed about the 365–6
good and bad leadership 98–9
good leadership 24–5
Google: Asia Pacific 287, 292–3; Latin America operations 287, 292–3; out of 289, 290
"gray zone": operating in the 234; reducing the 44–5
grounded: important for a leader to be 252, 255–6; staying 122-3, 170–1
guidance, role of a mentor 152

habits, preventing character development 13, 14
Hard Rock 179
hard work 44, 63–4, 68, 77, 119, 124, 145; leaders as hardest working 81, 356; and long hours 214
Harris, Michael Deane ("Mike") xx-xxi 24, 107–17, 327, 329, 332, 334, 339, 360, 363
Hasenfratz, Linda xxi 129–36, 327, 331, 332, 363, 366
helping other people, to achieve what they want to 292
high-pressure situations, staying calm and addressing the challenges 269
Hošek, Chaviva xxii, 185–96, 328, 342–3, 343, 346, 359; an immigrant with mindset that doesn't assume 90, 348
honesty: examples of 30–1; importance of 6; in your communication 59, 360
Honoré, Russel L., Lt. General USA (Ret) xxii 20, 25, 197–204, 327, 328, 338, 348, 358, 364
honour, "the greatest lesson I learned" 30–1, 360
humanity: virtues of a business leader 10, 10, 12; willingness to be human 33
humility: acknowledging somebody else's perspective 164; important aspect of leadership 68, 234; influence of family and

friends 145, 274–5; mistakes keep you
  humble 89; suppressing one's ego 37–8, 122,
  155, 364–5; virtues of a business leader 10, *10*,
  11, 17–18

Ian O. Ihnatowycz Institute for Leadership 5
impact: leaders' 158, 229; motivated by creating
  a positive 274
"impossible", making the impossible possible
  259
Indian biotech enterprise, pioneering an 168
Indian culture, reticence, part of 261
influence: ability to make things happen 19, 44,
  73, 96, 155, 315; of father 315, 316; having an
  impact on somebody's life 101
influences: of family 38, 44–6, 63–4; formative
  35–6
information: absorbing as much as possible
  78-9, 366; environment where information
  flows up 230, 363; opening up to 121-2, 221;
  people hoarding, not sharing 263
information flow, creating a network and
  system for 244–5
Infosys 173; importance of benchmarking 37–8;
  working in teams 39–40
inhibitions, overcoming 78
initiative, taking, to get things done 315
initiatives, hesitation to embrace new 241–2
innovation: Biocon as an example of 169;
  creating new knowledge that helps patients
  207
input, everyone's equally valued 363
insecurities, unfounded, the biggest enemy 174,
  340
inspiring confidence in people 170
instinctive management 140
Intact Financial Corporation 227
integrating, pathway to becoming a better leader
  352–4
integrity: acting with 231; attributes of a good
  leader 56–7; examples of 30–1, 317, 324;
  importance of 6, 54; virtues of a business
  leader 10, *10*, 11
intellect: as a barrier to learning 165, 363;
  underpinning leadership competencies 2, 2,
  4, 19
intelligence, as a barrier to learning 124
interaction, with people 132
interdisciplinary complexities, understanding
  353
introspection: and behavior adjustment 21–2;
  on impact you have on others 229
introspective, leaders need to be 259
Ivey Business School 5, 13, 23, 101, 102, 118,
  131, 312, 358; the Ivey experience 158;
  research on dimensions of character 9–12,
  10

job, learning how your job fits in the
  organization 179, 183–4
journey, leadership a 157
JOYUS 289, 291
judgement: building good 44–5; suspending
  immediate 366; virtues of a business leader
  10, 11, 12
judging, not quickly enough 192
justice, virtues of a business leader 10, *10*, 11

knowledge: broadening through diversity of
  experiences 353; respect for other people's
Kuhlmann, Arkadi xxii-xxiii 3, 20, 118–28, 330,
  332, 338, 340, 342, 357, 364

leader: a devalued word 186; inspired by one
  person 328–9; is always "on", always observed
  311, 357; learning more from a bad 57; only
  as good as high-performing team 82; raised to
  be a 247; realization of self as a leader 44, 327
leadership: an art 86; concept of 185;
  engendering followership 157, 158, 167; in
  First Nations 251; good and bad 98–9; new
  model needed 275; price of 123–4; setting a
  vision 154; a very lonely sphere 94; why we
  want to lead 285
leadership burdens: of accountability and
  responsibility 56, 59, 333, 343
leadership challenges, in a large organisation
  308
leadership character 6–15
leadership characteristics, real differences
  between men and women 273–4
leadership development 17–22, *19*; determined
  by opportunities 237; GE's commitment to
  45, 53; a learning process 3–4; within an
  organization 258
leadership experiences: in changing
  environments 197–8; learning from 328
leadership failures *see* failures
leadership framework xxxii 2–3, *2*
leadership insights, for the next generation of
  leaders 355–67
leadership qualities: boldness, persistence and
  tenacity 60; exhibiting 35, 327–8
leadership skills: enhanced by a personalized
  development plan 225; innate in all of us 237
leadership style: adaptation to managing more
  senior people 228, 348; little to do with
  success 139; more reflective in later years 116
leadership styles: exposed to different 130;
  respecting different 101–2
Leadership on Trial project 1–2, 6–7, 19, 283
leadership values: candor and directness 163–4;
  experiences underpinning 267
leading, not to be confused with managing 86,
  87

learned knowledge, experience of past errors and mistakes 301

learning: barriers to 100–1; deriving pleasure from 74; from your life 228, 235; key element to moving organization forward 230–7, 342; learning the things which are meaningful to you 91, 124; never stop 4, 365–6; outside your areas of knowledge 228; requires reflection 222; to be an even better leader 32–3, 342–4

learning curve, learning to lead 21

learning process, leadership development as a 3–4

learning to lead: competencies, behaviors and qualities needed to excel 17–22; conclusions on 336–54; as dynamics change 49; evolutionary, continuous process 45

legacy, creating shared value 275

letting go 135–6, 288, 363–4; building trust 207; of the control factor 254–5; getting out of the way 298, 364

life events, influencing character development 14

limitations: reasonable sense of your 191; understanding your 241

Linamar 130, 131–4, 363

listen: good leaders 221; truly listen before you speak 324

listening: actively, to synthesize information 87; benefits of good 361; but not really hearing 242–3; and getting people engaged 136, 324; and learning 70, 76, 317; show that you have listened 281

listening skills: based on years of experience 61, 61–2; to become a better leader 67

long-term, structural trends, having an outside-in perspective 77

lose with grace 30–1

luck, "equals opportunity plus preparation" 105–6

lululemon, bringing in a board of directors 298–9

McCain, Michael xxv-xxvi 3, 22, 157–67, 327, 328, 333–4, 340, 344, 345, 349, 351, 358, 360, 363, 367

managing, not to be confused with leading 86, 87

Maple Leaf Foods: listeriosis crisis 3, 163, 166, 358, 360, 361, 367; restructuring of 160–1; values-based leadership model 162–3

Martin, Paul, The Right Honourable xxiii-xxiv 255, 315–25, 327, 329, 339, 346, 349, 359–60, 360

Mazumdar-Shaw, Kiran xxiv-xxv 140, 168–75, 328, 356, 357, 358, 365

media: dealing publicly with an issue 51–2; talking to the 200–1

mediocrity, not acceptable 59–60, 361

memories, a great leader has great 127

mental time-out, having a hobby 126

mentoring: and leadership development 223; pathway to becoming a better leader 349–50; young people, particularly women 216

mentoring relationships, time required to develop 350

mentors 120–2, 151–2, 177, 258; benefits of 30; formative influence of a vice-president 96–7; wife as mentor 309

mentorship, with sponsorship 270, 273

Mercier, Eileen xxvi 25, 212–18, 327, 329, 334, 341, 343, 351, 356–7

merit, career driven first by merit 292

meritocracy: importance of 171; instilling sense of, in organization 41

middle ground, finding, and resolving issues 277–8

military leadership, best example of care 131

mind never at rest, cost of leadership 291

mindset, challenging the mindset of unspoken rules 257

mission, sense of 241

mission accomplished, credit in 200, 338

mistakes: burden to correct 198; handling 324, 364; in health care 208–9; learning to take accountability 89, 91; not taking action quickly enough 192, 359; part of the learning process 42, 80, 221; in a political career 186

moral compass, establishing an internal 44–5, 51

moral responsibility, to innovate 207–8

motivation: having the influence to shape outcomes 81; how not to motivate 96; to achieve greatness 18

moving on, realising when it's time to 178

multidisciplinary experience 132

multiple dimensions: experience in 353; women seeing problems in 83

multitasking, women 81

Murthy, N. R. Narayana xxvii 17–18, 35–44, 173, 356, 360

National Action Committee on the Status of Women 188-9

nature or nurture, role in leadership development 17, 157

negative criticism, dealing with 29–30

negative leaders, "helped me become a better leader" 177

network, developing a strong, at Ivey 159

networking 102–3; at international meetings 275; women need to find ways to 273–4

networks: informal, in organizations 49; relying on staff support to reach decisions 244;

relying on in tough times 334; start to
    develop them early 217
not-for-profit sector, leadership in the 72–3

obligation, understanding the concept of 57–8
observation: leadership demanding constant
    281; pathway to becoming a better leader
    351–2; people watch you all the time 357–8
obstacles, dealing with 29–30, 102
"off the record", is never off the record 51
Olympic Games, Vancouver, 2010, CEO of
    Organizing Committee 27–34
Ontario Teachers' Pension Plan Board, peer
    review 218, 343
open communication, importance of 254
open and constructive debate, creating 77, 362
opening up, to information 121-2
openness 255-6; be open, listen with intent 361;
    relating to people 25, 232
opinions: getting different, helps leadership
    evolve 210; getting people to express before
    decisions made 179–80, 324, 363; never state
    yours first 77, 362
opportunities: creating 202; recognizing and
    seizing new 18–19, 339; response to 52, 101,
    278; there are always 135; to lead 35, 85, 335
opportunities and burdens, of leadership 94–5
opposing perspectives, resolving tension in 164
optimism, intensity as optimism 292
organization, integrating learning about
    functions of 352–4
organizational commitment, to character
    development 14–15
organizational values, true to, in a crisis 163
Osler, Hoskin & Harcourt LLP 220, 221, 222,
    223
outcome, you can't control the whole 288
outcomes: having the influence to shape 81;
    taking ownership of disappointing 310
outside-in perspective 77
outsider, leadership as an outsider 112
overanalyzing a problem 140
overconfidence in what they know, a barrier to
    learning 165, 363

paradoxes, learning to manage 164, 182, 234,
    300
passion, leaders demonstrate 56–7, 130, 158
pathways, towards becoming a better leader
    337–54, 337
patience, learning to be patient 199, 366–7
peer reviews 217
peers, chosen to manage my 286–7
people, assessing, utilizing and encouraging 152
"people knowledge", becoming a better listener
    67
people skills 222, 223

PepsiCo Asia, sub president of 266
PepsiCo Frito-Lay organization 266
perfect, you don't need to be 183
perfection: don't try to be perfect 71; nothing in
    leadership is done perfectly 304
performance: high- and under-performers 82;
    improved in financial crisis 235; leader's role
    to evaluate 59–60; takes you to next career
    move 137; transition to more senior roles 119
performers, being too patient with average 230
performing: learning to lead 20; pathway to
    becoming a better leader 338–9
peripheral vision, ability to look beyond the
    organization 353
perseverance, patience goes hand in hand with
    determined 366–7
personality traits: defined 8; representing good
    leadership 68–9
perspective: leaders gaining integrated and
    holistic 353; putting things in 233, 235;
    valuing 165
perspectives: research to develop multiple 229,
    365; should be offered in balance 164
planning: leadership behaviors 130-1; long term
    319
play fair 27
points of view: getting different, helps
    leadership evolve 210; getting people to
    express 179–80, 324, 363; never state yours
    first 77, 362
political skills, need to develop, to deal with
    government 206–7
Polyvore 289; analyzing short stay with 290
"positional authority disrespect", everyone's
    input equally valued 363
postmortems: "we don't do them enough"
    120–1; where the value is 342
power: ability to make things happen 19, 44, 73,
    96, 155, 262-3,315; centre of power in an
    organisation 292–3; mediations on, in drama
    278
Power Corporation of Canada 316–17, 318
power struggle, understanding a political 188
practice, "deliberate practice" 18
pragmatism: demonstrates good will 323;
    hardest when involving political realities 216
predecessors, learning from 228
Premier of Ontario 109–17
preparation: for an interview 28–9; for a
    meeting on a new subject 222; for the week
    ahead 138
presence, importance of, in business
    environment 104
pressures: of taking unpopular decisions 114; as
    you grow into new roles 272 see also high-
    pressure situations
price of leadership 32, 51, 124, 333

principle, matters of 323
principles: standing for something, as chief
    financial officer 215; staying true to 139
priorities: in business and politics 319;
    determining 141–2
priority, having a clear sense of 233
proactiveness: tempered with humility 122;
    translated into leadership 118
problems, very thorny 214
problem solving 204
procrastination, overcoming 90
promotion, derailing careers by over-promoting
    313
public speaking: a learned skill 78, 89; learning
    from Pierre Trudeau 27–8; working at 320–1
purpose, finding your 274
purposive leadership 24–5
putting others first 300

reacting too quickly 223
reading 79, 222; about people who demonstrate
    leadership 88; about what organizations go
    through 235; devoting extra effort to 352
realities, refusing to accept emerging 317
reflection: on leadership provided 124–5;
    learning requires 120-21, 222; learning
    through 343
regional roles, managing several countries and
    cultures 266–7
regrets: over a decision taken 32; over a poor
    performance 64
relationships: ability to interact in a crisis 79–80;
    building 67, 159; good with 222; having
    people you can talk with 90; leadership as a
    relational quality 185; terminate if not
    working 268; where values not shared 271–2
relocation, being open to 271, 341
renewal, constantly having to look at 262
reputation: first, last and most important 216,
    356–7; open to interpretation 357; precedes
    you, it doesn't follow you 357
resilience: developing 40, 69, 161, 233; from
    hospital staff and environment 209; from
    personal experience of growing up poor 201;
    importance of 333–4; pushing on a problem
    builds 259
respect: earning 31, 356; for everybody's
    contribution 40; importance of 190, 267–8;
    "making respect more respectable" 39; a
    primary objective 38; showing 146, 281
responsibilities: leadership coming with 307; of
    a young naval officer 55–6
responsibility: accepting 343; burden of 134–5,
    189–90, 201; coming with leadership 27, 241,
    268; to young people 279; for what you say
    251, 357
results, leaders deliver 158

retrospection: and behavior adjustment 21–2;
    on impact you have on others 229
review, 360-degree review process 343
Richard Ivey School of Business see Ivey
    Business School
risk: dealing with, in ambiguous situations
    49–50; embedded in making decisions 269
risk control, with board of directors 301
risking: learning to lead 20; pathway to
    becoming a better leader 339–40
risk management, having your own process 90
risk taking, preconditions for 230
role, changes in leadership 352
role models: engaging with people 212–13;
    leadership influenced by 295; look for
    leadership role models 352

sacrifice, to achieve greatness 18
sailboat, metaphor for leadership 331–2
scandals, loss of public trust 4–5
self-awareness: as an immigrant in a new
    country 93; good leaders have acute 166;
    important especially for younger people 103;
    learning to lead 19, 21–2, 332; pathway to
    becoming a better leader 344–5; and self-
    criticism 61
self-confidence: in my ability to contribute 227;
    to make decisions, and make mistakes 221,
    359 see also confidence
self-criticism, capacity for 191
self-discipline, earning respect every day 145,
    356
self-recognition, a healthy dose of 191
service, real leadership is about 122
setbacks, dealing with 29–30, 102, 120, 192–3
Shakespeare, William: leadership a central
    theme 279; learning from different plays
    277–8
Shindler, Michael xxvii–xxviii 176–84, 330, 343,
    351, 352, 363
shop floor, leader should be present on the 209,
    358
Singh Cassidy, Sukhinder xxviii 3, 286–96, 327,
    329, 333, 352
situational awareness: critical to good leadership
    33, 81; developed when exposed to crises 234;
    every decision has a clock on it 199; learning
    from misjudging a situation 100, 348; relying
    on networks for information 244
skepticism, about our own abilities 77
skills, needing skills well beyond own 307–8
skill set, anyone can have, but a reputation...
    216, 357
skill sets, recognise diverse 313
slipping up, and earning back trust 261
slow things down, times when you have to back
    off 142, 366

smarter people: being comfortable working with 108, 109, 136, 170, 363; than oneself, there are 17, 37, 39
smartest person, don't try to be the 362–3
Snyder, Stephen xxviii-xxix 20, 25, 137–48, 327, 331, 332, 340, 344, 356, 366
social change: disagreement on how to make 189; empowering our citizens to lead 251–2
social conscience, inherited from father 315
social media: be careful what the world is telling you 312; emergence as a powerful force 47
solution mindset, being in the 233
speaking see public speaking
speaking your mind 260, 359
speed: acting quickly/taking more time 104, 129, 242; importance of 140, 142, 262
stakeholders: dealing with 88–9, 92, 283; understanding the motivation of 47
standards: of acceptable behavior 6; setting oneself high 98
standing up, for what you believe is right 237–8
station, taking on tasks beneath one's 40, 356
status quo: blinded by investment in 317; challenging the 237–8, 257; fear of moving beyond the 250–1
Stephenson, Carol xxix 1, 23, 96–106, 330, 331, 336, 340, 348, 349, 353, 357
stories, that connect with people 321
strategic decisions, taking more time on 135
strategic direction, set, then "let the staff do their job" 152, 154
strategic vision, and ability to drive the execution 46
strategy, understanding 187
Stratford Festival, Ontario 285, 362; love of working with others 277
strengths: integrating the value of other people's 229–30; recognising our, and how we can work together 252
strengths and weaknesses, choosing the right people 41
stress, coping with 40, 102
stretching: learning to lead 20–1; pathway to becoming a better leader 340–2
Stymiest, Barbara xxix-xxx 72–84, 330, 349, 353, 356, 362, 366
success: breeds success 250, 260; corporate world's choice of wrong attributes 39; sharing 362; "The higher the monkey climbs..." 173–4, 358; Western system grooming for 257–8
success beyond expectation, sustains a leader 93
succinct, takes effort and discipline to be 222
support: building 278; people looking to you for 251, 357; professional and personal, needed in transitions 289

supportive leadership 36
surprise, people will surprise you 280, 362

talent, for leadership 17
tasks, none is insignificant 40
team: bringing the team along with you 111; coaching the team to excel 46; create synergies in the 362; delegate to a team you trust 313; no individual bigger than the 314
team building 83, 361–2; a cycle of change 141; with people chosen for their skill sets 308; with people from different backgrounds 219; as Premier of Ontario 109–13
team development: addressing individual differences 271; preparing for more responsibility 179
teammates 69–70
teams, drive everything in business 310, 361–2
team selection 193
telecommunications industry, leadership in the 306–14
temperance, virtues of a business leader 10, 10, 11
Thapar, Gautam xxx 18, 257–64, 327, 328, 342, 343, 344, 349, 359, 363
think big, giving ourselves permission to 90–1, 346
thinking: across disciplines 353; becomes more integrated 353
"thought partners", informal mentoring 76
time: required to develop mentoring relationships 350; spending time together 68
time frames, in business and politics 319
time management 121; at work and home 141–2, 143; being prepared 138
tolerance, being tolerant of others 155
Toronto Community Foundation 93
Toronto Stock Exchange 353; shifting public perception of 74
track record, confidence from a good 310
traits see personality traits
TransAlta Corporation: decision to step down as CEO 144–5; learning moments at 146; a very steep learning curve 143
transcendence, virtues of a business leader 10, 10, 12
transformation agent, being a 35
transitions: adaptation to managing more senior people 228–9; adjusting to all sorts of changes 239–40; communicating the vision 282; a great preparation for general manager 266, 268; managing with support 289; multidisciplinary experience 131–2; problem of each role expanding 206, 363; to more senior roles 45–6, 88, 97–8, 109, 119, 160, 260
transparency: building credibility 228; in critical conversations 50–1

trends, perspective on long-term structural 77
trepidation, when taking on a new role 149
trust: abused or damaged 268; bilateral relationships with subordinates 61, 311, 346; inspired "by my father's trust in me" 267–8; learning to trust and foster trust 22; loss of public 4–5; trusting yourself 87, 88, 90–1
trust building 61, 67–8, 140–1, 232–3, 243, 346, 357; eight ways to build trust 347; and learning to trust others 310–11; letting the team go 207; requiring authenticity 92
trusting, pathway to becoming a leader 345–7
trusting others 233, 244–5, 346; related to them meeting expectations 208; to do the right thing 294
trusting yourself 345
trustworthiness, rooted in how you treat people 135, 346
truth, leader looking for approval rather than the 364
tunnel vision, leadership careers derailed due to 353

underestimation: facing the challenge of 28–30; leaders initially underestimated 334–5
understanding yourself 259, 344
United States Naval Academy, early training in leadership 55–6
University Health Network, Toronto, CEO of 205, 206, 207–11, 358–9
unknown, stepping out into the 281–2, 339
urgency, always acting with 289

values: establishing an internal compass 44–5, 57; influence of parents 98; influencing behavior 8–9; integrating organization's statement of 14, 54; need for alignment between company and leader 51; products of our circumstances 38–9; questioning yourself is important 272-3; relationships where values not shared 271–2; staying true to core values 153
values-based leadership model, Maple Leaf Foods 162–3
Vancouver Olympic Games 27–34
victim, always the 290-1
view of the world, critical to have a well-rounded 224, 365
virtues: becoming vices in excess or deficiency 12; of business leaders 9–12, 10; products of our circumstances 38–9

visible, leader should be 209, 358
vision: combining strategic vision with execution 46; communicating a 29, 57–8, 282; important to set a 274; leadership driven by a cause 27; people have to buy into your 111–12, 360; setting, with involvement of the team 268; setting, then "let the staff do their job" 152, 154 see also peripheral vision
volunteer opportunities, helped leadership development 86
vulnerable, willingness to be 33

watched: leader always "on", always observed 311, 357; for the tone you set in the organization 99, 357
watching: people watching you all the time 357–8 see also observation
weaknesses: good understanding of 220; identifying one's 90, 91
Wilson, Dennis("Chip") xxx , 25, 297–305, 329, 334, 345, 359, 364
Wilson-Raybould, Jody (Puglaas) xxxi, 247–56, 331, 344, 357, 360
win with class 30–1
winning, against expectations 65–6
winning formula, giving 100 per cent 300, 359
wisdom, comes only with age 312
woman: never wanted to be the token 217; operating in financial and technology sectors 80–1
women: cultural constraints on 194–5; decision making 53; in First Nations communities 248–9; and leadership 53, 273–4; should support other women 105
women leaders: in more senior positions 105
women and men, differences in leadership characteristics 273–4
women's movement, leadership in a 185–6
work see hard work
work ethic 78
work-life balance, learning the art of 90
worry, unable to shed 291
writing skills, emphasis on, at Ivey 159

young leaders, to embrace people unlike themselves 313
young people: empowering 278–9; rewarding to watch them take off 216